PROPHETS OF YESTERDAY

THE MACMILLAN COMPANY
NEW YORK · CHICAGO
DALLAS · ATLANTA · SAN FRANCISCO
LONDON · MANILA
IN CANADA
BRETT-MACMILLAN LTD.
GALT, ONTARIO

PROPHETS OF YESTERDAY

Studies in European Culture
1890-1914

GERHARD MASUR

New York · The Macmillan Company · 1961

First Printing

The Macmillan Company, New York
Brett-Macmillan Ltd., Galt, Ontario

The author wishes to express his gratitude to the publishers for permission to quote from the following books: *An Autobiographical Study,* Sigmund Freud, translated by James Strachey (The Hogarth Press, London, 1935); *Buddenbrooks,* Thomas Mann, translated by H. T. Lowe-Porter (Alfred A. Knopf, New York, 1952); *Civilization and Its Discontents,* Sigmund Freud, translated by Joan Riviere (The Hogarth Press, London, 1930); *Creative Evolution,* Henri Bergson, translated by Arthur Mitchell (Henry Holt and Co., New York, 1911); *De Profundis,* Oscar Wilde (Philosophical Library, New York, 1949); *The Forsyte Saga,* John Galsworthy (Charles Scribner's Sons, New York, 1933); *From Max Weber: Essays in Sociology,* H. H. Gerth and C. Wright Mills (Oxford University Press, New York, 1946); *The Fruits of the Earth,* André Gide, translated by Dorothy Bussy (Alfred A. Knopf, New York, 1949); *The Life and Work of Sigmund Freud,* Ernest Jones, M.D., Vols. I, II, III (Basic Books, Inc., New York, 1953–1957); *The Lyrical Poems of Hugo von Hofmannsthal,* translated by W. Storck (Yale University Press, New Haven, 1918); *Mind Energy,* Henri Bergson, translated by H. Wildon Carr (Henry Holt and Co., New York, 1920); *The Philosophy of Nietzsche,* reprinted by permission of Random House, Inc., and copyright 1927, 1954 by The Modern Library, Inc.; *The Selected Prose of Hugo von Hofmannsthal,* translated by Tania and James Stern (Bollingen Series XXXIII, New York, 1952) and reprinted by permission of the Bollingen Foundation; *The Tragic Sense of Life,* Miguel de Unamuno, translated by J. E. Crawford Flitch (Macmillan and Co., Ltd., London, 1926); *Wilhelm Dilthey,* H. A. Hodges (Oxford University Press, New York, 1944); *The Works of Stefan George,* translated by Olga Marx and Ernst Morwitz (University of North Carolina Press, Chapel Hill, 1949).

Printed in the United States of America

Library of Congress catalog card number: 61-9729

To Helen

PREFACE

The idea from which this book developed dates back to my student days. At the age of seventeen I attended a lecture on the inheritance of the Renaissance given by Ernst Troeltsch at the University of Berlin. My ambition to write one day an intellectual history of Europe took root at this time. The men to whom I felt most deeply attracted during those years were working along similar lines; besides Troeltsch, there were Friedrich Meinecke and Ernst Robert Curtius in particular.

But the world of events, of which I was both observer and victim, prevented me from carrying out my original plan. When, after many a detour, I returned to my favorite project, it seemed superfluous to add another history of the European mind to the numerous volumes already in circulation. Consequently I decided to tackle my subject in reverse, as it were, and to begin with an analysis of our present age and the epoch which ushered it in.

I have been conscious of the obstacles that lie in the path of such an undertaking. The historian who deals with a period close to his own life does not have a neatly defined object before him; his selection and his emphasis will be conditioned by his own background and his own experience; his perspectives will, of necessity, be limited and may even be biased. On the other hand, he brings to his subject a passionate concern and a vital knowledge of its urgency. In my own case, these considerations are evident in my choice of those trends and personalities which seemed to me decisive in the formation of our present intellectual situation. Whatever has been omitted was omitted after long and sometimes painful deliberation, as irrelevant to the phenomena I wished to explain. If I have invited criticism (and I am all too cognizant of the shortcomings of this book) let it be directed against what I have said and not against what I have excluded.

It has been my aim to write cultural rather than intellectual history; hence, the scope of the book may, in this regard, strike some readers as too encompassing, and therefore pretentious. Historians of the arts, of philosophy, of literature, and of society may be inclined to think that their disciplines have not been accorded proper attention. I am aware that this attitude will manifest itself; I am even sympathetic to it, but the project on which I embarked seemed to justify the acceptance of the risks involved.

Although this book deals with certain aspects of the "Decline of the West," I have felt no desire to emulate the prophets of doom and gloom. The decadence of one historical phenomenon contains, in most cases, the seeds from which other forms take their growth. This is particularly true for the change of the European position from one of hegemony to one of partnership in our contemporary civilization.

Nor do I think that any single element, material or intellectual, can be designated as the responsible factor in the great transformation which came over the world in 1914. The present volume is intended to be one of sober and empirical analysis, applying whatever tools may best fit the case under consideration. The endeavor to describe the prevailing trends in the period between 1890 and 1914 was the foremost idea of my undertaking, but I also wished to give full understanding to the complex structure of the intellectual life of the early twentieth century. In certain cases this has demanded a backward glance at earlier aspects of the nineteenth century, and in others a brief venture into the years following 1914.

If history is "the intelligible form in which a culture accounts for its past," we must bear in mind two separate though closely related approaches—the search for causes and the search for values.* The historian, especially the historian of ideas, cannot choose between them; he must apply them both. That a reference to values implies an element of subjectivity is well recognized. Yet it cannot be eliminated from historical research, and less from historical writing, since it is the life-giving impulse without which we would

* Friedrich Meinecke, "Kausalitäten und Werte," in *Schaffender Spiegel* (Stuttgart, 1948).

never turn to the past. It was, I think, for this reason that Nietzsche called the past an "oracle" which everyone would have to interpret in his own fashion. But to be conscious of one's subjectivity does not mean to renounce the criteria of objectivity. It simply means that such is the human condition in which the historian partakes, as does every other individual who is engaged in the pursuit of knowledge. It is not for me to say to what extent I have been successful in overcoming this dilemma.

It is customary to preface books of this type with the statement that they "could not have been written had it not been for. . . ." Like most conventions this too bespeaks a situation that, if not permanent, is at least so enduring that it has frozen into a cliché. It is the complexity of modern academic life which has made productive scholarship the exception rather than the rule. One would look in vain for similar declarations in Ranke or Burckhardt. Yet my case is not different from that of any other American scholar whose freedom for research has been made possible by the generosity of our great foundations.

I acknowledge with deep gratitude the assistance given me by the Rockefeller Foundation in the year 1954–1955. The officers of the Foundation have accompanied the progress of this book with sympathy and encouragement. I was fortunate in receiving a Guggenheim Fellowship in 1956 which enabled me to continue my research. In 1958 I held a summer grant from the Southern Fellowship Fund, and in 1960 I received a Fulbright Lecture Award to teach at the Free University of Berlin. It was during this period that the book was completed. President Anne Gary Pannell, of Sweet Briar College, has taken an enlightened interest in the advancement of my project, granting me more than the average leave from my academic duties.

I am also deeply indebted to the staffs of the great libraries where I carried out most of my research: the Widener Library of Harvard University, the Library of Congress, the British Museum, the Bibliotèque Nationale in Paris, the Friedrich Meinecke Institut der Freien Universität, Berlin. The staff of the Sweet Briar College library has likewise been most helpful. Several parts of this book have been read or discussed by friends and colleagues, and I have profited from their advice. Among these are Dr. Fritz Redlich of Harvard

University, Professor Leland Jenks of Wellesley College, Professor Lilly Rappaport of Sweet Briar College, and Mr. Herbert Steiner. But it goes without saying that I am responsible for any errors that may be found in the following pages.

My wife, Helen Gaylord Masur, has edited the entire manuscript. It would be immodest to praise her work at this juncture, but whatever readability the book may have is due to her labor and her critical judgment. In its final stage, Mr. Peter V. Ritner, of The Macmillan Company, has given me the support of his counsel and his enthusiasm from which the book has greatly benefited, to say nothing of my morale as an author.

GERHARD MASUR

Lynchburg, Virginia
December 26, 1960

CONTENTS

CHAPTER I

The Stress of Triumph

In the early morning darkness of April 15, 1912, R. M. S. *Titanic,* the largest ship the world had ever known, struck an iceberg in the North Atlantic and went to the bottom with a loss of 1,500 lives. The catastrophe moved the Western world deeply. In a dim and half-conscious way it was felt that the event forecasted greater dangers which would shake the very foundations of European civilization. It seemed to reveal the *hubris* of Western man, who prided himself on having attained control of the forces of nature both within and around him and who now learned, overnight, that he might become the victim of inner compulsions which could smash his arrogance to bits.

The observer who in the mid-twentieth century tries to comprehend the powers which sweep his life toward unexplored shores will inevitably be struck by the contrast between the period which followed 1914 and the preceding age of security in which his parents spent their days. But from experience he knows that the discrepancy between the present and the past is always more apparent than real, that every age has been formed in the womb of time, and that the laws of heredity apply to civilizations as they apply to individuals. Just as we see today that the Renaissance and the Reformation were prepared by the emotions and the ideas of the late Middle Ages, that the tremendous outburst of the French Revolution was nurtured by the thought of the "effeminate eighteenth century," so are we compelled to look to the past century for the wellsprings of our own complexities. That such sources exist we may take for granted, but it is the role of the historian to point to those causes which produced the cleavage between the late nineteenth century and our own and which transformed the controlled transitions of former ages into the infinite dynamic of the present. It is his business to define what is characteristically new in our troubled time as well as what still links it to the tradition of Western culture.

In 1914 the influence of Europe on the world stood at its zenith.[1] Not only did the European nations control directly an unwonted portion of all the lands of the globe, 85 per cent to be exact; not only were European immigrants pouring into other continents at an unprecedented rate; but Europe presented herself to the world as a cultural entity of inexhaustible vitality and undisturbed growth. Leopold von Ranke believed that nothing could arrest the "spirit of the Occident." "Irresistibly . . . armed with weapon and science," he wrote in 1879, "the spirit of the Occident subdues the world."[2] Who could have foreseen that this moment of extraordinary triumph was in reality a culmination that permitted no further ascent, and that the apogee once reached entailed, as in all tragic drama, a catastrophic declension. The short period of Europe's unlimited sway over the world came about because of many successes in the fields of politics, science, economics, and population-growth. Taken singly they would not have produced so stunning a conquest. But they were blended in a cultural pattern; they fused with and enhanced each other to the point where the dynamic of each depended on the dynamics of all. Not one element nor one trend can account for the dazzling success which the Europeans reaped from 1870 to 1914; nor did any one element or trend bring about their downfall. They must be seen together, intertwined as they were, gradually enmeshing the outside world in a net that seemed to be woven of indestructible fibers.

If, on the following pages, we attempt to single out elements in European civilization, we must ask the reader to bear in mind that they presented themselves not as isolated influences, but as the combined energies of a civilization which, sometimes by force, sometimes by persuasion, assured this culture its unique preeminence. Whole generations assumed that the powers which Europe was unleashing would always work in an ultimate unison, that their inevitable strife and competition would at all times end in a harmony conferred as the birthright of the white race by a benevolent Providence. No one anticipated that ruthless expansion, unbridled rivalry, and internecine strife among the European nations might finally endanger the organic whole of their civilization. But the tensions which developed and which eventually rent Europe asunder are as much a part of the picture we have to give as the preestablished harmony in which the world believed prior to 1914. These tensions made the coming of the Great War inevitable. Just as individuals torn by conflicting emotions become the easy prey of illness, just so do civilizations explode into war in the effort to rid themselves of conflicts that do not allow of peaceful adjustments.

I

By 1914 Europe stood in a relation to the rest of mankind never before achieved by any other civilization. She was the hub of the world, or, as Mazzini expressed it in 1848, she was "the lever that moved the world." Her unparalleled position was not alone the result of imperialism and capitalistic enterprise; it was based on cultural foundations truly unique in the history of mankind.

In its powerful expansion to the most remote corners of the earth European civilization had acquired an ecumenical character. No other culture had gone so far; all had been content or resigned to remain within geographical boundaries, however broad these may have been. If they claimed superiority for their own way of life, they did not, or could not, undergo the test of imposing their cultural pattern on all people and all nations. Europe itself had not in any earlier period made the attempt to assert the global validity of its cultural life. European expansion had, it is true, reached distant shores and had, as in the New World, established settlements oriented toward Western values and ideals in government and religion, art, and society, but these enterpises had been scattered over the face of the globe and were no more than Western islands in an ocean of alien life.

Not until the eighteenth century did Europe embark on her more temerarious adventure. It was then that the secularization of thought reached a density permitting philosophers to design schemes for humanity on a world-wide scale. Kant, Lessing, Condorcet, Thomas Paine, and Bentham were among the first whose thoughts aimed at the whole of the human race.

It was not, however, accidental that Europe was the only civilization to develop cultural molds sufficiently ample to accommodate the whole earth.[3] During its long history Europe had been the recipient of three great heritages which indicated the part it was to play in nineteenth century history. Greece had taught the universal validity of a truth which all men could perceive; Rome had given the idea of a law universally valid for all men; Christianity had bestowed the ideal of human brotherhood and the belief in one God whose essence is love and ultimate redemption. The philosophy of the Enlightenment was the fusion of these tenets; their crystallization was belief in the perfectability of man and the progress of humankind through the steady advance of reason. Carl Becker has called this eschatology the heavenly city of the eighteenth century.

The century following confirmed this faith in reason by the extraordinary triumphs that rational thought and empirical observation scored in all fields of scientific endeavor. In geology, biology, and medicine, in history, economics, and jurisprudence, the advancement of reason brought fruits beyond all expectation. While the world of supernatural commands grew dim, man's natural universe increased in perspectives—rich, tantalizing, confusing, and many times contradictory. Navigating on a boundless sea of reality, reason was, more than ever, man's rudder and progress was "the golden harbor" where he hoped to drop sail.

Nor was it a coincidence that European civilization produced the phenomenon of the Industrial Revolution at the same time. Mankind had displayed inventive genius in other ages, but never with the onrushing intensity with which new devices were now introduced in the economic process. Industrial and agrarian production began to rely more and more on science for the solutions of all problems in output, transportation, and distribution. Scientific discoveries in turn opened up new avenues to economic success. The story is well known. The power loom, the steam engine, and the use of chemical fertilizer marked only the beginnings of this "permanent revolution" that has affected the lives of all peoples more deeply than any other historical event.

The nineteenth century carried the products of the Industrial Revolution into countries and continents that had enjoyed autochthony for thousands of years. While scientists and entrepreneurs of the Old World were busy planning and discovering improved methods of production, merchants and salesmen began to penetrate nations which had been sealed to Western trade. These were the foot soldiers who carried out the orders drawn up in laboratories and workshops by a general staff of scientific minds. The steady trickle of goods became a mighty stream. Soon the surface of the globe was inundated by new types of transportation—steamships, railroads, streetcars, and automobiles; by new ways of communication—telegraph, telephones, cables, and the wireless. Together they facilitated the arrival of manufactured goods, and in turn, assured the shipping of raw material on which Europe depended for her survival.

One could, of course, argue that the capitalist expansion did not in reality produce a transformation of the non-European world, that all it did was to cover these people with a veneer of cheap consumer goods which endangered the time-honored production of the non-Europeans and jeopardized their deep-rooted customs and habits. Those who adhere to the German distinction between culture and civilization will also insist that the Industrial Revolution did not carry the best or the most intrinsic European thought overseas, but only a conglomeration of conveniences. But is not this argument fallacious? The ecumenical character of European culture in the nineteenth century is the direct result of its belief in the universality of scientific truth, valid under every sky. Western technology is the consequence of this belief, and the Industrial Revolution is, finally, the practical application of technological victories. It is based on the trinity of science, labor, and capital.

It is true that when Western technology conquered the earth from pole to pole it came in contact with civilizations radically different from its own. Religious institutions, everyday habits, social customs were opposed to those of the West. Clashes were inevitable and led to developments of tremendous significance in Japan, China, India, Persia, Turkey, and Mexico. It soon became apparent that these countries could absorb Western technology without embracing Western rationalism, which is the spinal cord bracing European control over nature. In such wise did Europe in the nineteenth century forge the weapons for its own defeat in the twentieth. Technology, though a creation of the West, was by no means a monopoly of the West. It was not the carefully guarded secret of a priest-caste, but the open findings of scientific brains, openly deduced. Just as it was employed to enforce European control, so could it be utilized to destroy it.

For the student of contemporary history few processes have been quite as stirring as this. During a single century Europe has toppled from unprecedented heights to political collapse. But the munitions for her defeat were produced in her own arsenal, and even in her humbling by the non-European world the triumphs of the Western spirit are many and obvious.[4] At the turn of the century few Europeans seem to have been apprehensive either of war or of defeat. It was a general assumption that the privileged position of the European countries would be maintained ad infinitum. It is only we who have come to know how really frail and precarious was their position.

Thus we return to our original quest. What accounts for this unique situation in which a small group of nations controlled the fate of so many millions whom they considered their inferiors and to whom they gave in return for economic exploitation and political domination only the fringe benefits of their highly sophisticated civilization? We have seen that, beyond all individual factors, a universal culture of ecumenical aspirations must be taken into consideration. Let us now review the elements that composed this culture.

II

Europe's political structure, both international and domestic, must first concern us. The nineteenth century, from 1815 to 1914, was a century of peace. If we compare it with the sixteenth, the seventeenth, or the eighteenth centuries, we find no such international conflagrations as the wars between the Valois and the Habsburgs, the Thirty Years' War, or the Seven Years' War. Nor do we find those international conflicts based on religious or ideological alignments which filled the periods between 1560 and 1600 or between 1792 and 1815. The Crimean War, the wars instigated by Napoleon III, Cavour, and Bismarck, and the Russo-Turkish War had limited objectives and were of short duration. The system of international relations which Europe embraced between 1815 and 1914 was characterized by a much greater elasticity and resilience than is generally supposed. It emerged from the Napoleonic period with basically the same organs and sinews that had controlled its activities before 1789, and it proved to be much more vital than its detractors anticipated. The balance of power was its regulating principle, and the European concert of nations was still harmonizing with remarkable success the movements of conflict and adjustment which govern all foreign policy. In 1815 there were five great European powers; in 1914 there were six. And although unification in Italy and Germany produced significant changes in the balance of power, it did not disrupt the function of the system as such.

The great statesmen of the nineteenth century, with the exception of Gladstone, were first and foremost diplomatists. Metternich, Napoleon III, Palmerston, Cavour, Bismarck, and Salisbury belonged by tradition and upbringing to the European aristocracy, and still showed in their policies and operations a European conscience and sense of responsibility. In pursuing the interests of the states and empires entrusted to their care they did not aim at the establishment of a lopsided hegemony in Europe in the hands of any single power. During the long period from 1815 to 1914 there were intervals of Austrian, French, and finally German preeminence, but these interims did not overturn the carefully calculated equilibrium on which the international system of checks and balances depended.

Bismarck's "limited imperialism" is a case in point. The policy of "blood and iron," of swift aggression, was followed by twenty years of peace.[5] Bismarck wedded Germany to a diplomatic system based on the coexistence of a number of equally stable powers. His great dispatches, such as the famous notes dictated in Kissingen in 1877, compel admiration, both for their perspicacity and their moderation. He never seriously entertained dangerous schemes like, for instance, the projected partition of the Ottoman or Habsburg empires. Today we are able to see the limitations of this basically conservative system. It took the European predominance for granted; it did not conceive of conflicts on a world-wide scale; nor did it foresee the tensions that the penetration of Africa and Asia might engender. The diplomats of the nineteenth century held that Europe would always be able to maintain its supremacy over the other races and continents. But it is only "the lucid view afforded by hindsight" that has taught us to detect these flaws.

Since the balance of power succeeded so well in securing and maintaining peace and prosperity, we cannot be surprised that its tools were accepted with little criticism or discrimination. The alliances, the secret treaties, the leagues and counterleagues were considered indispensable implements of international politics. In the hands of accomplished masters of the fine art of diplomacy they served their ends: the guaranteed survival of the European concert of nations. After Bismarck's dismissal the system deteriorated. The men who were at the helm at the close of the century depended on the alliance system instead of controlling it. This situation led to the breakdown of European solidarity in 1914. But forty years of peace had made the Europeans fear war rather than believe in its possibility. As Bergson phrased it: "War was probable but impossible." Complacency was largely responsible for the feeling of security that impregnated Western society before 1914.

The successful operation of the international system during these hundred years has, however, still another aspect worthy of mention. The balance of power principle had proved itself to be sufficiently elastic to admit of an idea unknown to previous centuries. We refer to the concept of the nation-state. Before 1789 the idea of national self-determination had been completely neglected by diplomatists: witness the partition of Poland. After 1815 it became one of the guiding principles of European life.

The idea of the nation-state had two aspects: one external, freedom from foreign control; the other internal, freedom from despotic rule secured by constitutional government. The French Revolution had proclaimed this new doctrine, and nineteenth-century European history was largely devoted to its application among those nations lacking in either or both of its implications. The independence of Belgium, the unification of Italy and Germany, the emergence of Slavic nations in the Balkans were the most important steps in this direction. They were accomplished by negotiations, by international congresses, by wars and by revolutions which were political rather than social in their consequences. After each convulsion the European balance of power returned to its labile stability and readjusted its functions to accommodate the new members. In others words, there was no fundamental rift between international and domestic politics in nineteenth century Europe.

The people had every reason to hope that their basic aspiration, that is, the right to live by the principle of national self-determination, could find expression in the existing system of international relations.

If we now turn our attention to the internal aspect of the idea of the nation-state, freedom from tyrannical rule, we will see that Europe had likewise traveled a great distance on this road. By 1914 the victory of representative government was almost complete. Even Russia had been unable to resist the magic attraction that the promise of personal freedom held for Western man. In different forms and to different degrees, sometimes radical and sometimes in compromises with institutions and traditions of the past, the liberal-democratic idea had swayed the Old and the New World alike. It was considered the fulfillment of long-nourished dreams of liberty under the law, inherent in European history since its earliest days. "The idea of representative government is typically European," remarks one of the masters of constitutional history.[6]

But, though typically European, it was no longer confined to Europe. The United States had given it original expression in 1776. Latin America had followed suit, though in an uneasy and vacillating manner. At the beginning of the twentieth century the idea of representative government was rapidly inflaming the political imagination of many non-European nations as well. The British Empire was a training center in constitutional government for Asiatic and African people. The English system of gradualism had many flaws; but it was and still is one of the most powerful instruments toward the Westernization of the world.[7] Similar developments took place in Japan, in Turkey, even in China. The world had come under the spell of Europe's political system. Its incentives were greatly enhanced because of the fact that, by 1914, most of the European states adhered to the system of constitutional monarchy. When the Great War started there were only three republics in Europe: France, Switzerland, and Portugal. The remainder were either true constitutional monarchies or, as Max Weber has called them, pseudo-constitutional regimes such as Russia, Spain, and to a lesser degree Germany, Austria, and Hungary. If the eighteenth was a century of enlightened despotism, the nineteenth was certainly the age of constitutional monarchy.

There are both political and sociological reasons for the general acceptance of this system.[8] In both respects it was basically a compromise. Constitutional monarchy guaranteed governmental stability to the body politic, which was now called upon to manifest its opinion at regular intervals by way of the ballot box. It could and did exist and function where the representation was placed on the broadest foundations: the German Empire proclaimed universal manhood suffrage in 1871, Norway in 1898, and England was well on her way by 1911.

On the other hand, the system of constitutional monarchy did not call for an equalitarian democracy. It permitted the aristocratic classes to survive in an age of increased mass influence. It was able to work out solutions whereby the aristocratic elements were deprived of their legal privileges without touching the property basis on which their existence relied, and without ignoring their efficiency in certain public offices such as in commands in the army, the diplomatic and the civil services.

Constitutional monarchy was more of a sham in Central, Southern, and Eastern Europe, where the position of the landed gentry was stronger than in the West. The Junker class in Prussia, the Magnates in Hungary, the grandees in Spain, exercised a powerful influence on the local, regional, and national level. They opposed electoral reforms and held a virtual monopoly over high offices in diplomacy, the army, and in the civil services; they also blocked any attempt at land reform, that crucial issue of the twentieth century. Here, then, constitutional monarchy tried to arrest the march of time. If it did not actually turn back the hands of the clock, it tried to prevent them from moving ahead. Tensions were building up under the façade of a representative government which was unwilling to grant an equitable share in power to the bourgeoisie, the peasants, and the workers. (It is significant that monarchy finally became extinct in Austria, Germany, Italy, and Spain.) But once more we must beware of hindsight. In 1914 constitutional monarchy was still the favored theory. It was in keeping with the preference for middle-of-the-road solutions, for compromise and adjustment, the outstanding characteristics of the age.

There is an old and blurred newsreel which shows the crowned heads of Europe gathered for the funeral of Edward VII. Another interment, to the sound of a more disturbing *marche funèbre,* was soon to bring them together again when they assembled for the entombment of constitutional monarchy. The German Social Democrat, Bebel, speaking to his opponents in the Reichstag, said, "The great *Kladderadatsch* [breakdown] will come; and it will not be brought on by us, but by you yourselves." [9] In other words, the system of constitutional government was doomed wherever it resisted the productive forces of society.

We shall return to this subject later, but before we approach the theme of class structure we must come to grips with a phenomenon closely connected with the nation-state yet surpassing it in scope and influence. I speak of nationalism. We have seen that the nineteenth century relied on the coexistence of independent nation-states. But the idea of the nation-state could not be applied to such supranational empires as the Habsburg monarchy nor to multinational states like Russia. In addition, most of the great powers controlled minorities which had no desire to be integrated into the life of a nation that they considered alien to their own. Instead, they aspired to a life of autonomy, or they looked forward to joining another nation of which they believed themselves to be a part. England had its Irish problem; Germany, Austria, and Russia were vexed by the Polish question; France had an Italian minority at the Riviera; France and Italy dreamed of redeeming splinter groups in Alsace and Lorraine and in the Trentino.

Although no one of these problems by itself was sufficiently pressing to bring the European peace into jeopardy, they did show, nevertheless, that the idea of nationhood did not coincide with the solid frontiers of the nation-state. When the war finally opened, a host of poisonous problems emerged; and one of the most dubious bequests of the past century was nationalism. It has proved to be a volcanic issue in international politics, and is likewise a tantalizing question for the social scientists. Recent studies list as many as thirty varieties of nationalism, and all attempts to define it have so far failed. [10]

Some common denominator may, however, be formulated. Nationalism is Western in origin. Occasional outbursts of national feeling had occurred in earlier periods of European history: in the Hundred Years' War, during the German Reformation, in the

British fight against Philip II. But not until very modern times have whole peoples been systematically indoctrinated with the tenet that every human being owes his first and last duty to his nation, that the nation is the ideal unit of political organization as well as the embodiment of cultural distinction, and that every other human loyalty must be subordinated to this supreme one.[11]

Nationalism, in the words of Carlton J. H. Hayes, is the fusion of two historical phenomena much older and more universal than itself: nationality and patriotism.[12] Nationality is composed of such various factors as language, historical destiny, cultural tradition, and a cohesive social fabric; it is either consciously or unconsciously shared by its members. Patriotism is the devotion to one's country and the willingness to defend it.

It was the French Revolution that made the fusion of nationality and patriotism imperative. Popular sovereignty replaced the old concept of royal sovereignty, and popular sovereignty led to popular solidarity. The nation consisted henceforth of citizens, and to be a citizen meant to be a patriot, conscious of the ideals that inspired the new state. This new loyalty superseded all others: to ruler, church, class. In order to repel the intervention of the European powers, France was obliged to raise an army of citizens by means of the *levée en masse*. Thus was nationalism born in the year 1793.[13] After the revolutionary armies had repulsed their enemies, French nationalism took the offensive, determined to propel antagonistic countries into democratic liberty by force of arms.

It soon became apparent, however, that nationalism was a multifaceted phenomenon and that it could thrive on sources other than French Jacobinism. A tradition-bound nationalism arose which allied itself with precisely those institutions which the revolutionary armies had threatened: the monarchy, the aristocracy, the church.

After 1815 still another form of nationalism appeared: liberal nationalism. It has been said that nationalism was essentially a middle-class movement, and although we know today that this is but a half truth, and that proletarian nationalism can and does assert itself, it is true that between 1815 and 1890 the bourgeoisie carried the torch for nationalism. Rapidly advancing in commerce and industry, the bourgeoisie felt itself to be the nation. This was the time when the nation-state surrounded by constitutional guarantees became the political ideal; it was promulgated by such varied minds as W. von Humboldt, Guizot, Dahlmann, Stahl, and Mazzini. Sharing in the general optimism of the age, they believed that the voice of each nation was indispensable in any harmonious choir of mankind, or as Mazzini said, fatherlands are but the workshops of humanity. Each nationality should be a political unity under an independent constitutional government which would undertake to terminate the rule of despotism, clericalism, and feudalism. These were the heydays of liberal nationalism, with the bourgeois millennium just around the corner.

But it soon became apparent that the dynamics of nationalism were not to be tamed by the niceties of bourgeois liberalism, that in reality it had no fixed creed, that it could ally itself with clericalism as it did in Ireland and Poland, that it could side with an autocratic regime as it did in Russia where Dostoevski and Danilevsky disparaged the aims of Western constitutional government and lauded the paternal wisdom of the Tzarist rule. Nationalism inspired the feeling of *revanche* in France, and added the spirit of ruthlessness to the economic expansion of England and Germany. It could use Darwinism and its dogma of the survival of the fittest as a frame of reference and interpret history as a struggle between higher and lower races. Anti-Semitism appeared on the political scene as one of its sinister by-products.

But perhaps the most significant shift occurred when nationalism begot a new form of imperialism. In 1792 nationalism had been a reaction against the European monarchs' intervention in France's internal problems. Now it developed its own imperialism. The late nineteenth century is characterized by movements such as pan-Slavism, pan-Germanism, pan-Anglo-Saxonism, and pan-Hispanism.[14] Each of these tried to establish closer ties between the mother-nation and those ethnical splinter groups which lived outside its political jurisdiction.

Of those movements, pan-Germanism and pan-Slavism proved to be the most dangerous for the peace of Europe. In the long wide belt that stretches from the Baltic to the Black Sea, nations and nationalities had lived for centuries in a crazy quilt fashion that admitted of no clear-cut political or ethnical solutions. Colonization, religious diversity, fluctuating conquests had left the map of these regions in multiracial, multilinguistic, multiecclesiastical confusion. To introduce the principle of nationalism here could only lead to chaos. Inevitably the Austrian monarchy and the Ottoman Empire became the preferred targets. Although the circles agitating for the new nationalism did not control the governments before 1914, they carried on a noisy and vociferous propaganda by press and pamphlet that poisoned the atmosphere. On August 8, 1914, the Tzar announced to the world: "We also fight for our Slavic brothers, our companions in faith, our blood relations." [15]

Thus nationalism exercised a twofold influence. Among those races who considered themselves suppressed, it supplied a strong force for breaking up supranational empires. And among the ambitious ruling classes of Germany, France, Russia, and England, it gave a powerful impetus to the revival of imperialism.[16] Integral nationalism in France, for instance, was defined as "the exclusive pursuit of national policies, the absolute maintenance of national integrity, and the steady increase of national power." It would seem obvious that a policy of integral nationalism, if followed by each and all, would of necessity lead to friction which must terminate in conflict. We touch here upon the basic weakness of nationalism: its inability to universalize its human aims. Unrestrained nationalism in one group could operate only at the expense of other groups.[17] We cannot leave the question of nationalism without touching on the factors in nineteenth century life that contributed to its tremendous influence. Sigmund Freud, in his essay "Mass Psychology and the Analysis of the Ego," has made an attempt to penetrate this problem with psychoanalytical tools. I feel, however, that we will remain on safer ground if we limit ourselves to more tangible causes.

As we have noted, the practice, introduced by the French Revolution, of fighting wars with large conscript armies, marked the beginning of nationalism. Eventually all continental countries adhered to this system. Consequently they depended on the mood of the masses and were, therefore, bent on transforming the defenders of the state into loyal citizens. It follows that the governments had an interest in spreading the new concept of national loyalty. Moreover, the masses were themselves a contributing element. The nineteenth century witnessed a growth of population unequaled in any other age. This growth was accompanied by a migratory movement from the countryside into the towns. Nationalism is essentially an urban movement. The new city dwellers lost their local and regional contacts; hence, if they were to take an interest in politics it would have to be on the national level. In addition, nationalism could give them a substitute for the regional links they had forsaken; it could provide them with that feeling of "belonging" without which human life is incomplete.

The rise of urban population carried with it a rise in the general level of education. Education was in reality a prerequisite to the needs and demands of the technical civilization so rapidly developing. But the ability to read and write made the urban population the potential victim of nationalistic indoctrination, which would begin in the school, would be continued in the army, and after the return to civilian life would be emphasized by the press.[18]

Modern large-scale production and modern industrial economy facilitated the ascendancy of nationalism: the workers as well as the middle class were gradually contaminated by the nationalistic virus. The workers had made progress in all of the European countries; their influence was guaranteed by the suffrage, and their economic standard, though it left much to be desired, had been improved through trade unions and measures of social security. And these advantages had come about within the framework of the nation-state; they were not the results of concerted international actions by the working class, of solidarity expressed by the proletariat. Thus, even the working classes developed a sense of loyalty to their respective countries. They refuted the Marxian dictum that the worker had no country. Nationalism, in the social structure of prewar Europe, had a firm rooting which went far beneath the middle class and the intellectuals to whom it is generally ascribed.

Nationalism is a further example of the tensions which this ecumenical civilization was building up within its precincts. At the same time that technical inventions began to encircle the globe and to exercise pressure toward the advent of one world, when international conventions regulated postal services, telegraphic communications, and overseas transportation, nationalism was slowly erecting barriers to impede the progress of these supranational trends.

A final comment may be added. Nationalism could appear only

in a thoroughly secularized civilization. Its tenets were contrary to the ideals of Christianity. In 1900 the masses who had grown up in an atmosphere satiated with mechanistic science had lost much of their faith in the established churches and were quite willing to accept a substitute. Nationalism did not replace the old religions outright; it overlaid them and gradually assumed a religious complexion of its own. The German, the French, the Russian, the English claims to hegemony and world leadership presented themselves as religious missions which would bring salvation to the world. That these claims were mutually exclusive seemed to produce little anxiety, but it made the frictions between them, and finally the open conflict, exigent and uncompromising. To those who were swept by the emotions of nationalism, it was, moreover, an assurance of immortality. In an age which no longer believed in the resurrection of the individual, it gave some comfort to cling at least to one association whose survival seemed guaranteed, even though the price was the sacrifice of the individual.

The close connection between nationalism and militarism has often been noted. According to one historian, militarism is the domination by the military over civilian life; its true counterpart is not pacifism but civilianism.[19] And it would seem one of many paradoxes that an age so bent on establishing constitutional controls should have ushered in a trend toward military ascendancy. Yet we discover the roots of modern militarism in the same events where we found the sources of nationalism: in the revolutionary wars and in Napoleon. All of the popular resources of France had to be mobilized to prevent the restoration of the absolute monarchy by the European powers. It is one of the ironies of history that the democratic expedient of the *levée en masse* paved the way for the rise of Napoleon. During the ten years of his empire he drafted 2,400,000 men into his armies. His regime shows the ascendancy of the military over the civilian; he stood and fell on his success as a general.

Napoleon's enemies found that his defeat required them to employ his own weapons. They were forced to adopt military conscription. Prussia led the way. The famous law of 1814, introducing military training in this state, proclaimed the creation of an army of citizens that would not only free the fatherland but that was further designed to intensify the civilian spirit among all who took up arms against the Corsican. This happy augury was not realized, however. Prussia remained an absolutism; no constitution was granted as a reward for the patriotic efforts of the population. While universal military training was kept on the books, the direction of the army was left in the hands of the aristocratic officer corps. The other European nations, however, returned to professional or semiprofessional armies after 1815.

There was no war between 1815 and 1854; hence it might seem that militarism had little chance of affecting civilian life. And indeed there was a widespread feeling of pacifism permeating all classes of European society during this period. It found its best expression in Lamartine's *Marseillaise de la Paix,* written in 1840. War appeared to be an obsolescence; armies were condemned to wither away in an atmosphere where "evil shall cease and violence pass away." [20]

An international peace congress met in Brussels in 1848. But into this tranquil scene there burst an event which, in the same year, brought about a complete reversal of position. The revolution of 1848 produced counterrevolutions, and the counterrevolutions depended on military support. In every continental state affected by the uprisings it was the army that reestablished the old order. Cavaignac in Paris, Wrangel in Berlin, Windisch-Graetz in Prague and Vienna, Radetsky in Milan were the men who crushed the revolution. Louis Napoleon was elected president of France, a symbol of the influence that the military myth had gained. The very word "militarism" was coined during the Second Empire.[21]

The social motivation behind these events is highly significant; it was the deep-seated fear of the bourgeoisie that it would be destroyed in a social revolution. At the beginning of 1848 the bourgeoisie and the working classes had fought together to overthrow the existing political order. But when it became apparent that the workers were fighting for a socialist society, the bourgeoisie severed relations with them. They preferred the upper to the nether millstone, and they were greatly relieved to see the military restore a state of affairs in which property, at least, would be respected. Thus 1848 marks the beginning of a growing authority of the military in civilian life. Napoleon III was, as we have noted, an example, and the event that led to the rise of Bismarck in Prussia is another.

Bismarck was appointed president of the Prussian cabinet as the champion of monarchical power in the conflict over the reorganization of the Prussian army. He sided with the king against the liberal majority and carried through the plans of his friend Roon, whereby the army of the Napoleonic period was transformed into the "Royal Guard" of Wilhelm I. This new instrument became the decisive weapon in Bismarck's foreign policy which, in three swift wars, completed German unification. The German Empire of 1871 retained military training, no longer as the corollary of popular rights, but as an efficient way of securing a large standing army. The officer corps preserved its aristocratic character.

More important still was the freeing from civilian control of all army promotions and operations. The general staff was, for all practical purposes, autonomous in its preparations of military enterprises.[22] The chief of staff, von Moltke, who had won military victories for Bismarck, was the first soldier to understand what war in modern times means, and he was likewise the first to apply the lessons and the tools of the Industrial Revolution to modern strategy. He foresaw that future wars would not be precipitated by princely ambitions but by the moods and desires of the people. He was the first to comprehend the management of mass armies by means of modern communications. He depended on railway and telegraph for the movement and rapid concentration of troops. Von Moltke mastered the technical intricacies of modern warfare with a self-effacing modesty far removed from Napoleonic ambitions, yet he is, nonetheless, representative of the new spirit in militarism that pervaded the European atmosphere after 1870. He considered war an inevitable concomitant of international politics. "The ideal of perpetual peace," he remarked, "is only a dream, and not even a pleasant one." He was also the first commander to object to political interference with wartime strategy.

One of his successors conceived the famous Schlieffen plan. This strategem, designed as a solution of the German dilemma of war on two fronts, advised the invasion of France through the Belgian lowlands. That it was made the basis of Germany's military operations in the Great War is clear evidence of the ascendancy of military over civilian considerations. Just as war was regarded as an inescapable reality, so were, necessarily, the instruments of war: officers and soldiers. The militarism of the leader caste led to popular militarism which aped the habits and outlook of the officer corps, and blended with the spirit of nationalism already discussed. The Prussian success on the international scene produced a new cycle of militarism. In a political system based on the balance of power this was inevitable. France was foremost in adopting the German model. Before 1870 her army had been a semiprofessional one; after Sedan she returned to the concept of an army based on universal conscription.[23] Soon Austria, Russia, and Italy were forced to enter the race. Only England and the United States continued to base their armies on voluntary enlistment.

In France, as in Germany, Austria, Russia, and Spain, the army was a society in a society, a state within a state. It lived under its own laws, and yet paradoxically enough it was considered by many as the embodiment of the nation. "La patrie," said Faguet, "c'est l'armée." [24] It was regarded as the great common denominator, the training ground on which the spirit of the Frenchman was shaped. Déroulède's *Chants du Soldat* are the most famous example of this glorification of French militarism, but there are many others.

It is difficult properly to assess the influence of this new militarism on European life. Economically, it deeply affected the average man. In the period from 1858 to 1914, during which the population of Europe was doubled, the outlay for defense increased four times in nearly all countries.[25] In addition, a study of the biographies of the intellectual leaders of the time shows that many of them came in contact with miltary institutions: Nietzsche, Gide, Renoir, Hofmannsthal, Tolstoi, Dostoevsky, Walther Rathenau, are but random examples.

There is no parallel to this phenomenon prior to the nineteenth century. In medieval times the warrior had been a permanent feature; small groups had been the units of combat. Now it was the army that penetrated the atomized millions of European life with its aggressive spirit. In reviewing this process we must also take note of the organizations of ex-servicemen, a novelty on the European scene. They became powerful pressure groups for nationalistic aims and were the self-appointed guardians of patriotism. The German *Kriegerverein,* the army and national service league in England, the *ligue pour le service des trois ans en France* were among the most vociferous. And they, in turn, worked hand in glove with such organizations as the pan-German league, the *Kolonialverein,* or the *ligue des patriots.* For the over-all picture of European society in the fifty years preceding World War I militarism had an added political importance. Since 1848, the armies were considered a bulwark against revolution. If they were not actually counter-revolutionary, they were the natural associates of reaction and conservatism. In all European countries the officer corps was recruited from the younger sons of the landed gentry with a sprinkle of both upper and lower bourgeoisie. It represented a class militarism that found ideological support in the established church, whether Roman Catholic or Protestant. In Germany, Austria, and Russia the class-conscious officer corps was the acknowledged champion of autocratic government.

On the whole the European West fared better, but the French Republic was obliged to undergo the Boulanger and Dreyfus crises before the victory of civilianism was ensured. Dreyfus was the only Jewish officer in a general staff composed of members of "les classes éclairées," the aristocracy and upper bourgeoisie. Of forty high-ranking officers, twenty-five had attended Jesuit schools.[26] The whole intrigue showed to what extremes a small clique would go in defense of the "integrity of the army." The victory of justice, belated though it was, came from the hands of courageous civilians such as Clémenceau, Zola, Anatole France, and others, and represented the triumph of the nation over the army. Thus France was spared the more fateful results of militarism although she, too, was a victim of that pugnacity which characterized the nation-state in an age that wedded nationalism to militarism.

It has often been said that militarism was the prime culprit in the case of World War I. The headlong race for bigger and better armies did lead to the outburst of 1914, but it was not the military mind alone that provoked the struggle. There were many officers who felt as did the Russian Grand Duke who said he opposed war because "it ruined the army." [27] The fury of the avalanche can be explained only by the fusion of nationalistic and militaristic emotions with economic rivalries and diplomatic entanglements. The study of militarism is revealing in still another aspect. It shows that the social pyramid of the age had not been erected on the substance and form of capitalism alone. Aristocratic forms of loyalty to the ruler existed side by side with the unconditional loyalty to the nation that the bourgeois age demanded.[28] We must then turn to the economic forces in order to determine their role in European civilization.

III

European capitalism is a unique phenomenon as characteristic of Western civilization as the constitutional monarchy or the system of balance of power. More than any other factor, capitalism has been instrumental in giving Europe global influence.

Nineteenth century Europe was the workshop of the world; it exported both capital and goods and viewed the world as an enormous market and an inexhaustible reservoir of raw material.[29] This release of economic energy was based on the disappearance of most precapitalist institutions in Europe, such as guild production and communal agriculture, on the rationalization and consequent depersonalization of economic activities, and, last but not least, on the ever-increasing use of new techniques in the production process.[30] Prior to the nineteenth century there had only been islands of capitalist economy in an ocean of village and urban economy. It was not until the second half of the eighteenth century that the process called the Industrial Revolution began to make itself felt. A new type of human being appeared and multiplied, dominated by the spirit of enterprise, profit-making, and rigorous calculation. The businessman became the new leader.[31] He combined the qualities of the technical expert who understands the intricacies of the production process with those of the salesman who knows the demands of the market and the financier who comprehends the function of the modern credit system. In many countries the business leader achieved heroic size; he was the tycoon who built industrial empires and whose name became a household word—Krupp, Thyssen, Rockefeller, Ford. Though occasionally inspired by religious motives, the entrepreneur was a thoroughly secularized type for whom business was a strictly objective, mechanized endeavor, measurable in terms of profit gained. He fought the ruling classes in his country to obtain his share in state control; his mode of life, his cast of mind, became more and more the decisive element on the social scene.[32]

Labor was the one item of the capitalistic system that the entrepreneur could not supply. It came to him from the disintegration of the older communal forms of economic activity: village, estate, crafts and guilds, and families. Capitalism destroyed or superseded these older centers of production and in turn absorbed the human beings who could no longer find their livelihood in them. It caused a growth of urban centers such as the world had never before known. But even the increased number of urban workers was not sufficient to assuage the man-hunger of capitalism; this was stilled only by the enormous growth in population which took place between 1800 and 1914. During these 114 years the population rose from 180,000,000 to 452,000,000. Even these numbers do not convey the full picture, because during the same period 100,000,000 emigrated from Europe to Canada, the United States, Latin America, Australia, New Zealand, and Siberia.

The story of the Industrial Revolution does not need to be retold. Beginning in iron and coal it started a chain reaction which continues to this very day. The tremendous increase in mining revolutionized consumption habits. Land transportation underwent a profound change. For a long time railroads were synonymous with industrialization. Very soon transportation in general was adapted to the new conditions of the world in an age of high capitalism. Steampower, electricity, the internal combustion motor, and finally the Diesel engine facilitated an exchange of goods and services on a tremendously accelerated scale. All commerce became world commerce, and production and consumption became independent of place and season. Security and legal protection were prerequisites for this inordinate traffic; indeed they became indispensable corollaries of capitalism.

While transportation improved in speed and security its cost declined, making it possible to have an ever-augmenting volume of goods ready for shipment to all corners of the earth. Shipping tonnage and railroad mileages showed incredible advances.

The tidal wave of the Industrial Revolution, starting in England around 1750, reached France by 1820, Germany by 1840, and soon engulfed both the Old and the New World with undiminished force. Capitalism moved ahead by a dynamics of its own and it carried with it new vistas for mankind that are all-important for the understanding of nineteenth century optimism. It assumed that man's ability to produce machines that replaced manual labor would eventually convert the globe into an earthly paradise, free from toil and drudgery. It was taken for granted that man was possessed of sufficient reason to control the irrational dynamics of rational machines, but these theories confused end and means. The machines which supplemented man's labor acquired an importance out of all proportion and blinded man's reason and his conscience as well. Although some thinkers, such as Jakob Burckhardt, foresaw the fatal consequences of this error, there was no hope of stemming the tide.

There was no check on the energies of capitalism except the law to which its own movements were subject. This is the law of boom and bust, or, as it is technically known, the law of the business cycle. Since its inception, the Industrial Revolution had shown a curve which followed the course from prosperity to depression to prosperity again. The Napoleonic Wars were followed by a lull which lasted until 1842. This was succeeded by thirty years of expansion that came to an end in 1873. From 1873 until 1893 there was another period of decline and contraction. But a long stretch of prosperity began in 1895 and lasted into the year when the Great War began.

The students of capitalism had, of course, given close attention to the movements of the business cycle. Marx had actually made it the principle link in the chain of his logic. He predicted the concentration of the means of production in fewer and fewer hands, a situation ending with world monopolies waging a relentless war of competition. With every new depression an increasing number of workmen would be thrown out of their jobs; the rich would get richer, the poor poorer, and finally the jobless millions would overpower the few capitalists by sheer weight of numbers and set up the dictatorship of the proletariat.

History, as we know, refused to comply with Marx's prophecy. Between 1890 and 1914 employment kept pace with the ever-growing population, and those who did not find employment in the old country were easily absorbed by the opportunities for industry and agriculture in the New World, especially in the United States, Argentina, Brazil, and Chile. Wages continued their upward trend, and many European countries followed Germany's example, passing social security laws which provided a minimum of economic security for the working classes.[33] The revolutionary impetus of the working class was on the wane. Between 1871 and 1914, Russia's 1905 revolution was the single example of this type of radicalism.

The growth of trade unionism expresses graphically the fact that the concern of the working classes was shifting from utopian hopes to practical problems, the solution of which might be achieved by legislation within the existing political order. They were more interested in working hours, factory conditions, and unemployment insurance than in bringing about the classless society. The progress of organized labor is reflected in the following table:

Trade Union Membership in 1912 [34]

Germany	3,753,807
Australia	433,224
Belgium	231,835
Denmark	139,012
France	1,027,059
England	3,281,003
Italy	971,667
Austria	692,681
Hungary	111,966
Russia	3,000 (?)
Sweden	121,866
Switzerland	131,380
Spain	100,000
U.S.A.	2,526,112

This long and sustained prosperity in a period of peace has contributed more than any other factor in giving Europeans that feeling of indestructible security so characteristic of the world of yesterday. In highly industrialized countries like England and Germany the national wealth increased at the yearly rate of 3 and 5 per cent respectively. Even the lot of the working class had greatly improved. A standard of living and the enjoyment of consumer goods, which had formerly been solely the privilege of the propertied classes, was now theirs even though they still considered themselves an exploited class. But capitalism, like all other elements constituting this particular blend of European civilization, added its share to the conflict between the contradictory principles that filled the century. While capitalism worked for progress, its concomitant tensions also enhanced greatly the dynamics of power politics.[35]

Ever since Adam Smith had proclaimed that an "invisible hand" directed the clashes between conflicting economic interests toward a preestablished harmony, the leaders of Europe assumed that the removal of economic barriers would lead to an elimination of political dissention. It was this hope that gave the fight for free trade a significance out of all proportion to the issue in hand.

Free trade was advantageous to England's privileged position as the workshop of the world and this country had been the first to embrace its principles. In the sixties France and Germany followed suit. The United States, Austria, and Russia, however, never abandoned protectionism.

In 1879 Germany reversed her liberal attitude and returned to protective tariffs in order to defend her agricultural interests and to safeguard her growing iron industry. The German reversal has not too accurately been called Neo-mercantilism. Whereas the state controlled and guided the economy of the seventeenth and eighteenth centuries, it was now the economy which exercised a significant influence on the policies of the European powers. Adam Smith's hopes were not fulfilled. Capitalism did not soften political power, nor did the economic drive supersede the rivalry between nation-states. On the contrary, economic competition, supported by popular movements and nationalistic ambitions, affirmed the selfishness of the great powers and led them to oppose each other even more vigorously on the international level.[36] Economic measures were used as political weapons, just as political action was applied to exercise economic pressure. Often the exportation of capital took the form of state loans or was channeled into public works to serve military purposes. Pressure groups gained influence in the conduct of foreign affairs. Even the prudent statesman, Bismarck, was obliged to yield to public agitation and to acquire colonies in Africa.

The German naval program is a still more telling example of the power that heavy industries could wield. The German battle fleet was built without any understanding of the international consequences it would of necessity produce. It was considered an instrument of international competition; the optimistic illusion prevailed that such competition was ultimately beneficial and that it would dissolve itself into higher forms of integration.[37]

The French financiers were persuaded to grant large loans to Tzarist Russia in order to cement the Franco-Russian alliance of 1894. Advocates of nationalism, like Déroulède, made such a policy palatable with slogans like "defeat is bankruptcy; victory is an investment." [38] Capitalism was becoming more and more expansionist. It had reached a state of density where it pressed inside a given nation for economic concentration in the form of trusts and cartels, and outside the frontiers of the body politic for control of foreign markets.

The harassment of alien commodities by protective tariffs, the line-up of the entrepreneurs in battle formation against the entrepreneurs of other countries, the adulteration of the competitive economic struggle, are all symptoms of a stage where capitalism was changing its complexion.[39] Industrial capitalism was being converted into finance capitalism. And finance capitalism, it has been contended, is the Siamese twin of modern imperialism. This theory was first advanced by the neo-Marxian school and popularized during the First World War by Lenin, who used this argument to explain the great cataclysm as the end stage of the capitalistic economy. But, as frequently happens, history proved to be more complex than the party slogan would have it.

Finance capitalism is as much the outcome of the Industrial Revolution in its advanced stages as it is the result of the European consolidation into nation-states. Because of her early start and her maritime supremacy, England had the lead over all other European nations. She was virtually assured of a monopoly position which lasted until France, Germany, Belgium, and the United States began to compete with her for the control of foreign markets. The coming of protectionism around 1880 closed some of the European markets to England and gave incentive to the idea that new markets must be secured if the high interest rate on accumulated capital were to continue.[40] Concentration in banking, which paralleled the trusts and cartels in the leading industries, facilitated the new direction in which capitalism released its energies. It began to look for profitable investments abroad. Europe, the workshop of the world, now became the world's banker.[41]

England, with the greatest amount of accumulated capital at her disposal, once more took the lead. By 1914 her investments abroad rose to 17,500,000,000 dollars. Finding the Europeans unwilling or unable to absorb more British capital she turned to the Empire, to Canada, India, South Africa, and in addition to the United States, Japan, China, and Latin America. The French were next in line, with 9,000,000,000 dollars invested abroad. The greater part of this sum went to Russia where France not only helped to finance the armament industry and the system of communications, but exercised control over coal mines, shipyards, and even the grain trade. Germany exported 6,000,000,000 dollars abroad, a considerable part of which was poured into the Ottoman Empire. These enormous amounts of money helped to build up new industries like the diamond industry in South Africa, rubber in Latin America and Southeast Asia, copper in Chile, tin in Bolivia, cotton in India, sugar in Cuba, and coffee in Brazil. By 1908 the oil industry became increasingly important.[42] Refrigeration was introduced and made the export of Argentinian and Uruguayan meat possible.

But by far the greatest investments went into the expansion of the transportation system. Harbors had to be converted to accommodate steamship travel; warehouses had to be built to allow for the stockpiling of goods. It was the age of grandiose railroad schemes. Whereas the European railroads were almost completed by 1880, other continents were still closed to industrial penetration. In the United States four great railroads were pushed through the continent to the Pacific Coast between 1865 and 1884. Cecil Rhodes dreamed of a railroad connection between the Cape of Good Hope and Cairo. The Germans advanced their plan of a Berlin to Bagdad railway.The trans-Siberian railway was completed in 1913. Similar to these transcontinental projects were those that opened up subcontinents like India, or that linked parts of a continent, such as the railroad that connected Buenos Aires with La Paz and Arequipa.

The outlay for these enterprises was phenomenal; the engineering skill and the labor involved were unprecedented. Gunnar Myrdal has observed that this expansion was made possible by the general rates of interest, which were below 3 per cent in the 1890's. In a way it was the heroic age of capitalism, but by our present standards it was not an enlightened capitalism. Would not the exportation of capital on such a scale lead inevitably to a neglect of the inner market? The European banker and capitalist of this period did not cater to the wage-earning class whose consumption capacity could doubtless have been increased by higher pay. Henry Ford chose to follow another pattern, and American capitalism in our time has followed his lead, that is, the maintenance of high profits through the expansion of industrial productivity geared to the inner market. Had Europe produced an industrial leadership of this kind, her tensions might have been eased and the resentment in foreign countries against exploitation by finance capitalism might have been avoided. On the other hand, finance capitalism kept employment in Europe on an even keel. And labor had, on the whole, adjusted itself to capitalistic procedures. While it still professed to work for a change in circumstances, it did benefit in the meantime from the steady prosperity. The European factory worker enjoyed higher wages, better medical care and legal protection than his fellow worker in the Bolivian tin mines or the Malayan rubber plantations.

The historian might also argue that the expansion of finance capitalism has ultimately benefited even those areas which, before 1914, it considered merely as its happy hunting grounds. Capitalism provided these countries, which had so far lived by an economy of extraction based on fields, forests, and mines, with industrial installations and demands hitherto unknown to them. It sucked these regions, now termed "underdeveloped," into the complicated domain of our global technical civilization. Although native production suffered and collapsed in many instances, new industries sprang up in its place. The process has proved irresistible. The fate of the modern world is inseparably tied up with the steady expansion of industrialization. Its means have been generally accepted, even when its aims may be in dispute. Finance capitalism, perhaps more than any other agent, drew the world closer together and paved the way for a global economy.

In view of the potential gains, in view of the risks that capitalism braved in its overseas ventures, it was logical that the influential groups in each country should use their power to gain the backing of their governments. In this manner, it has been said, was modern imperialism born, the child of finance capitalism. But the economic motivation in the history of modern imperialism, important though it is, does not entirely explain it. In the first place, imperialism was not an untried experiment in Europe. Spain had practiced it in the sixteenth century; Holland, France, and England in the seventeenth and eighteenth. The new imperialism, however, was distinguished from the older form, administered by Charles V, Louis XIV, and Napoleon, by its pluralism. The goal now was not a single empire, but a number of empires existing side by side. In other words, modern imperialism is an outgrowth of the European political system and the idea of the balance of power. The latter had operated successfully, whether applied to princely rule or to national sovereignties; now it was employed to control a number of empires competing for possessions outside Europe. But these empires had the core of their strength in the Old World. Thus all the trends which characterized Europe in the nineteenth century—nationalism, militarism, population growth, consciousness of the superiority of the Western way of life, and eagerness for high profits—entered into modern imperialism. World history between 1880 and 1914 is stamped by the appearance of nation-empires.[43]

By 1900 the European powers controlled 90.4 per cent of Africa, 98.9 per cent of Polynesia, 56.5 per cent of Asia, and 27.2 per cent of America.[44] These conquests were achieved with relatively little bloodshed, by jockeying for position, by international agreements and impositions. The colonial possessions of the great powers were of such magnitude that the European nations were completely dwarfed by the territories they controlled. This was true, however, only in point of size. The actual picture showed a small portion of mankind imposing its will, its administrative practices, its business procedures on every country of the world.

Of the six great European powers only four participated in the imperialistic race: England, France, Russia, and Germany. Italy's attempts were abortive, and the Austrian empire remained aloof. England, France, and Russia had a head start over Germany since the latter was able to consider the acquisition of colonies only after 1871. The idea of Germany's holding overseas territories had been viewed with apprehension by Bismarck. For fifteen years he used the Anglo-Russian and the Anglo-French rivalries in Asia and Africa with great finesse in diverting pressure from Germany's frontiers. In the end, however, he yielded to popular demand. The first international congress to concern itself exclusively with colonial affairs met in Berlin in 1884. Bismarck presided over a meeting of fourteen nations whose deliberations resulted in the partition of Africa into "spheres of influence" between France, England, Germany, Portugal, Belgium, and Spain. A few islands of independence remained: Ethiopia, the two Boer republics, Liberia, and Morocco. Most of these were, however, doomed to be swallowed up by the rapacious big powers. By 1900 the partition of the black continent was 90 per cent completed. Yet the awakening was not slow in coming; the African National Congress was founded by four Christianized lawyers in 1912.

In 1878 Europe had claimed 3,000,000 square miles of African territory; in 1913 her dominions included 10,784,000 square miles. And, obviously, "sphere of influence" was the projection of "balance of power" into the world of the colored races. The partition of Oceania proceeded along similar lines. Here it was Great Britain, Germany, Holland, France, and the United States who divided the spoils.

Although the development in Asia followed the familiar pattern, European conquest was not achieved there on quite so easy or unchallenged terms. The most complacent imperialist was obliged to admit that the Asiatic civilizations were not to be dismissed cavalierly as "lesser breeds without the law." Certain Asiatic nations, such as Japan, adopted the white man's example rather than contribute to the white man's burden, and then engaged in imperialism on their own. Others, like Persia, Tibet, Siam, and Turkey, escaped direct political domination by the European powers, but were not immune to more insidious influences. As a result, we find zones of influence, protectorates, and outright colonies side by side. In Central Asia, where Russian and British imperialism balanced each other, an uneasy peace prevailed. In Southeast Asia, France concluded the conquest of Indo-China and the British imposed their rule on Burma and the Malayan peninsula.

But it was in the Far East that imperialism produced its most unexpected and far-reaching consequences. We have noted the Westernization of Japan; the reaction to imperialism in China was even more significant. With their eyes on China's potentialities, the European powers paid no heed to Napoleon's prophetic words: "There lies a sleeping giant. Let him sleep, for when he wakes he will move the world." [45] They sowed the wind and left it for us to reap the whirlwind. France advanced toward China from Southeast Asia; Russia descended from Siberia; Germany, not to be outdone, looked for naval bases. Britain found it easy to strengthen her already established position by seizing ports. Imperialism wedged its way into China by means of loans, extraordinary privileges for foreign traders, the renting of naval bases in perpetuity, or outright annexation. Mining concessions, railway constructions, and other devices were the screens of "peaceful penetration" behind which loomed the possibility of final partition.

When the Chinese, in the Boxer Rebellion of 1900, attempted to prevent further encroachment, the European powers were still able to muster a united front and force China to bow to their demands. European civilization presented at least an outward solidarity to the "yellow peril," the specter of which was threatening the supremacy of the white race.[46] Inwardly, however, the harmony between the European powers was giving way to discord. In 1902 the British, anxious to escape from their splendid isolation, concluded a treaty of alliance with Japan. The treaty of 1902 led to the Russo-Japanese War, and Russia's defeat in this war made possible the conclusion of the Anglo-Russian treaty of 1907.

The United States was the only great power to view China's fragmentation with misgiving, and as a result proclaimed the "open door" policy in the way of a countercheck. In her own back yard, however, she was less timorous. The Western hemisphere did not experience any outright aggression during this period; the Monroe Doctrine was generally respected by the European powers. But Theodore Roosevelt was in his own way as much of a ruthless imperialist as his European colleagues and would brook no opposition to the interests of the United States as he understood them. The severing of Panama from Colombia in order to ensure the construction of the Panama Canal is the most flagrant example of a policy that made the United States the self-appointed police force in the Western Hemisphere against "chronic wrongdoing."

The "big stick" became a watchword comparable to Kipling's "white man's burden" or the Kaiser's "place in the sun." The period called forth a great many of these hypocritical slogans. The wolves had all kinds of sheep's clothing for disguise. Wilhelm II was particularly prolific in boisterous pronouncements, but he was not more aggressive than the other diplomatists who ran world affairs; he was merely more tactless.

Nationalism overflowed into imperial channels. The French spoke of their "civilizing mission"; the Germans of *Kultur* with a capital *K;* Lord Rosebery called the British Empire "the greatest secular agency for good known to the world." [47] Imperialism was sometimes declared to be a responsibility; at other times it was said to be the logical outcome of the struggle for existence and of natural selection whereby the lower races had to yield to the higher ones. The press, the popular review, the music hall, the best-seller, contributed to make imperialism attractive to the public. The masses were easily convinced that a large empire was the best argument for a larger empire.[48] There was without doubt an element of romance and drama in the story of imperialism; included within its aura were such men as Stanley, Cecil Rhodes, Peters, Lyautey, and Lord Curzon. But the romantic aspect was incidental; the stark reality behind the glamorous façade was less appealing. Its imperative was not to live dangerously, but to live profitably. "One cannot study this period," says W. Langer, "without marveling at the exuberance and optimism which went hand in hand with recklessness and confidence in the conduct of foreign affairs." It was taken for granted that the world was marked out by Providence for exploitation by the European white man and that the principle of every man for himself and the devil take the hindmost was natural law. In the writings of both statesmen and journalists there is little trace of a deeper understanding. The rise of Japan, the Aduwa disaster, the Boxer uprising—none of these epoch-making events really opened the eyes of the rhapsodical European. Even the astute Lord Salisbury divided the world into a handful of virile nations and an indefinite number of dying nations. The basic problem of international relations was, who should cut up the victim.[49]

It must, however, be stated that imperialism by itself did not engender the great conflict. It produced a number of local wars, some of which were sanguinary enough, but the struggle of the great powers for territorial possessions outside Europe never did reach the point of forcing the nation-empires into a general war. The devices of partitioning a helpless third party, of drawing new boundary lines, or of staking out new zones of interest were successfully utilized throughout the period to preserve the peace of Europe. Neither Fashoda nor the first or the second Morocco crisis led to war. From the time of the Anglo-French agreement of 1902 to the Anglo-Russian treaty of 1907 there was always the possibility of patching things up and letting someone else foot the bill. Even in 1913 there still seemed to be a chance for Great Britain and Germany to iron out their differences by disposing of Portugal's colonial empire. It was over European issues that Europe went to war in 1914.

The balance sheet of imperialism is, therefore, not a simple account of assets and debits. Most of the arguments listed in its favor fifty years back seem fallacious, or at least inconclusive, today. Imperialism has been defended as an outlet for population pressure, but the greater part of the Europeans who left the Old World went to live in the New World, or in Australia and New Zealand, not in regions where imperialism was rampant. Nor were the economic benefits beyond doubt. The German colonies, for instance, were never a paying proposition, and their share in the national economy was in reality negligible. This cannot be said of England, France, Belgium, or Holland. It can be and has been argued, however, that imperialism did not serve the nations as a whole, that it catered only to certain classes, that the profits went to bankers and entrepreneurs in a much larger measure than to the middle or the working classes, and that it was a parasite living on the sweat and toil of the colored races. Its greatest threat consisted perhaps in creating a state of mind among the Europeans which habituated them to the self-deception of a perpetual and unchallenged political preeminence, thus rendering them incapable of self-criticism.[50] They did not anticipate the frightful harvest of African and Asiatic nationalism, anti-imperialism, and anticolonialism which boiled up after 1919. Yet the handwriting on the wall was there to be read: the first Indian National Congress gathered in 1885; the Boxer Rebellion took place in 1900; Japan defeated Russia in 1905.

From our contemporary vantage point we recognize that imperialism had at least one lasting result. It speeded up the industrialization of the world begun by capitalism. This process has proved irreversible even where the agents of imperialism have been driven out. The people who had become accustomed to railways and airplanes did not return to the horse and buggy; they moved along the trail that imperialism had blazed. When the war of 1914 interrupted the flow of goods on which their economy depended, they found themselves obliged to begin industries on their own. Certain observers have attempted to explain imperialism as a relic of an older, autocratic way of life which continued to exist tangential to the capitalist economy, "a class oriented toward war maintaining itself in a ruling position." [51] But this argument is inconclusive. Salisbury had at his side Chamberlain and Cecil Rhodes, who came from the middle class. The Kaiser found imperialist seconds in Tirpitz, Krupp, Mannesmann, Thyssen, and Kirdorf. France had its Ferry. All European classes share the guilt of imperialism, though the working class derived only indirect benefits and was conscious that even these were purchased at the cost of injuring foreign labor which was kept on a starvation level. It is one of the paradoxes of history that the working class has developed an imperialism of its own in the twentieth century.

The historian who tries to profile these fateful decades finds it easy to fall into Hegelian terms. There seems to be a true dialectic at work, where every position becomes its opposite, yet preserves some of its original elements and carries it forth to new evolutionary stages. The carefully balanced compromise of constitutional monarchy gave way to radical forms of popular government, either equalitarian or totalitarian. The balance of power deteriorated into the setting up of superpowers of continental dimensions. The century of peace and prosperity gave birth to an era of exaggerated unemployment and protracted war. A period bursting with humanitarian sentiments, in arms for every good cause, was followed by a recrudescence of barbarism. Total war led humanity to the brink of self-destruction. The general feeling of security and optimism was replaced by deep-rooted anxiety. But, as we have seen, the seeds that in so short a time could produce the gigantic transformation, were nurtured in the different segments of European civilization. It is only natural that those who knew the world in the days before 1914 think of it as a gilded age and believe, to rephrase Talleyrand, that those who were not alive before 1914 will never know how sweet life can be. It was a glorious era—provided you were born on the right side of the tracks.

I am here reminded of my grandfather, a general practitioner in Berlin. Sometimes he found it difficult to decide on a vacation spot. With the trunks ready and the suitcases packed, he still remained uncertain and would say to the coachman, "Johann, drive me to a nice station." And thus Johann would decide where the old gentleman should go: to Baden-Baden, Merano, the Engadine, Ostende. There were indeed no obstacles for a traveler in those days. He was not required to carry a passport, let alone a visa. All he needed in the way of identification was a letter of credit or a sufficient number of those golden coins which everyone could lawfully carry in his purse. Wherever he went he would find that comfort to which he thought himself entitled and the goods to which he was accustomed. In Paris, in Vienna, in London or Berlin he could attend the favorite upper-class form of entertainment, the operetta. Those were the days of Lehar, Oskar Strauss, of Gilbert and Sullivan, of light folly that glossed over the cracks and rifts in society. Many of the leading personalities of this period appear to us now in the reflected glow of musical comedies: the Kaiser, Prince Bülow, Boulanger, Edward VII. But the relationship between this surface frivolity and the underlying tensions was in general disregarded. The warnings of the great prophets, Nietzsche, Dostoevski, Kierkegaard, Burckhardt went unheeded.[52]

From time to time the sound of a shot would shatter the over-all confidence and would send a shiver along the spine of the bourgeois age. There were occurrences of terrorism and violence which no one paused to comprehend. Isolated individuals, influenced by Nechayev's and Bakunin's theory that the state is evil and that terror is the only weapon against it, used political murder as their tool.

A wave of political crimes such as Europe had not before seen swept the land. Alexander II was assassinated in Russia, King Humbert in Italy; the Empress of Austria was stabbed to death. Spanish and Russian prime ministers became the victims of terrorism and presidents of France and the United States were no exception. But though these murders produced a feeling of horror in Western society, the stout shell of overconfidence did not break. With the exception of the anarchists no group was willing to identify itself with violent and irresponsible acts—least of all organized labor which condemned and abhorred terrorism. After each assassination the people settled back into their old routines convinced that such acts could originate only in the lunatic fringe of society and that, once the guilty were safely put away, there was really nothing to fear.

Nevertheless, terrorism as a political means was no casual or short-term visitant. Again, paradoxically, it had been born in the very century that had tried so hard to eliminate violence from all walks of life. The extremists found it a convenient instrument for the disruption of a social structure that resisted more civilized methods of persuasion. Terrorism was first put into practice on the home front, but in 1914 it emerged on the international scene. The Serbian nationalists who shot the Austrian archduke in Sarajevo on June 28, 1914, adopted political murder as the mechanism most suitable to their aims. The war then made violence a daily occurrence.[53] Thus we find the thread of continuity linking the two centuries even where they seem diametrically opposed.

There are few spectacles in the history of civilization comparable to this picture of Europe, basking in fruitful opulence under the autumn sun of its glory, ripe for the slaughter. The crusading spirit which had borne her forth on her journey of discovery and expansion in 1492 was a distant memory. In those days the white man had controlled 9 per cent of the earth's surface; by 1914 he had subjugated 85 per cent of it. Nor was this latter-day Europe any longer the country that Novalis had identified with Christendom. Europe in 1914 was essentially a secular, rationalistic, and mechanistic civilization; at one and the same time beneficent and Machiavellian, humanitarian and feral, with a rule which extended from Siberia to Tierra del Fuego and from Transvaal to Singapore.

No outside power was strong enough to challenge her; her destruction was brought to maturity within her own confines.

Together with so many of my contemporaries, I have been, over a long period of years, deeply perplexed by the profound transition which took place between 1890 and 1914. The war-guilt clause of the Versailles Treaty has led to a thorough search in all European archives for the arsonists who ignited the great conflagration.[54] Diplomatic events and economic causes have been exhaustively studied, but the cultural trends have not received the same close scrutiny. The cultural evolution of a period is not simply the superstructure of the socioeconomic infra-structure that Marx would have us accept. Neither does it exist independently of its sociological setting. The political and economic situation does not produce culture automatically, but it conditions its forms and actions, favoring the appearance of certain features and excluding or harassing others. The interests of society, as Max Weber says, are the great rails on which humanity moves, but the ideas throw the switches.[55]

CHAPTER II

Founding and Destroying Fathers

The extent to which ideas determine the course of human events is a matter of controversy. Whereas some historians interpret the great gait of history as the unfolding of spiritual forces, others grant to these forces a superficial importance only. Whatever the final answer may be, there seems to be one aspect of the problem that has been neglected: the influence of ideas is not a stable coefficient; it is subject to change according to the general conditions of the period. In other words, the influence of ideas has varied and will continue to vary from age to age. Any endeavor to ascertain the role which ideas have played in coloring the tapestry of time must start from here.

The nineteenth century has often been accused of materialism, but its very materialism was the expression of a new intellectual approach to reality. Its two foremost accomplishments, the national state based on constitutional guarantees and the technological revolution, were both legitimate offspring of European rationalism. Over a long period rationalism had questioned all existing human relations, had probed all answers heretofore taken for granted, and had gradually instilled in European society a dynamics unknown to previous ages. The Industrial Revolution was only one, albeit the most spectacular, feature of a process that had long been under way; the undermining of religious dogma, the centralization of all societal forces by the state are hardly less important.

During certain periods of history the stabilizing forces prevail over the dynamic forces; during others the process is thrown into reverse. The nineteenth century saw the static energies give way to revolutionary tidal waves which are still surging up in our time. In such periods the influence of ideas increases in direct proportion to the general weakening of the social fabric.

We have asserted that the influence of ideas cannot be expressed in formulae applicable to all times. This statement also holds true for the progenitors or, let us say, the embodiments of ideas: the thinkers. Every era has the thinkers it deserves. The question then is, what thinkers does an age deserve? One may assume that all modes of thought and all moods of emotion exist in mankind at all times. But in what way shall we account for the spiritual and temperamental differences which we find in the course of history? The general condition of an age favors some and proves hostile to others. Minds like Nietzsche and Kierkegaard, Baudelaire and Schopenhauer, have surely existed in previous epochs, yet only the nineteenth century activated them.

Change is perhaps the most obvious characteristic of reality; assuredly it is the most outstanding trait of history. But there have been times when the change was slow and almost imperceptible, and others when it flowed forth like lava, rapid and torrid. Moreover, the changes experienced by nineteenth century Europe were man-made and man-willed. These circumstances proved propitious for a type of thinker who might be called the professional revolutionary of the mind. Among the great thinkers of the nineteenth century there were few who like Hegel advocated the preservation of the *status quo,* and even Hegel became a ferment of the most explosive character. It was only natural that the prophetic utterance should flourish.

Under the title "Founding and Destroying Fathers" I have assembled a group of thinkers and artists who are, I believe, the godfathers of our century. The idea of *foundation* as one of the basic categories for the understanding of history has rarely been discussed. In America the term "Founding Fathers" is used, and occasionally Goethe and Stefan George referred to the concept of "Gründung" (the laying of foundations), and I myself am of the mind that this is one of the most crucial principles of historical understanding.

Historical founders and historical foundations imply a special quality. It is not identical with genius, though most founding fathers have shown that evasive trait we call genius. But it is not genius alone that I speak of; it is rather the plenitude of possibilities, the planting of seeds that will nourish future generations, which makes for founders. We find examples of this potential in all fields of history, and it would be a fascinating undertaking to scrutinize world history from this point of view. Here it must suffice to establish this concept as a criterion for our approach.

If some of the great figures of nineteenth century culture are missing it is because, in my judgment, they do not participate in the process of laying the foundations for our present-day civilization. Mazzini, Treitschke, and Mill, for instance, spoke more to their time than to ours and their echo has gradually grown dim. Ricardo, List, Proudhon, Fourier, recede into the mists of the past, but no one questions the significance of Karl Marx. Stirner, D. F. Strauss, and Renan are of interest to the scholar only, but the sufferings of Kierkegaard and Dostoevski burn like the scars on our own bodies.

But every foundation presupposes destruction—"to raise a new sanctuary, a sanctuary must be destroyed; that is the law." [1] It is our task to determine which of the great thinkers whom we shall now consider succeeded in laying new foundations and which merely bequeathed to us a "landscape of ruins."

I

"It would be possible," wrote Georg Brandes in 1881, "to study Goethe in his relation to every civilized nation and measure its stage of development in modern times by the degree of understanding of this single genius. . . . The twentieth century will receive him from the nineteenth as that century received him from the one preceding it." [2] Brandes assumed that there is *one* Goethe whom every generation shall pass on to the following, yet we know, as Goethe himself knew, that history is constantly rewritten.

It would not be difficult to catalogue the great writers of the nineteenth century who lived under his spell, or to list the statesmen and the scientists who found solace in his poetry, and the philosophers and educators who looked to him as a model. Such an approach would obviously prove nothing. It is the "why and how" of spiritual influence that interests the historian of ideas, not the "that and what." Goethe's ascendancy over the years from 1830 to 1918 is indeed an intriguing problem, but we are aware of it precisely because Goethe's authority is challenged in our time, and challenged not by iconoclastic rebels, but by thoughtful and responsible critics like Ortega y Gasset.

Goethe's lifework lies before us like a landscape; one look seems to embrace its entirety. Yet the more we fix our gaze on it, the more the panorama appears to shift. As Karl Jaspers says: "The constant communication of this infinitely rich mind conceals a profound silence. In vain do we try to define Goethe's character. . . . His being is full of tensions, polarities and opposites." [3]

Who then was Goethe? The answer may sound trite, but it must nonetheless be given. He was a poet. He was also during his long life a lawyer and minister of state. He became a theater director and a courtier. He spent a large—too large—part of his time in varied fields of the natural sciences. But all these side interests cannot dim the fact that the basic condition of his existence was to be a poet and "to give to the real," as his friend Merck remarked, "a poetical form."

No other poet has done so much to obscure his vocation. Goethe's Odyssey, the voyage of his mind during sixty years of discoveries, was maintained at the price of constantly jeopardizing the poet within him. Yet poet he was and poet he continued to be from his eighteenth to his eightieth year, his creations breaking forth like a geyser, heartwarming and beautiful. His lyric, rarely equaled, has never been surpassed. However, the most superficial glance at his work tells us that to be a poet "only" was not enough for him. In *Wilhelm Meister* he has given us some idea of the poet he wished to be: "The sensitive soul of the poet, easily moved, proceeds like the circling sun from night to day, and his harp is tuned with gentle transitions to joy and pain. . . . Out of the ground of his heart, the beautiful flower of wisdom grows. . . . He lives the dream of life as an awakened one and the rarest events are to him at the same time past and future. Thus the poet is also the teacher, prophet, friend of gods and men." [4]

When Goethe awoke to realize the intensity and originality of his genius, the eighteenth century had almost run its course. To be a poet in 1770 did not and could not mean the same as it had meant to Dante or Ariosto, Spenser or Shakespeare. Three great revolutions were in the making; to be a poet in this time could only mean to "live the dream of life as an awakened one."

The feeling of universal love *(All Liebe)* is the force that links and binds all Goethe's creativity and activity. When it first burst through the eighteenth century shell it expressed itself in symbols as contradictory as Ganymede and Prometheus, Mahomet and Faust. He discovered in himself a gift which he called by that great and ambiguous name: Nature. It seemed to embrace everything. It was superior to any teaching or custom with which it might conflict. It was even superior to experience, because, as Goethe said, he knew the world "by anticipation." [5] The man who knows the world by anticipation must of necessity become a titan; his genius will encourage him to proclaim his prerogative.

The two great symbolic creations which we find in Goethe's work, *Werther* and *Faust,* are the fruits of his titanism. But whereas *Faust* gestated for sixty years, from conception to completion, *Werther* was thrown upon the world almost before the tears of its travail had dried. *Werther* is a book full of explosives, as Goethe said, and its effect was truly explosive. It ushered in the movement of subjectivism which engulfed all Europe. Written twelve years after Rousseau's *Social Contract,* it was both antisocial and anticontractual, proclaiming the supremacy of emotional individualism—"I turn in upon myself and find a world."

It may seem strange to call *Werther* the fruit of titanism—Werther, whose sole manly act was his suicide. And it does show that all was not well with Goethe's titanism.[6] It has been said that his work displays a whole "gallery of weaklings," and that this gallery is one of self-portraits. No one knew it better than Goethe himself. Actually the most important decision of his life, that of taking roots in Weimar, was based on his knowledge that the titan had failed. The evolution of his mind after 1775 has its inception here. The leit-motif was still that of universal love, but the ways to achieve it were no longer those of rebellion or ecstasy. They became instead introspection, education, observation, and science. Goethe now throws a "calm backward glance" on the self-complacency of his youth and finds it wanting. He wrote to Lavater, "This desire to raise as high . . . as possible the pyramid of my existence, whose foundation has been given to me, outweighs everything else . . . perhaps fate will break me in the middle of my career . . . at least it should be possible to say that it was boldly projected." [7]

Thus the great business of living, of managing and directing his life began to crystalize in him, permeating every day and every minute of his life. "May my strength suffice for me to reach the summit."

The third great myth, after *Werther* and *Faust,* was born, the myth that was Goethe himself. "Werther and Faust," says Borgese, "are projections of the author's actual experience into the poetic possible, his might-have-beens; Goethe is the projection of the poetic possible in the actual experience, what he was and is under the dominance of his ought-to-be or ought-to-have-been." [8] It was through himself that Goethe wished to show the world a new image and a new possibility of man, an idea of humanity beyond the rational or irrational, a blend of science and poetry, of intuition and reason: the beautiful flower of wisdom, teacher, prophet, and friend of the gods and of men. "Have I ever before quoted to you the phrase, *Individuum est ineffabile,* whence I deduce a world?" The world deduced is a world of reverence for the individual, for life itself, and for the inscrutable, the Godhead.

Had Goethe succeeded in expressing his image of man with the directness he marshaled in *Faust* and *Werther,* his message would be clearer, but his great concept remained imbedded in his life as a promise only. He chose rather to freeze himself in the attitude of a demigod; a gradual metamorphosis took place; the man became a monument.

His efforts in the field of natural science furnish a pertinent example. Poet and thinker that he was, he had a vested interest in the nature of nature. He established a whole set of new evolutionary concepts: Urphänomen, metamorphosis, Gestalt, which have found universal acceptance in the organic sciences. As for his actual discoveries, they were great not of themselves, but because the foremost poet of the age had made them. His Theory of Colors was proved wrong by later science, and his pigheaded opposition to Newton will always remain a block to unconditional admiration. Goethe's fight against the microscope and the telescope, his hostility to the application of mathematics to natural sciences, were errors characteristic of his wish to build frontiers and to set limits upon the inherent curiosity of man.[9] Neither the nineteenth nor the twentieth century heeded his interdict; the human spirit cannot be halted by proscription. But while Goethe's humanistic short cut failed to arrest the development of physics, today's appraisal of his moral position in this controversy is more discerning: Goethe was trying to prevent further advancement in a field where mankind becomes the sorcerer's apprentice unable to arrest those forces which threaten it with self-destruction.

When Goethe, with hesitant fingers, lifted the veils from *Faust*, he set the imagination of his contemporaries on fire. By the time of its conclusion, in 1831, it had become a colossus in which historical periods, styles, and modes of thought were blended in the most imperious fashion. I shall not attempt to give full homage to Faust, that strange hero who stands condemned by any standards, whether pagan or Christian, legal or theological, rational or emotional, and whom Goethe decided to save in the end.

The nineteenth century was not greatly perturbed by the enigma of Faust's redemption. It sensed in him the myth of European self-interpretation which intrigued the philosopher and the scientist, the poet and the musician, with persistent magic. On any level the attraction of Goethe's *Faust* has never been exhausted. Many a reader is enchanted with the multiple objects of Faust's pursuit: knowledge, drink, sex, wealth, beauty, power, even social welfare; whatever the interest, it may be found singly or in combination in *Faust*. And since Faust's destiny is based on the foregone conclusion that he will test them all and reject them all, the scientist and the politician, the seeker of pleasure and the seeker of beauty, will find here not only his goal, but also the disillusionment that inevitably follows its attainment. Yet nothing more cruel or bitter has ever been written than the fifth act of *Faust*. The centenarian Faust, completely blind, experiences his supreme moment as he listens to the spades that, so he thinks, are breaking the ground where a free people shall rise, a people who will deserve life and freedom because they will each day conquer it anew. In this vision he feels the satisfaction which, according to the letter and the spirit of his wager with Mephistopheles, will lead him to eternal damnation. But the spades are the spades of his own gravediggers. Even his last goal is an illusion.

The nineteenth century did not comprehend the irony of this finale; it was content with Goethe's explanation:

Wer immer strebend sich bemüht,
Den können wir erlösen.

But the philosophy that "he who always striving labors will be saved," is just another ambiguity.

What saves Faust is not mercy and certainly not merit, but "das ewig weibliche," the "eternal feminine," that draws us onward. The eternal feminine is not grace or charity, it is love for creativity.[10] Faust is not saved; he saves himself. Nothing attainable could quench his thirst. Error and guilt are better than inertia. To strive is all; it is the redeeming virtue of the human race, its autosalvation.

The interest which *Faust* provoked in the nineteenth century fell short of understanding that Faust's love was not for Gretchen or for Helena, but for creative evolution, as Bergson would have said. But they did feel his activism, his ceaseless effort, his disgust with metaphysical speculations, his attempt to spread freedom through conquest. *Faust* seemed to fit the pattern of the age: restless enterprise, humanitarian endeavor, even imperialism, could turn to Faust and call him as witness for the defense. It is highly significant that two philosopher-historians of our time have adopted the Faust myth for their own purposes. Oswald Spengler in his *Decline of the West* christened the European culture in the name of Faust. Arnold Toynbee has gone even further, finding in Faust a clue for the comprehension of all historical growth.

To what extent may Goethe be called a founder of the past century and of ours? "Our teacher," he says, "is he under whose direction we constantly practice an art. In this sense I have been nobody's teacher. But if I would have to say what I have been to the Germans, I might call myself their liberator." [11] Teacher of no one and liberator of generations would be an accurate description of Goethe's relation to the times that followed him. His singular position in an age when the time-honored symbols of faith had lost their binding force imposed upon him the necessity of creating his own myths. He was the first European to be confronted with this necessity.

Croce has given us a summation of the forms which Goethe piloted into the nineteenth century: the autobiographical and utopian novel, the psychological drama and contemplative poetry, admiration for the pure form of Hellenic origin and the folk song, the enchantment of oriental wisdom and medieval exaltation, the storm of conscience, and the voice of conscience. However, Goethe and the nineteenth century do not meet on the simple ground of acceptance. At more than one point they seem to be at cross purposes. The great assignments of the century were: the formation of the nation-state, the establishment of constitutional government in continental Europe, and the triumph of the exact sciences which brought in its train the technological revolution. Conversely, Goethe was essentially supranational; constitutional government was no concern of his. His clairvoyant mind had glimpses of the industrial age, but he did not fully evaluate its ground-shaking character. However, the bourgeois society whose life was based on work, reason, and education did claim that its virtues were akin to Goethe's. It interpreted Goethe's existence as the incarnation of its most cherished belief, that of progress. Gradually Goethe's reputation superseded that of all other poets. Carlyle and Emerson, Stifter and Grillparzer, Keller and Nietzsche, Barrès, Gide, and Suarès saw in him a civilizing force permeating the entire age. But inevitably the nineteenth century saw Goethe in its own image. Predominantly an age of optimism, it disregarded the note of suffering and torture in Goethe's life.

The Goethe cult reached its height around 1900. By then the Goethe quotation had become the indispensable gear of the public speaker; Goethe's capacity for love served as an excuse for irresponsible sentimentality; his universality was less understood by those who seemed most devoted to the interpretation of his work. Few, like Nietzsche and George, sensed the danger of confusing Goethe's cosmic optimism with the belief in unbridled technical progress. It took the great crisis of 1914 to bring this problem into the open.

II

The latter part of the nineteenth century was an age of realism in science and art, novel and drama, politics and history. However, this realism was ushered in by three philosophical systems. It would seem as though the European mind had required the blessings of speculation before it dared to embark on its career of positive conquest. The three philosophers who sanctified reality by their interpretations were Schopenhauer, Comte, and Hegel.

Many European students in the era before 1914 experienced the emotion that overcame Nietzsche when with anticipatory awe he opened one afternoon Schopenhauer's *The World as Will and Idea*. Perhaps it was the provocative title that lured them into this world at once so lucid and so opaque; perhaps it was the tone of its somber and serious prose.

Born in 1788, the son of a wealthy merchant, Schopenhauer completed his great work at the age of thirty. His efforts to compete with Hegel's powerful influence at the University of Berlin were unsuccessful, and he resigned his position as lecturer in disgust, dedicating his remaining forty years to expounding the infallible truth of his system, to belittling the ideas of other philosophers and to scorning mankind in general and women in particular.

Schopenhauer's position as a thinker is post-Kantian: we live in a phenomenal world and the absolute cannot be apprehended by rational procedures. This is the meaning of Schopenhauer's statement, "The world is my idea." This truth holds good for everything that lives and knows, but man alone can bring it into reflective and abstract consciousness. If he really does so he has attained to philosophical wisdom, or at least has taken the first step in that direction.[12] But Schopenhauer was not only Kant's heir; he was also heir to the vast realm of German culture from Goethe to Beethoven, and would never have been content to know the phenomenal world only. We wish to know, he says, the significance of these ideas; we ask whether this world is merely idea . . . or whether it is something else, something more than idea, and if so, what?[13] The answer is given in his famous title. Will, and will alone, gives man the key to his own existence, shows him the inner mechanism of his being, of his action, of his movements. Schopenhauer finds will at work not only in men and animals, but also in plants and crystals, in magnetism and electricity; . . . it is the inmost nature, the kernel of every particular thing, and also of the whole. It appears in every blind force of nature and in the considered action of man; there are only differences of degree in its manifestations, not in the substance that manifests itself.[14]

Philosophy, as well as art, may be called "the world seen through a temperament." It was Schopenhauer's temperament that made him put the emphasis on will. His concept of the World as Will was a master stroke of explanation, less of the universe than of his century's view and estimate of the essence of the world. Indeed, the climate of the nineteenth century could not be described more accurately. If one may call the sixteenth century the age of religious conscience, the seventeenth that of power, and the eighteenth that of reason, the nineteenth century may well be designated as the century of will.

Thus Schopenhauer gave to the age-old quest for the absolute an answer that admirably suited his time. Whereas knowledge perceives only the phenomenal order of things in space and time and causal connection, philosophy penetrates to the core and understands the working of the will. Man is a citizen of two worlds, the world as will and the world as idea, and his grandeur as well as his misery rest on his unique place in the universe.

What was so extraordinary in this interpretation of the absolute as will? Negatively speaking, it was Schopenhauer's turning away from reason. Positively speaking, it was his picturing the world as filled with a dark and demonic force. Life is will and will is life. Following the interpretation of man and nature that Machiavelli and Hobbes had once advanced, Schopenhauer brought forth a vision of the world as the work of the unmotivated, causeless, unevaluated life-urge which is always at variance with itself.

Schopenhauer is the philosopher and the psychologist of the will. From his viewpoint the intellect is reduced to being a servant of life merely—"Thought is the slave of life." Man's organs, the brain no less than the organs of sex, have functional significance only; they do the pleasure of the will. Schopenhauer's will motivates human beings by and through its own cunning, very much as Hegel's Spirit of the World uses the "cunning of the idea" to obtain its ends.

Schopenhauer's discoveries in this field are far-reaching. He not only paved the way for Freud; he led Freud and the subconscious onto the stage. He revealed man's consciousness as the plaything of stronger and darker instincts that command its performance. The pages in which Schopenhauer describes the symptoms of desire in human beings, where he interprets their symbolic traits as the revelation of the great life force, are of exceptional beauty and depth, and would in themselves justify Schopenhauer's being ranked with the founding fathers of our time.[15]

It is obvious that Schopenhauer anticipated yet another of the great themes of the nineteenth century: evolution. If the world is will and will is life, the world is forever becoming. But Schopenhauer's concept of evolution is of a special kind; it is an evolution without goal. The life-urge, forever wishing and desiring, forever creating and destroying, has no aim; it moves onward, not upward. Or so Schopenhauer thought, since it suited his pessimistic bias.

Superimposed on his philosophy of the world as will is his conviction that the basis of all willing is need, deficiency, and pain, that all the satisfaction the will can give is essentially negative, and that eternal suffering outweighs happiness. More than ever we feel that philosophy is the world seen through a temperament, a mood, and a bitter and disappointed one at that.

To reason with a pessimist is as hopeless an undertaking as to discourage an optimist. We can, therefore, do no more than accept Schopenhauer's contention that life is will and will is life and that each should perish, for such is the conclusion he reaches. There were two ways, he believed, whereby man could free himself from the obsession that the will produces in him. One is transitory: art. The other is permanent: religious asceticism.

As a philosopher of art, Schopenhauer may well outlive all his other titles to fame. He has given us the deepest interpretation of the arts that has yet been produced by the European mind. "So long as our consciousness is filled by our will, so long as we are given up to the throng of desires with their constant hopes and fears, so long as we are the subjects of willing, we can never have happiness or peace." But through the arts, that peace which we are always seeking comes to us of its own accord, and we are content. We are then in a painless state, in the state of gods. "We are for the moment set free from the miserable striving of the will; we keep the Sabbath of the penal servitude of willing; the wheel of Ixion stands still."[16]

Obviously this is a romanticist's conception of the arts. It is art as delivery from the untamed ego with its uncontrollable urges and

desires. It is too negative in character to be entirely satisfactory.
Great art brings more than peace and freedom from want; it does
not act like a sedative, but produces a state of bliss very positive
in its fulfillment. But even with these reservations, Schopenhauer's
interpretation remains the most profound elucidation of the role
the arts play in man's life. Again, it is as a romanticist that he
exalted music above all other arts. Music is not the copy of Ideas,
but of the Will itself. "The composer reveals the inner nature of
the world and expresses the deepest wisdom in a language which
his reason does not understand. . . . Music, therefore, if regarded
as an expression of the world, is in the highest degree a universal
language." [17]

Schopenhauer resembles a Faust all too willing to cry to the
passing hour, "Oh, linger yet; Thou art so beautiful." But ultimately he was obliged to admit that these hours give no more than
short intervals of forgetting between long nights of desperation.
Esthetic happiness offers man only a fictitious respite followed by
an awakening where the blind urge of the life-will it tried to escape
still confronts it. The final solution for man's affliction cannot
come from the arts, it must come from moral sources. But can
there be an ethical code where the will is supreme and all-powerful?
Schopenhauer's answer is well known. Just as the moment of esthetic bliss is for him essentially negative, just so is his ethical teaching essentially abstemious.

The way to ethical awakening leads through two important
grades. When man begins to realize that life consists in constant
passing away, vain striving, inward conflict, and continuous suffering, he will recognize the truth of the Hindu saying, *tat-tvam asi*.
Man will recognize man as his brother and fellow sufferer. Love
becomes sympathy, or, as the Germans have it, *Mit-leiden*. But
sympathy is only the initiation. It is a virtue, but virtue provides
merely " a few cool places on the path of red hot coals" that is life.
Virtue must be superseded by asceticism. Only when man disowns
his nature can the will be overcome; only through self-negation
and self-conquest will man find salvation—in nothingness. The
man who attains this goal "looks back smiling and at rest on the
delusions of this world which once were able to move and agonize
his spirit, but which now stand before him as utterly indifferent to

him." [18] Nothing can trouble him more, nothing can move him, for he has cut all the thousand cords of will which held him bound to the world. Thus, the essence of Schopenhauer's teaching is nihilistic. *Life should not be.*

The nineteenth century was ready to accept the diagnosis but not the remedy. Although will became the keynote of the times, Schopenhauer's praise of a Buddhistic nirvana convinced few. To be sure, his own life seemed to disavow his teaching. He was too venomous, too disappointed a man to set an example of the dispassionate self-abnegation which was supposed to be the path to wisdom. He was also too much a cosmopolitan of the ancient regime to show any understanding for the pressing problems of his century. His thinking, contrary to Hegel's, was definitely ahistorical, if not antihistorical, and antisocial to boot.

For a long time Schopenhauer's following was limited, but eventually Wagner's music translated "the world as will and idea" into a language of emotional symbols, and it thus became one of the most potent influences of the time.[19] For Nietzsche the combination of Schopenhauer and Wagner proved the key to the burning problems of education and culture. Jakob Burckhardt expanded the contemplative pessimism of Schopenhauer into historical visions of great beauty and depth. Through von Hartmann the discovery of the unconscious and the interpretation of sex as the most powerful manifestation of the life-urge reached Freud, and through Freud, Adler and Jung.

III

Schopenhauer and Comte present immediate and spectacular contrasts. On one hand, there is the solitary thinker, the misogynist, the pessimistic hermit; on the other, the founder of the "positive religion," the Frenchman who extolled the ennobling influence of woman, and the advocate of progress. Yet both were sons of the same century, and express in their own divergent ways its tremendous dynamic drive.

A child of the merging eighteenth and nineteenth centuries, Auguste Comte was keenly aware of the historical situation that surrounded him. He hailed from a royalist and Catholic background, but, though he broke with the family tradition at the age of thirteen, the Catholic stamp was burned deep into his soul. His break with his monarchic and Christian legacy would indicate that young Comte was a follower of the ideas of 1789, but such an assertion must be made with reservations. Comte himself said that without the French Revolution neither his theory of progress nor the positive philosophy would have been possible.[20] But his philosophy rose in the aftermath of the Revolution, and Comte's first question was not how the Revolution should be perpetuated, but what social institutions should be established in its wake.

Comte learned his approach to politics from such antagonistic godfathers as de Maître and Saint Simon. During his close association with Saint Simon he came to grasp the social and economic issues of the industrial age, but he was too imperious a personality to remain the disciple of one master. Moreover, he was stimulated by other than political events. The scientific trends demanded his attention in the same, or even to a higher, degree. He read voraciously: the great mathematicians Descartes and d'Alembert; the Scottish philosophers Hume and Adam Smith, and also Turgot, Montesquieu, and Condorçet.

It was one of Comte's deepest intuitions to recognize that the crisis of the age had resulted from the impact of the scientific spirit on the sociopolitical institutions, and that it could be successfully resolved only if and when the two were no longer at variance. "Institutions," says Comte, "depend on morals, and morals in their turn depend on beliefs. Every scheme of new institutions will, therefore, be useless so long as morals have not been 'reorganized,' and so long as . . . a general system of opinions has not been founded which is accepted by all minds as true." [21] At the age of twenty-four he published a pamphlet that contains the program for all his later work.[22] He had been struck by one observation from the beginning. He had encountered the results of anarchy in the whole of society and in many sectors of the emotional and intellectual life of his time, but he observed that the province of the exact sciences had maintained its stability and independence.[23] "There is no freedom of conscience in astronomy, in physics, chemistry, or even physiology," he wrote, "in the sense that everyone would find it absurd not to believe with confidence in the principles established in these sciences by competent men."

From this point he advanced to the discovery of the *Law of the Three Stages*. According to this "law" each branch of human knowledge passes successively through three stages: the theological or fictional, the metaphysical or abstract, and the scientific or positive state. The first state is the necessary point of departure for the human intelligence; the second serves as transition; only the third is final and definite. "In the positive state the human mind has given over the vain search after absolute notions, the origin and destination of the universe, and the causes of phenomena, and applies itself to the study of their laws, that is, their invariable relations of succession and resemblance." [24] If this law was of universal validity, and such was Comte's conviction, it could lead not only to a general classification and hierarchy of all sciences, but would provide for a foundation on which to build the new science of society. Sociology in turn would direct the evolution of the human race toward a situation of harmony with the final and positive state of human intelligence.[25]

What is meant by positive? "Positive means real, utile, certain, precise, organic, relative, and even sympathetic." [26] The confusion of criteria in this definition points already to the difficulties inherent in Comte's enterprise. It shows that the law of the three stages was for him an open sesame like Hegel's dialectic. However, Hegel was an absolutist; Comte, a relativist.

Comte assumed that we have no knowledge of anything but phenomena, and that our knowledge of these phenomena is not and can never be absolute. "Everything is relative"; he says, "that is the only absolute." But there are constant resemblances and constant sequences observable in these phenomena, and these we term laws.[27] Comte never undertook to investigate the human claim to knowledge. Epistomology and psychology are conspicuously absent from his table of sciences. The omission led him into an untenable position in which he first substituted the relative for the absolute and ended by deifying the relative.

Once in possession of the philosopher's stone, Comte dedicated his life to bringing about a reorganization of the sciences, to be followed by the advancement in education, both to culminate in the reorganization of society.[28] A smaller mind would have recoiled from such an enterprise, and it is not surprising that even Comte's

mighty intellect cracked under the weight of its self-imposed burden. He became the victim of nervous disorders and was obliged
to spend a year in a sanatorium. Many of the extravagances of his
later work may have been the result of the strain under which he
labored to realize his great design.

The first part of his work to reach completion was the "Course
of the Positive Philosophy." Comte arranges the sciences in series
of which each represents an advance in speciality beyond the one
preceding it. Increasing speciality is accompanied by increasing
complexity, that is to say, the more advanced sciences deal with
a set of phenomena determined by a more numerous combination
of laws. Comte presents the sciences in this order: 1. mathematics,
2. astronomy, 3. physics, 4. chemistry, 5. biology, 6. sociology. He
asserts that the sciences have developed in this progression because,
according to the law of the three stages, they had no choice. Moreover, the historical sequence of their development is the only order
in which they can be understood.[29]

The contemporary critic still reads Comte's *Course of the Positive
Philosophy* with interest. It was a prodigious attempt, even though
the author fell into the common error of declaring that his own
time had reached a final scientific level.

The positive philosophy arrived at its zenith with the new science
that Comte sometimes calls social physics, but more often sociology.
It is based on his belief that social phenomena are, like all other
phenomena, capable of being grouped under laws, and that the
true destination of philosophy is to be social.[30]

Comte distinguishes between the static and the dynamic aspects
of sociology. The static gives the conditions of the existence and
permanence of the social state. The dynamic studies the law of its
evolution. Comte represents a reaction against the "revolutionary
theory" of society, which based the state on the individual only.
Against the theory of man's innate selfishness, Comte sets his concept of sociability. Sociability is the "instinct of instincts," just as
sociology is the science of sciences.[31]

Man, says Comte, is at the same time selfish and cooperative,
but always more selfish than cooperative. Under these circumstances, can we prove that there is an evolution in human affairs
and that this evolution shows improvement? Comte answers both

these questions in the affirmative. The evolution of mankind is caused by its wants. Want forces man to work, but not blindly. The law of the three stages demonstrates that man works under the guidance of the intellect; actually Comte sees the intellectual development as the main agent of progess. Improvement in human affairs results from the increasing strength of the social instinct which arms itself with the growth of man's intellectual activity. Thus philosophy of history becomes the crown of sociology. Comte's achievements in this field are great. The survey of human affairs from the vantage point of the law of the three stages was in itself an intellectual event of the first order and had a tremendous effect on other sciences such as anthropology, ethnology, and comparative religion. Comte saw the cumulative influence of past generations on the present. He spoke of the communion of the living with the dead as one of the deepest lessons that history teaches us. He saw discoveries and inventions as the necessary manifestations of the intellectual evolution, a concept from which all cultural history has benefited.[32] In a word, his philosophy of history remains a landmark in the development of historical consciousness.

Nothing so good can be said of his later attempts to erect a new political system and a new religion. A profound admirer of the Catholic Church, he thought that mankind in its positive state should enjoy a similar organization. Humanity, the only entity that is "positively known," was therefore raised to the rank of "le grand être"; it took the place of God. Few would follow Comte on this path, but no one can read his elaborate prescriptions for private and public devotion, for the nine sacraments, the calendar, and the saints, without being provoked to mirth. When Comte finally introduces a trinity of his own making, when he speaks of "la vièrge positive" the result is "positively" hilarious. His is a remarkable case of driving out transcendent thought through the front gate and smuggling it in again by the back door.[33]

His political system, too, is a mixture of deep thought and misguided conclusions. Basing everything on the social instinct, Comte sets down as the golden rule of morality the necessity of living for others, "vivre pour autrui." The word "altruism" is his coinage. But his moral system suffers from the same weakness as his religion: it is based on laws, not on values. He had a sovereign contempt for the principles of liberty and equality, and considered the parliamentary system not only incapable of aiding the reorganization of society, but a serious impediment to it.[34] As mankind is passing from the metaphysical into the positive state, the military spirit declines in direct proportion to the rise of the industrial spirit. The two powers in Comte's republic were, therefore, the leaders of industry and the positive thinkers, the former holding the secular, the latter the spiritual power. Since positive knowledge had already been reached, it was more important to defend and protect it than to question and discuss it. Men's opinions should be formed for them by a small number of highly trained minds, properly prepared for this laborious task. Comte was so authoritarian that he welcomed any autocratic figure on the contemporary scene, regardless of whether it was the Tzar Nicholas I or Louis Napoleon.[35]

But the follies of his religious and political programs did not curb Comte's influence. In reality his philosophy became the ideology which blanketed most of the Western world in the years between 1850 and 1900. He had followers, both critical and uncritical, in England: John Stuart Mill, Grote, Buckle, George Eliot, Spencer. In France their number was legion. He influenced as fine-grained a thinker as Dilthey. His philosophy appealed to the United States through its pragmatism and was a powerful influence in Mexico *(los cientificos)*, Brazil, and Argentina. His thinking stimulated men who publicly opposed him, like Renan and Taine, and it became the frame of reference for the powerful movement of naturalism which invaded the European scene around 1870.[36]

Yet the positive age has not arrived, or if one wishes, it has come and gone. And it is not Comte who holds for millions of people in the twentieth century the promise of a world organized according to "scientific principles," but Marx.

What was Comte's cardinal mistake? John Stuart Mill lists as the *fons errorum,* Comte's mania for systematization, but I think we must look deeper.[37] His was a world without transcendence. The law of the three stages did not permit any positive evaluation of the creative forces in man, and the cult of humanity was, in truth, self-idolatry. Much of Europe and America, before 1914, worshiped no other god than humanity and progress. In this respect Comte was an influence and a symptom at the same time.

But he cannot be summarily dismissed. For many his formulae had the strengthening effect of a prayer that they repeated to themselves for the reaffirmation of their belief in man. "Ordre et Progrès"; "famille, patrie, humanité"; "l'amour pour principe et l'ordre pour base; le progrès pour but"; "savoir pour prévoir, afin de pourvoir." Thus he remains a leaven in our age. His greatness consisted in seeing that the crisis of the Western world was first and foremost a moral and a religious one; his failure lay in the fact that he thought science could resolve it.

IV

It has often been observed that Comte's positive system and Hegel's philosophy move along parallel lines. Both interpret the world in progress; both adhere to a single method of explanation; both consider their achievements to be the beginning of the millennium.[38] But here the resemblance ends. Hegel's thought is rooted in quite different soil from that which fed the positive philosophy, and he rises to heights which Comte was never able to envisage.

Hegel spent his youth in close communion with Schelling and Hölderlin.[39] Like them he was moved by a nostalgic admiration for the Hellenic world, by the unrest that the French Revolution produced all over Europe, by the speculations that followed Kant, and by the contradictory inspirations of the romantic movement. Theological thought held a great attraction for him. The personality of Jesus and the future of Christian thinking in a world overshadowed by rationalistic ideas claimed his attention. But so did political reality and it found in him a genius to whom the elements of power were as self-evident as they had once been to Niccolò Machiavelli.

Hegel's position must be understood in the light of his struggle to find an answer to so many queries and to present a synthesis of so many antithetical elements. His achievements may be summed up in a single phrase: he understood the world as history. The labor which brought him to this understanding is not so easily summarized.

Hegel began like all post-Kantian philosophers with a reflection on the nature of thought and its position vis-à-vis reality. Whereas the eighteenth century thinkers had opened a cleavage between thought and reality, Hegel endeavored to close the gulf between the rational and the real. All Hegel's thinking is expressed in the well known words: "the real is reasonable and the reasonable is real." [40] Behind them lies the basic premise of his system which, says Croce, "recognizes that life is a struggle, but nevertheless a harmony, that virtue is a combat against ourselves, but that it is nevertheless ourselves. It recognizes that when an opposition has been overcome, a new opposition springs from the bosom of the unity, so there must be a new conquest, then a new opposition, and so on, but it recognizes, too, that this is just the way of life." [41] For Hegel, philosophical thought is concrete and universal at the same time; the whole is expressed in it and by it as vividly as the particular, and both are combined in the motion of thought. This then is the definition of his famous dialectic: thought in motion. It explains how the contradiction between being and not being can be overcome by becoming. Evolution is its watchword. The world is in flux, moving from thesis to its negation, the antithesis, which in turn will be negated by the synthesis, in which both opposites shall be reconciled and conquered *(aufgehoben)*.[42]

For many a reader this may sound like so much philosophical gibberish, but in truth the consequences of Hegel's discovery were vast. He elaborated on it in work after work until he believed that he had encompassed the universe. This is its essence: reason, or as Hegel calls it, *Geist* (spirit), is the very core of reality and can be apprehended only in motion. It is finite and infinite; it reveals itself in a process in which every fact is a fact of the idea and belongs to the organic whole of the idea. History is the very reality of the idea because the spirit is nothing outside its historical development.[43] Already, in his earliest attempts (1802), Hegel shows himself to be convinced of the significance of his interpretation of the world as history. In his *Phenomenology of the Spirit* (1807) he tried to prove that only his idea of God could explain what Kant and Spinoza had tried to explain in vain, that is, why God has to "release Himself" and become form in multiple manifestations. It is, says Hegel, the very nature of the spirit to release itself, because only through the realm of finite spirit does the infinite spirit disclose itself.[44] Knowledge of God can be achieved only through the memory of all the individual spirits in which He has embodied

Himself. Recollection is, therefore, not a detour, but the only possible way to gain complete knowledge of the divine mind. Thus history is lifted to a new dignity; it becomes the self-understanding of the divine mind, that is, of God in the mind of Man.

The understanding of God in history must proceed along the lines of dialectic motion, because it is in dialectic motion that God makes His historical appearance. In this manner Hegel ventured into one of the most ambitious enterprises ever undertaken. He believed it possible to show the pattern in the growth of human civilization at the same time that he stated its final goal. Philosophy of history became his supreme aim. But in the philosophy of history the ideas of law and society, of the individual and the state, found their place as well. Nor were religion and the arts to be forgotten. "The one thought," writes Hegel, "with which philosophy approaches history is the simple thought of reason: that reason rules the world, and that . . . there is rational progress in the history of the world." [45] For the steady and majestic pace of the world-spirit he found a definition which has become celebrated: it was "the progress in the consciousness of freedom." This statement, which intoxicated many minds during the nineteenth century, shows Hegel's greatness but also his ambiguity, because anyone could put the accent where it pleased him and thus come to a very different understanding of what history means.

In Hegel's progression the national spirits *(Volksgeister)* represent single but necessary steps by which the universal spirit manifests itself. This was Hegel's contribution to the role that nationalities play in history and his attitude proved very palatable to his century. The great individual, too, was recognized; he became the executive secretary of the world-spirit. Great men are the indispensable agents of progress. Inspired by personal ambitions and desires, they bring, nevertheless, the necessary achievements characteristic of each period. The world-spirit makes them do its work through "the cunning of reason"—another of Hegel's significant contributions to the way in which history advances.[46] Although no one element is completely neglected in this architecture, it must be obvious that Hegel sets the community high above the happiness of the individual, and that the forms of community life embodied in the state occupy the topmost rank. Hegel was an enemy of the discontented in life and spoke with contempt of "the laurels of good intentions . . . dry leaves which had never been green." [47]

The abstract philosophy of the Englightenment had, Hegel thought, collapsed, and his own was to take its place disclosing objective standards for religion and law, society and government. One cannot deny that this vision of history was full of grandeur; neither can one deny that it was utterly lacking in transcendence. In Hegel's thinking, values had ceased to be guides: they had become goals.[48]

Hegel viewed his system as the final one. It included the achievements of all preceding thought; it was the ultimate synthesis and the reconciliation of all opposites. Art and religion would find a "refuge" in philosophy and become the science of art and the philosophy of religion.[49] He was particularly determined to prove that Christianity and reason, so long at daggers' points, were finally at peace. With his extraordinary gift of interpretation, half intuition and half sophistry, he construed the mysteries of the Trinity, the Incarnation, and the Resurrection in terms of his dialectic. Thus Christianity was incorporated in the massive picture he gave of his epoch as the Era of Reconciliation. In reality it was just one more attempt to secularize Christian thought, and desperate souls like Kierkegaard were bound to rise against it.[50]

One question in particular has puzzled many a student of Hegel. How was it possible that the prophet of evolution could have conceived of an end stage in historical development? How could the same man be eschatological and dialectical at once? Hegel knew full well that when a form of life has grown old it may be understood only, never rejuvenated.[51] One would like to conclude from these words that Hegel looked upon his system as an expression of European culture in its latest phase rather than as the gospel which should usher in the millennium. But, alas! he indulged in ambiguity here too. Although he sometimes pointed to Russia and America as the stages for future events and stressed their "gigantic possibilities," he avoided a true approximation of the limitations of his own philosophy. The heavenly city was founded; this and his dialectic were the doubtful legacies he passed on to his disciple, Karl Marx.

But it would be unfair to limit the appreciation of Hegel's influence to Kierkegaard and Marx. In width and depth Hegel's philosophy extends beyond them. It was the first coherent "study of history." Hegel elucidated the inner meaning of that constant flux of which man is both part and victim. He bestowed significance and logical order on all events. Every historical position could be explained in terms of thesis or antithesis, every hope glorified as synthesis, bound to come. Hegel's philosophy made the *beati possidentes* secure, the opposition courageous, the oppressed fanatical. "The progress in the consciousness of liberty" was used by reactionaries as a shield and by radicals as a banner. The advocates of state power as well as the partisans of constitutional government, even the Communists, found it a useful slogan. Nor is this all. D. F. Strauss and Feuerbach hastened to bring the secularization of Christianity to its logical conclusion. The Russian intelligentsia was deeply attracted by Hegel as were English and French thinkers who, like Taine, admired his method and his comprehension.

At the end of the nineteenth century Hegel's philosophy, like all idealistic thought, was buried under an avalanche of materialism, but the beginning of the twentieth century saw a remarkable renaissance in Hegelianism, heralded in Germany by Dilthey and in Italy by Benedetto Croce. It is not accidental that the three countries, Germany, Italy, and Russia, which embarked on totalitarian experiments are the ones that had felt Hegel's influence most deeply. This fact in itself explains why there are few, if any, pure Hegelians among us today. Hegel's ambiguity, of which we have spoken, is not his only and perhaps not his greatest error. The present age shrinks away from the simple equation of might with right; we are aware of retrogressions in civilization for which there is no place in a scheme that makes history the result of a dialectic slide rule.

V

Hegel's reconciliation of theology and philosophy, of reality and reason, of state and society, seemed the perfect expression of the period of restoration following the downfall of Napoleon. But when Hegel died, the July Revolution had already demonstrated that any hope of sealing the European volcano was built on illusion. Many of the men who reached maturity in the years from 1830 to 1840 were rebels by temperament and no one surpasses Marx's claim to revolutionary fame. There was nothing in his early environment which might have predisposed him to the role he chose.[52] He grew up in an atmosphere of intellectual freedom and economic security. His biography reveals a process in which he found himself gradually advancing toward ever more radical positions until his view matured in uncompromising completeness. A revolutionary temper was his most intrinsic gift, inducing him at a very early stage to name Prometheus "the most noble saint in the philosophical calendar." [53]

Logically he took his stand among those disciples of Hegel who attacked the validity of Christian dogma. Marx called the disintegration of the Hegelian school "the putrefaction of the absolute mind." In the name of realistic humanism he fought against the transcendence of religion. Man, he said, is potentially free, wise, and creative, but his potentiality is yet to be consummated.[54] Earthly happiness can be achieved only by surrendering the illusion of a heavenly beatitude. When, in 1839, Feuerbach undertook to demolish the Hegelian metaphysic and tried to show that religion is "a dream of the human mind," Marx acclaimed him with enthusiasm. However, Marx had already advanced beyond any position that the Hegelians were prepared to accept. His own stand is revealed in the famous "theses" in which he took issue with Feuerbach's criticism. "Philosophers," he said, "have merely given different interpretations of the world; the point is to change it." [55] This celebrated proclamation marks his break with Hegel.

Before we inquire how Marx planned to change the world, it is important to recollect that his break with Hegel was of a distinctive nature. In an oft-quoted phrase Marx stated that whereas Hegel had turned man upside down, he, Marx, had put him "right side up again." In other words, Marx rejected Hegel's idealism but retained his dialectic method; moreover, he saw "matter in motion" rather than "ideas in motion." Although the term, "dialectic materialism," was not used by Marx (it was coined by Engels), it describes precisely enough the new position. That this position entailed a logical absurdity which would have caused Hegel to turn in his grave never troubled Marx. He gave contradictory appraisals of his relations with Hegel, sometimes saying that his own method was the very opposite of Hegel's, at other times asserting that he had salvaged the rational kernel from Hegel's idealistic shell.[56] It is not difficult to ascertain the truth. Marx kept the dialectic method because through it, and only through it, could he interpret history as an intelligible process of social evolution. Marx had an unshakable belief in the progressive character of human society; this is the central theme of all his thought and action. Freedom is for Marx social freedom exclusively. Consequently any abstract liberal idealism is rejected as wishful thinking. "The standpoint of the new materialism is human society or social humanity." [57]

The philosophy of social humanity was thus in a broad way enunciated, but it received its flesh and bone from the most passionate inquiry into the actual conditions of the living human matrix of the European West. Marx's early attempts to voice his radicalism had led to his expulsion from Prussia and he took refuge in Paris. Here he studied the capitalistic society of his day at close range. In the process he absorbed the vast amount of analysis and criticism already amassed by his contemporaries against bourgeois society. Most of Marx's famous concepts, such as "class struggle," the "labor theory of value," the "means of production," "proletariat," "communism," and so forth, were adopted from forerunners and corunners—Saint Simon, Sismondi, Rodbertus, Proudhon, and Ricardo. Marx acknowledged his indebtedness in rare cases, but more often than not he preferred to discount his obligations by heaping polemic insults on his intellectual creditors.[58] It was, however, not so much his ingratitude (though colossal) which determined this attitude, as his practical concern for the future of mankind. He believed that unity of theory and practice were fundamental, and this conviction permeates both his writing and his revolutionary activities.[59] By 1845 Marx's intellectual outlook had crystallized into a world view composed, in uneven proportions, of social science, prophecy, and political strategy. It is this combination of prophet, scientist, and politician which makes Marx a unique figure.

Marx claimed that he had overcome Utopian as well as anarchic socialism and that he had presented scientific socialism to the world for the first time. But even a superficial reading of his work makes it evident that his thought is not purely "scientific." It is based on a creed which defies proof.

This creed embraces Marx's conviction that man's right to justice, that is, social justice, will be realized, and it includes Marx's a priori certainty that in the process of history this ideal will assert itself. Man, declares Marx, is not doomed to live forever in a state of servitude or exploitation: "By acting on the external world and changing it, man changes his nature." [60] More explicitly still, he states, "All history is the progressive modification of human nature." A further article of Marx's faith was his belief that all history prior to the great and imminent change was only "prehistory." The revolution would establish a state in which exploitation would be nonexistent; a classless society would arise in which there would be no division of labor, consequently no specialization; no inequality between the sexes; in one word, the millennium would have arrived.[61] Such hopes may constitute a powerful motivation to touch off revolutions, but they are not demonstrable by any standards of objective evidence. To the extent of these beliefs, Marx's theory is messianic, but it is not difficult to understand the fascination that Marxism exercised over both intellectuals and masses wherever they felt the need of hitching their own fates to the star of an inexorably advancing destiny.

Of course Marx had other and more solid reasons for calling his doctrine "scientific." Said Engels, "Marx discovered the simple fact . . . that human beings must have food, drink, clothing, and shelter first of all, before they can interest themselves in politics, science, art, religion, and the like. This implies that the production of the immediately requisite material means of existence, and therewith the existing phase of development of a nation or an epoch constitutes the foundation upon which the state institutions, the legal outlooks, the artistic and even the religious ideas are built." [62] This is a neat summation of Marx's own thoughts found scattered throughout his work: "The mode of production in material life determines the general character of the social, political, and spiritual processes of life. It is not the consciousness of men that determines their existence, but on the contrary, their social existence determines their consciousness." [63] The prime mover in history is man's need. "Need gives man strength; he who must help himself will do so." To obtain his needs man has but one solution: labor. Marx's view of history is, therefore, essentially the history of human labor; the development of human labor is the key to any understanding of human history.[64] Man's answer to his need does not derive from instinct by which the animal provides for its needs; it comes to him through reason. It is, therefore, not labor alone, but rational labor, technology, which explains man's progress.[65]

The onward march of mankind takes form in class struggle. "The history of all hitherto existing society is the history of class struggle." The ruling class controls the means of production—land, capital, implements, whatever may correspond to a given state of technology, while the exploited class is forced to provide the labor.

Other historians before Marx had found class struggle in history, but no one had ever tried to construct world history in terms of class war. It was a discovery of the first order by means of which Marx gave all students of mankind, in Croce's words, a mass of new data and a canon of interpretation. But the great conception is marred by the preconceived notion of an inevitable outcome: the social revolution. "At a certain stage of their development, the material forces of production in society come into conflict with the existing relations of production, or—what is but a legal expression for the same thing—with the property relations within which they had been at work before. . . . Then comes the period of social revolution." [66] Marx denied any other issue of class struggle, such as adjustment or reconciliation, because he was determined to see the revolution come to pass and take part in it. Even before the revolution of 1848 took place, he had published his declaration of war, the Communist Manifesto.

Few books written in the nineteenth century equal this proclamation in historical perspective; none surpasses it in influence. In 1852 Marx summed up what he himself thought he had accomplished in the Manifesto. "What I did," he wrote to Wedgemeyer, "that was new, was to prove: 1. that the existence of classes is bound up with particular, historical phases in the development of production; 2. that the class struggle necessarily leads to the dictatorship of the proletariat; 3. that this dictatorship itself only constitutes the transition to the abolition of all classes and to a classless society." [67]

This claim seems at once too modest and too presumptuous, and there are other observations in the Communist Manifesto which demand comment. Marx was not the first to denounce the bourgeoisie as a class which "has left no other nexus between man and man than naked self-interest, than callous cash payment." But Marx was the first to describe, with a kind of love-hatred, the revolutionary character of the bourgeoisie. "The bourgeoisie cannot exist without constantly revolutionizing the instruments of production . . . and with them the whole relations of society." Marx recognized the planetary character of the permanent revolution we call capitalism. "The need of a constantly expanding market . . . drives the bourgeoisie over the whole surface of the globe. . . . The bourgeoisie has, through its exploitation of the world market, given a cosmopolitan character to production and consumption in every country. . . . We have intercourse in every direction, universal interdependence of nations. And as in material so also in intellectual production." [68] Recognition of the planetary nature of modern economics permitted Marxism to woo the labor forces of all countries, western and eastern alike, and it explains, I think, the extraordinary success that Marxism experiences today in the Afro-Asian world. Marx furthermore concluded that the proletariat, which will inherit and liquidate the bourgeois world, can exist only on a planetary scale.

Other discoveries which Marx announced in the Communist Manifesto included his insight into the economic crises which, with increasing vehemence, shook the body of society.[69] Marx's description of the proletariat was accurate for his time, but his prophecies and the realities of the twentieth century have not proved easy bedfellows.

Marx's diagnosis of the proletariat as the dialectic antagonist of the bourgeoisie had fateful consequences. Since he considered the bourgeoisie, with its penchant for replacing all human relations with "naked, shameless, direct, brutal exploitation," as the incarnation of all evil, it was necessary that the proletariat should represent the opposite pole.[70] Consequently Marx advocates the abolition of private property, the disappearance of class culture, the exit of the family, and the dissolution of national differences. "The working men have no country." The proletariat should abjure every social, sentimental, or cultural contact with the bourgeoisie because it would become contaminated and thus endanger its class-consciousness. Wherever Marxian ideas were accepted, an iron curtain de-

scended which cut society in two. Marx's predictions did not come
true in the West; there the working class continued to live by inheritance and by tradition in a hundred associations not determined
by class. Wherever Marx's prescription has been applied, however,
it has led to a wholesale destruction of the social and cultural fabric
of the past.

The ambiguity of Marx's image of the classless society has often
been noted. Once the dictatorship of the proletariat has done its
work, it will have swept away forever the very conditions which
produced class antagonism.[71] Then "we shall have an association
in which the free development of each is the condition for the free
development of all." [72] The state would "wither away," and so
would the division of labor. "Each can become accomplished in
any branch he wishes, society regulates the general production and
thus makes it possible for me to do one thing today and another
tomorrow." [73] The economic reward is likewise couched in cryptic
terms: "to every one according to his needs, from everyone according to his ability." "The government of persons is replaced by the
administration of things and the direction of the process of production." [74] That the working classes were willing to pin their hope
on such equivocal statements reveals their profound despair. Marx's
generalities are no more "scientific" than the promises of Utopia
which he and Engels so despised.

The revolution of 1848 had fallen short of Marx's expectations.
In exile in London, he devoted himself to a study of the capitalistic
society and to the direction of the proletarian movement. Although
he made tactical concessions to the changing political scene, his
over-all strategy never wavered; it remained faithful to the road
and the goal to which the Communist Manifesto was committed.
His later historical attempts, especially *Das Kapital,* show his consistent attitude distinctly. In *Das Kapital* Marx undertook "to discover the economic law of motion of modern society." Yet this book
is not a historical treatise, properly speaking. It is rather an attempt
to describe and analyze the economic laws and the social morphol-
ogy of modern society in its processes of production, exchange, and
distribution as they actually occur at this particular stage of class
struggle. "While there is progressive diminution in the number of
capitalist magnates there is, of course, a corresponding increase in

the mass of poverty, enslavement, degeneration, and exploitation
. . . the centralization of the means of production and the sociali-
zation of labor reach a point where they prove incompatible with
their capitalist husk. This bursts asunder. The knell of private property sounds. The expropriators are expropriated." [75] Like so many
other predictions of Marx this has not transpired. He failed to see
that control of the means of production is not identical with its
ownership, that capitalism could develop a legitimate interest in
labor as a consumer group, and that higher wages and not subsis-
tence wages would be the answer to economic crises. Capitalism,
especially in the Anglo-Saxon world, has shown remarkable resilience and a tendency to work out its problems in an experimental
manner.

Nevertheless, *Das Kapital* became a landmark in the history of
socialism. It provided the intellectual foundation for international
socialism, and became the holy writ of a movement resolved to
establish the validity of its dogma in all particulars. In the period
which concerns us here, Marx exerted the strongest influence in
central and eastern Europe; it was weaker in the Latin countries,
where the syndico-anarchical tendencies gained ascendancy; ironically enough, it was weakest in England, Marx's second country.
As for America, the importance of Karl Marx remained latent until
the Russian Revolution.[76]

Marx's spectacular impact derived from the combination of
scientist, prophet, and politician which we have already noted. But
it was precisely this combination which proved fatal to the many
who believed that Marx had solved the riddle of the sphinx.

Napoleon said to Goethe: Politics is fate. Marx would have said
economics is fate. Just as history was declared inevitable by Marx,
even so was Marx, malgré lui, declared infallible by his followers,
and his glaring mistakes lay uncorrected: his ignorance of agrarian
problems, his underestimation of nationalism, his materialistic blindness to religious motivation. Nor did events in the socioeconomic
realm come to pass as he had predicted them, or where he had
predicted them, or for the benefit of those to whom he had predicted
them.[77] But this was no deterrent to the faithful. It is paradoxical
that Marx, like Nietzsche, who wished to free mankind from prejudice and hypocrisy and to heal its self-inflicted wounds, provided

new and powerful means of oppression, slogans for self-deceit, and articles of faith for a new religion that is as tyrannical as any of the old ones, but lacks their spiritual luster.

It will forever seem anomalous that Marx was a contemporary of Baudelaire and Nietzsche, of Turgenev and Dostoevski. He seemed to be made of coarser material than they; the causes of his unhappiness lay outside of him in a society which he despised and cursed.[78] He was not plagued by internal conflicts. He had no individual problems and he thought that the answer to all queries must come from the reorganization of society. He underrated the individual and overrated the community. He taught us much about mankind, but very little about man.

VI

There is a close resemblance between Marxism and Darwinism which has been the subject of frequent comment.[79] Marx, indeed, wished to dedicate *Das Kapital* to the author of *The Origin of Species,* a homage politely declined by Darwin. Just as Marx summed up the fertile thought preceding him and passed it on to following generations as "scientific socialism," so did Darwin bring into focus the great amount of evolutionary thinking that existed in the eighteenth and nineteenth century and made it a scientific hypothesis. Both men took "matter in motion" as the clue to the enigma of human existence, Marx explaining societal forces and institutions by dialectical materialism, Darwin using it to show man's kinship with animal and plant life. Both viewed struggle as the principle of causal connection, Marx looking to class struggle, Darwin to struggle for survival in nature. The great idea of becoming was used by both as a guiding concept to understand man's position in the universe, blending a merciless rule of relentless strife with an optimistic outlook for man as a whole.

And yet it is difficult to conceive of greater contrasts between personalities. Darwin developed his intellectual habits much more slowly than Marx. Coming from a well-to-do family he could afford to waste his time at school and university in hunting trips and marksmanship; he was bored by classroom teaching and seemed quite unaware of the vocation awaiting him. Darwin's ample means secured for him a freedom of research which was never encum-

bered by want or professional duties. His autobiography is an enchanting document reflecting the best of the Victorian traits. The
exiled Marx was less blessed. Moreover, it was not in his nature
to reveal the attraction of pure intellectual pursuit with the humane
charm and sincerity that Darwin displays.

Darwin, in speaking of the voyage of the *Beagle,* a circumnavi-
gation of the earth covering the years 1831 to 1836, says it was
"the most important event in my life and has determined my
whole career." [80] Before he sailed for South America he had read
Humboldt's *Personal Narrative* and Lyell's *Principles of Geology*
and had already accepted the idea of gradual change in the history
of nature. In South America he observed the glories of tropical
vegetation, the great deserts of Patagonia, and the forest-clad
mountains of Tierra del Fuego.

"I had been deeply impressed by discovering . . . great fossil
animals covered with armor like that of the existing armadilloes,
. . . by the manner in which closely allied animals replace one
another in proceeding southward over the Continent. . . . It was
evident that such facts . . . could only be explained on the supposition that species gradually become modified, and the subject
haunted me." [81] Thus Darwin hit on a theme already discussed by
Buffon, Goethe, Lamarck, and a host of others. The idea that the
plants and animals of the present day are the lineal descendants of
ancestors on the whole somewhat simpler, that these again are
descended from still simpler forms, and so on back through the
ages, was not new, but Darwin made it "current intellectual
coin." [82] The manner in which he arrived at his conclusion was
strictly intellectual. He had no axe to grind. That he broke with
the Hebrew-Christian concept of creation and replaced it with the
idea of evolution was the result of his "love of science, unbounded
patience in long reflecting over any subject, industry in observing
and collecting facts and a fair share of invention as well as of
common sense." [83]

On his return to England he saw "how many facts indicated
the common descent of the species." He opened his first notebook
on the subject. Convinced that species had not been created in
separate molds, but had developed and become gradually modified,
he was still at a loss to explain "the innumerable cases in which

organisms of every kind are beautifully adapted to their habits of life." [84] In October of 1838 he read "for amusement" Malthus, *On Population*. Being well prepared to appreciate the struggle for existence which goes on everywhere, it at once struck him "that under these circumstances favourable variations would tend to be preserved and unfavourable ones to be destroyed. The result would be the formation of new species." And he concludes, "Here then I had at last got a theory by which to work." [85] The first abstract of his work was written in 1842, but it was not until 1859 that Darwin published "The origin of species by means of natural selection or the preservation of favoured races in the struggle for life." The moment seemed preordained for its spectacular success. Other scholars, independent of Darwin, had reached uniform conclusions, and positivism had created an intellectual climate in which Darwinian laws would be readily accepted as the most plausible explanation of a large collection of biological facts.

The Origin of Species is one long argument. Its persuasive force is a result of its having been built on true Baconian principles.[86] Darwin started from the geological record, which showed clearly that some species had become extinct whereas others, closely related to them, survived. In the next place, the geographical distribution of plants and animals over the globe offered to the scientific mind a question that could be answered only by applying a unifying principle of explication. Darwin perceived that the keystone to these problems was variation and selection.

Since the geological record spread over hundreds of millions of years and the scientist was carrying on a work of synthetic reconstruction, it was natural to look for a laboratory test to confirm or disprove any hypothesis. Domestic breeding seemed to offer ideal opportunities to test the idea of selection. "Under domestication we see much variability, caused, or at least excited, by changed conditions of life. . . . Variability is not actually caused by man; . . . but man can and does select the variations given to him by nature, and thus accumulates them in any desired manner." [87] Could the same principle be applied to organisms in the state of nature? Darwin's answer was in the affirmative. "In the survival of favoured individuals and races, during the constant Struggle for Existence, we see a powerful and ever-acting form of Selection.

The struggle for existence invariably follows from the high geometrical ratio of increase which is common to all organic beings. . . . More individuals are born than can possibly survive. A grain in the balance may determine which individuals shall live and which shall die—which variety or species shall increase in number and which shall decrease, or finally become extinct." [88]

By Darwin's own admission the term "natural selection" is a misleading one since it indicates a conscious agent, a concept which is not at all in keeping with his views; he preserved it because it had become a biological household word, but he really preferred Spencer's expression "survival of the fittest." What Darwin endeavored to show was that the variations which appear in nature are random variations or accidental variations. He never succeeded in explaining why they appear, and he wrote to Huxley, "If, as I must think, external conditions produce little effect, what the devil determines each particular variation?" [89] But this difficulty did not change his belief that the species had resulted from accidental variations by means of which, in the process of natural selection, the profitables had been continued and the unprofitables had been eliminated.

Darwin was not concerned with explaining the origin of life; nevertheless the universal perspective implied in his book produced an extraordinary impact. "To advance natural selection," says Barzun ". . . meant that purely physical forces, brute struggle among brutes, could account for the present forms and powers of living beings." [90] But Darwin did not feel that his conclusions were discouraging. At least an unbroken development was guaranteed, and that this development moved upward was for him and his Victorian contemporaries a foregone conclusion.

"As all the living forms of life are the lineal descendants of those which lived long before . . . , we may feel certain that the ordinary succession by generation has never once been broken, and that no catastrophe has desolated the whole world. Hence we may look with some confidence to a secure future of great length. And as natural selection works solely by and for the good of each being, all corporal and mental endowments will tend to progress towards perfection." [91] "Thus from the war of nature, from famine and death, the most exalted object which we are capable of conceiving, namely, the production of higher animals, directly follows. There is grandeur in this view of life." [92] I am inclined to think that it was this "grandeur of view" which explains the dramatic reception of *The Origin of Species*. Huxley thought this book was difficult to understand, but within eleven years it had reached its fifth edition.[93]

Twelve years after its publication Darwin acquired an even larger audience when he addressed himself to his great derivative problem: *The Descent of Man*. That no honorable person should accuse him of concealing his views, he had stated in 1859 that "light would be thrown on the origin of man and his history." [94] He was now ready to unveil his thought on the subject.

The Descent of Man asserts once more the community of all living beings. "It is only our natural prejudice," says Darwin, "and that arrogance which made our forefathers declare that they were descended from demi-gods which leads us to demur to this conclusion." [95] The basic ideas under which Darwin organizes human development are those with which we are already familiar: variability, rapid multiplication of the human race necessitating the struggle for existence, and natural selection. Just as, in his earlier work, he did not concern himself with the origin of life, so now he did not try to solve the problem of the birth of intelligence. "In what manner the mental powers were first developed . . . is as hopeless an enquiry as how life itself first originated." [96] However, he emphasizes those traits which link men to the animal world. He denies that the sense of beauty is an exclusively human feature, pointing to numerous cases of animal esthetics. As for religion, we find the following sentence: "Numerous races have existed, and still exist, who have no idea of one or more gods." [97] Consequently the moral sense must be explained genetically as derived from social instincts. We do not need to follow Darwin through his long discourse. His concluding words, however, deserve to be remembered: "There can hardly be a doubt that we are descended from barbarians. The astonishment which I felt on first seeing a party of Fuegians on a wild and broken shore will never be forgotten by me, for the reflection at once rushed into my mind—such were our ancestors. . . . Man with all his noble qualities, with sympathy which he feels for the most debased, with benevolence which extends not only to other men but to the humblest living creature, with his god-like intellect . . . with all these exalted powers—Man still bears in his bodily frame the indelible stamp of his lowly origin." [98]

Any attempt to evaluate Darwin's influence must distinguish between his scientific merits and the moral climate which his ideas engendered. Most scientists accepted evolution as a fact which was as clearly proved as other historical facts.[99] But whereas evolution became evident enough in dim outline, the concepts which Darwin advanced to explain the origin of species have been exposed to searching criticism.

The most important progress beyond Darwin took place in the field of genetics. Although the Mendelian laws were discovered while Darwin was still at work (1865), it was not until 1900 that the new science of genetics was firmly established. After a century biologists give a picture that is infinitely more complex than the Darwinian. As far as the layman can understand, we have reason to believe that new species arise quite suddenly.[100] While natural selection may still be considered the main cause of evolutionary changes, it does not account for the actual steps by which the off-spring differ from their parents; the causes of these differences are still matters of conjecture.

One fallacy of Darwin's reasoning must be mentioned; it is his assumption that natural selection will always make an organism fitter in its struggle for survival. In the picture that Darwin gave us, the idea of progress and advancement is unduly emphasized; the elements of deterioration and degeneration are neglected. This leads us logically into a discussion of the ideological repercussions that Darwin provoked.

It is one of the paradoxes of history that the mild-mannered Darwin, presenting his conclusions so cautiously, was able to deal a fatal blow to the religious attitudes of his day. For him the change from religious tradition to agnosticism had come almost imperceptibly, and consequently painlessly. But his contemporaries were from the beginning cognizant of the revolutionary consequences implied in his theories. The concept of a Creator had been damaged beyond repair; an impersonal, ruthless life force had replaced it. The idea of religious revelation seemed destined to fade. Of course, the idea of revelation had been under fire for a long time, but Darwin's views were much more devastating than all previous attacks because they did not aim at destroying the Bible story. They simply replaced it with a version which was more convincing since it seemed to be based on empirical evidence. The evidence was indeed so strong that most Christian denominations were forced to accept a "symbolic" interpretation of the first chapter of Genesis.

On the other hand, Darwin proved to be a godsend for the school of materialism. It saw in Darwin the confirmation of its belief that matter and energy could explain nature as well as history. The Darwinian outlook became an infallible philosophy. Haeckel's *Welträtsel (The Riddle of the Universe)* is the classic example for this materialistic monism. Darwinism followed Darwin.

In Darwinism evolution and natural selection were not only combined, they were hopelessly confused. The idea of natural selection had greater impact on Darwin's contemporaries than the idea of evolution, because it undermined the validity of any ethical ideal. If that only has persistence which can be adapted to a given physical condition, what will be the fate of moral values? What remains of our standards of good and evil? [101] Darwin himself had traced the ethical values back to parental and social instincts; the conclusion seemed inescapable that ethical ideals have no value in themselves but only in their capacity to strengthen our chance for physical survival. Social Darwinism made its appearance. Life was considered as an arena and human beings the gladiators, as Huxley expressed it. History was rewritten from the new viewpoint which seemed to blend admirably with the teachings of *Real-politik* and the struggle for power. Sociology was reconstructed on the basis of natural selection, the struggle for existence became an explanatory principle for the fight in society and between societies. Racism became a pseudo science intoxicating the half-educated. It could serve as a justification for imperial conquests, or for Teutonic predomination over the whole world; it was the opportunity for anti-Semitism to make its hatred appear scientific. But social Darwinism had other fields of application; it seemed to fit in with every doctrine that preached relentless struggle, whether socialistic or capitalistic. Ruthless competition could be vindicated in its name as well as the dictatorship of the proletariat.

It would, of course, be ridiculous to lay the blame for the excesses of Darwinism at Darwin's doorstep. His Socratic mind would, I am certain, have shrunk from the ill-founded conclusions to which his followers jumped with glee. They took his hypotheses as a package deal and insisted that if you wanted to have your evolution you could not eat your natural selection. Thus Darwin's impact on the climate of public opinion was, on the whole, a destructive one. It contributed to the general atmosphere of nihilism. It helped to make the masses indifferent to Christian or humanitarian ethics, and left them without comfort once the optimistic belief in an ever-ascending evolution was shattered.

Darwin, like Schopenhauer and Marx, was concerned with man's position in the universe. It was the problem of the descent of man that had finally emerged from the welter of biological facts as the most important question. Those who started where Darwin left off felt that the evolutionary outlook had to be accepted as one of the consequences of the scientific revolution that had started with Copernicus, Galileo, and Newton. By his own volition man had abdicated his privileged position in the universe; he had dethroned himself. It was imperative to restate man's position in the light of evolutionary premises. To say that this has not yet been accomplished would be an understatement, but only in this perspective can late nineteenth century thought be properly evaluated.

Nietzsche shows the consequences of Darwin's theories very clearly. The idea of the fluidity of the species disturbed Nietzsche so profoundly that he found it necessary to set new tables before man since the old ones had been broken. If man had descended from the animals, superman would ascend over man.

VII

The men whom we have so far considered were, in one way or another, preoccupied with the collective problems of mankind; their minds were engaged with the lofty issues which concern humanity as a whole rather than with those which perturb the individual. Neither for Hegel nor Marx, neither for Comte nor for Darwin were their own lives or their personal affairs of more than accidental importance.

A far different vista comes into view when we turn to the three great individualists of the nineteenth century. The biographies of Baudelaire, Nietzsche, and Kierkegaard cannot be dismissed with a casual glance. In them we find youthful experiences which etch themselves forever in the memory, maladies which deform the body and open the mind to perilous notions. The work of these men reflects a personal and indelible stamp.

From earliest childhood Baudelaire experienced a feeling of solitude. Regardless of family ties and young companions, his destiny lay in an eternal isolation, and this he knew.[102] From the beginning he is a being posed above his own reflection, a narcissus. Today we know what precipitated the singular development of his soul; it was his love for his mother. Baudelaire's letters to his mother have the inflection of a case study, and scarcely need psychological interpretation in their naked emotionalism. "There was in my youth," he wrote on May 6, 1861, "a period of passionate love for you, listen and read without fear. . . . Ah, that was the best time of motherly tenderness . . . all the time I was living in you and you were uniquely mine." [103] Baudelaire never recovered from the shock of his mother's second marriage; the little Charles was driven out of a paradise where his idol had been uniquely his.

"Still as a child I felt in my heart two opposite sentiments: the horror of life and the ecstasy of life." His work is the voice of this strange combination.[104] Who among us, he asks later, is not Homo Duplex? I speak of those whose minds have been touched with pensiveness from their childhood, always double, action and intention, dream and reality. At another time he says, ". . . the precocious taste of the feminine world makes for superior genius." [105] And what is genius? "L'enfance retrouvée à volontée."

But as the child grows older he realizes that the paradise cannot be regained, that it is in reality a paradise lost. The grief Baudelaire felt for his ravaged Eden was to make him sympathetic to satanic states of the mind. It was also to produce an antipathy toward those whom he held responsible for his loss. His stepfather, General Aupick, was the first victim of his impotent hatred, but he soon developed a loathing for everything that encroached on his dreams, that is, society in general. There are in Baudelaire's life typical encounters with the representatives of organized society, the soldier, the master of a ship, the counsellor at law, the priest. At such times he felt like an albatross lured to the boat deck for the entertainment of the crew; he, a rider of the storms, was an exile on the earth surrounded by the jeering throng—"ses ailes de géant l'empêchent de marcher."

The conviction that he was a poet and that immortality awaited him came early to Baudelaire and led to further conflicts with his family. In an attempt to alter his decision they sent him on a voyage to India. The splendor of the tropics but fecundated his imagination and created within him "a new world of ideas." His faith in his destiny as a poet remained firm.[106] He returned to Paris and after reaching his majority he encountered no further opposition.

At the age of nineteen he contracted syphilis. Today it is difficult to appreciate the full penalty that this illness entailed in past centuries. With antibiotics it has become a clinical accident. In Baudelaire's day syphilis was generally incurable, and his disease increased the horror of life that the poet had known since his boyhood. It explains the absence of quietude in his work and the pervading atmosphere of sadness and death. It accounts also for the feeling of ennui, the deep melancholy which blankets the whole of existence. Unwittingly he echoes Schopenhauer when he writes "vivre est un mal." [107]

Baudelaire's ennui was, of course, an inheritance from the preceding generation, the mal du siècle. But in Baudelaire there is a poignant quality which is missing in the work of Byron, Vigny, Musset, or Heine. In Baudelaire's dreams a higher certainty than reality had become known to him, but in this world "L'action n'est pas la sœur du rêve." [108] When action is not the sister of dream, escape becomes a necessity. Baudelaire's alleys of escape were two: the orgy, the refuge into an artificial paradise of lust, wine, opium, hashish, whatever a tortured imagination might suggest; and the attitude of the dandy. Baudelaire's dandyism was the defense of the artist in a utilitarian world. Dandyism is an attempt to found a new élite in times of transition from aristocracy to democracy; it is the last outburst of heroism in an age of decadence; it is a sunset full of melancholy.[109] Although Baudelaire was by no means the first to adopt the attitude of the dandy, he was the first to develop it into a weapon for keeping the world at arm's length. His example was followed by all who accepted his esthetic creed: art for art's sake.[110]

The doctrine of art for art's sake had been in the air since 1830. Gautier had given it expression. But Baudelaire imparted to it a tone of sincerity and provocation which made him one of the great artistic initiators of his time. Whereas his contemporaries thought that art should serve progress (Hugo), or humanity (Dickens), Baudelaire wished to ban from art all that was moralistic, all that might justify its existence in the eyes of educators, manufacturers, philistines, or hypocrites. Art should have no other purpose than its own existence. The new creed soon became a pseudo religion; it had its high priest, Baudelaire, its acolyte, Flaubert; and a whole choir of minor voices.[111]

In this doctrine we have the philosophy of a generation which was no longer at home in a society that paid lip service to the idea only. Unfortunately l'art pour l'art overstated the truth inherent in its program and became as fallacious a doctrine as the one it was eager to refute.

Baudelaire's own work testifies to deeper beliefs than the battle cry of art for art's sake. The little volume which has given him the immortality he was so sure of obtaining contains but a few hundred pages; yet though the nineteenth century produced poets who were greater and more powerfully endowed than Baudelaire, none was more influential.[112] The glory which has fallen on the *Flowers of Evil* is the result of a combination of Baudelaire's own gifts and the conditions of his time. When he began to write, romanticism had reached its peak. Although a romantic by temperament Baudelaire did not wish to follow Lamartine, Vigny, or Musset. He felt obliged "to do something else." Such a declaration suggests a change in subject matter, an impression enhanced by his famous title, but we must look further and deeper for his diversity. The title was adopted rather than discovered, and while it is true that his poetry is sometimes lascivious, shocking, scandalous, and revolting, nevertheless these poems, the flowers of evil, of doubt, of grief, torture, weakness, disgust, and blasphemy, are flowers of extraordinary beauty. And here lies the secret of Baudelaire's work. By means of an alchemy all his own he transformed his hatred and his revolt, his adoration of the foul and the degraded, into forms that have never lost their power to enchant. The magic of his spell is the result of an ability to transform reality, both natural and human, into a transcendant world of symbols. For Baudelaire the whole universe became "a storehouse of images and designs." [113] Man passes through the universe as through "des forêts de symboles."

The phrase "forêts de symboles" opens up a new epoch in the consciousness of modern man. He no longer identifies himself with the rhythm of nature; he is divorced from cosmic forces, immobilized, as it were, in the self, the only reality of which he can still be assured.[114] And in a kind of "ecstatic horror" he makes the world his symbol. Baudelaire thus creates what Comte has called an "antinature." He scorns the poetry of "sanctified vegetables" and develops a universe that is metallic, sterile, and luminous. In the process he discovered the fantastic beauty of the great city; he sings of urban lanscapes as poets before him had sung of lakes and mountains.

Valéry attempted a further explanation of Baudelaire's ability to transform ugliness into beauty when he wrote, "*Les Fleurs du Mal* contain neither historical nor legendary poems; nothing based on narrative. There are no flights into philosophy. Politics make here no appearance. . . . But all is charm, music, powerful abstract sensuality . . . there is a combination of flesh and spirit, a mixture of solemnity, warmth and bitterness, of eternity and intimacy, a most rare alliance of will and harmony." [115] In Baudelaire's own words, all is "luxe, calme et volupté."

By a process of painstaking labor his poetry reached a degree of intensity and power of expression unknown till then. Thus the best poems of *Les Fleurs du Mal* have the magic force of incantations. While this explains, I think, why almost all poets who came after Baudelaire confessed their indebtedness to him, it does not exhaust the spiritual significance of his work.

A great deal has been written about Baudelaire's religious attitude. After he had been defamed as blasphemer and atheist, attempts were made to picture him as mystic and saint. I think the truth lies elsewhere. Baudelaire was neither skeptic nor atheist, but a suffering human being.[116] At all times he found in man two conflicting desires: to invoke God and to embrace the devil. Although he had experienced the spiritual pleasure of lifting himself step by step, he had also known the joy of vertical descent into animality.[117] Divided between the wish to raise himself to the throne of God and the impulse to taste the bitter brew of sin, he became aware of God as fully when he broke the law as when he fulfilled it.

"Soyez béni, mon Dieu, qui donnez la souffrance/ Comme un divin remède à nos impuretés." To the poet a place in heaven is promised. "Je sais que vous gardez une place au Poète/ Dans les rangs bienheureux des saintes Légions." Baudelaire finds only one redeeming feature amid the paralyzing horror of life: the thirst for beauty. And it is, therefore, through poetry and music, through painting and sculpture that man is assured of his immortality. The last stanza of *Les Phares* gives voice to Baudelaire's religion:

> Car c'est vraiment, Seigneur, le meilleur témoignage
> Que nous puissions donner de notre dignité,
> Que cet ardent sanglot qui roule d'âge en âge
> Et vient mourir au bord de votre éternité.

Again we see that the spiritual conflict that occupied the most eminent minds of the century had but one concern: the restatement of man's position in the universe. The individualist Baudelaire, who could never leave his self behind (L'artiste ne sort jamais de lui-même) finds solace only in his conversations with God. God is the eternal confidant in this tragedy where everyone is the hero.[118] Only the individual and his work are of importance. If every human being would make progress his goal, humanity as a whole would progress.[119] The spiritual effort of the individual alone is worthy, even though it die away like a sigh before God's eternity. Baudelaire was the first to define the position of Western man "in tenebris," surrounded by mysteries and conscious of the silence that will greet his incertitude.

We cannot take leave of Baudelaire without mentioning his critical work. The poet who wrote *Correspondences* was a discoverer of the first order; witness his translations of Poe, his appreciation of Delacroix and Manet, and his early understanding of Wagner. But his greatest glory was the inspiration he gave to later poets: Swinburne, Verlaine, Rimbaud, Mallarmé, Stefan George, Rilke, d'Annunzio, Valéry, and T. S. Eliot. Baudelaire, says Léon Daudet, is an event; he marks the passing of one era to another, of one form of desire and voluptuousness to the other. He transmuted the intelligence, the emotion, and the concept of beauty.[120]

In perspective, Baudelaire shows clearly destructive features: his venomous disdain for all bourgeois morality, his devotion to cruelty, depravity, ugliness, lust, perversion, and outrage. But to a far greater extent he was a purgative influence. After reading Baudelaire, says Marcel Proust, Victor Hugo seems shallow. And, we may add, so do Tennyson and Browning. By introducing the most appalling aspects of reality into poetry and by transforming them into terms of the highest imaginative expression, he broke down conventional barriers and encouraged all future writers to listen to the heartbeat of reality no matter how disturbing or convulsed the sound. He was the discoverer of a new concept of beauty, the beauty of an urban civilization hitherto unsung, and he voiced it with the sincerity that through him became the canon of all contemporary poetry.

VIII

Sören Kierkegaard was born to suffer. Like Baudelaire, he was the child of an old man, and just as Baudelaire was forever dominated by the image of his mother, so Kierkegaard's life was eternally shadowed by the austere and guilt-conscious personality of his father whose towering figure filled his entire horizon. He was a child "crazily reared by an old man." [121] In his diary there is abundant evidence of the effect his father had on him. "I have been since childhood in the grip of an overpowering melancholy . . . my sole joy being . . . that no one could discover how unhappy I felt myself to be. I have never really been a man, even less a child or youth." [122] His statement was literally true and has opened the door to many speculations concerning the pathological conditions of his genius. That such conditions existed was acknowledged by Kierkegaard himself ("the thorn in my flesh"), but their causes and their nature have never been revealed. They were his secret, his terrible secret, that was to die with him and that no explicator should ever be able to unfold. His "genius for concealment" was wholly successful. A great number of hypotheses have been advanced: that he was a hunchback; that he was sexually impotent; that other difficulties existed.[123] But for all the research,

Kierkegaard's secret remains his own to this very day. All we know is that he was a spindly, deformed little man, with a goodly number of manias and phobias which made him an eccentric in the eyes of his native Copenhagen. It is a misfortune, he remarked, to be a genius in a small town. His life was uneventful and moved in circles whose very narrowness increased his capacity for suffering. But it was from suffering that his thought arose.

Steeped in humanistic tradition, he absorbed at the University of Copenhagen and in his travels to Berlin the classic and the romantic ideas of the age of Goethe. Mozart's music moved the strings of a heart forever destined to house an "unhappy lover." He encountered Hegel's philosophy, and, although he later launched a devastating attack on this philosopher, he had in himself abundant elements to be attracted by Hegel's dialectic. Growing up amid internal strife, his whole thinking was in terms of conflict, of dialogue with himself, that is, dialectical. Romanticism and Hegelianism were for Kierkegaard temptations which he was never able to conquer completely. His intellectual profile shows traces of the metaphysician, the poet, the mystic.

He came to be the expounder of Christian doctrine and Christian conduct in a time that was ready to declare Christianity defunct.[124] The historical-critical arguments that his contemporaries, Strauss, Bauer, and Feuerbach, hurled at Christianity never touched him. He had moments of doubt and, during his student days, even prolonged periods of remoteness from God, but his faith in the tenets of Christianity was never shattered. He therefore did not try to prove God's existence to an unbelieving world.[125] He understood that his mission was to become a Christian in Christendom. He worked toward a second reformation that would make all Christians "contemporaries of Christ."

On my tombstone read only these words: "That individual," said Kierkegaard. All his thinking begins in subjectivity and ends there. "The thing is to find a truth which is true for me, to find the idea for which I can live and die," he wrote in 1835. To his last day he lived for this truth: the individual.[126] Whereas Schopenhauer, Comte, Hegel, Marx, and Darwin submerged the individual in generalities of will, society, state, class, and species, another group of thinkers lifted him high above any social imperative, making him a law unto himself: Stirner, Kierkegaard, Baudelaire, Bakunin, and Nietzsche. Between these two groups the social fabric of European civilization was torn to shreds; on the one hand undisciplined anarchy, on the other overdisciplined authority.

The Kierkegaard family was bourgeois and the son lived an outwardly bourgeois life. He was free from financial worries and once confessed, "That I became a writer was due to my melancholy and my money." [127] His suffering was his castle; that he was allowed to dwell in it was the result of his privileged position as a member of the leisure class. The *vita activa* was a sealed book to him. "I have been blessed by Providence with an outstanding comprehension of the truth such as rarely has been granted to any man . . . in this matter I have reason for humility in only one respect: it is that I have not had the strength to be myself what I understood." [128]

With amazing foresight he predicted "the total bankruptcy" toward which Europe was heading. He anticipated such terrors of modern civilization as the Nazis were to perpetrate a hundred years later. He was aware of the damage that the increasing dissemination of information might do to man's soul. But he was essentially a conservative and saw in every revolt a rebellion against God. A single man, he said, cannot help a time or save it; he can only express its fate. The individual, the single man, remained the basis of his creed, not in the sense in which everyone is an individual, however; he was concerned mainly with the exceptional individual or the individual exception that was Sören Kierkegaard. "Truth is subjectivity." [129] This was the radical position which Kierkegaard occupied in the history of European thought. All Western philosophy had traveled from reality to reality via the human personality: Kierkegaard traveled from the human personality to the human personality via reality. [130]

On this voyage reality has been weighed and found wanting. Man thinks and exists; God does not think, he creates. God does not exist; he is eternal. The only reality which man faces, then is God. Man stands "before God." Thus Kierkegaard made one, if not the most important, step in the history of Western thought. He removed himself from the reality of the world. He faced nothingness and could save himself from nothingness only by a leap into faith. Kierkegaard is the most determined counterpart to

Descartes' famous "cogito ergo sum," but Kierkegaard's postulate was not "I am, therefore I think," but rather "I despair, therefore I exist." His way leads from the nihilism of despair to the "uncertainty of belief." [131] Belief is the contradiction between the infinite passion of the individual's inwardness and the objective uncertainty of faith. The only authentic existence is that of the individual "before God," which is a self-committal. The Christian truth is a paradox, an absurdity, and demands from the believer a decision, or rather, a leap. Kierkegaard has summed up his foremost concern with Christianity in these words: Christianity is spirit, spirit is inwardness, inwardness is subjectivity, subjectivity is essentially passion, and at its maximum, an infinite personal passionate interest in one's eternal happiness.[132]

It is characteristic of Kierkegaard that in his journey to eternal happiness he encountered so few moments of joy and so many days of despair, of "fear and trembling." Behind all his dialectical efforts to attain the unattainable, there was, as in the case of Schopenhauer, a heart in dire need of repose. Kierkegaard was deeply attracted by *The World as Will and Idea*. He was in sympathy with its pessimistic outlook and felt its "melancholy voluptuousness" to be akin to his own. And Schopenhauer's world view, exclusively concerned as it was with the esthetic and the ethicoreligious attitude of man, found its parallel in Kierkegaard's three stages.

Every man, says Kierkegaard, lives esthetically, ethically, or religiously. These stages are not levels in an evolutionary process, as Comte or Hegel might have conceived them; they are, on the contrary, enclosed worlds. Man must decide on which stage he wishes to belong and then take citizenship in one of the three. This idea is most clearly expressed in Kierkegaard's first masterpiece, *Either-Or*. Man has a choice, but to have a choice includes the necessity of decision. This is not as in Hegel's dialectic "both and," but literally "either-or." [133]

The esthetic attitude is described by Kierkegaard as romantic hedonism in eternal chase after pleasure. "See him in his season of pleasure; did he not crave for one pleasure after another, variety his watchword . . . change was what he was crying out for when pleasure pandered to him, change, change." Kierkegaard was able to give this analysis of the esthetic type because he had in himself all the elements that constitute a romantic poet. He had felt "the vertigo of possibilities" as is evidenced in his portrait of Mozart's Don Juan and in *The Diary of the Seducer*.[134] But we also know that he renounced the esthetic principle as he renounced all forms of personal happiness. In drinking the bitter cup of "infinite resignation" he came to understand the existential mistake made by the romantic esthetitian. The hunt for pleasure ends in boredom and disgust, and produces despair and a longing for death. Kierkegaard has given us a profound study of despair in *The Sickness unto Death*.

Despair can be overcome only when the self is grounded "in the power that constituted it . . . as an individual man, this definite individual man, alone before the face of God." Despair is the gateway of human life through which we must pass if we choose the "eternal validity" of existence.[135] It leads men to the second stage, the ethical, because it is the eternal validity of his being of which man becomes assured if he chooses the ethical stage. He feels the intensity of duty. The awareness of duty raises man above the pleasures of the moment, above the passions that come and go. By obeying the absolute duty the individual can hope to realize the synthesis of the universal and the particular in his person.

But the ethical fails if it tries to deal with the exceptional individual, Kierkegaard's prime concern. Furthermore, ethics are based on the knowledge of the universal good. But man may choose to ignore the law or rebel against it. It is really man's sinful nature which forces him to reach beyond the ethical into the transcendental or religious. Man is God's creature; he may forget this and live in guilt, but he cannot rid himself of his existential condition. "Revelation is signalized by mystery, happiness by suffering, the certainty of faith by uncertainty . . . the truth by absurdity." God is the Other, and no one has described this otherness as dramatically as Kierkegaard. God hates all existence, we read; and again, Christianity exists because there is hatred between God and men.

Sören Kierkegaard was an "unhappy lover of God"; he did not know the "peace that is beyond all understanding." There is a hostility to life in his writings which is unchristian rather than Christian. He describes marriage as a crime and human life as "a community of criminals."[136] One must come to the conclusion that his physical and social disability rendered him incapable of ever accepting life on human terms, and that his hunger for God was the attempt of a desperate soul to leap across the abyss of nothingness into the cruel love of God.

Kierkegaard's religion is a religion for the exceptional individual, but in arguing the case of the exceptional he made it the rule. Mankind is not so constituted that it passes only through the three stages of the esthetic, the ethical, and the religious. Man has an economic basis of which Kierkegaard does not speak because he never knew the bitter lesson of sweat, toil, and tears. Man has a political side, which Kierkegaard ignored because he believed that civic obedience was a Christian virtue. Equality between men could only mean equality before God.[137] The crowd was for him the untruth. He confused the masses with public life.

Marx wanted to change the world, Kierkegaard the individual. Both fell short of the truth. Marx makes economic man the basis for everything and denies the individual; Kierkegaard bases everything on the individual and sees in humanity nothing but an "indifferent multitude." He was a citizen of eternity, a man who had come under the spell of the absolute, but he had little conception of fellowship either on earth or in heaven.[138] The only way he could conceive of acting upon a world in which he felt himself a stranger was by being a witness for his faith. He pondered the question of whether a man has the right to have himself killed for his faith and predicted a "government of martyrs" who would change the world. When, shortly before his death, he launched his attack on the Danish state-church and abjured any form of organized priesthood together with religious rites and sacraments, he chose to become a martyr. He was convinced that Christendom needed "a jolt," that he had been called to administer it, and that his act would be the greatest accomplishment of his life. He failed not only because his fellow citizens dismissed his accusations with scorn, but because he disregarded the foundations on which every church is built. In the name of "human honesty" he discarded human nature. There was some quixotism in Kierkegaard's fight, something Utopian just as there was in the work of his companions, Marx and Nietzsche.

Kierkegaard spoke of himself as a "corrective." In a time that recognized only the temporal and the profane, he emphasized the eternal and the divine. He fought against all the forms under which the individual became subordinated, that is, philosophical systems, the concept of world history, the asphyxiating bourgeois world. It was his mission to proclaim the exception, the paradox, fear and trembling, dread and despair, in a time which throve on technical progress, material advancement, and economic betterment. He brought back the knowledge of man's loneliness before the absolute, his perilous position which could never be made secure by rational or scientific victory, because man carries in his soul "the sickness unto death."

But Kierkegaard was a man of problems and conflicts. As Professor Jolivet sums it up: "contradiction beset him on all sides, because he lived, as it were, divided up between the religious man and the poet, between the rationalist and the Christian, between the believer and the unbeliever, between the dialectician and the ironical critic of Christendom; he was these all at once, lacking any higher means whereby they might be reconciled and pacified. . . . He was assuredly a martyr, not to Christianity, as he said, but to himself." [139]

We cannot leave the "unhappy lover of God" without raising a final question. In his struggle to be a Christian in Christendom Kierkegaard was ready to let human culture go by the board in order that Christianity should conquer. It was one more case of *fiat justicia pereat mundus*. The future of the Western world cannot lie within this alternative, within this either-or. It must be a future of continuity, as it has been for nineteen hundred years.

The final evaluation of "God's policeman," as he called himself, will to a large extent depend on the strength of Christianity to prevail in Christendom. Kierkegaard did not succeed in what he thought to be his mission, and perhaps success was impossible given his own premises and the conditions of his time. When he finally came into his own in the early twentieth century, first in Germany, Spain, and France and soon after in the Anglo-Saxon world, it was not so much as a teacher of Christianity but as a master of psychological analysis for agnostic intellectuals, "paralyzed

Hamlets," who had gone through one catastrophe and were preparing for the second cataclysm.[140]

IX

Now, more than sixty years after his death, the essence of Friedrich Nietzsche's teaching and its import to our Western culture are still matters of controversy.[141] There is little hope that new discoveries will shed greater light on this twilight figure. The texts, the letters, the memories of his friends are open to us, and commentaries are numerous and acute. But a sustained and critical reading both of his own work and that of his interpreters produces an agonized perplexity as to his sum and substance. His life and his work bring to mind the picture of a desolate landscape illumined by flashes of lightning.[142] "To these men of today I will not be light . . . I will blind them: lightning of my wisdom, destroy their eyes." [143] Is there not here the indication of a new type of intelligence that prefers to obfuscate rather than to enlighten?

Nietzsche belongs among those disinherited minds about whom Rilke and Heller have spoken: the battlefields of two ages; no longer at home in the old, not yet rooted in the new; citizens of a spiritual no-man's land.[144] Torn by their own contradictions and intoxicated by extremes, they wish to anticipate the future by a simple fiat. Such figures have been rare in the realm of philosophy; they are hybrids of poetry and religion, metaphysics and politics. Pascal and Rousseau, Dostoevski and Kierkegaard, are the closest parallels to Nietzsche in European thought.

It is a pity that Nietzsche did not and, of course, could not deal with the phenomenon that was himself after the manner in which he dealt with so many other psychological phenomena. It would have produced a remarkable page in *Human, All Too Human.* But, alas! "Each one is farthest away from himself—as far as we ourselves are concerned, we are not 'knowers.' " [145] To be sure, his writings abound in statements in the first person singular and we have his *Ecce Homo,* but he was unable to describe the inner structure of his being which corresponded so amazingly to his position between two eras.

"An incarnation of dissonance—and what else is man?"—thus he defined himself in his first book; and in his last we read, "Agreed that I am a decadent, I am also the very reverse." [146] One more confession may be added: "I must be profoundly related to Byron's Manfred; I discovered all his abysses in my own soul—at thirteen I was ripe for this book." [147]

But was he not the expounder of the Dionysian lust for life, the philosopher with a hammer, the prophet of superman and the will to power, the champion of eternal recurrence? The contradiction is flagrant and has been noted by such keen observers as Thomas Mann and Stefan Zweig.[148] There is a pathetic contrast between the miserable, lonely, precarious existence endured by this German ex-professor and the life forces that he exalted in such unmeasured terms. There is a deep cleavage between the bourgeois existence of a "petit rentier" and the master race he glorifies. There is finally a patent disparity between the wretched physical state in which he passed most of his days and the state of the superman he envisaged. But such a picture of discrepancies remains two-dimensional. The most outstanding trait in Nietzsche was not the rift between his being and his teaching, but rather the challenge presented to him by that very rift to pursue his voyage into the unknown. His human condition was, as Stefan George said, to destroy in himself whatever was most dear to him, only to long for it anew in trembling.[149] An alien to his own time, at war with all his instincts, he decreed that he was destined to overcome pessimism and establish himself as the great yea-sayer. It is the truth, however, that there was no new yea in Nietzsche. All he could do was to switch the symbols of operation, to change plus to minus, minus to plus, "to transvaluate the values." But new values do not come of volition; they come from constructive insight, and this was denied Nietzsche. Thus he never reached the new continent; the land of Zarathustra remained a mirage. But the importance of his voyage must not be minimized, for in the course of it he discovered other realms in psychology so far uncharted.

"Morality . . . is the idiosyncracy of decadents actuated by a desire to avenge themselves successfully upon life." [150] Could Nietzsche have rejected the application of this comment to his own life, he who said, "My danger is the loathing of mankind"? In reality, Nietzsche was a moralist, a disillusioned moralist, whose disappointment propelled him toward the question of the genealogy of morals.

Only a man so deeply hostile to his age and to his self could lift
the veil from psychological secrets such as the driving force of
resentment in the architecture of morals. But, as with Kierkegaard,
his discoveries stem from a deep-rooted desire for self-annihilation.
And though many of Nietzsche's psychological achievements have
become the pandect of our day, his philosophical imperatives have
remained empty formulae. This is easy to understand. His philosophical ultimates are basically weapons of defense invented to
curb his desire for self-destruction. His relativism arises from an insatiable hunger for the absolute; his "yea" is but the wishful negation of the destructive "nay" that devoured his whole being. I do
not mean in this manner to reduce Nietzsche's philosophy to a
psychological problem. Rather, I am attempting to explain the insoluble contradictions which Nietzsche presents to the reader and
to show why he was claimed by power-drunk totalitarians and good
Europeans alike. There are not two Nietzsches (as Crane Brinton
oversimplifies the matter), a gentle and a tough one. There is a
single Nietzsche who, fighting his own self, constantly wavered between extremes and opposites, who endeavored to overcome and
to sublimate his human condition by switching, as we have said,
symbols of operation and by calling his "nay" his "yea." [151]

When the young Nietzsche had outgrown the pious devotion
that had surrounded his boyhood he seized upon three elements
that lay ready to his hand: classical antiquity, the work of Schopenhauer, and the music of Wagner. His first book, *The Birth of
Tragedy from the Spirit of Music* amalgamated these heterogeneous interests in a daring fashion, combining analysis and prophecy
in a typical Nietzschean manner. The prophetic utterance asserted
his faith in an impending rebirth of Hellenic culture "from the
womb of Wagner's music," a faith he soon relinquished. The significance of this work does not, I think, lie in its famous thesis that all
art derives from a matrimony of Apollonian and Dionysian forces,
because this thesis was but a rephrasing of the older contrasts between classic and romantic poetry. The importance of *The Birth
of Tragedy* consists in Nietzsche's discovery of the Dionysian life-
force—the eternal joy of becoming which involves also the joy of
destruction—and of reason as its opposite. Nietzsche saw in Socrates
the incarnation of the intellect which constantly jeopardizes the

Dionysian life-force, the very instrument of decadence. This is the basic theme of his first work and was to remain with him to the end.

The Birth of Tragedy is an a-Christian rather than an anti-Christian work. *Thoughts out of Season* is also a-Christian in attitude. The subject matter is identical with Nietzsche's earlier attempt: human greatness, German culture, Schopenhauer, Wagner. But *Thoughts out of Season* speaks in a different voice; this voice is polemical, critical, even iconoclastic. Nietzsche was awakening to the realities of the second German Empire, to its crude materialism and shallow complacency. Its orgies of bad taste provoked his fury and he gave free vent to his spite and contempt. The books that make up this tetrad are not the most important of Nietzsche's works but in many ways they are his most revealing. They show the critic of European culture in a present which he condemns, looking back upon a past and forward to a future which he exalts alternatively. They also give evidence of the particular Nietzschean love-hate with which he was to approach all the subjects of his career—Wagner, Germany, Christianity, Socrates, decadence, and so on. They reveal his basic approach to culture as essentially German with a fundamental German bias. It was centered in poetry, philosophy, and music to the exclusion of every other interest. Its social corollary was the idea of a spiritual aristocracy, the men of cultural genius who alone represented the superior type. His viewpoint was typical of pre-Bismarck Germany, lacking both political and social consciousness. Nietzsche admired Jakob Burckhardt but Burckhardt never succeeded in making him understand the importance of institutions and customs, of law and social regulations. A solitary throughout his life, he failed to comprehend the significance of the human community.

Nietzsche arrived at the body of ideas that can rightfully be called his philosophy in a moment of deep crisis. "I was suffering from a general aberration of my instincts." He had denounced Wagner, resigned his professorship at Basel, and his health was at its most precarious.[152] It seemed to him that he had neglected his life task: that is, to meet the religious crisis with determination. He had called himself "an atheist by instinct," but he began to realize that he had not known what it meant to be an atheist. Looking about him he saw that he had contemporaries who occupied more advanced positions than his own. In an abrupt turn he became a positivist, rather a psychological positivist, since the scientific positivism of Comte held no interest for him. "Everything has developed," we read in *Human, All Too Human*, "there are no eternal facts, just as there are no eternal truths." But positivism was a steppingstone only. With a characteristic mental somersault he took his revenge for the necessity of becoming a relativist.[153] To be a relativist means to be a nihilist, to understand that God has died and that all values have lost their validity. The famous formula, "God is dead," has a very special ring; an undertone of fear is sounded reminiscent of the ancient lamentation: the great Pan is dead.

God's death is for Nietzsche the greatest event in history. But man in killing God is unaware of the consequences of his deed. Although Nietzsche systematically obscured the fact, it was really the impact of Darwin's *The Origin of Species* that caused him to cry out, "God is dead." Through Darwin the doctrine of sovereign becoming had triumphed; the fluidity of all species had been established. Any cardinal distinction between man and animal had been erased; man had become human, all too human.

Nietzsche directed attention to some of the philosophical consequences of Darwin's hypothesis. He saw that man's position in the universe was at stake and had to be redefined. That God was dead, that the distinction between man and animal had been removed, marks the turning point of Nietzsche's philosophical existence. He baptized the ensuing vacuum in the name of nihilism. The word was already in existence, its meaning ardently discussed in both France and Russia, but Nietzsche's repetition was incremental. He defined nihilism in terms of value; he saw it as the final result of the religious crisis. "What does nihilism mean? That the highest values disvalue themselves . . . the goal is lacking; the answer is lacking to our why." [154] A new goal had to be set, a new answer to be given. In Nietzsche's creed both goal and answer are summed up in: the superman, the will to power, and the idea of eternal recurrence. In this manner he progressed from the diagnostician of nihilism to the prophet of a new God. "If there is a God, how could I bear it not to be God myself?" [155]

The new message was first unfolded in *Thus Spake Zarathustra*. Here is no gospel. While it will always attract the adolescent, it repels those who look for taste, discipline, and maturity of mind in a writer. This book which Nietzsche deemed without parallel in history and which has for so long sustained his fame, is an intellectual miscarriage. In reading it one is constantly obliged to recall that Nietzsche called himself "the buffoon of the eternities." Fortunately, the concept of superman and the will to power are better elucidated in other writings of his last period.

Man is something that is to be surpassed, so reads Nietzsche's new tablet. Man is the rope stretched between the animal and superman—a rope over an abyss. Nietzsche rejected any evolutionary interpretation of superman as constituting a new species, but he also excluded any spiritual explanation. If we seek for a positive answer to the question, what iconography reposes in superman? we find ourselves thrown into a maze of contradictory suggestions. Goethe, Napoleon, Cesare Borgia are brought forth as examples: "a Roman Caesar with the soul of Christ" is the ideal.[156] But who can fail to recognize the Utopian frame of such a vision. By neither Roman nor Christian standards can it take on reality.

The idea of eternal recurrence is likewise not a new vista of metaphysical depth, but the result of Nietzsche's wishful thinking wherein he hoped to convert his instinctive "nay" into a conscious "yea." "The eternal hourglass of existence is turned around ever again—and you with it . . . how well disposed toward yourself and life would you have become to crave nothing more fervently than this ultimate eternal confirmation?"[157] Obviously this is Munchhausen endeavoring to extricate himself from the swamp of nihilism by the shoestring of his own thought. Nietzsche had now arrived at an appalling dictum: nothing is true, everything is permitted. But he did not advocate a nihilism of indifference; instead he tried to supersede it by a "nihilism of strength." *The Will to Power* (though not revised by himself) remains Nietzsche's most important work. This "history of the next two centuries" with its amazing prophecies of world wars, world tyrants, and world unity shows the final stage reached by his mind.

"Know you what the world is to me? . . . A marvel of power without beginning, without end . . . bounded by nothing save its own bounds . . . a sea of tumultuous and torrential power, eternally changing, eternally returning, with immense cycles of recurrence

. . . this Dionysian world of everlasting self-creation, of everlasting self-destruction, this mystery world of doubled delight . . . this . . . is the Will to Power." [158] Power, then, is the essence of the universe and the only criterion of appraisal. Nietzsche uses the phrase "power quantum" in judging the importance of human phenomena. It permitted him not only to predict but to welcome the great despots even then germinating in the womb of the twentieth century and with them the afterbirth of disciplinary regimentation and oppression. Nietzsche split humanity into master races and slave races and pondered the question of breeding and training necessary for the propagation of a generation of supermen who would dominate the earth.

The world has seen how the Nazis capitalized on Nietzsche's *Will to Power*. Although it is absurd to call Nietzsche a Nazi or a half Nazi, he who was both antinationalistic and antisocialistic, it is equally absurd to deny that some of the elements of the Nazi ideology can be found in *The Will to Power*. Perhaps Nietzsche's greatest mistake lay in the belief that he could overcome nihilism by reducing mankind to herd and superman and that nihilism could be conquered by "a few lucky accidents." He did not see, as did Dostoevski, that "we arrive all or none." The crises which have shaken our society have proved that the separation of individual genius from the masses is not only wrong but pernicious.

It is impossible to take leave of Nietzsche without noting the pathological aspects of his genius. Over a period of fifteen years, from 1874 to 1889, he suffered long stretches of ill health interrupted by spells of inspiration and an illusionary feeling of well-being. This condition not only influenced his writings but structured it to such an extent that it became shot through with madness. His last books forecast the impending collapse with a shrill and awe-inspiring voice. Truth for Nietzsche was something unbearable that must nevertheless be pursued even beyond the borderline that separates clairvoyance from lunacy. His final breakdown may have been a clinical accident, but his madness is a symbol for the state of mind of Western man. Had there ever before been a mad philosopher?

Nietzsche's effect on the twentieth century is difficult to assess. He did not wish to found a school, even less a religion: ". . . of what account are all believers?" The parlor admirers who chanted his praises at the turn of the century would have annoyed him as much as the Fascists of the 1930's who borrowed from him. In general it may be said of Nietzsche, as of Marx and Kierkegaard, that his errors made a deeper mark on the age than his intuitions.[159] In a period of hubris he provided the catchwords and the slogans. The tyranny of superman led to the despotism of sub-man. Without doubt the history of the twentieth century would have run its course if Nietzsche had never written a line. His imperatives: vital energy, will to power, hostility toward religion, were already rampant in the political, social, and military trends of the period. Nietzsche but provided the philosophical and poetical expression, the ideological justification.[160]

Nietzsche was by intellect observer, by temperament prophet. It was his fate that neither gift could be fully consummated; the diagnostician hampered the prophet and the visionary dimmed the clarity of the observer. As a result his accomplishments as a critic are many; as a builder they are paltry. No construction followed the demolition. Although he hastened the process of secularization in Western society, his influence is less than that of Comte or Marx or Darwin.

Wherein, then, lies his importance? He recognized and with great vehemence set forth the critical condition of our civilization. He felt the impact of rationalism on our religious, political, and artistic traditions more profoundly and with more distress than any other thinker, and he had the courage to state the logical conclusion. He sensed the clash between old and new, and refused to abide by any hypocritical attitude that would avoid the conflict by ignoring it. He was primarily concerned with the human condition, and it is here that he made his greatest contributions, all of which fall into the realm of psychology. He practiced depth psychology long before Freud; he studied the phenomena of human emotions before Scheler, vitalism before Dilthey and Bergson, irrationalism before George and Klages. His most important bequests were his intellectual honesty and his demand for uncompromising sincerity. He helped a whole generation of writers to view themselves without pretense and without equivocation. But though he manifested man's plight in this age with unmatched intensity he was unable to rebuild a new image of man to replace the one he had been so intent on destroying. His philosophy is sterile; it leads nowhere, save into madness. Thus, his greatness remains but symptomatic and symbolic.

X

The conflicts inherited by our age from the nineteenth century may, in large part, be attributed to the belief that reason conquers all. Western man had sworn allegiance to the faith that his eyes would be opened and that "he would be as God." But already Byron had known that "the tree of knowledge is not that of life." Baudelaire, Kierkegaard, and Nietzsche had voiced their hostility to rationalism. For them truth was subjectivity. During the past century there were comparatively few who were aware of the implications of this great struggle. One writer, however, was fully cognizant of the stakes and brought the fight into the open with a vengeance.

Dostoevski's biography resembles so closely the lives of his protagonists that his novels seem as much a part of his existence as his existence is a part of his novels.[161] On three separate occasions fate lifted him up, and three times cast him again into the depths from which no resurrection seemed possible.[162] But the recurrent rhythm of triumph, catastrophe, and catharsis was not merely a characteristic of his mind; it was the indispensable condition of his creativity.

Feodor Dostoevski's childhood was joyless and overshadowed by sinister occurrences that he never revealed. A significant silence envelops most of his youth. We have reason to believe that "something terrible, agonizing and unforgettable" happened to him then which lacerated his soul forever, though its exact nature has never come to light.[163] His mother died when he was sixteen; his father was murdered by rebellious serfs when Feodor was eighteen. The connection between his father's death and the motif of parricide in Dostoevski's work has struck many a biographer. "Who does not desire his father's death?" asks Ivan in *The Brothers Karamazov*. Sigmund Freud has diagnosed Dostoevski's trauma and the resultant epileptic seizures from which he suffered throughout his life as the outcome of a subconscious wish for his father's death. The evidence is, however, too sparse to venture further than conjecture.[164] But we are safe in assuming that the sense of sin and guilt which overwhelmed his mind were brought into focus by his father's assassination. The conviction of man's sinfulness is in his make-up when we first peer into his mind. So also is the concept of suffering: "We shall have to work out our future happiness somehow by suffering; pay for it by fresh miseries. Everything is purified by suffering." [165]

His was "a raw youth." As a student in the school for military engineering, the drill and skill of which he despised, he became enraptured with his mission as a writer. "Man," he wrote to his brother, "is a mystery. It must be unraveled, and if you give your life to this task, do not say that you have wasted it. I devote myself to this mystery because I wish to become a man." [166]

His first literary attempts gave him the fame to which he aspired. But the literary glory did not last and Dostoevski soon found himself attracted to a group that concerned itself with the political transformation of Russia in accordance with socialistic ideas. What seems to the modern observer to have been a mixture of debating society and political club had for the officials of Tzardom all the marks of conspiracy. There followed his imprisonment, his conviction, and the mock execution on the Semionovsky Square. "There the death sentence was read to us; we were given the cross to kiss; the dagger was broken over our heads, and our funeral toilet . . . was made. . . . Finally retreat was sounded . . . and it was read to us that His Imperial Majesty granted us our lives." [167] This was the turning point in Dostoevski's existence. In that terrible moment he had felt that his soul had outrun death and knew itself to be alive.[168]

In this crisis the gospel of suffering revealed its full meaning. He was able to accept the sentence of four years of hard labor in Siberia and to justify it. "Even in prison there dwell not beasts but men, and many of them are possibly better and worthier than I am . . . and when once I have the prison behind me, I'll write regularly. During these months I have lived through much in my soul. . . . I shall truly have plenty of material for writing." [169] And after he had completed his sentence he said to his brother: "Decidedly I have not spent my time there in vain. I have learnt to know the Russian people." [170]

The House of the Dead is the picture of his Siberian inferno, and, as Turgenev said, it is worthy of Dante. Its place in nineteenth century literature is unique. To a period of optimism it showed man as "a being who becomes accustomed to everything"; it presented him as a mixture of naïveté and cynicism, of blasphemy and awe, of courage and baseness, of generosity and vileness.[171] He was right in saying that the days in Siberia had brought him to the most critical pass in his life and that he was now ready to cherish hopes "of which I never thought in other days." [172]

It is not easy to summarize the impact of these experiences. Brought up in the orthodox faith, he came to realize the necessity of religious fulfillment. "I am a child of this age, a child of unfaith and skepticism, and probably (indeed I know it) shall remain so to the end of my life. . . . And yet God gives me some moments of perfect peace . . . in such moments I have formulated my creed . . . I believe that there is nothing lovelier, deeper, more sympathetic, more rational, more manly and more perfect than the Saviour; I say to myself with jealous love that not only is there no one else like Him, but that there could be no one. I would even say more: If anyone could prove to me that Christ is outside the truth, and if the truth really did exclude Christ, I should prefer to stay with Christ and not with the truth." [173]

The notion that Christ could be outside the truth was, of course, a heresy, a heresy very typical of Dostoevski. He presents himself in this confession as divided between his unfaith and his longing to believe. He knew of the profound dualism in his make-up, a dualism that emotionally, mentally, and spiritually, made him a divided and contradictory person. Indeed, he could not overlook the intellectual difficulties into which faith would lead him, but, as one of his characters says, "Without God what would I be?" Therefore, by repeating in his own life the historical process of Christianity, he hoped to bridge the gulf; in adhering to the Christ-ideal he expected that his own suffering would redeem his guilt.[174] The essential condition of human existence, says another of his figures, is that man should always be able to bow down before something infinitely great. If men are deprived of this, they cannot go on living; they will die of despair.[175]

Such random quotation must not lead us to bestow upon Dostoevski a unity of view which he, in reality, never achieved. Tolstoi said of him that his whole life was a struggle between good and evil. This struggle is maintained throughout his work; it, in the final analysis, is the "true message" which he left us, not the Utopian prophecies with which he tried to console himself and his contemporaries.[176]

Although Dostoevski's existential problem was similar to Nietzsche's and Kierkegaard's, his approach to "the mystery of man" was different. Nietzsche and Kierkegaard were poet-philosophers; Dostoevski was first and foremost a creator of human beings. His genius gave him the power to express the contradictions of his heart in a variety of contrasting figures; he was not under the logical compulsion of building a system or a doctrine of philosophical consistency. By giving free rein to his intuition he could picture the murderer and the saint, the lecher and the innocent, the man-god and the god-man, each with his own problems and confusions, as he saw them in those troubled hours when they fought for the possession of his own soul. Like Baudelaire, he saved himself from shipwreck amid the storm of human emotions by the process of objectivization; his novels might well have been called the flowers of evil. What Baudelaire expressed in lyrical form, Dostoevski expressed in his novels—novel-tragedies, rather; that is "tragedies in epic dress." [177] It was his inner conflict that propelled him toward this form, typical of his divided self, where he could practice his "cruel talent" of vivisecting the soul.[178] One other characteristic of his novel-tragedies must be noted: all have crime at their core. This is not the crime that appears in all pictures of human life, in Shakespeare, Schiller and Balzac, but the crime that is the essence of human existence. Dostoevski's own tendencies may have inclined him toward this singular viewpoint, and his Siberian experiences strengthened further the belief that the criminal came nearer the true human being than the law-abiding citizen. It was his plan to show that those who believe themselves to be in good health are in fact infected by the most fearful self-inflation and self-admiration. He was bent on unmasking these deeply ailing individuals in order that "they might get cured." [179] Dostoevski gives us a portrait of inverted humanity in which there is more joy over one sinner than over a hundred just men. His sociology is the sociology of the insulted and injured, of life's expatriates, of those who have been

tortured by mankind and by God—a hospital of neuropaths, said
one of his French critics; the Marquis de Sade of Russian literature,
said Turgenev. It is among these outscasts, these extremists of good
and evil, that Dostoevski unrolls the tragedy of mankind.

The rebellious passion of a man who confessed: "In all things
I go to the uttermost extreme," appears in the self-centered and self-
willed natures that people his novels.[180] This man who was starved
for faith finally projects his mystical hunger in a gallery of saints
who experience no greater happiness than complete submission to
God's ordinances.

The problem with which Dostoevski wrestled all his life was not
so much the existence of God, but "the meaning of His creation,"
not God but his relation to man. Man was a battlefield in the
eternal fight between God and the devil. And thus it is that he is led
into the further problem of human freedom. We know already that
for Dostoevski human freedom could be achieved only by a surrender to something higher, by submission to the God-man, to Christ
and His Gospel. But we also know that he had felt deeply the
temptation of an absolute freedom. The vehemence with which
he later fought the "false tendencies" of his time is one more proof
of the marked cleavage in his heart and mind.[181] All his novels, from
Notes from the Underground to *Brothers Karamazov* are one long
and passionate dialogue between the rationalistic and the mystical
Dostoevski. It is well known that he scorned Western Europe for its
belief in reason and enlightened self-interest, that he thought it impossible to construct either personal or communal life on rational
principles, that he condemned positivism, liberalism, socialism, and
anarchism as elements in the same deadly witch-brew. Like Tolstoi
he harbored a profound distrust of the scientific and industrial civilization of the West and condemned its good and bad alike as the
final convulsion of the bourgeois world he believed to be doomed.[182]
Notes from the Underground was written at the time he first came
into direct contact with Western culture. Its hero is a prisoner of
his own reason and of his restless self-analysis. Thought has corroded
his will. Science, he feels, has only succeeded in shrinking a boundless domain to the limits of a prison cell. In impotent rage he batters
his head against the stone wall of arithmetical certainty. Dostoevski anticipates Unamuno's protest when he says, "I will not be

reconciled to it just because it is a stone wall." The whole purpose of man must surely consist in his proving to himself that he is a man and not a cog in a machine. The underground man forecasts Dostoevski's next creation: Raskolnikov.

In the person of Raskolnikov, Dostoevski made his first attempt to probe the social consequences of a human attitude that is guided by nothing higher than its own reasoning. This "Napoleon of the slums" divides humanity into the extraordinary and the ordinary, the leader and the herd. In order to prove to himself that he is one of the extraordinary, he murders an old pawnbroker, a "human louse." But Raskolnikov soon realizes that he is not a Napoleon; he is just another louse, and his crime has brought about a severance of all his ties with mankind. Only by confession and atonement can he extricate himself from the isolation which he finds intolerable. Dostoevski, according to his notes, wanted to show in Raskolnikov the idea of immeasurable pride, of arrogance and scorn toward society, an idea even more clearly expressed in *The Possessed*.[183]

The picture of Russian terrorism and anarchism which Dostoevski painted in *The Possessed* brings the reader into the presence of a group of men he has come to know all too well: the nihilists turned politicians. *The Possessed* is not Dostoevski's most accomplished novel, but for us who have witnessed the experiments of totalitarianism it has a truly prophetic ring. "Starting from boundless freedom I end with boundless despotism," says one character of *The Possessed*. Slaves must have leaders, leaders who will know how to corrupt the tissue of human society by attacking family ties, love and property, by teaching schoolboys to laugh at God and children to kill old people for the thrill of it.

Thus Dostoevski anticipated Nietzsche's position by almost two decades. He pictured the nihilism that finds no answer to our Why, the superman who thinks himself beyond good and evil, the will to power as the ultimate goal. But the solutions that Dostoevski envisioned are deeper than the ones given by Nietzsche. For the Russian writer superman has only two alternatives: to end the process by committing suicide or to fall on his kness and confess his errors with humility.

The novels we have mentioned deal with the corroding influence of human reason and the destructive power of self-centeredness.

We have witnessed the battles between God and the devil, but the question of man's victory or his salvation must be answered. Here we must distinguish between Dostoevski the pamphleteer and Dostoevski the poet. As a publicist he paid a heavy toll to the pet ideas of his century. He was a nationalist of the first water, as rabid in his belief that Russia would save the world as Treitschke was in his idolatry of Prussianism. He believed in a Russian God, the God of the Orthodox Church; he defended Russian imperialism as a crusade to rescue the world from Western corruption for which he blamed the Roman Catholic Church, liberalism, capitalism, and socialism alike. As one of his biographers puts it: Unwilling to consider the beam in the Russian eye he went ferociously about the business of casting the mote out of the Western eye.[184] *The Diary of a Writer* spills over with the most spurious kind of prophecies and has contributed its share in placing Dostoevski in the position of being the ally not only of Tzarist expansionism but also of Communist imperialism. In spite of his Cassandra songs Europe has stood the test of defending Christianity far better than Russia. It is Russia that has handed over her fate to "the possessed."

But Dostoevski the artist applied a more severe criterion of truthfulness than Dostoevski the publicist. In two of his greatest books he has dealt with the problem of how human beings could be saved in a world dominated by demonic forces. *The Idiot* was his attempt to depict a "positively good man." [185] After showing the man-God in his failure, he undertook the portrait of the God-man. But Prince Myshkin, although Christlike, is not Christ. He is a suffering human being who subordinates action to feeling because he believes that a sinful action can be more easily forgiven than a sinful state of mind.[186] It is Myshkin's tragic fate to end in madness, but that does not lessen the intense attraction which emanates from his being.

Dostoevski's final answer is to be read in *The Brothers Karamazov*. The chapter called "The Legend of the Grand Inquisitor" discusses in mythical greatness the conflict between the man-God and the God-man. The Grand Inquisitor is the symbol for all forms of authoritarianism which in the name of security and happiness deprive man of his divine birthright. Freedom includes man's inclination toward sin, but it also includes his willingness to expiate his sin through suffering.

Although the man-God, Ivan Karamazov, hands back to God his entrance ticket to a world of injustice, Zosima and Alyosha accept the irrationality of the world and their role in it. Dostoevski's most profound idea, as revealed in *The Brothers Karamazov,* is the idea of solidarity. Human guilt is as universal as God's forgiveness. All have sinned before all men in all things; every human being bears his quota of the universal guilt. "Equality is to be found only in the spiritual dignity of man." It is this equality which Dostoevski called pan-human and which he thought to be the unique province of the Russian people. Whatever the truth of this claim, the idea of pan-human solidarity would seem to be Dostoevski's great bequest to our century. I would rank it even above his more tangible contributions to the realms of psychology and literature. It is true, however, that he transformed the psychology of the novel as deeply as he transmuted the novel as an art form. He was the first to present human beings as a compound of irrational conflicting forces. The masters of modern psychology have acknowledged how deeply their concepts are already imbedded in Dostoevski's studies of the human soul. As for the change in the novel as an art form, there is hardly a writer of distinction who has escaped his influence.[187]

Dostoevski's fame was at its height thirty years ago but has now suffered an eclipse. He prophesied the Great War and the decline of the bourgeois world of security and comfort as did Marx and Nietzsche, Kierkegaard and Baudelaire. He sensed the illness that afflicted Europe long before its symptoms had become apparent, but the remedies that he recommended will convince no one today. He sided with the forces of oppression and advocated the continuance of the old autocracy until a "change of heart" should make all men brothers. But the belief in a change of heart that would purify man's nature is as Utopian as Marx's belief that by changing the ownership of the means of production one could change man's nature.

Dostoevski shares with many of the *Founders* of the twentieth century the fate of having his premises accepted and his conclusion denied.[188] This century is convinced of the irrationality of human nature and that it must be controlled by moral forces. This is our debt of gratitude to Dostoevski. But we cannot share his belief that to accept the antinomies of life as part of the human condition would entail the resignation of every effort to improve the human lot. Like Kierkegaard, Dostoevski made his own exceptional condition the rule for mankind. But humanity will hardly agree to live by the rhythm of sin and atonement, crime and punishment, as concepts of social conduct.

Yet the fact remains that his idea of pan-human solidarity has a significance for the present hardly surpassed by any other idea advanced during the past century. By it and through it Dostoevski anticipated, as Keyserling said, "the extreme tension belonging to the type which alone seems to be quite adequate to the tasks of an ecumenic civilization." [189] To have heralded the coming of an ecumenic civilization is Dostoevski's legacy to our time.

CHAPTER III

The Self-Enchanted

The last two decades of the nineteenth century witnessed the crystallization of a movement that embraced many of the ideas advanced during the long period since the death of Goethe. It has been referred to as the esthetic movement, neo-romanticism, or art for art's sake, but these are merely surface characterizations which fail to reveal the essence.

"We, we!" wrote Hugo von Hofmannsthal in 1895. "I know only too well that I am not talking of the whole great generation. I talk of a few thousand people, dispersed in the great cities of Europe. . . . Nevertheless, these two or three thousand people have a certain significance . . . they are not necessarily the head or the heart of the generation; they are its conscience." [1] Hofmannsthal thus sensed, not only the intimate kinship of this new group which was about to occupy the European scene, but, going further, calls it the conscience of the age. It was indeed a generation of which he spoke, if we take the word in its recently defined sense, that is, as a group born in a certain time span which determines both its inheritance and its living environment, a group which, because of its historical position, is confronted with identical or parallel problems, even though the solutions offered by its individual members may differ widely.[2] By this definition the group that we are to consider was in every way a generation. Its representatives were born between 1850 and 1880, roughly speaking; Wilde in 1854, Barrès in 1862, d'Annunzio in 1864, Stefan George in 1868, Gide in 1869, and Hofmannsthal in 1874, to mention only the figures of universal renown.

By 1880, when the older members of this generation began to assert themselves, naturalism had reached its zenith. In reality, this movement was little more than the application of positivism to the world of the arts, an attempt to compel the imagination to surrender to natural laws, whether mechanical or biological. Emile Zola was its chief exponent. While the subject matter of literature had vastly enlarged its scope under the influence of the naturalistic movement, the creative impulse of the artist had been sold for a "mess of facts." Yet the victory of naturalistic ideology was not complete, nor was it ever undisputed.

Romanticism as a legacy of the Pre-Raphaelites lived on in England. Schopenhauer's concept of the arts continued to be a decisive element in Wagner and in Nietzsche. Against the mechanistic enslavement of the soul, Paul Bourget in his novels and the "Essais de psychologie contemporaine" proclaimed understanding through self-analysis, symptom of that greater revolution in the realm of psychology soon to come. And from the solitary protest of Baudelaire against the vulgarity of his century stems a new literary movement devoted to pure form and symbolic expression.

However, the naturalists seemed to have the "Zeitgeist" on their side. By 1880 the tide of industrial progress had engulfed all Europe and was rapidly reaching out toward distant shores. The gaslight cities of the period with their revolting slums and the equally revolting elegance of their suburbs seemed in accord with an art that was respectively argumentative and descriptive; its intellectual appeal was directed toward the proletariat or the bourgeoisie.

But there were some who refused to conform, and a new élite began to proclaim its otherness. "We, who are born at the close of this wonderful age, are at once too cultural and too critical, too intellectually subtle and too curious of exquisite pleasures, to accept any speculations about life in exchange for life itself. . . . Metaphysics does not satisfy our temperaments, and religious ecstasy is out of date. The world through which the academic philosopher becomes 'the spectator of all time and of all existence' is not really an ideal world, but simply a world of abstract ideas. When we enter it, we starve amidst the chill mathematics of thought. The courts of the city of God are not open to us now. . . . It is enough that our fathers believed. They have exhausted the faith-faculty of the species. Their legacy to us is the scepticism of which they were afraid." [3] Thus did Oscar Wilde challenge the beliefs of both his fathers and his brothers.

I

The final verdict on this man who voiced so distinctly the consciousness of his generation has not been spoken, but today, more than half a century after his death, neither his memory nor our judgment can be clouded by his aberrations and their social repercussions. He has gradually emerged as one of the greatest wits of the nineteenth century, as a critic of considerable acumen and originality, as a moralist—strange as it may seem—of courage and foresight, and as a playwright, novelist, and storyteller of indelible character.

André Gide, his friend and admirer, has declared, "Wilde n'est pas un grand écrivain," [4] and certainly by classical standards he cannot be called "a great writer." His style is uneven, sometimes ornate and precious, at other times diaphanous and trenchant, and always pretentious. He borrowed freely and even unscrupulously. But no critical comment can bypass the fact that through his work and even more through his life, he has moved into the sphere of intellectual history as a symbol of the fin de siècle.

Wilde's self-evaluation—portrait of the artist as a broken man—elucidates the position in which he saw himself and in which he wished others to see him. "I was a man who stood in symbolic relations to the art and culture of my age. I had realized this for myself at the very dawn of my manhood and had forced my age to realize it afterward. . . . The gods had given me almost everything. I had genius, a distinguished name, high social position, brilliancy, intellectual daring; I made art a philosophy and philosophy an art; I altered the minds of men and the colours of things . . . I treated art as the supreme reality and life as a mere mode of fiction. I awoke the imagination of my century so that it created myth and legend around me. I summed up all systems in a phrase and all existence in an epigram." [5] Subtracting the self-esteem whereby the defeated man sought to make Reading Gaol, where he wrote these lines, somehow more bearable, subtracting the exaggerations, there remains enough truth in Wilde's words to command attention.

Recent studies have brought us closer to an understanding of the basic problem of Wilde's existence. The form of expression most congenial to his mind was the paradoxical epigram; his plays, his prose poems, his novel, his essays all bear out this observation.

"The contradictions," writes G. Woodcock, "which became evident at a very early period in his writing and which continue until his death, were the result of a very deep cleft in his mental process. . . . It is likely that Wilde loved the paradox because it suited the peculiar duality of his attitude toward the world." [6] Two opposite creeds strove for precedence within Wilde, hedonism and suffering. He was the esthetic poseur and the serious critic, the snob and the social thinker, and, most tragic conflict of all, the playboy and the prophet.[7]

A psychoanalyst might solve these contradictions. As a historian I am satisfied to trace some of them back to his heritage and environment. His father, a surgeon of great distinction and an archeologist of renown, was also notorious as a philanderer. He was stirred by a perpetual store of physical and intellectual restlessness. Wilde's mother, too, was a turbulent and mettlesome woman. She longed always for some impossible splendor of character or circumstance, "because I was an eagle in my youth." Oscar preserved an affection for this mother which was based on admiration and on an awareness of their close affinity. Like Wilde himself, she was a noted conversationalist, "remarkably original, sometimes daring, and always interesting." Like her son, she had a passion for showmanship and sartorial exhibitionism.

There were two events that Wilde considered of paramount importance in his life: his father sent him to Oxford; society sent him to prison.[8] Of the Oxford dons, Ruskin and Pater exercised the most profound influence on his mind. Through Ruskin he made contact with the Pre-Raphaelite movement in its double aspect of ethical and esthetic reform, and through Walter Pater he reached the nerve center of his own existence. Ruskin's rhetorical fervor, so very different from Wilde's own nonchalant and disengaged temperament, became the formative influence on that part of Wilde's personality which secretly thirsted for religious comfort and which eventually emerged in the demand for social reform.[9] But the influence of Pater was even more decisive. It was not so much his personality, evasive and reticent, that impressed Wilde; it was his work, and especially his famous essays on the Renaissance. This collection of essays with its description of the Gioconda, its analysis of Botticelli and the della Robbias, fulfilled for the Anglo-Saxon world a function similar to Jakob Burckhardt's *Kultur der Renaissance,* which so stirred the intellectual thought of the Continent. Both are, to a high degree, responsible for the Renaissance mythos, for what has been called "renaissancismus." [10]

But Pater's "philosophy" left a deeper mark on Wilde's mind than did his historical conceptions. "To burn always with this hard gemlike flame, to maintain this ecstacy, is success in life. In a sense it might even be said that our failure is to form habits. . . . While all melts under our feet, we may well grasp at any exquisite passion, or any contribution to knowledge that seems by a lifted horizon to set the spirit free for a moment, or any stirring of the senses, strange dyes, strange colours, and curious odours, or work of the artist's hands, or the faces of one's friends." These sentences, that sounded so rebellious in the stifling atmosphere of Victorian righteousness, have become the cliché of prep-school compositions, but their ardor has not completely faded, and one may well understand why the undergraduate at Magdalen College said that "Mr. Pater's essays became to me the golden book of spirit and sense, the holy writ of beauty."

It was only natural that the admirer of Pater's "intellectual impressionism" became a disciple of Greek culture, the Greek ideal of life, the Greek concept of art, during his years at Oxford.[11] Here Wilde strikes a chord that we will find echoed in George and d'Annunzio, in Hofmannsthal and Gide. "Like Gautier," Wilde confessed, "I have always been one of those 'pour qui le monde visible existe.' " [12] He believed the Greeks had bequeathed to the modern world the two supreme arts, Life and Literature, life and the perfect expression of life.[13] Thus we arrive at the core of the esthetic movement, the relation between life and the arts, and between life and the artist. The problem is age-old, inherent in all forms of higher cultural endeavor, but the solutions advanced by this generation were novel. The tensions that always have and always will exist between Life and Mind had increased dangerously with the emergence of modern subjectivism. Goethe had still dominated the conflict between his life and his work. As the effects of the French Revolution and the Industrial Revolution became steadily more decisive in European society, the conflict between the artist and life seemed to be leading toward open cleavage. Life took more and more the form of material advancement, of industrial production, of output and the selling of the output. The triumph of utilitarian criteria seemed to Flaubert and Baudelaire a triumph of vulgarity, ugliness, and idiocy, and they admitted freely the breach between life and the arts.

Wilde's position was akin to theirs in many ways, but he constantly vacillated between praising and cursing life, between denouncing its ugliness and shapelessness and hoping that it would one day become the crown of the arts. Wilde's first appearance in the market place was, in any case, more a propitiation to life than to the arts, or perhaps he thought to conquer life by the esthetic approach. He, like Baudelaire, took up the pose of the dandy, and, though there was nothing new in the attempt to gain attention by startling attire and immodest speech, he met with a great deal of success from an advertising point of view.[14] Gilbert and Sullivan parodied him as "the apostle of the high aesthetic band," and so great was the appreciation of this burlesque, that he became for many of his contemporaries an attitude rather than a personality.[15]

Yet he was indeed a personality; the mannerisms of the dandy merely served to reinforce his individuality, accommodating both the actor and the clown. He confounded a multitude of people, but he himself remained unperturbed, his ideas, constantly focused on the great problem of Life and Art. His wit rather than his dandyism secured him admisison to society, for which he had as much of the snob's admiration as Proust. He defined happiness as a state wherein the individual was in harmony with himself and his environment, and it does not seem strange that he believed himself to be happy at this stage.

Wilde adopted rather than created the forms through which he communicated his ideas to his age. Although gifted with a Celtic imagination, his mind was articulate, and this rare combination found expression in countless epigrams. His poetry was seldom more than an echo of the poets he most admired, but he showed a remarkable independence in other fields. He introduced into English literature the prose poem invented by Baudelaire and Rimbaud. Wilde's prose poems show his constant preoccupation with the themes of guilt and sin, themes he was to pass on to André Gide.[16] Other forms he chose, intimately related to the prose poem, are the lyrical drama and the fairy tale.

In view of his artistic premises, it was only logical that he selected the fairy tale rather than the short story as a means of revealing both the artist and the moralist in his make-up. It is not the fairy tale of Grimm, but rather that of Goethe, Novalis, and Hans Christian Andersen.

The blending of different and even opposed art forms to which Wilde's ambivalent mind inclined is even more apparent in his lyrical drama, *Salomé*. Its emotional content, with its sadistic overtones, sets the pace for much of the literature of the twentieth century. The plot interest has been drastically reduced; the drama relies exclusively on diction and atmosphere.[17]

Wilde approached the novel with a similar divergence, and while the plot of *Dorian Gray* may fade, the paradoxes of Lord Henry continue to be repeated and enjoyed. The theme concerns the granting of a human wish by supernatural powers. Balzac and Poe had dealt with the idea, but Dorian's wish is peculiarly Wildean; he desires eternal youth and everlasting beauty. Typical of Wilde are also the three protagonists: Lord Henry, the cynical wit and seducer; Basil, the artist; and Dorian, who would rather lose his soul than submit to the ravages of time. *Dorian Gray* makes manifest the self-condemnation of esthetic individualism, and discloses Wilde's subconscious awareness of the abyss toward which his path was tending.

Wilde's work as critic is substantial in volume and surprising in its freshness. It is also novel, epigrammatic, and audacious. In this writing he does not present himself as a "tired hedonist." The dialogues on *The Decay of Lying* and *The Critic as Artist* are attempts to reestablish esthetic values in a world of pragmatic and utilitarian behavior. Art, says Wilde, expresses only itself; like thought, it has an independent life. "It is not necessarily realistic in an age of realism, nor spiritual in an age of faith. The moment art surrenders its imaginative medium it surrenders everything." When, from this position, Wilde goes on to maintain that Life imitates Art far more than Art imitates Life, he is obviously carried away by the sophistry of his own dialectic. But we must remember that he was "intent on shocking people out of their complacent faith in the realistic theories of art." [18] Wilde looks at criticism as "a creation within a creation" and believes that it provides a perpetual stimulus to culture and thought. Contemplation is the highest aim of thought and life, and "the contemplative life, the life that has for its aim not doing but being, and not being merely, but becoming . . . is what the critical spirit can give us." [19]

In *The Soul of Man under Socialism,* Wilde turned to social criticism.[20] The title indicates his reason for conerning himself with the question which occupied the minds of Shaw and his Fabian friends. The true perfection of man, says Wilde, lies not in what man has, but in what man is. He advocated socialism because he thought it would lead to individualism; poverty should be abolished because it debased people and retarded their individual development. "There is only one class in the community that thinks more about money than the rich, and that is the poor." As a contribution to economic theory, the essay is worthless: Wilde speaks as a moralist about the moral aspects of an economic problem, but his approach is intellectual, not emotional. "Starvation, and not sin, is the parent of modern crime." "It is through disobedience that progress has been made, through disobedience and rebellion." He discards the idea that manual labor and drudgery enoble man; machines should be the slaves and not the competitors of man. But he balked at State socialism, and his premonition of its hazards is astounding: "If Socialism is authoritarian; if there are Governments armed with economic power as they are now with political power; if, in a word, we are to have industrial tyrannies, then the last state of man will be worse than the first."

By 1890 Wilde had reached the summit of his career. André Gide gives us a memorable description of him: "Wilde avait alors ce que Thackeray appelle le principal don des grands hommes: le succès. Son geste, son regard triomphaient. Son succès était si certain qu'il semblait qu'il précédait Wilde et que lui n'eut qu'à s'avancer. . . . Certains le comparaient à un Bacchus asiatique; d'autres à quelque empereur romain; d'autres à Apollon lui-même—et le fait est qu'il rayonnait." [21]

But success had ceased to satisfy Wilde. He craved some flagrancy of beauty and pleasure, and like Dorian, was ready to sell his soul for it. Lord Alfred Douglas was only a minor emissary of Satan; Fate needs but small bait for its willing victims. Wilde became a practitioner of his perhaps always latent homosexual inclination. Though he evoked in his defense the lofty names of Plato and Michelangelo and Shakespeare, his own companions were frequently male prostitutes. In *De Profundis* he described this phase of his life: "I let myself be lured into long spells of senseless and sensual ease. I amused myself with becoming a flaneur, a dandy, a man of fashion. I surrounded myself with the smaller natures and the meaner minds. I became the spendthrift of my own genius, and to waste eternal youth gave me a curious joy. Tired of the heights, I deliberately went into the depths in the search for new sensation. What the paradox was to me in the sphere of thought, perversity became to me in the sphere of passion. Desire, at the end, was a malady, or a madness, or both. I grew careless of the lives of others. I took pleasure where it pleased me, and passed on . . . I ceased to be lord over myself." [22]

There is some indication that Wilde was prepared for the last great emotional experience of his life. Gide, who saw him just before the debacle of his trial, wrote: "Une fatalité le menait; il ne pouvait pas et ne voulait pas se soustraire." And Wilde himself said to Gide, "Il faut qu'il arrive quelque chose, quelque chose d'autre." After a reading of the trial testimony there remains a distinct impression that Wilde chose to go to prison from a feeling of guilt, and from a desire for atonement. "I must say to myself that I ruined myself, and that nobody great or small can be ruined except by his own hand. . . . Terrible as was what the world did to me, what I did to myself was far more terrible still. . . . There is only one thing for me now, absolute humility." [23]

That Wilde's sentence was a judicial accident is now openly admitted. Viewed as part of the long struggle between the artist and society, it assumes the characteristics of a long-delayed and carefully nurtured revenge; the bourgeois society of the nineteenth century finally imposed its authority on the mocking and defiant artist who had dared its power for so long. It was Abel who put Cain into Reading Gaol.

Ready though he may have been to atone for a life of waste and sin, Wilde could hardly have imagined the ordeal that awaited him.

But the shame and humiliation, the hardship and sickness that now became his lot, laid bare the soul of the poet in him. *De Profundis,* written in prison, carries one motto through all its pages: "The supreme vice is shallowness. Whatever is realized is right." Of the two works conceived in Reading, the famous ballad seems the more homogeneous one. It sounds in somber tones the two chords in Wilde's heart: pity and terror. Terror lay at Wilde's heart; each day was like a year, a year whose days were long. And he who had lived more lives than one, more deaths than one had to die.

One wishes that his Letter to Lord Alfred Douglas had the same consistency of tone, but, alas, it is a document in which great confession and petty rancor, philosophical introspection and self-pity are curiously blended. In a way it is Wilde's artistic testament, yet he marred it with reminiscences of the restaurant bills that he had paid for the naughty Alfred.

He thought that he had now come to an understanding of Christ's teaching; Christ was the incarnation of the perfect individualism for which he, Wilde, had been striving all his life with mistaken means. "In a manner not yet understood of the world He regarded sin and suffering as being in themselves beautiful holy things and modes of perfection." [24] But once released from prison, Wilde learned that society had been much stronger and he himself much weaker than he had realized.

Sebastian Melmoth, the name under which he tried to hide his shame, had longed for the day when he would see the sun and the sky again, could smell roses, lilac, and laburnum, and feel the good earth under his feet. But Wilde could not hold to this key. He slid back into the old groove of brandy, overeating, and the sordid pleasures that his "friends" could still give him. His few remaining years have become as legendary as his early life. The legend of a homeless, shabby Wilde is, whether true or not, part of the symbol into which he himself and society had rendered him. That he preserved much of his temperament, so akin to joy, is certain. If he did not die with an epigram on his lips, like Chamfort, it was only because his speech was impaired. But when a few days before his death he told his friend, Robert Ross, that he had dreamed he was dining with the dead, Ross grinned. "Well, Oscar," he said, "I am sure you were the life of the party." [25]

Oscar Wilde's life span covers a significant period. Heine died in the year of his birth, and the year of his death is shared by Nietzsche. First to apprehend the symbolic implication of Wilde's position in the history of the European mind was Hofmannsthal.[26]

Wilde was only the "sketch of a great man"; his failures as well as his achievements become apparent when he is regarded as part of the movement of European individualism that proclaimed the primacy of the arts over life, and that suffered such a defeat at the hands of life.[27]

II

Wilde's idolatry of the arts provoked a notable reaction in Germany, where Stefan George and Hugo von Hofmannsthal represent important and complementary counterparts to Wilde's position.

At a very early age Stefan George had felt within himself the burning knowledge that he was destined to be one of the elect, a prophet and a seer, whose mission was not to be confined by nationality or profession. He was born in Büdesheim, a little village of the Rhineland, on July 12, 1868, and spent his childhood in Bingen. Even as a young boy he showed a deep interest in language. He invented a secret vocabulary just as many other children have done, but George did not forget his childhood game, and he preserved its memory in his poem, "Origins," where specimens of it have puzzled many a reader. In nearby Darmstadt, he acquired proficiency in Latin, Greek, French, English, and Italian, to which he later added Polish, Danish, Dutch, and Spanish.[28]

Aware of his gifts and with more than a confident belief in his ability, George set out to found his kingdom. He left Germany because he sensed the kinship that bound European artists together in a free-masonry of their own; moreover, contemporary Germany, the Germany of the Wilhelminian era, held little to attract him.

The way stations on his European peregrination were London and Amsterdam, Montreux and Turin, but Paris left the deepest impression. In all the European capitals he found those who shared with him the conviction that a literary renaissance was imperative— Ernest Dowson and Albert Verwey, Albert Saint Paul and Waclav Rolicz. In Paris he was soon introduced to Mallarmé's famous Tuesday evenings in the Rue de Rome. Here he met the poets of France, who left an indelible mark on him: Verlaine, Hérédia, de Régnier, and many others. George readily accepted their belief in "l'art pour art," but from the beginning he placed the accents differently. The elimination of all reality, social or political, on which the French symbolists prided themselves, engaged George's interest only because of his distaste for the social and political realities of his homeland.

He returned to Germany with a literary program styled on that of Mallarmé.[29] Once more he found himself offended and repelled by the cultural climate of his country. Contemporary German poetry seemed to him an anemic imitation of classic and romantic models. Naturalism was alien to his temperament; like Wilde, he felt that the reproduction of reality makes photographs, not works of art. His despair was deep and genuine, because he believed poetry to be the innermost manifestation of a nation's life compared to which all other revelations weighed but little.

The renewal of German poetry became his ambition. His own experiments in poetry were continued, sometimes in French, sometimes in a language of his own invention, sometimes in German. Of equal importance to him was his attempt to prepare an appropriate atmosphere for the propagation of a new poetry.

Seer and prophet though he was, George's personality embraced some aspects of the statesman and the man of action. He was a dominating and domineering individual, who demanded complete loyalty and unremitting adherence to his ideas, recognizing neither neutrality nor tolerance, voracious in his friendship, implacable in his hatred. His social ideal was a religious order in which he could celebrate, high priest and prophet at once. But in 1891 these characteristics were embryonic; his name was unknown and the appearance of a small volume called *Hymns* seemed unlikely to sanction any such pretension. He had failed to find sympathetic companions and had drawn about himself a cloak of solitude which threatened to smother all his human and artistic impulses. In a desperate attempt to free himself, he went to Vienna, and here met Hofmannsthal.[30]

With all the force of his passionate nature, George wooed the young Austrian poet in the belief that he had found the companion for whom he had been searching. But his very impetuosity frightened Hofmannsthal, whose reticent, feminine, and sensitive nature retreated before the imperial George. The result was a painful, but inevitable, process of estrangement. Hofmannsthal always showed a genuine sympathy for the poet in George, but he was unable to lend himself to that human identification which George desired, fearing lest he surender to an alien temperament.

Hofmannsthal did not altogether decline George's offer to join him in his literary venture, a publication all his own which was designed to demonstrate the new poetic principles. This journal, *Die Blätter für die Kunst*, published at irregular intervals and only for subscribers, was different from other literary magazines in presentation, spelling and content.[31] Its divergence expressed George's intention of separating himself from the literary public, the "stupid crowd." It was a propensity which he also revealed in his personal appearance by cultivating a blend of Beau Brummel and robed priest. André Gide has best succeeded in preserving his appearance: "Complexion bluish white, skin pale . . . beautiful bone structure; impeccably shaved, compact and abundant mane . . . thrown back in a solid mass; a convalescent's hands, very slender, bloodless, very expressive. . . . Large clergyman's frockcoat with two clasps at the top, opening on a black velvet stock tied on top of the collar and flowing over it. The simple gold slide-ring of a cord that holds watch or monocle introduces a discreet brilliance into all this black." [32]

The program of the *Blätter für die Kunst* would seem eminently Wildean. Its guiding idea was art for art's sake: beauty is a supreme value; it does not serve society. What we aspire to is simple, said George; we want an art that is free, an art that transcends Life after having penetrated Life. Art alone reaches the eternal, and the artist is the guardian of its sacred flame.[33] A severe condemnation of current conditions accompanied this proclamation of the new art. The whole body of recent literature, said George, was bourgeois and moralistic or vulgar and diverting. It aimed at the poor in spirit, while he addressed himself to the noble in spirit. George demands a new attitude which would revolutionize the arts, and bring about a renaissance in life. He believed the new attitude to be more important than science, philosophy, or "ten conquered provinces." The cleavage between the man and his time seems completed.

George is distinctly aristocratic, antidemocratic, antirational, and hierarchic. Of the great forces that had guided the nineteenth century, natural sciences and technology stand condemned from the outset, and only that part of history which fits his pattern is admitted. Greece is the cultural inspiration around which the new art should rally—"A ray from Hellas fell on our path." Dante, Shakespeare, Goethe, and Nietzsche, as well as Baudelaire and a handful of contemporary European poets, receive his homage, but ultimately it was not as a poet only that he addressed his decade. He was the center of a new movement. His followers referred to the impetus which he generated in the intellectual life of his time as "the spiritual movement." His title became "the master" and he was seldom mentioned by name.

We have already said that George's was a commanding mind, in which the will power was perhaps greater than the imagination. Despising tolerance, he was completely lacking in a sense of humor. In the many photographs of him, the observer will not detect a smile. He prided himself on his resemblance to Dante, and in the masquerades which he and his group devised, he frequently represented the great Italian.[34]

George conceived himself as the progenitor of a new law, which others were expected to abide by. Since reality refused to bow before him, he chose to condemn it and to dissociate himself from it. This highly personal attitude colored much of his criticism of the times, and gives it a decidedly egotistical twist. It is marred by a haughty and derisory note of contempt for his fellow men, by his insistence on the right of the genius to claim infallibility, and to express himself in words and symbols of extravagant daring. He presented his conclusions as dogma: the novel was declared to be a dead art form; the theater was a vulgar entertainment to which no real poet would stoop.[35] His attitude toward music was still more recreant. Music, he declared, was an inferior manifestation of artistic impulses which corroded the mind because of its extreme subjectivism. Such verdicts might be overlooked as the misconceptions of a superior mind had he not elevated them to the position of profound intuitions destined to cure the modern world of its illnesses.

There is, however, one realm where George's personal predilection struck at the core of human life. Woman, he asserted, was an inferior being; even her body was a mere caricature of the male. He emphasized this idea in his poetry:

The spirit that is always male has shaped the world we know.
The woman's gift is substance, no less a shrine to bow to . . .
In council she is evil and nefarious.[36]

George's attitude toward woman and toward love between the sexes paralleled his attitude toward music. Melchior Lechter said to Cyril Scott, "He is seldom attracted by women; he tries to justify himself by declaring that they are inferior beings." [37] George's bent is more than a personal accident; it is a basic condition of his poetry and takes him further than Wilde or Gide, raising his personal predilections to the rank of a pseudo-religious message which he passed on to the German youth of his age.[38] No full appraisal of George's poetic work is possible without a recognition of these human and esthetic foundations.

The *Hymns* and the *Pilgrimages,* his two earliest books, are important to us in estimating young George's mastery of the language, which he had found in a state of degradation. The mode of utterance in these first attempts is sparse and stern, and the desire to avoid common usage makes it overcompressed and precious, obscure and harsh. There are undertones of human loneliness and abandonment which will continue until the mature George has found the love that answers his quest.[39]

The third book, *Algabal,* is George's interpretation of the Roman Emperor, Heliogabalus. The boldness of its imagery and the extreme daring of its human substance make it the most significant of George's earlier works. Algabal is a priest-king, who wishes to attain his own divinity by building a subterranean realm, independent of the light and air of the upper world. He has no desire to be a romantic spectator of life; he wishes only to enjoy the dream world of his own making. All that is natural or alive is banned from this phantom palace built of polished metal, littered with jewels. "My garden requires no air and no sun."

George's artistic models were Baudelaire, Mallarmé, Huysmans, and Wilde, but experimentation along these lines was new in German literature. And in George's hands the melancholy that finds its only outlet in cruelty, that longs to see the "mob perish and groan," that yearns to see everyone "who laughs . . . nailed upon the cross," became a symbol of esthetic isolationism. "Beauty is death and death beauty." [40] The world of Algabal is a world of psychological terror, completely devoid of grace. [41]

Although George outgrew the theatrical Caesarism of his dream world, something metallic, artificial, and overornate remained in his poetry. George must have felt that *Algabal* was a dead end, because he turned away from the agony and sickness of these verses to a primitive world where he might again discover the beauty of the world around him. He still employed historic backgrounds, finding them now in idyllic antiquity, now in medieval legend and lay. Some of these poems disclose with great force the tensions which crowded his soul to the breaking point. The "Lord of the Island" is one of the most perfect poems written in this decade; it expresses George's deep and melancholy knowledge that supreme beauty will always be stained by human anguish. Hofmannsthal commented that the work of this period showed "the innate royalty of a mind entirely its own," and added, "Nothing is more alien to this time; nothing is more valuable to the few." [42] In this volume, George already makes clear that he has freed himself from his models and from the dark and obsessed compulsions of his first attempts. In the *Year of the Soul* he reached maturity. This book remains one of the most delicate manifestations of lyrical inspiration in the German language; for many it represents the purest expression of George's genius. [43] The title, reminiscent of a verse by Hölderlin, suggests the cycle of the soul reflected in the seasons of the year; nature is a mirror where the emotions of the soul become visible.

The soul's pilgrimage begins in autumn. This is characteristic not only of George's own disposition, but of that whole generation of Europeans who felt the winter of their civilization approaching. For him, as for so many who had a premonition of "the Decline of the West," spring was far behind, was indeed no longer expected. In the *Year of the Soul* this season of rebirth is altogether omitted. But there is an autumnal splendor in the landscape matched only by poets like Keats. Winter, too, is in this book, and summer, but the feeling of nostalgia and of resignation is all-prevailing. The impression that neither autumn nor summer can heal the wounds of loneliness is deepened by the "Mournful Dances" which end the volume. "Gedämpfter Schmerz," muted grief, is the keynote. George never again achieved the same musical cadence of verse, the same awareness of shades and colors, both in the outer and the inner world.[44] The *Year of the Soul* shows a George still under the spell of his self-chosen isolation. "In this universe without God," says Claude David, "in this world which is nothing but a spectacle, where everybody plays his solitary role, without faith or support, the soul preserves a new dignity in its despair." [45]

George's next work, written at the turn of the century, removes him still further from the twilight of the subterranean garden; to Nature and Soul he adds Life and Mind. The *Tapestry of Life* and the *Songs of Dream and of Death* open with a message: "Das schöne Leben sendet mich an Dich." The Angel who speaks to the poet is the herald from a life where beauty rules; but his voice resembles that of the poet, and is in reality the poet's "daimon," his superior and commanding self. The name "Angel" should not mislead us; it is not related in any way to Christian mythology, any more than is the Angel of Rilke's *Elegies*. The angel gives comfort and an ear to his sorrows, but he also frames laws and conceives the ideals which are to guide the poet's life. George's feeling has become unified; the alien, the exotic, and the dazzling no longer threaten the integrity of the work. Here we find him ready to accept the fluctuations of life, the rise and descent of the creative force, even the anguish of utter loneliness. The Angel alone can compensate him for the disillusionment that love engenders, for the despair of those hours when inspiration fails the poet.

The tone of these poems is to a surprising degree didactic. The message is directed to the whole age, or at least to those who had been initiated into the inner circle. In this phase of George's work he bids farewell to the perilous journeys, the haunts of Venice and Rome, the magic of distance. It is the Rhine that now attracts the poet, the treasures of his people ". . . your waters green with life, O surging stream." Here we receive the first indication of George's shift toward nationalism, a theme which was to become an integral part of his later work.

For a man who had scorned his time with so much bitterness, and who still held aloof from the imminent problems of his nation, this development seems strange indeed. George continued to criticize Germany mercilessly for all that he hated in her—commercialism, vulgarity, mediocrity, majority rule—but an increasing conviction that the redemption of the West would come from Germany becomes ever more evident in his writings.[46]

George had come to the stone wall before which all esthetic individualism must halt. If Narcissus does not wish to drown himself in the mirroring pool, he must drown himself in life; he must become again a part of the human community, because in no other way can the individual survive. Each of the great personalities of the esthetic movement eventually bowed before this law.

It is difficult to describe, let alone analyze, the crisis by which the earlier George became the "Master," as he wished to be known to our century. In his *Preface to Maximin* he gives posterity a certain amount of enlightenment concerning these strange events which now catch him up in their web.[47] Half of his life had passed. He saw himself surrounded by a society which prided itself on its inventions and its sophisticated feelings, while the great deed and the great love were nowhere to be found. At this juncture a unique human being appeared on George's horizon and restored his confidence in the future. "When we first met *Maximin* in our city (Munich), he was still in his boyhood." In this lad George found his ideal of sovereign youth, a being created to be his heir and to widen his realms. George's disciples asserted that Maximin is, in his poetry, the counterpart of Dante's Beatrice.[48] And after Maximin's early death George did not hesitate to compare him with Alexander and Christ.

Today the mythical veils that George wove about the memory of this youth have been lifted and enough is known to permit an impartial judgment. Maximilian Kronberger, who died of meningitis at the age of sixteen, wrote a handful of tender and pious verses of little merit. As the inspiration for one of the great poets of the time, however, he may not be dismissed with few words.[49] Those who cannot sympathize with this source of George's poetic ecstasy would not hesitate to respect the profound grief into which George was plunged at his death. But the poet was not content to receive this sorrow merely as the prelude to a renewed belief in the power of love and beauty. Instead he undertook the deification of this youth. A new god had appeared and George had been chosen to deliver his message to an incredulous world. Thus be becomes now the prophet of a new salvation, complete with cult, dogma, and excommunication for the unbeliever.

Obsessional traits had been evident in George's personality from his early youth. Now they are elevated to the sphere of revelation, and challenge the time with a private god and a private religion. The hubris of esthetic individualism could go no further. Both writer and reader might be spared this chapter in the history of frenetic subjectivism were it not for the quality of work which George produced at this period. He continued to write great poetry, and even reached a new mode of expression as a result of his experience.

In George, as in Wilde, the adoration of beauty had led into despair. The "love that dare not speak its name" had been Wilde's perdition. George spoke its name, and set it up as a new religion, but it remained a frail and tawdry substitute. Before the unalterable forces of history, the prophet took on the semblance of a madman and his religion appeared a travesty.

How is it possible to do justice to so extraordinary a personality? It cannot be denied that George restored its birthright to German poetry. By applying the most severe standards to his own life, by serving his ideal with an exclusive passion, he instilled in a generation accustomed to formlessness and relativism a new responsibility and a new belief. Hofmannsthal and Rilke acknowledged their indebtedness to him. For the youth of antebellum Germany, he was the incarnation of spiritual devotion, of heroic identification with work and mission, the only man who continued the German Renaissance of the early nineteenth century beyond Nietzsche. But George never overcame the esthetic imperative: he raised the poet to the rank of prophet, he made him infallible. Consciously he poured his life into a mythical mold, so that, little by little, the man disappeared in the monument.[50] Who can deny the greatness of his attempt to impose a new myth upon a resisting and rationalistic time? But who could assert that he succeeded?

George's later works, *The Seventh Ring* and *The Star of the Covenant*, must be seen in this perspective: as part of his attempt to restore the heroic myth. But the cleavage between the artist and his time was bridged by George no more than by Wilde. The efforts to find religious solutions in esthetic premises were doomed from the outset. The criticism of the times, sincere and profound as it was, remained essentially negative. From the days of *Algabal* to the end, there was something Neronian in George, and while no poet could have extinguished the flames that were to consume the Continent, only the anesthetized could have remained impervious while Rome burned.

III

Any anthology of European poetry written between 1890 and 1914 would, I am certain, include most of the poetical work of Hugo von Hofmannsthal. In the abundance of his productivity, the maturity of his thought, and the perfection of his presentation, he borders on the miraculous.[51]

Hofmannsthal was the youngest member of the generation we are here treating. His background, abounding in the oldest of European traditions, was of great importance in the early ripening of his talent. Born in Vienna, the only child of an Austrian lawyer, his ancestors reveal German, Italian, and Jewish origins. He grew up in the protected atmosphere of a patrician home, but it was the home of Austrian patricians, close to Italy and the Balkans, close also to imperial dreams and Roman Catholicism. Broch has very well described the "vast ellipse of landscape rich in heroic culture and heroic nature" which forms the setting of Hofmannsthal's creativity.[52]

The literati of Vienna were surprised and curious when, in 1891, they first read some specimens of a poetical talent penned by one who called himself Loris. Upon inquiry, they were presented to a boy still wearing the apparel of the high school student. In order to appreciate the phenomenon that was Hofmannsthal, we must look into the springs of his genius and try to define the type of poet he came to be.

As we have noted, the problem of the esthetic movement lay not only in the exclusive preoccupation with creating and enjoying beauty, but more particularly in the relationship of the artist to the world and to life. In Wilde this relationship had come to rest in open cleavage; in George it took the form of a messianic mission.

Hofmannsthal's approach was of a different nature; he did not wish to challenge the world or to dominate it. He wanted to become one with the world. Divergent as his approach was, however, the essence of the problem remained the same: the self versus the world. It was in his encounter with George that the seventeen-year-old boy became aware of his otherness.

In a number of diary entries, Hofmannsthal tried to give an account of his psychological constitution.[53] He saw in George a poet who "exalts the ego," while he saw himself as one who "comprehends the universe"; he uses the expression *la présence de l'univers*. He looked upon the self and the world as coexistent and indivisible. He is not antagonistic or hostile toward the world; on the contrary, he feels that there is too much of the world in him, so much that the self becomes endangered. As the self becomes a dovecote for every impression, it places its identity in jeopardy.

Hofmannsthal's dilemma was then of a very special nature: how was he to explain the *présence de l'univers* in his soul, how was he to account for being interwoven with the fabric of past and present? He believed in "preexistence," in a state where there was no separation of subject and object, of space and time, a state akin to childhood, yet lacking the nescience of childhood.

Goethe said that he could not have pictured the world had he not known it by anticipation; such anticipation is Hofmannsthal's "preexistence." He carried a thousand souls in his own, and was tortured by the question, Who am I? He sensed an identity with his ancestors, and felt in his veins the beating pulses of lives that had ceased a hundred years before. The fatigue of bygone nations lay heavy upon his frightened soul, and he was filled with an awe like "the silent fall of stars."

The nostalgic longing for a state of preexistence is as endless as it is hopeless. In Hofmannsthal's work it determines his constant preoccupation with death; only the mystery of death could resolve the mystery of life, could assuage the emotions of loss and desolation that the self experiences in the flux of life. Death is omnipresent; the very mutability of life reveals it—"we die of life" ("denn lebend sterben wir").

To reconcile the preexistent with the contemporary in himself became Hofmannsthal's existential problem.

From the endless fusions within him
His ardent soul pursues in symbols
The fusions in the outward life.[54]

It was the labor of a poet, this poet's labor. To reveal the wealth of preexistence that he observed in himself, he must create, but his creations will be like dreams, and a curtain of unreality will separate them from life. But perhaps life itself is only a dream. He felt deeply that "la vida es un sueño y los sueños sueños son." Life and death, dream and rebirth, are the permanent chords on his "fragile lyre."

For a man whose thoughts were on so mystical a plane, an encounter with George could result only in tragic misunderstanding. Hofmannsthal was aware of George's genius, and he acknowledged that he had received force and love and hope from their meeting, but George as a human being filled him with apprehension. George's further importunities but increased his anxiety; he was repelled by George's desire to seduce and dominate: "He could kill without touching his victim." [55] Yet the encounter is memorable in the history of the esthetic movement because it reveals the polarity of possibilities that it encompassed.

In the *Book of Friends* Hofmannsthal says, "Plasticity develops not through observation, but through identification." [56] Identification with the world was indeed his need and his ambition; only thus could he return for moments to that preexistence where there is no separation between object and subject, time and space. In hours of exaltation, Hofmannsthal experienced a sense of unity with the world similar to that of the mystic; his poetic intuition might be called esthetic mysticism. The highest moments of bliss, he said, I experienced always in complete solitude, without any relation to a woman or to any human being, equidistant from all of them, the center of a sphere. Unlike most lyrical poets, Hofmannsthal sought to efface his ego rather than to assert it:

If I only knew more of these adventures,
For somehow I am woven in them all,
And know not where the dream and life divide.

His cardinal motive is found here: "Many fates with mine are interwoven; subtly mingled are the threads of being, and my share is more than one Life's narrow flame or fragile lyre." [57] Hofmanns-

thal has been called an impressionist but his problem was more
complex. He wished not simply to mirror the beauty of impressions,
but to discover what linked his responses to the world, or, as he so
often puts it, to life.[58]

But life is in constant motion, and the poet is impelled to protest
that there is nothing stable, that life is mutable and erratic, a river
where the bridges from which we look down into the whirling torrent
provide the only permanence. Hofmannsthal's poetry centers around
the nostalgic desire of the I to overcome its limitations. In *Welt-
geheimnis (Cosmic Mystery)*, he speaks of the secret that once in
silence and wonder was known to all. In the beautiful *Lebenslied*
he praises the poet, the heir who, unfettered and unreflecting, casts
away his heritage.

> For every place delights him,
> And every door invites him,
> Each passion-wave incites him
> As lone he wandereth.[59]

In *Manche Freilich* he reveals the interdependence of all life,
where the shadow of those who live in darkness falls on those who
sit with kings and sibyls, and where the light of heart are bound
to the heavy of heart, as to air and earth. This is again the theme of
Ein Traum von grosser Magie (A Dream of Great Magic); he feels,
dreamlike, the fate of all men, the great gait of all life in which near
and distant, great and small, are one. But a grief too deep for trivial
tears is sung in *Mutability*; the poet admits that the unity of preexistence, *la présence de l'univers*, can never be permanently restored. In a like mood he conceived the "Ballade des äusseren
Lebens" ("Ballad of the Outward Life"), which depicts the melancholy of the perennial rupture between the outward and the inward
life. He speaks of the soul that looks at children and fruits, at birds
and cities, at roads and trees, that listens to words and winds, and
then he asks, Why are all these created, each to the other strange
in form and fashion, and why do tears and laughter intermingle?

> What boots it much to have seen the while we roam?
> And yet he sayeth much who "evening" saith,
> A word whence deep and solemn meanings run
> Like heavy honey from the hollow comb.[60]

Hofmannsthal's lyrical dramas are also built around the insoluble problem of concurrent self-effacement and self-preservation.

His first dramatic attempt, *Gestern (Yesterday)*, shows Hofmannsthal in a Renaissance costume rented from Burckhardt.[61] The hero, Andreas, surrenders himself to every beautiful moment in an attempt to make his life a work of art. He instructs his mistress in this line of conduct and she becomes an all too willing disciple, finally betraying him on the principles of his own unstable creed. From this hour, the Today becomes overshadowed by the Yesterday which Andreas is unable to relinquish even in the presence of his avowed philosophy. Here we have Hofmannsthal's *reductio ad absurdum* of the esthetic attitude; the individual who declines the responsibility inherent in all life destroys itself. Those who, like Andreas, do not wish to make decisions, for whom choice is suffering because all life attracts them, are the architects of their own doom.

The command of language in this sketch by a seventeen-year-old boy is striking, but the precocious and clairvoyant analysis of his own precarious existence is even more surprising. Even in these early years he is harried by a fear that he may not reach the highest, the deepest, the best. "Weil eine Angst nur ist in meiner Seele: Dass ich das Höchste, Tiefste doch verfehle." [62]

Hofmannsthal's next work, *The Death of Titian,* remained a fragment, ironically enough because he was obliged to work for his high school diploma. But in its few pages, pregnant with a luxurious beauty, there is a recurrence of the problem found in *Gestern.* Renaissance Venice provides the setting chosen by Hofmannsthal. A group of young men and women follow the death agony of their old master. He is the center of their life, an artist such as Hofmannsthal hoped to become, one in whom life finds its completion and perfection, who gives soul and significance to man and nature.[63] His pupils pass the long night in evoking the magnificence of his creation; they have learned from him to revel in the flux and flow of everyday life, to comprehend the beauty of all forms, and to be the spectators of their own lives. But they are *epigoni,* the second generation, and the pulse of life in them beats at a slower tempo. With the death of the master, their lives will become dull and empty unless some force from the outside world, some hope, some sorrow, breaks through the shell of their isolation. The truly great artist, however, is he who feels no need beyond the inspiration of his inner life and who ennobles whatever he touches:

> Die aber wie der Meister sind die gehen
> Und Schönheit wird und Sinn wohin sie sehen.

The unique character of this fragment cannot be shown in summary. Hofmannsthal reveals himself here for the first time as an essentially visual artist.[64] The sleeping Venice below the garden where the young men are gathered is a picture of slumbrous and Bacchanalian beauty. If Venice were to vanish without a trace, it might, to vary a phrase of Carlyle's, be rebuilt from these lines.[65]

In *Der Tor und der Tod (Death and the Fool)*, Hofmannsthal gives the most penetrating and heartfelt expression to the anxieties that disturbed his youth. The fool, Claudio, has been called "the little Faust of the decadence," but in reality Hofmannsthal's Claudio has nothing in common with Faust. He is no suppliant for knowledge, or magic, or power, as was Faust: "What do I know of the life of man? I viewed it as an outsider; I was unable to weave myself into it . . . I could never forget myself." [66] Neither religion nor the treasures of art could save him from the snares of life's masquerade. Never quite conscious, never entirely lost in the unconscious, Claudio goes through life as a spectator only. Disillusioned, he inveighs against an existence "wherein no race was ever won by speed . . . where sorrows sadden not nor joys make glad, where senseless answers senseless questions breed . . . and chance rules all, the hour, the wave, the wind." [67]

Finally Death comes to teach him the meaning of life. His mother, his beloved, and his friend are evoked, and in sad succession they bring to Claudio a realization of his mother's anxiety and loneliness, the ache of his beloved's tears, and the wild despair of his friend. In bitter contrition he learns that he has moved through life recreant and nugatory. "Now that I die, I feel at last I am . . .", but his enlightenment comes too late; Death denies him a second chance, and thus he passes "from out of life's dreaming into death's awakening." [68]

Since its appearance in 1893, Hofmannsthal's *Death and the Fool* has been accepted as one of the representative works of the period. Compared with Dorian Gray, Algabal, or Andrea Sperelli, Claudio's guilt seems mild; he has not committed a crime, or indulged in cruelty or vice. Au fond, however, Dorian and Algabal, Andrea and Claudio are equally guilty; they have divorced themselves from life; they have escaped into the counterfeit which mocks at life. There is an ethical perception of the untenable position of the esthete that gives to *Death and the Fool* a singular position among the books of this generation. It was Hofmannsthal's first attempt to extricate himself from the corroding influence of an unrestrained egotism which would serve art for art's sake alone. His story, "The Tale of the Six Hundred and Seventy-Second Night," reflects the same predication.

Hofmannsthal's diary contains this observation: "The beautiful life impoverishes. One would lose all force, could one always live as one desires." [69] And indeed, though the Beautiful Life still called forth his rapture, he sounds continually the note of fear for its unremitting hazards. "The Little Theater of the World" expresses this attitude; the beautiful moment is a bridge flung across the river of time, whereon men and women appear and reveal their souls. "The White Fan" and "The Emperor and the Witch" repeat the theme.

For a decade Hofmannsthal clung to the hope that the poet might establish a balance between the artist and the world. The poet, he wrote, is the spectator, nay, the hidden companion, the silent brother of all things—his sensitive soul suffers, not from lack of perfection, but because of his own receptive nature, and in his suffering he finds happiness. "Dies Leidendgeniessen ist der ganze Inhalt seines Lebens." [70] "Melancholy passivity" was the keynote of Hofmannsthal's life and poetry until 1899. [71] All his characters are blessed in one way and cursed in another: the rich whose wealth sets them apart from mankind, the beautiful to whom love is denied, the haughty who linger in solitude, the young who fear life, the pure who remain immaculate and sterile, the dreamer who anticipates life and is disillusioned by reality, the adventurer who wastes his days. [72]

Hofmannsthal knew that admission to the elect might well entail ostracism from life by that law of existence which demands a price for everything—love must pay in the coin of pain; arrival includes the fatigue of the road; periods of apathy follow periods of increased comprehension; and an empty heart may reward our deepest emotion. Our whole existence demands its price, and the price is death.

At the age of twenty-five, he who so deeply realized the immutable law of human life was overtaken by a crisis which threatened his very existence and drove him to the verge of insanity.

Hofmannsthal was not an exhibitionist like Wilde or d'Annunzio, nor was he a self-styled prophet like George. His external biography is calm and to all appearance bourgeois. In 1901 he married and set up a home in Rodaun, near Vienna. He had nothing of the Bohemian in his make-up, and held the bogus artist in distrust and contempt. Goethe, whose work, he said, might easily replace a whole civilization as the basis of an education, was his master in a determination to shoulder any responsibilities that life should offer. With fatherhood and the management of a conventional household, he reached a satisfactory relationship with the world about him. Later in his life he confessed: "I would not like to live without the unspeakably gratifying harmony between outside and inside, between the world and myself. I do not regret that I am a man like other men, that I have children and keep a house for them, although it seems sometimes strange to me." [73] But this "unspeakably gratifying harmony" was his only after he had passed through a gate so narrow that only a man of great resilience could survive the experience.

The springs of his inspiration had dried up, and as an artist he faced an appalling void. Hofmannsthal had written all his poetry and most of his lyrical dramas before he was twenty-five. It seemed now that he had exhausted himself in this premature outburst. Many of his contemporaries thought so, and the cruel comment was made that he would have been the greatest poet since Goethe, had be but died at the age of twenty-five. It is difficult to come to any adequate conclusion on so complex a subject as the sudden subsidence of the creative impulse, and in Hofmannsthal the truth seems to lie buried in issues that were as enigmatical to the poet as to his biographer. In any case, it would seem that in the last days of the century Hofmannsthal found himself propelled toward that iron rock where esthetic individualism is bound to shipwreck. His earlier belief in the redemption of the world through the medium of the poetic word—his medium, that is—had been shattered, and without faith in his tool he found it beyond his power to create. The melodramatic solutions and psychological somersaults to which some of his generation reverted in this same predicament, were at variance with his moral taste.[74] His own case he attempted to clarify in one of the most illuminating documents of European literature, the *Letter of Lord Chandos to Francis Bacon*.[75] Though clad in Elizabethan garb, this letter is the explanation which Hofmannsthal (Chandos) ventured to give for the sterility which had overtaken the exuberant creativity of his youth.[76]

"In those days," wrote Hofmannsthal, "I . . . conceived the whole of existence as one great unit; the spiritual and physical worlds seemed to form no contrast. . . . The one was like the other, whether in dreamlike celestial quality or physical intensity . . . at other times I divined that all was allegory and that each creature was a key to all the others; and I felt myself the one capable of seizing each by the handle and unlocking as many of the others as were ready to yield." [77] But, continued the writer, this marvelous state had come to an end. No longer was he able to experience the act of mystical identification, because words, the only means by which this identification was possible, had become devoid of sense. On ecstasy followed panic.[78] "For me everything disintegrated into parts, those parts again into parts; no longer would anything let itself be encompassed by a single idea. Single words floated around me; they congealed into eyes which stared at me and into which I was forced to stare back—whirlpools which gave me vertigo and, reeling incessantly, led into the void."

The catastrophe which befell Chandos-Hofmannsthal is the tragedy of the esthete for whom the substance of life and the power of decision have been torn asunder. Chandos realizes that he has seen the world only through the medium of art, just as Hofmannsthal in his early work had seen it.[79] But some light shines through his despair; there are hints of a rebirth into the simpler and truer life. "A pitcher, a harrow abandoned in a field, a dog in the sun, a neglected cemetery, a cripple, a peasant's hut—all these can become the vessels of my revelation." [80] And with these familiar objects of everyday life, he feels that a new and hopeful relationship with the whole of existence is possible if he can only begin to "think with the heart." [81]

Although Chandos told Francis Bacon that he would never write again, Hofmannsthal's own future was fortunately less drastic. His break with the esthetic creed was complete, and he turned to modes of expression in which he could reveal the genuine humility of one who had passed through the debacle of art for art's sake. Dramatic and narrative works take the place of the lyrical search for the *présence de l'univers.* Hofmannsthal's essays of this period are likewise high in suggestive power, and the lyrical comedies which were written for Richard Strauss have a value far beyond mere libretti.

The atmosphere which surrounded the later Hofmannsthal was no longer that of mournful lethargy or artistic intoxication. It was rather the climate of ethical conflict in which could be found a reverence for real life with its infinite possibilities forever oscillating between good and evil. *Die Frau ohne Schatten (Woman without Shadow)* and *The Tower* are the greatest examples of his later art.

Hofmannsthal is the only representative of the esthetic movement to have plucked from its failure the flower of humility; he alone found the way from the temple to the street. "Since my childhood, I have had the feverish desire to discover the spirit of our confused age in the most different ways and in the most different disguises." [82] He did not enter the lists for nationalism, which indeed, Austrian as he was, would have been difficult, nor did he don the robes of high priest for a new cult. "As intellectuals," he wrote to Barbusse, "we are challenged by a world that chooses chaos because its ideas are crumbling. Our value as individuals is modest and problematic; the enormity of the situation is without example." [83] For the few who did listen to a voice as pure and as serious as that of the old Goethe, Hofmannsthal embodied the civilizing force of literature; his concern was neither to remain aloof nor to fight, but to educate. It was a heavy burden for so fragile a spirit. Paul Claudel felt rightly: "il pésait une fatalité terrible sur lui." [84] The fate that burdened Hofmannsthal was the fate of the Occident.

IV

"One has sometimes the sensation that our fathers, the contemporaries of Offenbach, and our grandfathers, the contemporaries of Leopardi . . . left us, the later-born, but two things: pretty furniture and hypersensitive nerves." [85] This comment accompanied Hofmannsthal's introduction of d'Annunzio to the Viennese public. The protagonists of the esthetic movement commonly recognized the family traits that linked them.

D'Annunzio's reputation has suffered much at the hand of time. His books have become period pieces. His first literary attempts show the influence of Carducci, but it was the formal touch only that he learned from Carducci. His real models were French, English, and Russian; it was a miscellaneous list of spiritual ancestors to whom he confessed himself indebted.[86] Zola, Ibsen, and Tolstoi appealed to him through their naturalism; Dostoevski and Bourget through their analysis of complicated psychological acts; Wilde and Baudelaire through their belief in beauty as an absolute; Flaubert through his ascetic devotion to artistic craftsmanship; Swinburne through his intoxication with word and rhyme.

As an Italian, he was deeply conscious of the classical heritage which was a more tangible force for him than it had been for Wilde, Hofmannsthal, or George. He found the vestiges of ancient culture in Sicily, or in Rome, or when, leaving his birthplace on the shores of the Adriatic, he crossed the sea to stand on the soil of Greece. The portals of the Renaissance opened to him with little need for the guidance of Pater or Burckhardt; the great century spoke to him from squares and palaces, from fortresses and cathedrals, with an ever-present energy. More than his fellows, d'Annunzio was attracted by the human ideal of the Renaissance, the *uomo universale* and the *cortegiano,* but the conditions of his age and his own limitations precluded any hope for the restoration of a vanishing perfection.

When d'Annunzio began his career, the unity of Italy had but recently been achieved. He was far from any feeling of disgust for political reality such as George professed. On the contrary, he saw in the political world one more stage on which the Renaissance genius could demonstrate his superiority. That his first attempt in the lower chamber turned out to be a dismal failure in no way discouraged him from later adventures of a more explosive nature. He shares with the generation of European estheticists the cosmopolitan outlook, but he was earlier and more easily contaminated by the nationalistic virus. He and Maurice Barrès are the two great examples of the move from unrestrained subjectivism to unrestrained collectivism.

So far the Risorgimento had produced no artist of great stature, and d'Annunzio envisioned himself as prophet and messiah of the movement.[87] Richard Wagner's figure impressed him deeply, but his admiration was tinged with envy. In the role of an artistic Machiavelli, d'Annunzio hoped to expel the foreign idols from the sacred soil of Italy and to unify her a second time through his poetry.

He liked to think of himself as the incarnation of Nietzsche's superman, but he was essentially a dandy and a snob. His mansion was as replete with works of art as the bourgeois dwellings of the period were full of bric-a-brac. He prided himself on concocting his own perfumes, he kept pure-bred horses and pedigreed greyhounds; he fought duels and the rosary of his mistresses is composed of many beads.[88] Everything about him became a mirror in which his vanity delighted to find its reflection.

Notwithstanding, he was the greatet poet that Italy produced in the years between 1880 and 1914, hélas! as Gide might comment. Like Victor Hugo, d'Annunzio could say anything and say it beautifully. He was more distinguished as a craftsman than as a poet, and more distinguished as a poet than as a human being.

He published his first verses while still at school, and, like Byron, woke up one morning to find himself famous.[89] These early poems give more than a prelude of what he was to become. In the four "hours" which divide his day— hora suave, hora tetrica, hora jocunda, hora satanica—we are given the four elements out of which his personality may be constructed.[90] The style, too, has many of the characteristics that the mature poet will later display. It is, one critic notes, as if the world had just been created and man were abandoning himself to its enjoyment. D'Annunzio was essentially a visual artist; he looked at the face of the world as a lover looks at the face of his beloved. He possessed a high degree of sensual vehemence and an instinctive feeling for life; he did not have to break through artificial barriers; life was here to be invaded and conquered.

From the provinces he came to Rome. "The success," he says, "was quick and extensive . . . flattery intoxicated me. I threw myself into life, avid for pleasure with all the ardor of youth. All the doors were opened to me. I went from triumph to triumph without looking back. I made blunder after blunder and walked at the edge of thousands of precipices." [91] What d'Annunzio himself calls his "demencia afrodisiaca" became the all-prevailing motif of his writings. His joy is as sensual as his sadness; this mind with the extraordinary splendor of its verbal orchestration is moved by the palpitations of desire to the exclusion of anything else.

Although d'Annunzio's novels spread his reputation through Europe, his genius was essentially lyrical. He was primarily a poet. "Il verso e tutto" we read in one of his poems. Even the best of his prose, whether narrative or descriptive, is musical in its intoxicating flow. Of the trilogy entitled *Novels of the Rose*, the most significant one is *Piacere (Child of Pleasure)*, an autoanalysis if not an autobiography. The principal figure, Andrea Sperelli, is the first of many self-portraits. It is d'Annunzio's own triumph of the flesh over the spirit, his own abuse of literature and art, his own voluptuousness and his egocentricism. In company with Dorian Gray and Algabal, Sperelli will remain the classical incarnation of European decadence. We have, so far, avoided the use of this ambiguous word, but the late flowering estheticism of d'Annunzio did indeed produce blossoms of evil. All human values of charity and self-abnegation are lost in the pursuit of self-aggrandizement and self-enjoyment found in carnal conquest.

Sperelli, scion of one of the great families of condottieri, had dreams of other conquests, of fights in which he saw "rivers of blood, mountains of gold," but the only thing that stirs him profoundly is the dream of love. The analyst of the European mind, however, will not fail to detect the undertones of cruelty and sadism in d'Annunzio which were too anachronistic to be noted at the end of the nineteenth century, but which were in the near future to make him one of the godfathers of Italian fascism.

Sperelli's battlefields are the salons of Rome; his goal, seduction; his strategy, deceit; his weapons, the refinement of the individualist. He lives condemned to rotate in the magic circle of his pride, a vacuum impossible to penetrate. He wishes to make his life a work of art; the concepts of beauty and love are one to him. "The concept of beauty is for men of intelligence, educated in this cult . . . the axis of their internal being, around which all other passions gravitate." [92] The passion for beauty, however, frequently turns toward the contemplation of furniture and engravings, and at times

Sperelli sounds more like an interior decorator than a condottieri. But only a reader blind to color or deaf to music would deny that there is beauty in his introspection and in his passion for Helena Muti, the would-be courtesan of the Renaissance as Andrea is the would-be condottieri.

The esthetic-hedonistic outlook is as destructive in Andrea as it is in Dorian Gray; it corrodes the will power and leaves the soul exhausted. Sperelli, like all d'Annunzio's heroes, fights passion with passion. The outcome is moral nihilism, or, at least moral anarchy. His protestations notwithstanding, d'Annunzio does not picture life; he escapes it through analysis. His characters live and die in a moral vacuum. They discuss their love and they love their discussions.[93] Behind the endless torrent of psychological reflections we see the indestructible ego raise its Medusa head; any sympathy or admiration we might have felt then becomes paralyzed. The other parts of the *Novels of the Rose* trilogy do not contribute new answers to our quest. They show the same beauty of form, the same sensitivity, with emphasis on the foul, on sickness, insanity, adultery, rape, incest, and murder.[94]

The spiritual void remains unfilled in d'Annunzio's next trilogy, the *Novels of the Lily,* where the "child of pleasure" wears the mask of the superman. The encounter with Nietzsche was not accidental in d'Annunzio's work, but it remained at the surface. It served as the intellectual justification for his dreams of heroism and ferocity, of violence and exuberance. On many occasions d'Annunzio voiced his regret that modern society rejected the reappearance of great conquerors like Cesare Borgia or Napoleon. He would like to have overcome the tedium of life by spectacular action. Claudio Cantelmo, the hero of *Maidens of the Rock,* thinks that he is destined to sire the superman who will impose his greatness on Italy and restore the Latin race to purity. Disgusted with the corruption of his country, Cantelmo goes to Trigento where a noble family vegetates, remaining faithful to the Bourbon dynasty which Garibaldi had driven from the soil of Italy. They carry on their lives in an atmosphere of memory, misery, and madness. It is among the three daughters of this house that Cantelmo hopes to find his bride, the mother of the superman.

The description of the three maidens, Maximilia, Anatolia, and

Violante, belongs to the most accomplished pages of Italian prose. Like Cantelmo, we soon find ourselves the prisoners of an enchantment that combines nobility and decay, purity and frenzy, in a dreamlike haze. The hero's desire to beget the future king of Rome all but vanishes before the tantalizing task of choosing between three perfections. He finally elects Violante, who symbolizes beauty rather than strength or faith, a typical d'Annunzian choice.

The poet took for this novel a motto from Leonardo da Vinci: "Jo faro una finzione que significhera cose grandi." That the *Maidens of the Rock* is great fiction seems an overstatement, but it is a significant work. It is also characteristic of a certain snobbism in the esthetic movement which turned back to a dim and vanished aristocratic life. The decision for beauty links the *Maidens of the Rock* to *Fuoco (The Flame of Life)*.

The autobiographical indelicacy of this book, depicting Eleonora Duse as the aging and discarded mistress, has today lost much of its scandalous attraction. What remains is the portrait of Stelio Efrena, as true a picture of frenetic subjectivism as that of Sperelli and Cantelmo.[95] Again superman is presented as an artist, beyond good or evil since good and evil can become combustible material for the flame with which the artist burns; the holy fire purifies everything as it consumes everything.

Fuoco arouses our interest for two reasons. In it d'Annunzio confessed his intention of rejuvenating the classical tragedy and making it the instrument of a national rebirth as Wagner had undertaken to do in Bayreuth. Where the barbarian had failed, the Italian genius was bound to succeed. Furthermore, the psychological aspects of *Fuoco* claim our attention. We already know that d'Annunzio's heroes use love as a mirror. Sperelli found supreme satisfaction in the moment when the beloved admits her love for him. But such simple contentment does not suffice for Stelio Efrena. His mistress, the great actress, endows him not only with her love; through her he comes to know the desire of all who have loved her, the torment and frenzy of thousands of men. In one of his early poems, "Pamphilia," d'Annunzio had already touched upon this strange craving to know through one woman the passions of all men.[96] It is a refined form of promiscuity that takes place in the realm of wish and imagination. Efrena wished not only to know the loves of his mistresses' bygone lovers; he longs to experience the passions which she arouses in the masses. The applause which she receives becomes for him an intoxication similar to but stronger than the sexual appetite. Through her, Efrena realizes how art can become a vehicle for communication with the multitude. Thus he dreams of investing the masses with heroic life through the power of his word. Esthetic individualism, facing nothingness, tries to escape from its career by again embracing the community. Fascism, with its exaltation of the masses and its theatrical display, was in more ways than one the brainchild of d'Annunzio's poetry.

It was natural that d'Annunzio should be attracted by the theater as a means of esthetic education, and it was equally natural that his drama should be lyrical like that of Wilde and Hofmannsthal. He dons Greek and Renaissance costume with the same ease as contemporary garb; he mixes mythical and realistic ingredients. But this decadent of the ending century did not comprehend the destiny that propels human beings toward a tragic end. His dramas, like his novels, are garlands of words, verbal cascades which induce a transitory euphoria in the spectator but move him neither to fear nor to pity.

Of all the writers we have considered, d'Annunzio was least inspired by ideas. He was essentially a temperament, a temperament whose mainspring was carnal obsession.[97] Was it the sexual desire that led to the cult of beauty, or did the cult of beauty stir the desire? It seems a vicious cycle, eternally veering from "Begierde zu Genuss."

Those who read him today will still feel the delirious force of his language but they will also tire of his rhetorical splendors. His magnificence becomes monotonous; his feasts last too long.[98] His lack of inner truth brings on fatigue. Except for the ever-powerful ego, d'Annunzio's inspirations came to him at second hand: through works of art, books, historical relics—shells which time had left upon the shores of his age. Like everything that is but the reflection of a reflection, his work occasions not only fatigue, but distrust. Even his admiration of beauty and his great love song of life leave us unconvinced, because his song of life is in reality a paean of praise for his ego. "Oh, Life . . . shall I one day have told all your beauty . . . oh, Life of a thousand faces, nothing was alien to me; my soul lived ten thousand times. I aspired to everything; I tried everything, and what was not done, I dreamed." [99] This is clearly reminiscent of Nietzsche, but as Zaldumbide says, it is a Nietzsche without intellectual substance, a Nietzsche without Nietzsche.

D'Annunzio introduced Italy to the dangerous teaching of Master-and-Slave-morals, to the imperative of living perilously, and he had sufficient vanity to live up to his own manifestoes. During World War I he made spectacular flights, one of which cost him an eye. His esthetic nationalism amalgamated easily with that of the irredenta; his eloquence spread catchwords through the body politic of a nation already affected by social ills of long standing. His role in the "coup de théâtre" of Fiume, the famous charter which he proclaimed there, are readily recognizable symptoms of the antidemocratic trend which engulfed Central Europe in the backwash of the Great War. Perhaps because he was intellectually less imposing, d'Annunzio shows patently the Neronic tendencies which we have noted in other members of this generation. He also manifests clearly the function which esthetic individualism played in the intellectual and social fabric of Europe.

V

Maurice Barrès is the spiritual twin of d'Annunzio and like him became the idol of the literary world only to be relegated to limbo by future generations. Novelist and political agitator, analytical writer and propagandist, Barrès is more easily recognized by his intellectual profile than by his widespread activities. By birth and by ideology he belongs to the group whose influence we are endeavoring to establish. He represents more clearly and certainly more vehemently than any other writer the turn from a decadent and fatigued skepticism to an aggressive nationalism, a psychological bent with which we are already familiar. His work was essentially concluded before 1914; since then his influence has steadily declined. [100]

Barrès was born in Lorraine and witnessed as a child the defeat of France by the Germans. His personality shows the tensions that are part of life on a European frontier. The literary masters whom he worshiped at the Lycée in Nancy were Gautier, Flaubert, and Baudelaire. His beginnings evidence a complete aloofness from the political problems which agitated France in the decade following the "debacle"; he scorned reality and abandoned himself to the "strange sensations" which only the elect are capable of experiencing. The romanticism of his life at the Lycée caused a powerful ferment in Barrès' imagination easily traceable in his later novels. With his debut in Paris two other personalities began to attract him, Renan and Taine. Barrès has given tribute to both of these men in his work; he has described Renan's amiable unbelief in "A week with Monsieur Renan," and has portrayed Taine in an impressive chapter of one of his novels.

Renan's flirtatious skepticism turned into relativism in the mind of the young Barrès. Taine's influence was even more profound. From him Barrès learned what was then termed "exact psychology," the belief that a personality can be explained by the racial and environmental elements that have entered its composition. Taine had used his famous "milieu-theory" to analyze literary works and he passed on to Barrès the technique of interpreting art as a manifestation of sociopsychological and racial realities. He was the first to call Barrès' attention to the concept of race.[101]

With these ideas Barrès blended other tendencies. Schopenhauer's pessimism had been absorbed in France under the impact of military defeat; to Barrès the German became an exponent of his lethal conviction that "all the gods were dead." [102] Wagner's music swayed him as it swayed most of the artists of the decade. The symbolist movement he noted with interest. He was constantly in search of new sensations however exotic, and he was fascinated by an artistic creed which had discovered that for "the most sensitive souls the ordinary vocabulary proved insufficient." [103] However, Mallarmé's aloofness could not long hold an author to whom popular acclaim soon became important. His first work, a trilogy like d'Annunzio's, gave him the fame to which he aspired. Its title, *Le Culte du moi*, aimed straight at the heart of esthetic individualism; no more telling phrase has been found to describe the intellectual position of the artist of the 1890's than Barrès' cult of the self. He called his books ideological novels: they are at the same time analyses of the era and intellectual autobiography.

The central figure—he can't be called a hero—that links the three novels is oppressed by the sensation that he is living in an age of incipient barbarity.[104] Like the last of the platonic philosophers, he awaits the invasion of the barbarians in the grove of Academe. He is the brother of Algabal and Sperelli and practices self-analysis as they do. He expresses the philosophy of this whole generation in a sentence that has deservedly become classic: "Il faut sentir le plus possible en analysant le plus possible" ("One must feel the utmost in analyzing the utmost").[105] But the old portals to experience are closed to him. The goals which the times propose to his ambition seem to him empty; herein lies the secret of his despair. His world does not proffer him a destination worthy of his activity. It seems strange that Barrès writes in this vein at a time when Cecil Rhodes was building his African empire and Lyautey was ready to undertake a similar assignment for France.

In the general disintegration of responsibilities and values the self alone constitutes reality. Since the self is the only stable point in a world corroded by relativism and skepticism, the self must be cultivated; hence, le culte du moi. But this self acknowledges nothing outside itself or above itself. These three books trace the *via crucis* of the intellectual at the end of the nineteenth century.[106]

The self cannot live forever by feeding on the I and is at length overtaken by the *horror vacui*. It attempts to fill this vacuum by giving itself over to the enjoyment of the perfect form. But Barrès himself admits that "the most perfect forms are only symbols for my curiosity." His curiosity refuses to resign itself to the stagnation of narcissistic emotionalism. Already in the "cult of the self" Barrès recognizes that even the most accomplished individualities are but fragments of the greater system of the race which itself is a fragment of God. The individual is ruled by the same law that governs the race. The candidate of nihilism pursues his apprenticeship from analysis to analysis; he proves to himself the nothingness of the self and awakens to the "sens social." This is the interpretation which Barrès himself has given of his first book.[107]

The impact of *Culte du moi* on Barrès' contemporaries was considerable. Its exquisite prose, its rare sensations, brought to premature bloom in the hothouse of his delicate nihilism enchanted the young. His "confessions in white tie and tails" became the favorite reading of the lycée seniors of 1890.

For a time he wavered. Though he felt, like all the other members of his generation, that esthetic individualism was an end beyond which there was nothing but suicide, he stood uncertain before the other road signs. What could quench his intellectual thirst and at the same time break the isolation in which the personality dessicated? Socialism attracted him for a short time but more as a problem than a solution.[108] He tried travel and discovered the tragic beauty of Spanish art and folklore, becoming one of the first to feel the fascination of El Greco. Like Hofmannsthal, d'Annunzio, and Mann, he evoked the morose charm of Venice, the Venice of Byron and Musset, of August Platen and Wagner. His impressions were gathered in a book that once more showed Barrès' gift of expressing the emotions of his time in one caption: *Du Sang, de la volupté et de la mort.*[109] The solemn and sinister chord of this legend has always struck me as profoundly suggestive of the moral climate that was to envelop so much of twentieth century writing: the work of D. H. Lawrence, Hemingway, Thomas Mann. No doubt Barrès was a genius in coining titles that often promised more than his books fulfilled. But he was too much a son of the nineteenth century to be content with violence, sex, and death. He clung to tangible panaceas and found them in identifying his restless and receptive self with the nation from which it emanated.

Barrès entered his final phase with the great crisis that shook France to her very foundations: the Dreyfus affair. His bent was antidemocratic and nationalistic, and he never hesitated to make his position clear. In the turmoil provoked by General Boulanger, Barrès had been elected deputy to the lower chamber, an avowed champion of the hapless general. He considered the bourgeoisie and its parliamentary constitution to be the enemy of the great personality that alone could redeem France. The Dreyfus affair found him at the extreme right. His political arguments are not worth consideration, but the national anxiety that the Dreyfus affair produced obliged Barrès to take a new stand. His next work, once more a trilogy, is called *Roman de l'énergie nationale (Novels of National Energy)*. He advances from the I to the community; what began as analysis of the self becomes exaltation of the nation. The first part of the trilogy is the most interesting, made famous again through its title: *Les Déracinés (The Uprooted).*[110]

In order to restore the national energy to its full dynamic, Barrès thought it necessary to scrutinize the trends that had led to the defeat of 1870 and were now showing their disintegrating influence in the Dreyfus scandal. Although he was himself uprooted and an intellectual, he points to the uprooted intellectual and the politician as the source of the evil. The book describes the lives of seven men who leave their native Lorraine and become entangled in the base intrigue of cosmopolitan Paris. The fault is not theirs but that of a civilization which had torn them from their roots. These roots are regional because Barrès believes deeply in the locality that nourishes the growth of its people; they are social because everyone should live in a stable frame of society; they are spiritual because they are a heritage from the great geniuses who have built up the treasure house of culture. Those who voluntarily or involuntarily cut loose from these roots become "les déracinés," the driftwood of modern society.

Barrès' analysis touched a vital spot in our social structure. There are few who have escaped the nostalgia occasioned by watching a once stable European society transform itself into an economic whirlpool where the industrial atoms no longer follow the bent of tradition and anchored habitation, custom, and family, but must comply with the merciless demands of job-seeking, going wherever economic necessity drives them. The mobility of modern society is both a blessing and a curse; and for Barrès the penalty was more potent than the reward. But though his comprehension of the problem of modern uprootedness is astonishing, his explanation is prejudiced and childish. He did not understand that the uprooted were the victims of the great technological revolution which was sweeping the globe from pole to pole. Instead he lays the blame at the doorstep of alien influences, German thought and Jewish immigration. To his anti-German and anti-Semitic bias he adds authoritarianism. Barrès did not believe in the people and he openly despised the masses. However, mass emotion intoxicated and seduced him as it did d'Annunzio, and he envisions a new Napoleon, "un être clairvoyant et fiévreux," who will restore the biochemical balance of the race. His evocation of Napoleon, "professeur d'énergie," is one of the fascinating parts of *Déracinés*.[111] We are reminded of similar ideas harbored by George and d'Annunzio, and it is clearly indicative of a growth in totalitarian tendencies in the European mind long before totalitarianism became an acute menace to Western society. In Barrès' novel it is not difficult to identify the unholy trinity of Caesarism, militarism, and nationalism.

Barrès' nationalism is grounded on a belief in forces more powerful than the intellect and the individual. "What a small thing is intelligence," he writes now, "a surface of ourselves merely." We are basically emotional beings (des êtres affectifs).[112] Thus Barrès moves not only from individualism to collectivism, but from skepticism to irrationalism.

His irrationalism differs from the older irrationalism of the romantic period by its lack of universality and its narrowed horizons. Because the emotions that Barrès finds in the depth of his beings are not universal, but only French; it is France with which he concerns himself. Since Barrès refused to consider reason as more than superficial, he must look elsewhere for France's essence. The eternal France is not the France of Descartes and Voltaire, of Rousseau and Mirabeau. It is "the earth and the dead," "a cemetery and the men of genius." As E. R. Curtius puts it, Barrès has progressed from the cult of the self to the cult of the dead.[113] Barrès' cult of the dead is the cult of the past.

The past had exercised a magic attraction for the minds of many representatives of the esthetic movement; Wilde had felt its lure, and George; Hofmannsthal and d'Annunzio bowed before its spell. But the past that captivates Barrès is confined to what he called the Latin genius. He was not receptive to "the splendor that was Greece," and Rome was important only because she had made France possible. France is the heir to the "génie Latin"; she is the citadel of civilization; she holds the "barbarians of the East" at bay. Thus Barrès becomes the herald of "litérature engagée." His later works are frankly dedicated to the cause of "revanche" and have contributed their share in preparing the overheated atmosphere of explosive nationalism that made 1914 possible.

Nor did his ideology gain in universal perspective by the attempt to interpret the Catholic Church as one of the great manifestations of the Latin genius. Barrès and Charles Maurras became the leaders of traditionalism, "French and Catholic." But Barrès had as little faith as Maurras and saw the Catholic Church as essentially an instrument of authority, of order and discipline. The indictment that the Vatican brought against the *Action Française* in later years could have been applied with equal validity against Barrès. His religion was a religion without God, very similar to that of Comte. Its church sprang from the "miraculous soil of Lorraine." According to Thibaudet, Barrès became one of those Catholics who form the guard of honor of the Church in France. If Barrès had ever undertaken to draw up a calendar, the majority of his saints would have been French, with a sprinkling of holy men from Italy and Spain thrown in for good measure.

The two books which Barrès devoted to religious problems, though moving in their descriptive beauty, suffer from the same psychological handicap that mars all his work after his conversion to nationalism. Their "mystique" is not Christian; their inspiration is not God, but the past and that vague atmospheric charm which surrounds the meadows and hills of Lorraine.[114]

Although Barrès was an important, perhaps the most important, link in the chain that joined the tenets of Catholicism to the ranks of the French intelligentsia, he never reached the plane of Claudel or Péguy. Doctrinal truth mattered little to him—"C'est l'élan qui fait la morale." [115] Until the end of his days it was the self that was all-powerful in him to the point where he could exclaim, "Que je suis las de moi-même." His prayers too are characteristic of the individualist who, much as he might strive, was never quite able to overcome the esthetic imperative: "Free me from living for vanity and let me enjoy in my brief life the infinitude of poetry." [116] Behind the fierce nationalism, behind the emphasis on tradition and race stands the ever-present temptation of nihilistic solipsism. His nationalism is a desperate attempt to entrench himself in an absolute. But the nation is not an absolute; it is itself a historical product and cannot be clothed in the unfading splendor of absolute values.

Barrès was the exponent of a society basically bourgeois in its outlook; for him extreme individualism, once proved destructive, admitted of no other cure than extreme nationalism. In reality it was the community he sought to embrace, but he could conceive it only in the form of the nation-state. Others of his generation, like Claudel, turned to the Church. There was always something hollow in Barrès' appeals to nationalistic passion, even in the evocation of his native Lorraine. The more ironic of the French writers might well say: It is not Lorraine that has created Barrès; it is Barrès who has created Lorraine. His ideology is an ideology "as if" and one can understand his enemies who called him "farceur sublime." [117]

Perhaps it would be more just to say that he was playing the role of the enraged nationalist while in his heart he knew that the values of history could not quench his thirst for the absolute. "Life has no meaning. I even believe that it becomes more absurd every day. To submit to all the illusions and to know that our desire . . . will never be stilled. To want only eternal possessions and to comprehend ourselves as a series of successive states. From whatever point one may look at the universe and at our existence they remain senseless tumults . . . however, we must adjust ourselves to them." [118] This is Barrès at his most honest. The man who had once tasted of the delight that beauty gave to his inflamed sensuality, took refuge in the community as a measure of mental hygiene. It is characteristic of him, as of so many of this generation, that he recognized his own outlook and his own melancholy as Neronic. He had planned to entitle one part of the *Culte du moi,* "Qualis artifex pereo." But the artist did not perish, and it therefore became his fate to long for an absolute that, more and more, he knew to be unattainable.

VI

The croaking of despairing frogs in their stagnating swamps— thus did Nietzsche characterize "l'art pour l'art." And indeed, none of the artists we have considered found it possible to remain in the atmosphere of exclusive estheticism. Each made an escape from his original attitude.

Many a reader will question the inclusion of André Gide in this group; certainly his work is not circumscribed by the esthetic movement. His protean personality defies not only this but almost any category. Yet no one has shown the position of European individualism at the end of the century with greater clarity.

Gide often dwelt on the subject of his inherited antagonisms. "Born in Paris, of an Uzès father and a Norman mother, where . . . would you have me rooted?" [119] The diverse character of the two families and the two regions cannot, however, have been entirely responsible for the intricate nature of his personality. We are obliged to probe further if we are to uncover the conflicts that perturbed his being.

Gide has himself asked us not to subject him to a hasty assessment: "Ne me comprenez pas si vite." At another time he remarked, "Les extrêmes me touchent." [120] Thus we are cautioned not to accept a simple formula or to take his own confessions at their face value. Gide's essence is not revealed in any single work: rather must we look for it in the ebb and flow of his dialectic, in the "internal dialogue" which began with him as a child and ended only with his death.

Gide was a sickly boy craving attention more than affection. He was surrounded and reared by women of all kinds and distinctions: his mother, devout, strict, ever conscious of her duties; Anna Shackleton, a spinster to whom the Gides had given a home; his aunt Claire, the embodiment of bourgeois pretensions; his cousin Madeleine (the Emmanuèle of his autobiography), later to become his wife. While still a child he discovered in himself a strong sexual urge. [121]

Gide's sexual impulse lies at the root of his deepest conflict; it demanded consummation at the same time that his outward existence required the denial of the flesh represented by the pious and austere women about him. The biological urge and the categorical imperative made him the victim of an endless struggle. He was forever torn between the rejection of his self and the affirmation of this same self. From self-discovery he switches to self-denial, from self-exploitation to self-chastisement. He has said that most of his books were "des livres de critiques." [122] He meant, of course, self-criticism. Gide's characters are not self-portraits but they indicate his potentialities; they are personalities imprisoned by a rule, fixed in a formula. [123] Invariably an attempt to understand his own drama, "each of his works is a chemical experiment in purifying some particular quality or vice which he pursues to its logical conclusion." [124]

The internal conflict determines likewise the rhythm of his life: his restlessness, his departure for unknown adventures and his return to the idyllic life of Normandy. [125] It sets the stage for his attempts to find a synthesis between paganism and Christianity; it explains Gide's freedom to use Greek myth and the Bible as canvasses for the picture of his own tormented self. "Ma valeur est dans ma complexité."

Gide's attitude toward contemporary problems was likewise conditioned by his basic conflict. He was attracted by Catholicism and by communism, but neither could hold him long enough to make "unconditional surrender" enticing. The comfort that comes from submission to authority was, for Gide, not worth the renunciation of the personality that with all its turmoil, through its turmoil, was the source of his creativity.[126]

His situation was not uncommon; it was his attempt to conquer it through his art that was unprecedented. It has been said that he understood how to give to his personal drama a universal significance that touched the anxiety of the following generations.[127] He is a writer whose chief concerns were moral problems, not a moralist who tried to express his ideas through the medium of literature.

But let us return to his biography. Under the benevolent despotism of the matriarchs who ran the household his reading was supervised, but this did not prevent his discovery of the romantic poets. He read Gautier, Hugo, and Baudelaire; Heine intoxicated him.[128] Two books, however, were more important to him than the whole galaxy of romantic poets—the Bible and the Arabian Nights.

No monetary problems interfered with his vocation; financial worries were as distant from him as they were from George or Hofmannsthal. Ample means for study and travel, or the printing of books in editions de luxe were his for the asking.

From the beginning there are in Gide's literary work two tendencies, one literary, the other psychological or therapeutic. In his first book, *Les Cahiers d'André Walter,* he endeavors through the poetic expression of his experience to sublimate his contest with the flesh. Unable to affirm his desires, he would repress them; he would become impervious to the countless temptations which assailed his sensuality day and night. The body must be denied; only the soul shall be asserted. "Les corps me gênaient; ils me cachaient les âmes. La chair ne sert de rien." [129] But there are also undertones which point to the later Gide: "La vie intense, voilà la superbe"; to multiply the emotions, not to enclose oneself in a single life, in one body only, in such phrases does André Walter foreshadow a future attitude.[130] There is the whisper of a question: is the soul first and foremost the negation of the flesh; does not virtue lead to pride, the greatest barrier between God and Man?

Reflections such as these give to *Les Cahiers d'André Walter* greater psychological interest than artistic value. The human conflict is overlaid with a heavy coating of literature and second-hand notions are expressed in a manner both "ejaculatory and indefinite." [131]

Gide believed that he had reached his "summa" in *Les Cahiers* but he had reckoned without his host; the public was indifferent to the life and death of André Walter. The book served only as a calling card to the literary circles of the capital. He met Henri de Régnier; he visited Hérédia; and Mallarmé welcomed him to his Tuesday evenings in the Rue de Rome.[132]

Mallarmé had conceived the idea that the poet should create in an atmosphere of metaphysical purity. Living at a time when language was abused by journalist and parliamentarian alike, he set forth to restore poetry to its spiritual birthright. His goal was Baudelaire's "infallibility of the poetic production." This led to his search for symbols which might assist him in his effort to liberate the spirit in its flight to an infinitely distant homeland where dream and reality, symbol and truth live in unison.[133] Gide's symbolistic phase was short, but it is indicative of the intellectual climate of the nineties that in his period of waiting, his *période d'attente*, he was attracted by this group alone.

In the myth of Narcissus who finds death in the embrace of his own beauty, esthetic individualism discovered its most congenial reflection. In his *Treatise of Narcissus* Gide declares Narcissus to be the perfection of beauty; he disdained the nymphs because he was in love with himself. Here Gide still wears the disguise of Mallarmé's symbolism but we hear darker chords in this prelude to the future Gide. It is the artist's function to confess. "All things must be made manifest, even those things that are the most baneful. Woe unto him by whom the offense cometh, but it needs be that the offense come." [134]

Le Voyage d'Urien, Gide's next book, still adheres to the symbolist creed. It is a "voyage du rien"; and the polar landscape of Ultima Thule symbolizes Gide's desperate soul hesitating between resistance

and acquiescence to the commands of his desire. When he finished
the book in the summer of 1892, he knew that symbolist poetry had
become for him a lie, and that he was waiting, waiting, waiting,
to tell the truth that must be heard.[135]

Gide has described his break-through with great veracity. As a
result of his inner discord, he fell ill. His father had died of tuber-
culosis and Gide feared he might be afflicted with the same disease.
He went to Africa in October of 1893, and at Sousse in Algeria
a native boy offered himself to Gide. After his return to Paris he
found himself a stranger in a literary milieu that had become stale
and meaningless to him. He returned to Algiers where he met Oscar
Wilde at Blida. Wilde introduced Gide to another "charming Arab
boy." What followed has been related by Gide himself; it was his
Declaration of Independence.[136]

As we have noted, he found himself a stranger in the Parisian
salons on the return from his trip to Africa. His disenchantment
with the literary world is the theme of *Paludes (Marshlands)*.[137]
It is a protest against the ivory tower existence of the intellectual
who, living of, by, and for books, becomes a spectator of spectators.
Gide's hero resembles Hofmannsthal's Fool whose lot was—"mein
Leben zu erleben wie ein Buch." But Gide's literary approach is
different; he is ironical, not lyrical, and his outlook is detached, not
dramatic. Its sardonic and derisive attitude marks it as one of the
representative books of the decade; according to Paul Claudel, it
is the most complete document of "that special atmosphere of . . .
stagnation which we breathed from 1885 to 1890." The conclusion
of *Marshlands* is, however, positive and very Gidean: the individual
should be itself and reveal itself in its action.[138]

The reputation of *Marshlands* has been overshadowed by the
other work in which Gide proclaimed his freedom from the fetters
that had restrained him. *Les Nourritures terrestres* [139] *(The Fruits
of the Earth)* is an assertion and a deposition. "You will never
know the effort it cost us to become interested in life; but now that
life does interest us, it will be like everything else—passionately." [140]
Do not hope, says the apostate Puritan, to find God here or there;
God is what lies ahead of us. Do not distinguish God from your
happiness. This God of whom Gide speaks is obviously not the
Calvinistic God to whom he prayed as a child; the commandments

of that God had wounded his soul. "All things are divinely natural." [141]

But it is not only the old concept of God that is sent to the wall. All that conspires to overlay man's self with routine and habit must go, too. Families, I hate you; books, a bonfire of all our books; I have no use for knowledge that has not been preceded by sensation; principles and commitments, they all estrange the self from the self. One must forget the laws to listen to the new law: to be one's self. The cardinal points of *Fruits of the Earth* are fervor, availability, and restlessness, and can be summed up in the word "desire." [142] Desire enriches more than possession. Gide carries the message of individualism to its logical extreme: assume as much humanity as possible; know all the passions and all the vices; consider this book but an invitation. "When you have read me, throw my book away and depart. I wish I could give you the desire to depart . . . from your town, from your family, from your room, from your thoughts. [143]

Fruits of the Earth holds an exceptional place in Gide's work. In a preface written thirty years later, he stated that it was the book of a convalescent. [144] And it is true that it was a therapeutic document of the first order. In it he affirmed life because he had learned to affirm himself and his complexities. It is a book that invites the reader to experiences and pleasures just as much as d'Annunzio's *Piacere* or *Dorian Grey.* Yet it differs from them in style and mood. In its loose composition, its dithyrambic prose, it seems closest to Nietzsche's *Zarathustra,* which Gide might well have read. [145] *Fruits of the Earth* became a landmark of emotional emancipations. For the young, however, Gide became a liberator not so much through this "manual of evasion" as through subsequent works in which his new position was expressed in a more objective manner: *The Immoralist, Strait Is the Gate,* and *The Return of the Prodigal Son.*

These later novels are not simple transpositions of Gide's newly won freedom. To understand them we must return briefly to the account of his life. He had sacrificed the liberty of his African days by marrying his cousin "Emmanuèle." It is difficult to understand why he took this step; we can only assume that his feeling of guilt had not subsided, that he continued to long for atonement, and that he was ill at ease without the spiritual love and Christian virtues he had just decried. His journal bears witness to this endless struggle. But a marriage in which homosexual pleasure and spiritual love existed side by side was no solution for Gide, and was a source of perpetual suffering for Emmanuèle. It was characteristic of the intellectual in Gide that he hoped "to convince her" by writing books, as if a literary effort, were it the best, had ever comforted a woman stricken to the heart.[146]

The three books which reflect the tension of Gide's existence must be understood as a whole; they are a triptych, two wings and a center panel. *The Immoralist,* too well known to call for analysis here, may be interpreted either as an indictment against or a panegyric on the audacity of sexual liberty. The book is a work of art and as such is essentially ambiguous in disclosing a conflict of life. Michael obtains his personal happiness at the price of his wife's anguish and death. Conversely in *Strait Is the Gate* ascetic youth and resigned virtue are condemned rather than exalted. Alissa (a portrait of Emmanuèle), who renounces her love from religious motives, realizes the futility of her martyrdom. Confronted with death she finds that the heaven toward which she had directed her whole being is empty. Neither her love nor her God proffer her comfort in the moment of death. The novel is a study in futility; an undercurrent of Pascalian despair runs through its pages.

Gide's analysis had brought him to the inevitable question: can the pursuit of happiness, that kills, and the joylessness of morality, that destroys, be reconciled? His attempt to give an answer is found in *The Return of the Prodigal Son,*[147] a parable that had always been dear to heretics.

The four conversations which the prodigal son holds with his father, his mother, his older brother, and his younger brother contain the essence of Gide's quest. The father is the child's image of God. He comforts the weary. It is I, he says, who has formed you; I know who you are. I was waiting for you—I was there.

The older brother represents order and dogma. He is the self-appointed interpreter of God. But the prodigal son finds it difficult to obey his commands, and he turns to his mother, the only one who can give him the solace of love. She asks him, "Que cherchais-tu?" and he answers, "Je cherchais . . . qui j'étais." But the journey has fatigued him, and he no longer understands how he could have left her. It is she who calls his attention to his younger brother.

The prodigal son seeks him out but is met with sullen questionings. Why had he returned home? Because he has suffered and suffering has made him think. Has he then come back defeated? Not exactly; resigned perhaps. What has made him despair? He has lost the liberty he sought; instead of a kingdom he has found servitude, doubts, humiliation. But when the younger brother tells him of his own resolution to depart, it is the prodigal son who cries, "Be strong; forget us; forget me. May you never return." And the younger brother leaves the house as the prodigal son lifts the lamp to guide his steps.

Eternally divided between desire and obligation, thirst and the quenching of his thirst, loneliness and the comfort of human companionship, Gide could not pretend that to depart was to conquer. He could not discard the embrace of the father, or the pity of the mother, or even the admonition of the elder brother. But neither could he restrain the younger one who hoped to triumph where the prodigal son had failed. The rebellion of the individual is eternal. "Let each follow his own bent."

Wherein lies Gide's importance? Certainly not in having made a creed of homosexuality. Nor does any one of his works, or their sum total, have sufficient distinction or transcendence to lend them symbolic value. Yet his figure remains an indisputable link between the nineteenth and the twentieth centuries. What explanation then may we offer for the enigma, André Gide?

A Christian who extolled the pursuit of all pleasures, a homosexual who paraded as the head of a family, an upper-middle-class bourgeois who embraced communism—paradox after paradox, and they lead to one conclusion: André Gide as a moral being was an impossibility; as an artist he is among the ranking figures of his time.[148] Gide was, as his friend Roger Martin du Gard said, a man of letters from morning to night. Not only was he an artist, but an artist whose organizing center was esthetic individualism. Essentially Gide was *homo aestheticus,* much as his disguises may suggest different interpretations. He belongs in the category of the esthetic individual who, according to Schiller, creates while he plays and plays while he creates. And it is in this category alone that his protean nature and the "moral impossiblity of being André Gide" may be resigned.

Gide was never a Christian, nor was he ever a Communist. Both doctrines ignited his imagination and troubled his conscience, but never to the point where they might become commitments. Such a statement obliges us to ask: how genuine was his approach to ethical problems? I believe that his approach was as legitimate as an artist's can be; that is, he could demonstrate the human dilemma involved, never its solution. It was his greatness to refuse man-made dogmas or attitudes as absolutes and to continue the perpetual dialogue of criticism and irony; it was his limitation not to realize that life without limitation is an impossibility, because life is not a dialogue and the most perfect prose cadence will not make it one.

Many of the ambiguities in Gide's work are cleared away when viewed in this light: his constant misuse of the word "God," the phantom problem in which he revolves the idea of human liberty, his attempts to make Christ a precedent for his own individualism. It is not difficult to understand why he was called "liberator" by some and "corrupter" by others. Yet I think he was neither. He believed that each individual was a law unto himself; how then could he obtrude? Let each follow his own bent; this was the esthetic center of the moral storm, André Gide, and like the eye of a hurricane it was a center of stillness around which the gusts of moral conflict raged endlessly.

VII: Conclusion

We have made no attempt in the foregoing pages to exhaust the literary potentialities of the period. Our task has been to indicate the prevailing temper of intellectual thought and behavior at the close of the century.

When Goethe asserted: "Wer Wissenschaft und Kunst besitzt, der hat auch Religion" ("He who has art and science has also religion"), he proclaimed the unity of art, science, and religion. During the nineteenth century this trinity of art, science, and religion had become dissolved. Hemmed in by an industrial society which valued only what was compatible with its utilitarian standards, the artist withdrew into a dream world and declared the divorce of art from

life. Since life did not offer the artist a proper medium for its manifestations, "art disdained what did not appreciate it" (Gide). Unable and unwilling to remain in a sterile atmosphere of resentment,
the artist affirmed the superiority of art (Wilde). Art was superior
to life because it was a law unto itself; whoever practiced it should
do so for its own sake. It was not long before this arrogant attitude
became untenable, and the artist began to invade the realm of religion. Religion, under the impact of the natural sciences, had lost
the power so save man; science refused to do so. The artist, therefore,
proffered his solution: man should be saved through the arts.

While the metaphysical grounds on which European civilization
had been built crumbled and the blessings of "progress" became
doubtful, the arts alone appeared to possess the power of redemption.

Shortly, however, the artist learned that he was not only the high
priest of this new cult but its victim as well; he had offered himself
as the sacrificial lamb. Furthermore, this was a cult to which only
the chosen few were admitted; art for art's sake came to signify art
for the artist's sake. The members of the esthetic movement formed
a closed corporation in which the poet praised the painter and the
painter portrayed the poet.

In the end, the artist found himself in a twofold isolation. He had
rejected the outside world, and his portentous ego was obliged to
reject all other egos. He was alone with himself in a solitude that
became unbearable.

Since it had been decreed that art and life were separate, there
could be little intake from the outside world. The artist had to
depend on his own emotion. This strange situation explains, I think,
why so great an emphasis was placed on Eros. The artist who did not
feel himself to be a member of society could find relief from his
loneliness only in a beautiful "Du," as the Germans would say. Only
the beautiful "you" could assuage the thirst for companionship. This
attitude marks the last phase of the romantic movement with its exaggerated appeal to emotion divorced from reason. But in this desperate attempt to cling to the value of beauty, the two other
Platonic values were lost, and the belief that beauty could take their
place proved to be a dangerous deception.

"A world should be sacrificed to polish a verse," wrote the poet.
But the world was by no means willing to be sacrificed and answered

the contempt of the poet with the heavy fist that crushed Wilde. And though other poets escaped his martyrdom, there was no reprieve from the ultimate judgment. Each realized that the isolated individual whose only recourse lies in eroticism cannot survive.

For the historian of the twentieth century their disengagement from individualistic estheticism is as important as their original attitude, because they contributed to the beginning century some of its characteristic trends: antirationalism, the revival of the myth, and a marked tendency to set the individual against the masses. Such influences led to Caesarism and autocracy.

From the sociological point of view, the esthetic movement was a bourgeois movement notwithstanding its antibourgeois aspects. Without exception, its representatives came from the middle class. None knew the struggle of the working class from direct experience; those who awoke to feel it at all, like Wilde, George, and Hofmannsthal, did so through intellectual channels. Estheticism would have been impossible in a theocratic society because it would have been condemned as a heresy; it would have been scorned by an aristocratic society where the "clerc" was kept in his place. Needless to say, it would not have been tolerated in a communistic society. Trotsky characterized Gide's work as "human records from an irrevocable past."

But all records are vestiges of an irrevocable past! The past can only be evoked, not recovered. And the esthetic movement left us a plenitude of records for the evocation of this "irrevocable past." Its fatigued beauty, its overripe delight in form and color, its mellowness, its spiritual awareness, will not be forgotten. More than this, the esthetic movement became one of the links in the chain that binds the two centuries to each other. Of the great writers of the twentieth century there are few who do not share in one or more of the problems that art for art's sake attempted to solve: Mann, Proust, and Joyce in the novel; Rilke, Valéry and Eliot in poetry; Dilthey and Ortega y Gasset in the fields of criticism and philosophy.

CHAPTER IV

The Disenchanted

I

Wilhelm Dilthey thought of poetry as "an authentic interpretation of life," and he was well acquainted with several of the writers whom we have noted in the preceding chapter. But Dilthey's own mission in life was not circumscribed by esthetic individualism; he went much further until finally his interests embraced nearly all of mankind's spiritual endeavors.[1]

The date of his birth, 1833, would seem to place him outside the time limits we have imposed on these studies. However, the impact of his work was scarcely felt before the beginning of the twentieth century. The nature of his numerous essays was disguised under highly scholastic titles, and the essays themselves were hidden away in learned journals. But gradually his fame began to spread, to the point that Ortega y Gasset put him down as "the most important philosopher in the second half of the nineteenth century."[2] He is, therefore, not a forerunner but a true member of the group of men who were deeply concerned with the future of Western culture and the place that science should occupy therein.

The word "science" in English has by now connotations mostly derived from the exact sciences, but we would do well to recall that its scope and meaning were considerably broader during the nineteenth century. John Stuart Mill spoke of moral sciences, as did many a French scholar, and the German term *Wissenschaft* covers both the natural and the cultural sciences with no discrimination against the latter. To defend the autonomy of the cultural sciences against the impositions by the exact sciences became one, if not the foremost, endeavor of Dilthey. But he was only the leader of many who were pioneering on this new frontier.

Dilthey's birth coincided with a great "Gotterdämmerung" in German culture. In rapid succession Hegel, Niebuhr, Goethe, and Schleiermacher disappeared from the stage. To all of them Dilthey paid tribute in his work, as he did to Lessing, Novalis, and Hölderlin. His spiritual origins were not rooted in the generation that filled the market place around 1840, the generation of Heine, Feuerbach, Marx, and Engels. They reached beyond this valley into the mountain range of Germany's classical period.

Dilthey was the descendant of a family of headstrong Calvinists who made their home on the lower Rhine.[3] Like Nietzsche and Lessing, he was the spiritual heir of Protestant ministers, and like Nietzsche he inherited from his ancestors, together with intellectual discipline, a musical sensitivity which led him to speak of listening to great music as an "almost religious act." [4]

As a student, he enrolled first in the faculty of theology, but soon bade it adieu. Historical studies began to attract him. In 1860 he wrote: "I saw my life before me today in a number of possibilities, some clear, some obscure, but the sum of them is that it is my business to trace in history the vital part of religion, and to give a moving exposition in an age that is stirred by politics and science alone." [5] However, Dilthey did not attempt to escape from his age into a romantic antagonism; quite the contrary. He sensed the conflict between his own predilections and the general trends of his time and decided to solve it.

He lived at a time when Europe had acknowledged a challenge to its tradition and had begun to feel a growing uneasiness about its future.[6] The solidity of its society, already shaken by the French Revolution, was further threatened by the consequences of the Industrial Revolution. The nations of Central Europe were striving toward national unity; the Slavs were awakening; science was making tremendous advances whose importance could not be ignored. However, Dilthey's initiation into the making of the human mind was, from the beginning, conditioned by the historical approach. He called it his good fortune that he lived in the time of Bopp, Trendelenburg, Boeckh, Grimm, Mommsen, and Ranke.[7] This school, he added, possessed a clear empirical eye for facts, a loving penetration into the details of the historical process, a universal outlook upon history, regarding the life of the mind as in every respect a historical product.[8] But Dilthey did not overlook its shortcomings. "Hitherto the historical school has not broken through the limitations which were bound to hinder its theoretical development and its influence on life . . . it had no philosophical foundations." [9] "It would not be worth while," he exclaimed, "being a historian, were this not also a way to understand the world." [10] This is the young Dilthey at his best. He told his daughter in later years that everything he had produced was but the execution of thoughts and projects conceived in his youth.[11] Only a few of his great enterprises were completed, however, and these were not the fundamental ones. Launched forth in a grandiose manner, they usually progressed to the conclusion of Volume I, and were then abandoned as the urge of new ideas became insistent. The term "creative instability" might have been coined to describe his type of mind.[12] Hence arose the discrepancy between the "rank of the man and the ring of his name." [13] But Dilthey was not disturbed by neglect or the possibility of oblivion. With ease he climbed the ladder of academic success leading him from Basel via Breslau to Berlin. Such success meant little to him. As he wrote, "It is strange how completely all external ambition has vanished as a result of the desire to complete my great undertakings. The tremendous crisis of European culture in which we live has captured my mind deeply and wholly, and the wish to become useful in its solution has eliminated all personal ambitions." [14]

We have seen that Dilthey was early moved by poetry, philosophy, and theology, but he harbored reservations in regard to all of them. In a letter to his brother he wrote, "Thought is fruitful only when it is based upon the special investigation of some aspect of the real." [15] The approach to the real became his problem.

During Dilthey's formative years Germany had begun to feel the positivist movement, which proclaimed as its goal the elevation of the study of man and society to the rank of a science. Dilthey read Comte and Mill with admiration, and he agreed with their proposition that the study of man and society should be given scientific validity. But he differed profoundly from them as to the method by which this end might be achieved. He thought that Anglo-French positivism was erroneous in assuming that the methods of the natural sciences could be applied to the field of Human Studies. The

Geisteswissenschaften (a term already in use, but enormously popularized by Dilthey) had their own methodology. What he deemed necessary, then, was the writing of a critique of historical reason, such as Kant, a century earlier, had given in *The Critique of Pure Reason*.[16]

In retrospect, Dilthey defined his quest in the following manner: "When I was introduced to philosophy, the idealistic monism of Hegel had loosened its hold over the natural sciences. Whenever the spirit of natural science sought philosophical expression, as with the Encyclopedists, in Comte . . . an attempt was made to conceive the mind (Geist) as a product of nature . . . and in the attempt the mind was disfigured. . . . I had myself grown up with an insatiable interest in the actual historical manifestations of spiritual life in all their variety and depth. The spiritual world embraces realities, evaluations, and a realm of ends of an infinite variety. . . . The great poets, Shakespeare, Cervantes, and Goethe, thought to interpret the world in this fashion . . . Thucydides, Machiavelli, and Ranke opened the world of history to me, a world telling its own story . . . the philosophical concepts based on natural science could not do justice to this world that stirred within me, and still less was I satisfied by the opponents of the natural science school. . . . In such a situation the dominating impulse of my philosophical thought arose, the desire to comprehend human life on its own terms. I had the urge to press even deeper into the world of history, to become aware of its soul; my philosophical efforts to find the way into the domain of reality, to lay valid foundations ensuring an objective knowledge of it,—this urge was but the other side of my desire to penetrate the historical world more deeply." [17]

In such manner did Dilthey become the historian of ideas and the philosopher of history. The two activities which held his life in suspense were but two different aspects of the same central idea. But this twofold nature of his work presents the historian with an almost impossible task. It would be necessary to demonstrate the interaction between the historical research and the philosophical construction put upon it by Dilthey, since he rarely chose a subject solely for its historical interest, but because, in addition, he hoped to derive systematic insights from its pursuit; witness his biographies of Schleiermacher and Hegel, or his studies of the sixteenth century and the Englightenment. Likewise, his systematic works are inter-laced with historical descriptions. The historian and the thinker in Dilthey fertilized each other, but they also crossed and jeopardized each other. If one looks for a general denominator in summing up his varied and fanned out activities, one might say that his writings were but one great *Einleitung in die Geisteswissenschaften,* an *Intro-duction to Human Studies.* The following profile must be drawn to show only the most basic achievement of Dilthey's efforts.

The problem of Dilthey, the philosopher, was to establish the scientific value of historical analysis. The problem of Dilthey, the historian, was to trace the origins and structure of the European mind. Both assignments were reconciled in his own person, the representative of a generation determined to free itself from the servitude to metaphysics in any form. Viewed from such a stand-point, Dilthey's endeavor was truly Kantian. But whereas Kant had applied his criticism only to the natural sciences, Dilthey was obliged to extend his criticism to cover the cultural sciences as well. A substantially different situation presented itself. In the latter case, one could not subordinate facts to laws, or apply methods which did not grow out of the facts themselves.

Dilthey wished to study the integral nature of man, "the whole man in the diversity of his own powers." Could such a knowledge be obtained by formulating an a priori idea of man and laying down the principles of his development? Dilthey's answer is No; a general science of man will find human nature revealed in experience, and in past experience remembered. Ortega y Gasset has summed up Dilthey's position in a neat aphorism: "Man does not have a nature; man has a history;" he does not have an immutable constitution; he manifests himself in varied and diverse forms.[18]

History is for Dilthey the deepest and most comprehensive mani-festation of life. He was a vitalist and never did tire of emphasizing that life is prior to knowledge. Like Bergson, he stressed the ever-floating stream of life which carries all human doings to unknown shores. However, life for Dilthey is not a biological, but a psycho-logical term, referring to all mental processes and especially to those creative activities which form the substance of history. "The whole psychological reality is not, but lives." [19]

Underlying all historical creativity, therefore, is a feeling of life (ein Lebensgefühl) that the humblest human being shares with the greatest. This feeling of life does not remain inarticulate. In life itself there is a potentiality of higher consciousness. Dilthey, though a vitalist, is scientifically minded. "Life imperiously demands guidance by thought." [20] When thought and life meet, the feeling of life crystallizes into a world picture (Weltbild). The world picture is the unifying element in every civilization; it explains the identity of style and expression in its various branches. This world picture, however, becomes clarified on a still higher level of consciousness as a world-view, or, to use Dilthey's own term, as a *Weltanschauung*. Although this concept was not originated by Dilthey (he inherited it from his teacher, Trendelenburg), it has received wide currency through his writings.[21]

What is world vision? It is the answer that man gives to the "riddle of life," to the eternal enigma of birth and death, love and hate, greatness and weakness, joy and sorrow.[22] There is in man a native drive toward unity of outlook in overcoming the flagrant contradictions in which his existence involves him. "All *Weltanschaungen* arise from the objectifications of the ways in which living man, perceiving and thinking, feeling and desiring, seeking to have his way with things, experiences the world." [23] Philosophy, poetry, and religion are the basic vehicles by means of which man tries to express his answer to the riddle of life. Dilthey does not single out any one of them; poetry ranks with him as high as philosophy. Throughout his writings runs his conviction that in the work of the poet an understanding of life in its entire reality may be found. "The genius appears and forces others to see with his eyes; he thus creates a school, a style, an epoch." [24]

One might be tempted to think that here was an interpretation of history based on a feeling for life, world picture, and world vision, essentially spiritual in character, an answer and a challenge to Marx. But nothing could be more erroneous. Dilthey never refers to Marx, and Dilthey's history of the human mind was realistic rather than idealistic. He knew full well that "the background of . . . ideas is force which the higher world has no power to overcome. And this is everywhere the case. Factuality of race, locality, or balance of forces is everywhere the foundation which can never be made spiritual. It is a dream of Hegel that the periods of history represent a stage in the development of reason." [25]

With the framework for a theory of history thus established, Dilthey had still to prove that the old concepts, so long in vogue, could never do justice to the living stream of human creativity. There was first the metaphysical approach to history which had been practiced from Plato to Kant. Here the lessons of history were dismissed in rather cavalier fashion as *vérités de faits* which could not hold a candle to the vérités éternelles. From the Greeks to the end of the eighteenth century, history had taken a back seat. With Voltaire, Herder, Hegel, and Comte, the attempts to discover the meaning of history appeared to have found an answer. But, objected Dilthey, ". . . there is no such last simple word of history, uttering its true sense, any more than there is such a thing to be abstracted from nature." [26] And as we know, Dilthey rejected with equal determination the pretense of the natural sciences that they held a monopoly on methodological truth. History deals with individuals. In words which remind us strongly of Ranke, Dilthey describes the specific structure of historical objects: ". . . the units which interact in the marvellous complex whole of history and society are individuals . . . each of which is distinct from every other, each of which is a world . . . and this singularity of each and every such individual who operates at any point in the immense cosmos of the mind can be followed out into several components, according to the principle, *individuum est ineffabile,* and only so does it become known in its full significance." [27]

The methods developed by the natural sciences cannot be used to appraise the individual. Dilthey acknowledged that the human studies can never give laws for the mind which might compare in number, importance, and precision to those established by the exact sciences. But, he maintained, this incapacity is more than outweighed by the enjoyment we derive from entering the inner life of other human beings which become comprehensible to us and thus bring us to an understanding of man. The faculty which is at work in human studies is the whole man, and intellectual satisfaction will be gained from studying any aspect of man.[28] In such manner did Dilthey strive to assure the human studies of their birthright.

They did not and should not aspire to the pretense of metaphysicians who gave to the world an artificial unity, contradicted and canceled by other metaphysicians who adhered to another set of principles. Nor should they insist on having the firmness and universality which distinguish the exact sciences, since such firmness and universality must needs destroy the very essence of history.

Historians from Thucydides to Ranke had, over the years, worked out their own methods for a proper evaluation of the uniqueness of historical phenomena, but they had worked on a trial and error basis. According to Dilthey, history still lacked a sound scientific foundation. We now approach the second part of Dilthey's endeavor. It was devoted to the question: how may scientific knowledge of individual persons and of the great forms of human existence be acquired? His answer was: through *Verstehen,* or as we can best translate the term, through sympathetic intuition.[29]

Dilthey had first encountered this problem while at work on his biography of Schleiermacher. Gradually the theory of understanding came to occupy a pivotal position in his thinking. Whereas the natural sciences explain facts, the cultural sciences penetrate into the workings of the human mind. How may an individual consciousness with a cast of its own attain objective knowledge of another such individual consciousness? As we have said, Dilthey believed it might be gained through sympathetic intuition, an act by means of which we transfer ourselves into a spiritual life which is different from our own; we relive it; we imitate or emulate it. In our capacity for sympathetic intuition is grounded our ability to participate in alien consciousness. From the simple understanding of words and sentences to grasping the significance of works of art or complex structures of human behavior, understanding follows its own rules. In this process of understanding, insisted Dilthey, we must start with the whole in order to make the particular intelligible, and in so doing we learn to distinguish between essential and nonessential.[30]

Understanding grows out of lived experience and must always be firmly rooted in life. Since its significance is not alone theoretical, it is not confined to the receptive reconstructions of the past by historians. Sympathetic intuition is anchored in many a roadstead: it is at work between people in love; it enables the statesman to read the mind of his opponent; it is at the root of all imaginative and artistic creation. What we encounter in the act of understanding is not only the stream of consciousness flowing through another life; it is much more, something which Dilthey at the end of his life called *Bedeutung,* or signification.

To understand is to discover—in the case of the historian, to rediscover. In the act of understanding we conquer for ourselves a whole world of meaning, and only in this way are we enabled to learn about the nature of man. To be sure, the path of understanding is strewn with difficulties. Understanding must correspond to the life it tries to understand, and the instances of misunderstanding are manifold. But even misunderstanding still bespeaks the importance which sympathetic intuition has in the process of human life.

No one would deny that the ideas which Dilthey advanced in his psychological studies were of the highest order. They definitely placed the Human Studies on the *globus intellectualis* and defined their frontiers; they showed them to be an integral part of man's creative ability, and demonstrated their significance for man's understanding of himself. Yet behind them rose a far greater problem, that of historicism, or, to be more explicit, of historical relativism. If metaphysics and scientific laws were equally banned from the cultural sciences, how could history expect to find an answer to the human quest for the absolute?

Dilthey was an avowed relativist. "History," he says, "does indeed know of various assertions of something unconditional, as value, norm, or good. . . . But historical experience knows only the process, so important for making these assertions; on its own ground it knows nothing of their universal validity." [31] What then was left to man? Dilthey answers: the knife of historical relativism which has made the wound must also be the instrument of cure. The mind which has pondered all the great systems of thought is not so much affected by their relativity, as by the sovereignty of the human intellect when confronted by each of them. "The contemplation of life makes one profound; history makes one free." [32] But if we ask, free for what, Dilthey leaves us without an answer. The anarchy of world vision (die Anarchie der Weltanschauungen) was the somehow tragic balance to which he admitted at the end of his life.

If the contemplation of the infinite variety of the human mind were all there is to life, Dilthey's position would be praiseworthy. Karl Mannheim, following Dilthey, sketched as the ideal of a scientific observer, that of the "free-roving intelligence." But we know that there is no such thing as the free-roving intelligence, that intelligence is always subject to the conditions of its own epoch. Dilthey's freedom of mind was the result of an age so embarrassed by historical riches that it lost its own firm grounding.

The only certainty which Dilthey thought he could establish in the pursuit of his lifelong quest was a typology of the world-views. The effort to find certain stable types, appearing and reappearing in the history of the human mind, runs through all his writings. He conceived this idea when he was only twenty-six years old, and followed it up in his *Introduction to the Human Studies*.[33] The first type of world-vision that he defined was that of Greek thought. The Greeks saw the world as a conceptual, mathematical order, which in turn reflected the cosmic order. He discovered the Romans to be a society of mutually responsible wills, linked by the ideas of liberty, law, and obligation. A third basic element was added by Christianity. Hebrew-Christian religion gave to the world a sense of salvation through communion with the living God. However, through contact with Graeco-Roman philosophy, Christianity was permeated with philosophical ideas, and from the fusion emerged new concepts: providence, creation, man's kinship with God, and, above all, the salvation of man's soul. On these concepts was based the *Weltanschauung* of the Middle Ages. The center of gravitation has shifted from the real world to the transcendental; the natural had become a symbol of the supernatural.

These three elements of European metaphysics held sway for well over one thousand years. It is not difficult to see that they correspond to the three elements into which philosophers had traditionally divided the human faculties: thinking, willing, and feeling.[34]

At the end of his life Dilthey returned again to these types of world-vision. Once more he stated that there were three basic types and he now defined them as objective idealism, the idealism of freedom, and materialism or naturalism.[35] The first of these forms is grounded in the affective life of mankind; it occupies the standpoint of life values; it searches for the meaning and sense of the world. All reality appears as the expression of something inward, of an immanent divine principle which becomes visible in the phenomena of this world. The Stoics, Spinoza, Leibniz, Goethe, and Hegel, are its greatest representatives.[36]

Such a world-vision was obviously based on the esthetic element. If, however, the volitional attitude prevails, the mind strives to prove its independence from nature. The sovereignty of the human personality takes shape. Plato, Cicero, the Christian thinkers, Kant, Fichte, and Carlyle, show the different stages of the idealism of freedom. If, finally, knowledge of reality is the fundamental motive of philosophy, the mind becomes subordinate to the physical world and materialism results. Democritus, Lucretius, Hobbes, and Comte are the champions of naturalistic thinking. Obviously, there are others in which these outlooks intermingle and in which intellectual consistency is often impaired. Each of the world-visions, Dilthey says in conclusion, has a power of attraction and a possibility of consistent development; each grasps the "ambiguous reality of life" from its own standpoint.[37]

The ambiguous reality of life seems thus the one elusive element which attracts philosophy but with which it wrestles in vain. Dilthey left the problem here. But two avenues are open to further research. The types, established by Dilthey, may be traced back to human attitudes and a psychology of world-visions may be developed. Karl Jaspers and Eduard Spranger have tried to do this. On the other hand, the sociologist may continue Dilthey's attempts in the direction of an advanced typology of human behavior.[38]

But neither typology nor psychology can hope to deal successfully with "the ambiguous reality of life." The historical consciousness lives in the comprehension of all ages and it observes in all creativity the accompanying relativity. Dilthey called this the "secret trouble" of our age that must be borne in silence, in calm surrender to the inevitable.[39]

Before we try to summarize Dilthey's manifold enterprises, a word must be said about his historical studies which, as we stated, resulted in many instances from his systematic quest. After he had traced the great themes of European metaphysics in his *Introduction to the Human Studies,* he became interested in a geneology of scientific thinking in modern Europe. He planned a second volume of his *Introduction* which would show the dissolution of the metaphysical approach to reality in the ages of the Renaissance and the Reformation. It was never written, but a great number of preparatory essays exist, which attempt to unfold the development of scientific consciousness.

In these essays, assembled today in the second volume of his collected works, Dilthey demonstrated how the Renaissance and the Reformation completed the disintegration of medieval metaphysics by affirming a new feeling of life.[40] Not only did a new science appear at the beginning of the sixteenth century, but also a new art, a new poetic outlook on life, and a radically different political theory. Modern consciousness is embodied in Luther's and Zwingli's theological doctrines as well as in Leonardo's paintings or in Machiavelli's writings. Dilthey did not follow Burckhardt's example of sketching a "man of the Renaissance"; for him the period was a kaleidoscopic picture of the most diverse personalities, figures, and types.[41] Impetuosity, a restless impulse to forge ahead, contented neither in the sensuous moment nor in a static existence, conceiving life as a form rather than a substance, sudden, spontaneous, abrupt —such was the tone of the new age.[42]

With loving care Dilthey examined those trends of humanistic thought which sought to vindicate man's moral autonomy: the philosophy of Erasmus, the "Christ within us" of Sebastian Frank. No doubt they were closer to his tolerant and unprejudiced mind than either Luther or Calvin. After the Renaissance and the Reformation had done their work, the seventeenth century set out to develop a natural interpretation of man and the world. Its triumphs were most noteworthy in the exact sciences, but gradually law, politics, and economics came under its influence. Dilthey called this system the Natural System of the Human Studies and devoted a number of related investigations to its description. A comprehensive title for this group of essays might be: How the European Mind Came of Age.[43]

This trend of thought led Dilthey quite naturally into the age of reason. He had never been hostile to the Enlightenment, but, conscious of its limitations, he turned his mind toward the German aspect of this great movement rather than toward the Anglo-French thinkers.[44] It was in German culture that the narrowness of the Enlightenment was overcome—in German philosophy, in German

poetry, and in German music. Dilthey's presentation expands to
include Bach and Händel, Klopstock and Leibniz, Frederick the
Great, and the Prussian law code. While the German *Aufklärung*
abandoned the old Christian dogmas, it preserved the essence of
Christianity, believing as it did in the progressive education of the
human race and in the moral perfectibility of the individual. It is
impossible to show within our framework either the scope of Dilthey's interest or the power of his penetration in mastering his subject. But today his fame rests less on his systematic achievements than
on these and related writings which set up the history of ideas as an
independent discipline on a level with the older, long-established
forms of historiography.[45] And perhaps there is something more
than his fame to be considered. The picture that we today have of
Dilthey is that of a man who returned from his odyssey through the
human mind "tired but not defeated." Though he declined to call
himself a Christian, he nevertheless belonged to the invisible community of men who have left sectarian loyalties behind and have
gained supreme freedom and nobility of the soul.[46] Dilthey felt a
fascination for sympathetic intuition much akin to that of Goethe
and Ranke, and it was a poet, Hugo von Hofmannsthal, who first
saluted Dilthey's desire for knowledge of all forms of human existence.

Yet it would be futile to maintain that his desire was granted him,
or that he even came near the goal he had set for himself. His work
remained fragmentary, perhaps inevitably so, since he had mapped
out a program that no human mind could hope to master. There
is some comfort in the thought that many of his enterprises were
carried on by his students and by those who wished to follow his
example—historians of the mind like Troeltsch, Litt, and Ortega y
Gasset, or psychologists like Spranger and Wach.

Dilthey's greatest achievement, the establishment of Human
Studies as a discipline independent from, but equal in goal and
method to the exact sciences, was accepted by many without the
realization of the tragic consequences it implied. From then on, the
human studies were split off from the natural sciences; the two
halves of man's cognitive effort were divorced from each other,
neither half paying great heed to the labors of the other. It was the
first time in the history of Western civilization that such a separation

had occurred. Hitherto the metaphysical approach, as Dilthey called it, had held the science together. Even the last great systems, those of Hegel, Comte, and Spencer, prided themselves on uniting the spheres of human comprehension, not on dividing them. With Dilthey the metaphysical approach had lost its validity in the Human Studies as it had for the exact sciences with Kant. Though its death was slow and more stubborn than Dilthey had anticipated, it could only be resurrected and reintroduced into historical pursuit under the guise of "empiricism" as in Arnold Toynbee's *Study of History*. The human studies had been cast adrift, and if they were to make port it would be through their own efforts. Psychology and sociology were but poor substitutes for the foundations of world-visions on which history had previously built.[47] The enjoyment of historical contemplation, the inner freedom by which consciousness breaks the last chain, could produce a new type of tolerance and wisdom such as Burckhardt and Dilthey reveal, but certainly no panacea for the great malady that had begun to afflict the scientific curiosity of Western man.

II

Dilthey had been conscious of the crisis in European culture, and he had hoped that his efforts would effect a solution in the realm of science. However, the essential ambiguity of his position constituted a stumbling block which his fellow philosophers pointed out with alacrity. The discussion of the relationship between the exact sciences and the Human Studies was most substantially advanced by the neo-Kantian school, represented by Windelband and Rickert. Their work, though highly technical, cannot be by-passed since it forms an important link between Dilthey and the men who followed him.

Windelband took issue with Dilthey's attempt to build the Human Studies on a science of psychology. No mean historian in his own right, he rejected psychology as being naturalistic to the core, choosing for himself the methodological approach.[48] He suggested that the difference between the natural and the social sciences was one of method rather than of object, and proposed the terms *nomothetic* and *idiographic* for the two branches.[49] Rickert, a student of Windelband, took the problem from here. His work is characterized by clarity and precision. He was a logician; his doctoral thesis had been devoted to problems of definition, and his logical equipment proved to be more incisive than Dilthey's.[50] His first difference with Dilthey concerned the question of nomenclature. Rickert was not satisfied with the term "Geisteswissenschaften" and submitted in its place "cultural sciences." [51] History, he said, was primarily the science of human culture. Although such arguments might be dismissed as the splitting of hairs and the squabblings of philosophers, other concepts in Rickert's work deserve our attention.

Rickert agreed with Dilthey that philosophy had so far neglected the imminent problems of historical thinking. Whereas the foundations of the natural sciences had been laid by Kepler, Galileo, Newton, and Kant, nothing similar had been done in the realm of the cultural sciences.[52] To this task Rickert devoted his life; the title of his most important book, *Cultural Sciences and Natural Sciences,* is a clear expression of his endeavor. The gist of his argument is as follows: the natural sciences take reality as their object in so far as it is determined by general laws; the cultural sciences aim at the element of uniqueness in reality.[53] Culture is opposed to nature on both logical and objective grounds.[54] Rickert was a disciple of Kant, and maintained that reality is not "given" to the human mind; it is constituted by it. From the inexhaustible variety with which we are confronted, we constitute objects by the application of scientific methods.[55] "Reality becomes nature if we consider it in regard to what is general; it becomes history if we consider it in regard to the particular or individual." [56]

The natural scientist is aware that every object he studies has the mark of individuality; no two leaves are identical, no two specimens of a mineral are the same. But this individuality is irrelevant to his pursuit, and he must ignore it, since he aims at general laws or rules. "Only that which is anonymous can be an object of natural science." [57] The situation in the cultural sciences is the reverse; here the goal is reality in its concreteness and individuality.[58]

It is obvious that Rickert rejects as strongly as did Dilthey the pretense of the natural sciences to possess a universal method valid for all reality. Such a universal method would make knowledge of the individual impossible. "The concept of a historical law is a contradiction in terms." [59] But Rickert goes a step beyond his predecessor in clarifying the concept of individuality, or perhaps we should say, uniqueness. The term had been loosely used by Herder, the romanticists, and Ranke. "I perceive," said Ranke, "spiritual substances, original creations of the human mind, I might say, thoughts of God." [60] Rickert was of a more sober disposition; he would not have admitted intuition as the source of historical knowledge. History's prime concern was with the unique event. Rickert conceded that the historian uses general concepts, but he uses them as means, not as ends. Ideas such as church, state, class, religion, art, or culture are introduced into historical descriptions only to define the individual phenomenon on which the attention of the historian is focused. [61]

Cultural life appears throughout as a meaningful, significant happening in contrast to nature, which is without meaning or purpose. [62] Cultural objects form a realm of signification; they are open to our understanding. [63] The natural sciences consider individuality only in so far as it may be brought under general laws, that is to say, as examples. History on the other hand, finds interest and value in individuality. Thus Rickert introduced the concept of value in the analysis of individuality.

We cannot here trace the genesis of this important idea. Ultimately it was derived from Kant's philosophy, but it made its appearance only in the latter part of the nineteenth century. Rickert was the first to perceive the significance of values in describing the structure of the cultural sciences. [64] All history, he says, is written by men and for men. Only those objects which possess social significance are historically essential. To phrase it differently, not every individuality is historically relevant, but only those which represent cultural values or whose activities are related to them. [65] History exists only for beings that recognize values. [66] It is the cultural value which lifts individuality from the infinite variety of reality and gives it meaning. Instead of mere otherness, we now find uniqueness. [67]

Hence, historical interest depends on a world of values. [68] Rickert links the idea of value to the concept of causality. Only what is related to certain values in a cultural context will arouse our curiosity, and only that which causes changes in such a structure is historically significant. Historical causality is, therefore, different from causality in the realm of nature; the latter does not stand in need of values. [69]

Rickert was aware that his reference to values might place in jeopardy one of the most cherished maxims of historical research, that of objectivity. But once more his dialectic talent came to his aid. Rickert asserted that values were indeed indispensable for any historical endeavor. Values determine the historian's point of view; they furnish him with principles of selectivity without which the mass of historical data would remain amorphous. But, says Rickert, there is a difference between value-relatedness and value-judgment.[70] Value-relatedness does not endanger historical objectivity, since historical interest would not even exist without it. He showed convincingly that such terms as "progress" or "retrogression" are value-concepts, and that they are used in every historical narrative.[71] (Comte's famous law of the Three Stages, for example, is not a natural law, as he wishes us to believe, but a value formula with which he measures the course of world history.) But, as we have already stated, value-relatedness must be distinguished from value-judgment. Value-judgments may indeed impair the objectivity of historical research.

In such manner did Rickert clarify a problem that had vexed historians for many years. He did not maintain, however, that the value-relatedness of historical knowledge warrants any claim to preference, in other words, historical knowledge should not be used to establish a hierarchy of values. Cultural values appear in a given historical context and must be comprehended as relative to it. They are valid only for a circle of beings who adhere to the same cultural pattern.[72] As a consequence Rickert admits that there are as many historical truths as there are civilizations.[73] Thus the problem of historical relativism, Dilthey's "secret trouble," remained; nay, we might say it was confirmed.

A man of Rickert's cast of mind was not likely to advance great innovations. He served best as a surveyor of the vast landscape of European science. The cleavage between the cultural sciences and the exact sciences that Dilthey had recognized was now acknowledged as a methodological necessity. Rickert voiced no regret about this situation. He denied that any other science could take the place of history. Neither a general sociology nor a comparative study of mankind could break this mold. Anticipating the attempts of Spengler and Toynbee, Rickert said: Universal history can only be the study of a universal individuality, that is, of mankind.[74]

Many of Rickert's German contemporaries were impressed by his achievements. Ernst Troeltsch and Friedrich Meinecke followed his ideas along diverse avenues. However, Rickert's most fruitful influence was on Max Weber.[75]

III

Weber was a colleague of Rickert at the University of Freiburg. Though only in his thirties, he had already made a name for himself in two fields: economic history for one, and agrarian policy in contemporary Germany for another. But we cannot hope to understand this extraordinary man through his scholastic achievements alone. He was one of the greatest analytical intellects in prewar Europe, but he was also a human being of demoniac force, deeply disturbed, divided in his impulses, and contradictory in his philosophy. The development of his genius has been described by Marianne Weber in one of the most moving biographies ever written by a wife about her husband. Although *Max Weber, ein Lebensbild* may not answer all the perplexities which his mind confronts us with, it will remain the foundation for all further inquiries.[76]

Max Weber was born in Erfurt in 1864. His father came from a well-to-do family of textile manufacturers in the Ruhr Valley, the same solid stock that produced Friedrich Engels. Weber's mother was from Heidelberg. She had the blood of French Huguenots in her veins and throughout her life preserved a deeply religious faith. Those close to her called her a saint.[77] Both parents exerted a strong influence on Weber; only after a long and bitter struggle did the example of the mother prevail.

Weber senior moved to Berlin in 1869, where he made a political career. He was a member of the Prussian Landtag, the German Reichstag, and municipal counselor of Berlin. His party affiliation was with the National Liberals, and the notables of this creed filled his house: Bennigsen, Mommsen, Dilthey, and many lesser lights. His wife had to care for a large circle of friends and relatives, as well as for a growing family. She bore her husband six children, of whom four survived.

Max Weber was born and reared in the German upper middle class. Financial worries never touched his childhood, but psychological conflicts did. His father was an easygoing bourgeois, amiable, selfish, and contented with the material success he had achieved. His wife, overburdened with the cares of her household, tried desperately to keep her religious convictions alive. Gradually the two drifted apart. Max was the eldest son and probably aware of growing tensions. Many years later he wrote about his father: "We all do him justice now . . . we rejoice in what he was . . . we understand his uncommon firm and pure bourgeois sense, we know that the break in his life was the tragedy of his whole generation. . . . His generation had lost the old belief in authority and yet it thought along authoritarian lines in matters in which we have lost faith." [78] So much objectivity, however, was gained only after his mother's influence had asserted itself over the self-complacency of the bourgeois father.

As a child Max was retiring, and his mother never ceased to complain that she could not reach him. He was sickly and precocious, and at least one grave illness is recorded. His only outlet was in reading, and this he did on an astounding scale. "I am not enamoured," he wrote at fifteen, "I don't write poetry; what else shall I do but read, and this I do thoroughly." [79] He read Machiavelli, Cicero, Walter Scott, Homer, and Ossian. Though the school routine meant little to him, he received from the Gymnasium a command of Greek and Latin and a reading knowledge of Hebrew. Intellectual obstacles did not exist for him, but there was something precipitate and unhealthy in this growth. He himself confessed: "Intellectually I matured early, in every other respect however, very late." [80]

It would have been surprising if this young mind, so keenly bent on intellectual improvement, had found spiritual comfort in traditional religion. Weber, who single-handedly established the sociology of religion, said that he was "tone-deaf" when it came to matters of faith. He received the instructions that preceded Confirmation with a detachment bordering on indifference.[81] His mother tried in vain to impress on him the momentous nature of the ceremony. Weber remained aloof. When the day of his confirmation came, the minister chose for Weber a motto that well expressed the law of his future life: "The Lord is the spirit, but where the Lord's spirit is, there is freedom." [82]

Weber's years in the Gymnasium were followed by two more in

Heidelberg, where he studied law as his main subject, with history, economics, and philosophy on the side. His teachers were Knies, to whom he later devoted a long essay, Kuno Fischer, and Immanuel Bekker. But there was also a good deal of free spending, drinking, and card playing. He joined the fraternity to which his father had once belonged and indulged with relish in their fencing practices. (To his last days he thought of duels as a proper method to resolve points of honor between men.) The results of the Heidelberg years were not altogether promising. When he returned to Berlin his mother hardly recognized the "scarred boozer" and greeted him with a slap in the face.[83]

In 1883 he served a year in the army at Strassburg. His letters describe vividly the perpetual boredom of the drill, but the service left its mark on him. He could not help admiring the power of the military machine. It was his first encounter with the Leviathan forces of the modern state, and it did nothing to dim the ardent nationalism of the twenty-year-old Weber.[84]

However, there were other influences in Strassburg. His mother's sister, Ida, was married to the historian, Herman Baumgarten, one of the few liberals who had kept faith with the ideas of 1848. Weber's aunt was an ardently religious woman and she opened to Weber the world of protestant faith. She introduced him to Channing's writings. "It was the first time that something religious had for me more than an objective interest." [85] It was probably Channing's idea of the autonomous moral personality that attracted Weber. On the other hand, Channing's radical pacifism seemed to him a mistake in judgment which he rejected passionately.[86]

Still another emotional influence came to him from the Baumgarten family. His cousin, Emmy Baumgarten, impressed him deeply. She was a lovely girl of eighteen, with the face of a German madonna, extremely sensitive, frail, and with a marked tendency to melancholic depressions. Letters and occasional visits kept this "amitié amoureuse" alive long after Weber's departure from Strassburg. The two families watched the sympathy between Max and Emmy with apprehension. The young people were closely related and there had been hereditary strains of mental affliction in the family. For ten years Weber felt committed to this young woman. When he finally married Marianne, he wrote to Emmy: "I have always . . . compared women and girls whom I met with the essence of your being. It was a kind fate for my gross nature that I felt intimately obliged to see the other sex through your eyes." [87]

Weber returned to Berlin in 1884 to complete his study of law. Among the teachers he most admired was Rudolf von Gneist whose idea of the Rechtsstaat was a guidepost for many liberals of the period. He also attended Treitschke's lectures with a feeling between admiration and revulsion. "I find (Gneist's) . . . lectures true masterpieces; really I have marvelled at his manner of directly entering questions of politics and at the way he develops strictly liberal views without become a propagandist, as Treitschke does in his lectures." [88] Thus Weber touches for the first time on one of the great issues of his life: how could science as a vocation and politics as a vocation be reconciled? Both fascinated him; for both he believed he was well equipped. He rejected the confusion of science and politics which the passionate Treitschke paraded in his classroom and which swayed many a student toward anti-Semitism, militarism, and the idolatry of power.

Weber wrote his thesis on the history of trading companies in the Middle Ages, picking up a reading knowledge of Italian and Spanish in the process.[89] Academic tradition demanded that he defend the thesis against the older members of the faculty. Theodor Mommsen took issue with him on one of the finer points. But when the debate was over Mommsen paid Weber a handsome compliment: "If my time comes to die, there is no one to whom I would rather say 'Son, the spear has become too heavy for my hand; go and carry it from now on,' than to my highly esteemed Max Weber." [90] Two years after receiving his doctorate, Weber became Privatdozent for German and Roman Law at the University of Berlin. The book which accredited him to the faculty on this occasion is entitled *Roman Agragrian History in Its Significance for Constitutional and Civil Law*.[91] Mommsen had been right to acclaim Weber as his heir; Weber followed Mommsen's example as a historian and as a politician. Mommsen, like Niebuhr before him, had shown profound interest in Roman social history, and had explained the rise of the republic as the history of a peasant people who came to conquer the world. Weber delved even deeper into the economic history of Rome. The transformation from Republic to

Empire he traced back to changes in agrarian property.[92] And just as Mommsen's *History of Rome* had been quickened by a political passion for the problems of his own time, so was Weber's agrarian history accompanied by a concern for the agrarian situation in his native Germany.

According to his conviction that science and politics should not be confused, Weber carried his investigations on two separate ledgers. That he would find his way into politics was preordained. Discussion of political problems was the daily fare at the family table. His mother's life was nurtured by a loving concern for her fellow men; but what was charity in her became reasoned argument in the son.

At the early age of six Weber had witnessed the creation of the second German Empire. Thus the nation-state became the frame of reference for his political thinking, never to be relinquished, rarely to be discussed. "Real-politik" was likewise accepted as a matter of course. "We are a power state." [93] His later studies were to dissect the techniques of power, but the phenomenon as such was taken for granted. On the other hand Weber did not close his eyes to the fact that the generation of liberals to which his father belonged had been cheated out of their finest expectations by the architect of the German power state, Bismarck. Weber realized how the chancellor had destroyed every independent-minded politician, how he had treated domestic issues as if they were problems of international politics, in other words, simply from the point of view of naked power. Catholics, socialists, liberals, and conservatives were but so many pawns that his Caesarian mind moved at will.

The majority of Germans bore Bismarck's constitutional dictatorship complacently and rejoiced in the prestige and the material prosperity that had fallen upon them. However, there was a group of men who were well aware of the necessity of advancing German social legislation and of integrating the working classes into the body politic.[94] Many of them occupied academic positions of distinction, like Schmoller, Brentano, Knapp, and Gneist. Their opponents mockingly called them socialists of the chair. In 1873 they founded the Verein für Sozial-politik (the association for social politics). In the 1880's the social and economic problems of Germany once more became acute. Bismarck had abandoned the free trade policy for protective tariffs. In order to suppress the social-democratic agitation, he made the Reichstag pass the anti-socialist laws, which remained on the books for twelve years. In the meantime he attempted to cure the evils of industrialism by introducing measures of social security on a scale quite novel for Europe.

It was during this period that Weber joined the association. Very soon he was given a special assignment: to study the situation of rural labor in Eastern Germany. In 1890 he presented his findings to the society. The problem was indeed a formidable one; it may be called the greatest in Germany's social history since it involved the economic foundations of the Junker class. For the first time there appears in Weber's writings the trenchant style so characteristic of his later treatises. "I shall consider the problem of rural labor exclusively from the point of view of the "raison d'état" and am not interested in the question whether they (the laborers) are well off or not, or how the proprietors can obtain cheap labor." [95]

Weber did not invoke an idea of social justice, nor did he wish to condemn the Prussian aristocracy on other grounds than those of power. What he did assert was that the Junker class, hard pressed by the capitalistic gains of the rising bourgeoisie, had been forced to become entrepreneurs themselves. After the liberation of the serfs in 1807, they had constantly expanded their estates at the expense of the independent peasants. As a result, large portions of the rural population had abandoned the soil, taking refuge either in urban areas or emigrating overseas. Their place had been taken by migratory workers from Poland and Russia, seasonal workers who were not allowed to settle in Germany. Nevertheless, every year small groups remained behind who endangered the national cohesion of Germany. Their standard of living and culture was far below that of Germany, and they had no loyalty for her.

In conclusion Weber suggested: the closing of the eastern frontier to migratory labor, a resettling of a sturdy peasantry with small holdings, and systematic recolonization. He stated bluntly that the economic interest of the Junker class in cheap foreign labor ran counter to the national interest and had to be sacrificed for higher considerations. "We do not engage in social politics in order to create a world of happy men . . . we wish to transform, in so far as it is in our power, the external conditions of life, not to make men more content, but to salvage from under the burden of the inevitable struggle for existence whatever in them is worthwhile, that is, those spiritual and physical qualities which should be conserved for the national good." [96]

Weber's work on the situation of rural labor was of consequence in many ways. The student of law had acquired a first-hand knowledge of economic conditions in contemporary society. At the same time he had come to realize that economic conditions do not operate in a cultural vacuum. "There are ideals at work in the economy, the power of which is more forceful than the questions of fork and knife." [97] From the recognition of such ideals it was only a step for him to become sensitive to the religious motivation of economic activities. [98]

Beyond the intellectual gains which his work afforded loomed an even larger human problem. Should Weber remain in the "quiet isolation" of his scholastic pursuits, or should he devote his energies to the political struggle? The fight for political freedom fascinated him as much as did the discovery of uncharted lands in the realm of science. "I feel a most extraordinary longing to do something practical." [99] He even took steps to secure a position in the municipal administration of Bremen which fortunately led nowhere. It was at this time that he was drawn into the circle of Friederich Naumann, promoter of a type of social Christianity which would be reconciled with the ideals of the nation state. [100] Once more Weber sounded the same note. "After all I am not a typical scholar." It is hard to say what tipped the scales in favor of an academic career. Perhaps it was his marriage to Marianne.

In spite of his success as a scholar-politician, Weber had been the victim of a gnawing depression. "I was," he wrote, "during the last years, which I remember with horror, plunged into a resignation which was not free from bitterness." He went about his professional duties like an automaton. Fighting fire with fire, he attempted to assuage his constant torment by working around the clock, never giving his mind or his nerves the slightest rest. [101] The crisis which broke his life in two might have come earlier, had he not found a human being who repaid his violent passion with an unflinching devotion.

Marianne was Weber's cousin on his father's side. She had spent a sad and joyless childhood in the care of foster parents. She was twenty-one when she was invited to visit her relatives in Berlin. Here she fell immediately under the spell of Weber's mother, but soon afterward Max began to intrigue her. The story of their engagement reads like an Ibsen drama.

Marianne heard rumors of Max's understanding with another cousin, the frail and enigmatic Emmy. At the same time a friend of Max's began to court Marianne, and Max's mother favored this prospective marriage. Did she still expect Max to marry Emmy, or was she unwilling to lose her first-born to Marianne? There is no answer to these questions. Weber himself felt the need to see Emmy, whom he had not visited for five years, once more. At his return he proposed to Marianne in a letter full of self-doubts and inner torment. "You don't know me . . . you don't see how I struggle . . . to tame these elemental passions which nature has put into me." [102] He continues to accuse himself, saying that as far as morals were concerned he had been his mother's problem child. And finally: "I have a twofold guilt to pay to the past." In spite of all he will go the road he must go.

Marianne was not discouraged, and after two months their engagement was announced. Weber was "a strange and pensive bridegroom" who only slowly overcame the idea that he could never be close to a feminine being. Even after his marriage he did not relax. He taught an average of nineteen hours a week, and constantly took on new assignments. In 1896 he accepted the chair for "national economy" at the University of Freiburg. The change from Berlin to the small town in the heart of the Black Forest relieved Weber somehow and, one would think, at least delayed the approaching disaster. He found many interesting colleagues at Freiburg. Besides Rickert, there were the psychologist Münsterberg and the economist Schulze Gävernitz. There was leisure for walks, for informal discussions with his students, and there was now, too, the additional advantage of his economic independence. As a politician, he maintained his alliance with Naumann.

In a public address on "Nation-State and Economic Policy," he expressed again his belief in the power state. His words had a pessimistic, one could almost say, a menacing ring. "We do not strive for man's future well-being; we are eager to breed in him those traits with which we link the feeling that they constitute what is humanly great and noble in his nature. . . . In the last analysis, the processes of economic development are struggles for power. Our ultimate yardstick is the *raison d'état*." [103] This sounded like the voice of an imperialist who did not shy away from the sinister implications of social Darwinism. But Weber also warned of the dangers that were threatening the very existence of the nation-state. His target was again the Junker class. "It is dangerous . . . if an economically sinking class holds political power in its hands . . . it is still more dangerous if those classes . . . are politically immature in their leadership of the state." The allusion to the Kaiser could not be misunderstood.[104]

In spite of his being known as an enemy of the ruling class, Weber was offered the chair for economics at the University of Heidelberg. Here the circle of his friends was even larger, and included the theologian, Ernst Troeltsch, the philosopher Hensel, and the jurist Jellinek. Everything augured a glorious future. But in the spring of 1897 Weber fell prey to a deep depression which ended in complete collapse. He suffered from insomnia, exhaustion, and anxiety. When he looked at his lecture notes, his eyes failed to focus; functional disturbances appeared; sometimes he lost control of himself and wept or fell into fits of rage.

Medical science knew very little about psychic afflictions at the time. All that the doctors could prescribe were cold water cures and a change of scene. Weber traveled, but to no avail. His family thought he should try "to pull himself together," but his illness was not to be cured by good advice. Most of the time he just sat and stared out the window. He had no hobbies to turn to; when Marianne tried to interest him in sculpturing, he copied in clay the dying lion of Lucerne.[105] He was obliged to interrupt and finally to cancel his lectures. An offer to tender his resignation was not accepted by the authorities, and he was instead granted a year's leave of absence. But after more travel and more therapy, he realized that he would not be able to return to his duties. He was an eagle whose wings had been broken. The government of Baden, under whose jurisdiction the university was, suggested a generous solution. Weber was appointed "Honorar Professor," best translated as research associate, without teaching obligations.

The reason for Weber's breakdown has puzzled many observers.

Shortly before his collapse he had a violent altercation with his father. It concerned Weber's mother, whose right to inner freedom the son upheld. The elder Weber died soon afterward from an internal hemorrhage, and the memory of this occurrence deeply troubled Weber, who was already given to feelings of guilt. It has been argued that a strong Oedipus situation existed.[106] But this does not seem to be a convincing explanation. His devotion to his mother cannot be questioned, but it became clear to Weber only as he matured. Even in his most intimate letters we find a restraint that bespeaks admiration rather than love.[107] As Weber grew older he came to appreciate his mother's life, encumbered as it had been by external difficulties, but harmonious within. His own marriage to Marianne, he confessed, would never have been so happy without the mother's example.[108] But these are measured words, the appreciative words of a good son, and one has only to compare them with, for instance, the letters of Baudelaire to his mother, to realize that an Oedipus situation hardly existed.

Of course, there are other explanations: a hereditary disposition toward mental disorder, constant overwork to the point of abuse. But these do not seem conclusive either, because overwork was for Weber a means of silencing the dark voices within. He actually wanted to feel "crushed under the load of work." [109] We are left with the riddle. Marianne either could not or would not answer this question. Weber himself alluded only once to the cause. In his later years he wrote to a younger friend who had accused himself of a moral guilt: "Believe me, there are good reasons why I do not berate someone who knows what guilt is . . . I have burdened myself with a *maximum* of outrage—certainly not without deep and lasting aftereffect." [110] But what this outrage was, we are not told.

That he was able to overcome the crisis was partly the work of Marianne who felt that the chained Prometheus needed her more than ever and who found her own happiness in serving him.[111] In the last analysis, however, it was Weber's own victory. In the letter in which he speaks of his guilt, he adds: "Moral rupture—that can never heal—exists only for very weak people. What has been, has been. . . . Guilt may or may not become a source of strength depending on how one copes with it. It would be bad if only the *integer vitae* allowed us to become a whole man. . . . In this case, I, at least, would have to renounce my claim to being a whole man." [112] He bore his fate with stoic strength. "Such a disease has its compensations. It has opened to me the human side of life . . . and this to an extent previously unknown to me. I could say with John Gabriel Borkman that an icy hand has let me loose." [113] Still, in July of 1908, he wrote to Karl Vossler: "Misery teaches prayer—always? According to my own personal experience, I should like to dispute this statement. Of course, I agree with you that it holds frequently, all too frequently for man's dignity." [114]

Weber was no weakling, and after four years of apparently hope-less struggle he found a way to wrest a few hours of work from his precarious condition. His sleep remained uneasy, and the idea of being without sleeping pills could bring on a nervous crisis. Depres-sions continued to occur, but their severity gradually abated. Trips to Holland, Italy, and the United States prevented that excess of work in which he had indulged in his earlier years. To everyone's surprise he bore the fatigue of prolonged travel quite well, as though his nervous system fed on new impressions and constant tension.

His most painful decision had certainly been to give up teaching, to forego the response of eager youth, and to lay aside his guidance of students. But in his enforced retirement, Weber did not lack either friendship or stimulus. The relationship with Troeltsch, who shared a house with the Webers, blossomed into a most fruitful cooperation. And many others came to get his counsel. In 1903 he joined Sombart and Jaffé as editor of a new journal, the *Archiv für Sozialwissenschaften und Sozialpolitik*. The main purpose of the new publication was the "historical and theoretical analysis of the cultural significance of capitalism." It was Weber's own scholastic goal. Most of his writings were first published in the *Archiv*.[115]

The *Archiv* could also serve him as a substitute for political ac-tivity; obviously a man in his condition could not hope to play a political role. Politics, he said later, was a "strong and patient drill-ing of hard boards," and he would fly off the handle at the slightest provocation. But he never conquered his desire to return to politics. He grew increasingly concerned with the amateur who occupied the imperial throne and who was squandering Germany's inheritance in boastful blunder. When Weber was invited to return to academic teaching at the University of Munich he wrote that he would be needed more in Berlin to counterbalance the lack of integrity there (Gesinnungslosigkeit). [116] But nothing came of it and he was obliged to be contented with making his voice heard at conventions or in newspaper articles.

However, it was not a bad life altogether. The Webers were able to purchase the house in which his mother had spent her girlhood, and it soon became an intellectual center. Southwest Germany, especially Heidelberg, had a cultural life of its own. Among the many visitors to call on Weber were Karl Jaspers and Gundolf, Robert Michels and Vossler. Even Stefan George agreed to visit Weber, though their meeting revealed only that two powerful minds were worlds apart.[117] When Weber grew restless, there were always the south of France or Italy where he might take refuge, but these were but temporary escapes from the prison of his fanatic quest. He rejected the pursuit of happiness as adamantly as any Puritan. Sensual enjoyment should never be an end in itself. Thus he would return from Mediterranean soil grateful but still deeply conscious of his Nordic mission and his Kantian duty.[118]

Weber produced the bulk of his work in the years from 1903 to 1914. It seems incredible that a man who could not give an academic lecture or enter a public debate without a *crise de nerfs* could have accomplished so much. But Proust and Darwin provide similar examples. Weber worked in spurts of frantic concentration, preceded by long periods of gestation. Who can say which of his ideas did not ripen during his illness? The chemistry of genius is still open to exploration. In any case, the main part of his work was completed by 1914.

At first glance Weber's intellectual output shows a bewildering variety and range. While still in a state of recuperation (1902), he plunged into the methodology of the social sciences. He relinquished these studies to investigate the religious origins of modern capitalism. From there he expanded his research into the social and economic premises of the world religions. He became immersed in Buddhism, Confucianism, and Judaism. But all of these studies were intended as a backdrop for the understanding of Western capitalism, and Western capitalism was, in turn, only a part of our Western culture. To understand it was his main endeavor.

According to Weber, by far the most important characteristic of

Western civilization is its tendency to an ever-increasing rationalism. He traced this rational element even in Western music. At the end he undertook to write a general treatise on sociology in which once more the progressive disenchantment of the world was the keynote. Most of this work came out in the *Archiv,* some remained unpublished, even unedited. Yet there is an Ariadne thread to lead us through the labyrinth. Weber worked all his life on three different intellectual levels: the methodological, the historico-sociological, and the systematic, but the wellspring of all his efforts was the desire to comprehend the impulses that moved our Western civilization.[119]

Chronologically as well as logically we must begin with Weber's studies in the logic of science.[120] His motive for entering the debate on the future of the sciences was prompted by his wish to explain to himself and to others what science could and what it could not do. He continued from where Dilthey and Rickert had left off, and accepted the division of human knowledge into two classes: the natural and the cultural sciences. He rejected the hope of the positivist school that the two halves could be reconciled by a universal method, and that, in the process, order and happiness would be advanced. The crisis of the sciences was a reality, revealing in turn an underlying crisis in culture.[121] What distinguishes Max Weber's studies from those of Rickert and Dilthey is the fact that here a master of law and economics reflected on the principles of his own research. His essays are replete with concrete examples flowing easily from the reservoir of his universal erudition.[122]

In opposition to the classical school of economics, Weber insisted that the social sciences belong in the category of the human studies. They do not aim at a system of general concepts but at an understanding of individual phenomena and relations. These relations we are able to understand (in the Diltheyian sense of the word). But Weber was not satisfied with the vague notion of intuition. All understanding must be controlled as far as possible; it must be intelligible explanation. No evasion of the responsibility of scientific judgment can be tolerated. The individual phenomenon must be explained by "causal imputation." [123] In other words, Weber maintained, contrary to Dilthey, that the cultural sciences share one important concept with the natural sciences, that of causal explanation. The cultural sciences, too, use empirical rules and general causes.

There is a common ground on which all cognitive efforts meet: the natural sciences explain and comprehend; the cultural sciences explain and understand.[124]

These words were not meant to obscure the differences between the cultural and the natural sciences; the empirical rules of the Human Studies are not laws like those formulated by the exact sciences. They are kulturwissenschaftliche Allgemeinbegriffe, or ideal types. (Weber took the term from his friend, Jellinek. He scorned the scholars who handled scientific terminology as though it had the personal qualities of a toothbrush.) [125] Every social scientist uses general concepts, such as *homo economicus,* capitalism, church, sect, Christianity, and so forth. The ideal type is not a representation of reality, but it makes a representation possible. It is not a hypothesis, but it points in a direction where hypotheses may be fruitful. Ideal types are not aims of knowledge, like the laws of exact sciences, but are a means of knowledge. Since the perpetual flow of cultural life leads constantly to new problems, new ideal types must and will be conceived to correct the old ones. Historical knowledge remains in flux. A "closed system" like that of positivism can never do justice to the evolution of mankind.[126]

These were highly significant contributions to the logic of science. But they would hardly deserve a place in the intellectual history of Europe, were it not that they lead up to an even more important problem: what role does science play in our lives, in the decisions we make, in the actions demanded of us from day to day? Can science tell us not only what to think but how to act? [127] Weber, a Kantian of sorts, admitted that our knowledge covers only small segments of reality. The historian, the economist, the sociologist, focus on problems in which they are interested. By relating data to values we constitute the subject matter of human studies. Such value-relatedness (Weber's argument closely follows Rickert's) adds an element of subjectivity to our studies, but it does not preclude valid results.

The problem that preoccupied Weber over many years, however, went beyond the realm of logic. Over and over he asked: how does value-relatedness differ from value-judgment? For Rickert this had been a logical problem; for Weber it assumes ethical overtones. Under value-judgments Weber understood: "practical evaluations of the unsatisfactory or satisfactory character of phenomena subject to our influence." [128] Obviously the accent is on "subject to our influence." Weber held that, of all types of prophecy, the professorial type was the most obnoxious. [129] Science and personal evaluation were two radically different attitudes. He does not even condone a "statesman-like compromise" where opposed evaluations are weighed against each other and scientific objectivity results from mixing black and white into a muddled gray. [130] His own solution may be called scientific asceticism: the rigorous separation of science which rests on evidence, and values which are adhered to but cannot be proved. It was a complete dualism, a dichotomy of being and obligation, and he held it to be the only intellectually honest position. There was in Weber's aversion to prophets and visionaries a certain savagery, as though he tried to convince himself that he had to live without the easy comfort furnished by illusions. I will see how much I can endure, he is known to have said. His famous pun: "Wer Schau will, soll ins Lichtspiel gehen" ("He who seeks vision may look for it in the movies") is but one of many such observations. Science, he insisted, does not point the way to the absolute or to personal happiness. Science is a technique. [131]

"All serious reflection about the ultimate elements of meaningful human conduct is oriented primarily in terms of the categories 'end and means.' Whether certain means are appropriate to obtain certain ends is a question accessible to scientific analysis. Likewise the consequences of the eventual attainment of the proposed end might be scientifically discussed. Thus we can answer the question: what will the attainment of a desired end 'cost' in terms of the predictable loss of other values?" [132]

But so much restraint made science the handmaiden of every possible attitude. Weber agreed with the elder Mill that a purely empirical consideration of the world would make polytheism the only acceptable metaphysics. He called himself a polytheist: "Over the gods and their battles rules fate, not science." [133] All that science can do is to clarify our choice; the choice itself is made by an act of preference to the values in which we believe. The various attitudes that human beings have toward life are incompatible and irreconcilable.

The full significance of Weber's appraisal of science must be understood in the light of his conviction that rationalization, intellectualization, and the disenchantment of the world were the signs of the times. "To the person who cannot bear the fate of the times like a man" there is left the alternative of sacrificing the intellect to the old churches, he said.[134] As for him, his mind was made up. To devote his life to science was an inescapable condition of the historical situation. "We cannot evade it as long as we remain true to ourselves." To live without illusions, to think cynically and to act ethically, that was Weber's lot "in a polar night of icy darkness." [135] One of his critics has observed the close correspondence to Machiavelli in this idea of the separation of science and life; the same kind of intellectual honesty is there, the same dry and often cruel approach to reality.[136]

Weber refused to admit that his attitude should be labeled relativism, but relativism it was, since no certainty could be given as to any scale of values. Obviously Weber was not indifferent to human values; he lived for the conviction that only ideals and duty give meaning and dignity to human existence.[137] But these ideals had to be accepted on faith, faith which was not a surrender to dogmas and institutions but a personal commitment. When he was asked whether his indictment of all unknowledgeable knowledge applied to philosophy, he answered with a cutting, "I don't know anything about it" ("Davon verstehe ich nichts").[138] That one of the greatest scientists of the age could make this remark characterizes him as much as it does the age.

Intellectually honest though Weber's position was, it was absurd. It implied the compartmentalization of life into science as a vocation and politics as another vocation. Nor was this ultimately true for Weber himself, because he felt a deep concern for the enigmas of life to which the great religions had given their own peculiar answer. It is perhaps the greatest paradox of his life that he turned from logical analysis to the sociology of religion.

"I am," said Weber, "a-musical as far as religion is concerned, and have neither the desire nor the capacity to build religious architectures in myself. But after a careful scrutiny, I may say that I am neither anti- nor a-religious." [139] The immediate impetus for his work on the sociology of religion came from his reading of a statistic which stated that the Protestants of Germany had a much larger

share in capitalistic enterprises than the Catholics. It took the eye
of genius to pick up this clue. From an interesting tidbit of information it grew into one of the longest undertakings in comparative
history. (One is reminded of Thomas Mann's observation that his
great novels, such as *The Magic Mountain*, evolved from short story
themes.) Weber's curiosity, once aroused, was further stimulated by
his visit to the United States, and he witnessed for himself America's
tremendous intensity in work and production. His visits to colleges
and universities showed him that the Protestant spirit was much
stronger in the communal life of this country than Weber had found
it to be in Germany.[140]

All these impressions fertilized a series of thoughts which can be
traced back to his earlier studies on rural labor in Germany. Even
then he had noted that ideas like liberty may triumph over economic
considerations. The whole problem led Weber logically to a critical
examination of the Marxian thesis that ideas play a role in history
only when they are used to justify economic interest. Weber saw in
Marx's economic interpretation of history a new and generative
principle, but he refused to believe that a monocausal explanation
was admissible. All spheres of cultural development, the political,
the economic, the religious, were interrelated. It was impossible to
make one the common denominator for all historical life.[141]

Weber's concept of the relationship between ideas and interests
differs from that of Marx in important points. Weber saw that under
certain circumstances "an elective affinity" between ideas and interests may develop. In the interrelationship of capitalism and Calvinism he thought he had found such an affinity.[142] But it would be a
mistake to speak of *The Spirit of Capitalism and Protestant Ethics*
simply as a case study. There was also an affinity between Puritan
ethics and Weber's own intellectual asceticism. No one can read
this study without sensing how deeply Weber himself had been
moved by "the course of human destinies which surged upon
his own heart." [143] His essay ranks in boldness and originality with
Burckhardt's *Renaissance*, Ranke's *Great Powers*, Tocqueville's *Ancien régime*, or Pirenne's *Mohammed and Charlemagne*. "It posed
a problem where once was universal agreement or a void." [144]

What, asked Weber, distinguishes Western capitalism from other
forms of economic activity? Greed, the lust for acquisition, and

avarice have always existed. Adventure capitalism, speculative capitalism, booty and colonial capitalism, can be found in every economy based on money. The idea that economic activities must be considered a moral duty is something new and typically occidental. It was brought forth by the European bourgeoisie, especially in the countries under Calvinist influence, that is, Holland, Great Britain, and the United States. It must be stated that the adaptability of Calvinist sects to business activities had been noted before, but Weber added a plausible explanation. He found it in the religious discipline derived from the basic beliefs, which he called inner-worldly asceticism. Weber, and later Troeltsch, insisted that the break between the Middle Ages and modern times had not been a radical one. From the other-wordly practices of monks and nuns, the Calvinists turned to an inner-worldly asceticism, a methodical discipline of everyday life, wherein they hoped to find confirmation of their state of grace. The central problem that loomed behind their inner-worldly asceticism was that of predestination, the will of the *deus absconditus,* the mysterious sovereign of the universe who, for reasons that the human mind cannot fathom, had chosen some and condemned others. Weber showed how the adherence to this belief had produced a psychological pattern in which incessant work was considered the panacea for the terrible uncertainty under which man lived. There is no need to follow Weber through his argument; the "thesis" is too well known and has produced a storm of controversy.[145] Some of the criticism leveled against Weber was rooted in misunderstandings. He had never tried to describe the origins of capitalism, nor did he wish to embark on a history of Calvinistic capitalism. All that he had hoped to demonstrate was that the dogma of predestination produced in the Puritan believer a behavior pattern conducive to economic work and gain. There are obvious gaps in Weber's argument and there are important omissions; even so, the essence of his thesis remains valid.

The impact of Weber's study was instantaneous, but few realized that it was but the prelude to a much greater enterprise: the social psychology of world religions. By world religions, says Weber, we understand the five religions . . . which have been known to gather multitudes of confessors around them . . . the Confucian, Hindu, Buddhist, Christian, and Islamic religious ethics.[146] To these Weber added Judaism because of its importance for Christianity and Islam. His goal was to lay bare the economic ethics in each. He did not look for ethical theories in the great religions of the world; rather was he interested in those practical impulses which may be found in the psychological context of a great faith.

Before we go further we must once more ask: why did Weber embark on an enterprise of such magnitude? At one point he called his studies a contribution to a "sociology of rationalism." In the introduction to his work he posed the questions: why does science exist only in the Occident; why do we find systematic thought only in the West; why was a rational doctrine of law known only to Roman and Canon law? The same spirit of rationalism, he insists, can be found in Gothic architecture, in European music, and in the linear perspective on which all painting since the Renaissance depended. More important still—the trained civil servant, this pillar of the modern state, exists only in the West. The state itself as an institution with a rational constitution, rationally ordained law, and an administration bound to rational rules, is known only to the Occident. And, of course, the same holds true of modern capitalism.[147]

It should be apparent that Weber wrote his treatise on the economic ethics of the world's religions in order to prove that only in the West was this powerful rationalistic spirit developed. Weber's comparative sociology may be called a negative experiment.[148] He used the criterion of rationalism to develop the structure of the non-European civilizations to ascertain why it did not come to fruition in them. Taking economic ethics as his focal point, he traces their consequences through the class systems, the legal orders, the art forms, the educational setup, and so on. These studies are not strictly historical, but they represent an important step in the comparative study of civilizations. Spengler's *Decline of the West,* which corresponds to a new global awareness of the historical consciousness, parallels Weber's approach.[149] *The Decline of the West* was published five years after Weber had outlined his program. It is interesting to note that the two men met and at least respected each other.[150]

An evaluation of Weber's sociology of religion would be out of place in our studies, but his method may be explained by token examples. Confucianism, for instance, is defined as the ethics of a bureaucratic class, the literati. Here the rationalistic ethics of self-control were applied, but the lives of this class, the literati, were separated from those of the peasant class. The followers of Confucianism tended to prolong their own rule by opposing any reform and by making tradition the regulating value in social life. These mandarin ethics have retarded China's development and have prevented her from taking up economic activities similar to those of the West.[151] In India the caste system made modern capitalism all but impossible. Early Hinduism was supported by a hereditary caste of cultured literati. They formed a stable center of religious orientation for the stratification of society. Islam was a religion of conquering warriors, a knightly order of disciplined crusaders, in contrast with Christianity which began its course as a doctrine of itinerant journeymen. It was a specifically urban and civic religion. The cities of the Occident have been the major theater of Christianity. Of course, such abbreviations cannot convey the wealth of thought and information contained in these volumes of Weber's. It is unfortunate that most of it is clothed in an indigestible prose, overloaded with sociological terminology and complex sentence structure.

Aside from these literary objections, there remain some basic doubts about the aims of Weber's inquiry. He had wished to demonstrate why an economic mentality (Wirtschaftsgesinnung) which made modern capitalism feasible had appeared only in the West.[152] But throughout the entire work the problem seems to be not so much how economic ethics determine the social order, but rather how this order has influenced economic ethics.[153] Take, for instance, the statement that Christianity was an urban movement. Is it more than a half-truth? The personalities of its founder and its apostles do not reveal urban traits. In the times of its expansion through the ancient world, urban centers were indeed of importance. But the Christianization of Ireland, England, Germany, and Hungary did not spread out from cities, nor were there any urban centers where the faith might be propagated. In the long period from the seventh to the twelfth centuries, monasteries like Monte Cassino, Fulda, Reichenau, and Cluny were as important as any of the cities then in existence. What could Weber hope to gain from an obvious misstatement of the historical circumstances? It reveals a tendency to reduce historical variety to sociological formulae. He was conscious that his problem was one of universal history, but his studies present types of civilization rather than evolutionary movements.[154]

We have seen that Weber advanced by slow stages from the study of law and economics to sociology. For many years he even avoided the use of the term "sociology." But toward the end of his career he felt the need to examine his tools once more, and the result was a systematical treatise entilted *Wirtschaft und Gesellschaft (Economics and Society)*.[155] It is a laborious book, difficult to read and difficult to place. Its first part is given over to the fundamental concepts of sociology, the second deals with the categories of economic action, and its final chapters are devoted to the categories that comprehend political action in the broadest sense. It is only in this part that Weber's gifts as a political anatomist are shown.

It has been said that Weber made an attempt to round out Marx's economic materialism by political and military materialism.[156] To us it seems that he propounded a sociology of power, or better, *his* sociology of power. This concept is embedded in his philosophy of history and cannot be understood by itself alone. We are already familiar with his idea that rationalization is the fate of the Occident. In his sociology of power he tries to show how this rationalization is implemented through the rise and fall of institutions, parties, classes, and rulers. The state is for Weber "the human community that successfully claims the monopoly of the legitimate use of physical force within a given territory."

The legitimate use of violence has found three types of justification: the traditional, the patrimonial prince of yore; the legal, domination by a bureaucracy; and finally, the charismatic, the authority of the extraordinary leader.[157] The most interesting of these types is to be found in Weber's idea of charismatic leadership, a term he borrowed from R. Sohm, which describes the leader who appears in times of psychic, physical, economic, or political stress.[158] This leader is neither an officeholder nor the incumbent of an occupation; he rules by special gifts which are accorded to only the few. Charismatic leadership may run the gamut from war lord to poet, from prophet to pirate.

Clearly, these charismatic influences puncture the social fabric woven by traditional or bureaucratic routine. They introduce an irrational element into history; they make it unpredictable. The movements unleashed by charismatic leaders are enthusiastic and revolutionary. But soon the mechanics of institutions make their weight felt again. Saviors become founders of churches; prophets gather sects; war lords set up empires. A process is initiated which Weber called "the routinization of charisma"; it is the tragic dialectic in which all charismatic leadership finds itself at length enmeshed.[159] The permament revolution becomes institutionalized, and traditionalism and bureaucratization take over.

The picture that emerges from Weber's sociology of power is an uneasy balance of charismatic movements and rational routinization. We might call it Carlyle's hero-worship substantialized by Karl Marx.

It has been noted that Weber himself was more interested in routinization than in charisma; he wrote about Caesarism, not Caesar; about Calvinism, not Calvin.[160] As for our Western world, he was convinced that rule by bureaucracy would be our fate in one form or another. "All economic weathercocks point in the direction of increasing servitude." Neither democracy nor socialism would be able to stem the tide.

The application of these concepts to our contemporary worlds rounds out Weber's political diagnosis. He was a liberal of sorts. Although he proclaimed personal freedom as the highest good, he could not anchor this belief in any body of ideas since it obviously presented only a value-judgment. In dealing with the contemporary scene, he fell prey to his own method of considering political structures exclusively as techniques. Thus, the democratic states have little more freedom than the autocratic ones. The party leader is for Weber a dictator on the battlefield of the ballot box; democratic Caesarism, or plebiscitarian Caesarism is his forecast for the Occident. There was, as usual with Weber, an element of truth capsuled in this statement. We are instantly reminded of Lenin, of Mussolini, or Hitler. On the other hand, Weber never fully understood the workings of Anglo-Saxon democracy. He did not seem to realize that charismatic leaders may appear in societies which will restrain their action, and that such restraint may be accepted by the leaders themselves. Both Churchill and Franklin D. Roosevelt showed gifts of leadership which may be defined as charismatic. Their activities were, however, curbed by existing constitutional frameworks which

they were obliged to acknowledge. Obviously there is more to politics than the study of techniques. In a conversation with Ludendorff
in 1919, Weber outlined his own type of democracy. "In a democracy the people choose a leader in whom they trust. Then the leader
says, 'Now shut up, and obey me.' People and parties are then
no longer free to interfere with his business. . . . Later the people
can sit in judgment. If the leader has made mistakes—to the gallows
with him." Small wonder that Ludendorff found this type of democracy to his liking. The death penalty for misguided executives
seems unlikely, however, to guarantee a successful functioning of
democratic government.[161]

Weber's concern for German politics became increasingly stronger
as World War I approached. He denounced Germany's parliamentary setup as "sham constitutionalism." When Bismarck's alliance
system fell apart under the bungling hands of Bülow and Holstein,
Weber wrote: "No man and no party which believes in democratic
and national ideals should accept responsibility for this regime." [162]
But he had little faith in the parties to remedy the situation.

When the war came, he offered his services and was put in charge
of a hospital in Heidelberg. "This war," he wrote, "with all its
ugliness is great and wonderful." [163] He was not immune to the
German war propaganda, or even to the fever for annexations that
swept the nation. But he saw, more clearly than his compatriots,
that the unrestricted submarine warfare would bring the United
States into the conflict. He estimated correctly the industrial potential of America and predicted that an expeditionary force of
"500,000 well equipped sportsmen" would tip the scales against
Germany. When his warnings went unheeded, he devoted his energies to bringing about a sweeping democratization of Germany. "I
do not give a damn about the forms of the state, if only politicians
and not dilettante fools like Wilhelm II and their ilk rule the country. . . . I see now no other way than ruthless parliamentarization.
. . . Forms of state are for me techniques like any other machinery." [164]

In the summer of 1917 he opened the debate on "Parliament and
Government in a newly-ordered Germany" in a series of articles for
the *Frankfurter Zeitung*. Perhaps it was his sense of responsibility
that made him return to academic teaching after a leave of twenty

years. He first became guest professor at the University of Vienna, and later professor at the University of Munich. The impression he made on his audience was extraordinary. Even through the restraint of his presentation, the students felt the demoniac fury that had motivated Weber's research. He himself refused to admit that his personality had anything to do with his listeners' response. In words both naïve and grandiose he said, "The facts themselves are so excitingly interesting." [165]

When Germany capitulated in the autumn of 1918 he was more calm than many others: "I have never felt as I do in this hour of shame that it is a gift from heaven to be a German." [166] Some thought that he was destined to play an active role in politics. He was invited to participate in the drafting of the new constitution, and his hand is easily discernible in those provisions of the Weimar Constitution that deal with the plebiscite election of the president of the republic.[167] He was a member of the German delegation that went to Paris to discuss the peace treaty. He advocated a rejection of the Treaty of Versailles. After it was signed, the politician Max Weber fell silent.

Thus Weber was once more thrown back into the academic field. In Munich he delivered two addresses: "Science as a Vocation" and "Politics as a Vocation," which are his last will and testament. We have already drawn freely on both and little remains to be added to our characterization.[168] Their title is reminiscent of Weber's studies in religion, but their content is frigidly sober. Science, said Weber to his students, is the affair of an intellectual aristocracy. He, the apostle of great comparative enterprises, insisted on the need for specialization, this "strange intoxication ridiculed by every outsider." He scorned the cult of personalities then very much en vogue in Germany. The scientist was only a cog in a large machine which was working relentlessly at the progressive disenchantment of the world. Weber evoked the shadow of Tolstoi who had damned all scientific and artistic labor because it blinded man to the ultimate question of human destiny. To these problems, Weber maintained, science can give no answer. Nor can it give practical advice in political problems. Only prophets and saviors may do this. "Science today is a vocation organized in special disciplines in the service of self-clarification." [169] The times are characterized by rationalization and intellectualization. The most sublime values have retreated from public life; even the arts have withdrawn. It would be to no avail to fake a monumental art or to create a new religion. What remains is intellectual integrity. They who tarry and yearn for new prophets are like those Jews who in exile asked: Watchman, what of the night? We, concluded Weber, shall neither yearn nor tarry; we shall set to work and meet the demands of the day.

This carries us into the second of the two lectures: "Politics as a Vocation." Here, too, Weber drew heavily on his previously for-mulated concepts. As a matter of fact, this address is an excellent synthesis of his political ideas. Yet there was a new tone. Weber warned the German students of rising demagogues who would be in search of power for power's sake. Alas! such warnings were all but wasted on the German youth. The professional politicians, in Weber's analysis, are the men who seek power only for a cause, and who apply it with the utmost responsibility.[170] This, of course, brought forth the question of ethics and power.

Weber confirmed his belief in the separation of ethics and power, and in the tragic dilemma that such a dichotomy implied. "The world is governed by demons . . . he who lets himself in for politics, that is for power and force as means, contracts with diabolic powers, and for his action it is not true that good can only follow from good and evil only from evil, but that often the opposite is true. Anyone who fails to see this is, indeed, a political infant." [171] Con-scious of his closeness to Machiavelli, he evoked the memory of the Florentine citizens who deemed the greatness of their city higher than the salvation of their souls. He who seeks salvation of the soul, of his own or others, should not seek it along the road of politics.

At the end of his speech Weber said: "I wish I could see what is to become of you who now feel yourselves to be genuinely princi-pled politicians." He was spared this experience. German youth found its leader, but he was one who lacked the prerequisites which Weber had listed, especially the sense of responsibility. The question whether Weber would have hailed Adolf Hitler should not even be phrased; here was nothing more than the strutting caricature of the truly charismatic leader.[172]

But fortunately Weber did not witness the events which surged be-low the horizon of his life span. In the summer of 1920 he fell suddenly ill. What seemed to be a harmless cold became bronchitis, and finally pneumonia. He had no wish to fight his illness. In the pauses of his delirium, he would wake and say: "I am beyond help." He died on June 14, 1920. His last utterance was "The truth is the truth." [173]

There was little in Weber that was not truthful. His friend, Jaspers, said of him that he did not teach a philosophy; he was a philosophy. But one may doubt whether Weber himself would have cared for this kind of praise—he who said: "Of philosophy, I understand nothing." [174] With as much logic, one could argue that all his teaching was a denial of the legitimate aspirations of philosophy.

As a social scientist, he stands head and shoulders above his contemporaries, Sorel, Pareto, Durkheim, and Sombart. He surpassed them both in erudition and in conceptual precision, but a final evaluation gains little from comparisons, which are, in any event, odious. Weber was, as were few others, the expression of the contradictions and antinomies that beset Germany and the rest of Europe before 1914. And much as he would like to have protested the characterization, he remained a figure of the Wilhelminian period.[175]

The word that rises most distinctly from Weber's description of our Western culture is "disenchantment." Weber was a thoroughly disenchanted individual himself. A partial explanation of this bent may lie in his long illness which denied him the natural outlet for his own charismatic gifts. But even before 1897 there were signs in his writings indicating a desire to tear through the veils of idealistic phraseology and lay bare the naked drive for power and greed in human beings. Since there was so much sham that cried to him for destruction in pre-1914 Germany, his attitude assumes the aspect of a protest against the hypocrisy of his time. Yet there was more than protest in Weber.

He inherited from Dilthey the crisis of the sciences as "the secret trouble" of our times, and he left it where he found it. Much as he refused to be called a relativist, he was exactly that; he merely preferred to call himself a polytheist. But wherein lies the difference between Weber's polytheism and Dilthey's anarchy of world-visions? Weber's methodological attempt to find a common ground for the natural and the cultural sciences in the principle of causal explanation failed of its effect for the simple reason that science in his hands became a technique for handling and interpreting data. Weber realized that all scientific endeavor in the Human Studies was value-related, but he did not claim any validity for values short of the strictly subjective ones. A hierarchy of values, such as Max Scheler tried to establish, he denied. We may well ask, what were the values in which Weber himself believed?

He discarded esthetic values because they lead to irresponsible pleasure. He believed in personal freedom and was willing to fight for it, but he could not and did not claim that it was more than his personal conviction. It was his categorical imperative, not an "inalienable human right," because the nation-state was for Weber an instrument of power, and human rights would have to be sacrificed to the demands of the power-state. Actually, one may call the idea of the nation-state his one unshaken article of faith. Even the great war did not corrode it. He remained convinced that Germany would have another spring: "Of that I have no doubt." [176] Weber's belief in the national community was almost "antique" in its naïveté, and in the face of it he forgot his own statement that the forms of government are only the techniques of power.

The perspectives which emerge from Weber's work are perplexing. There is science as a vocation, and there is politics as a vocation, both techniques in the service of values that cannot be proved. And above the earthly battle for values there rules an inexorable destiny.

Weber has been compared to Marx, but he is a Marx without Marx's motivating belief in social justice. He has been linked with Comte and his "savoir pour prévoir, prévoir pour pouvoir." Yet Comte's faith in the triumph of the positive philosophy is notably lacking in Weber. Others have found him to be the heir of the Enlightenment. If this be so, it is an Enlightenment that no longer believes in the light, and that, on the contrary, predicts a polar night of icy darkness.[177] Reading Weber is like reading Marx or Freud: an unsentimental education.

Unsurpassed as a diagnostician of the Western world, he had no expectation to offer beyond that of a renaissance of the German nation-state. His picture of world history is not a great tableau like those of Ranke and Hegel. Weber had neither the faith of the former nor the philosophical imperialism of the latter. But one sentence of Hegel well describes Weber's position in European civilization: "If a form of life has grown old, it can only be understood but not rejuvenated . . . Minerva's owl begins her flight only in the gathering dusk."

Epilogue

If Blaise Pascal could have attended the inquiry into the aims of the exact and the cultural sciences, he might have remarked that its gist had already been encompassed in his aphorism concerning the two types of mind: L'esprit de géometrie et l'esprit de finesse.

It may seem strange that none of the men who defended the autonomy of the Human Studies was aware of the great crisis which occurred in the exact sciences during the same period. The reason for this neglect lies in the fact that the philosophical implications of the new theories in physics were then barely formulated; even today, fifty years later, they are still in dispute.

An adequate description of the revolution in physics would be out of place in this book; it could be undertaken only by using the mathematical symbols which alone can represent the strange world of modern physics. Here we can do no more than round out the intellectual picture of the period by listing the new ideas which involved a change in our mode of thought about the world.[178]

Ever since the Greek philosophers speculated on the elements of nature, the human mind had been searching for laws by which the manifold diversity of material phenomena could be reduced to principles, which, in turn, might be expressed in mathematical terms.[179] This aim seemed to have been realized with Newton's *Principia*. They provided a pattern which all subsequent developments might be expected to follow.[180]

By the end of the nineteenth century it was generally assumed that the atom with its fixed mass was the real substratum of matter, and that the elementary process in nature, motion, could be explained by the equations of dynamics. In Schroedinger's words: "There was a piece of matter that had never been created (as far as the physicist knew) and could never be destroyed . . . moreover, this matter . . . was with regard to its demeanor, its motion, subject to rigid laws." [181] As has been said, the foundation for this set of principles had been laid down by Newton, but the great advances in physics and chemistry during the nineteenth century seemed to corroborate them; notably, the atomic theory in chemistry, the kinetic theory of matter, and the researches in the fields of light, electricity, and magnetism.

Following the work of Lavoisier and Dalton, Mendeleev discovered the periodic law of atomic weights. Helmholtz and Lord Kelvin formulated the laws of thermodynamics, great generalizations concerning the conservation of energy in the universe. As with Newton, varied phenomena were united under fundamental laws which seemed to support the scientific faith in an interpretation of nature in materialistic terms.

The discoveries in the field of electricity were even more significant. Light was found to be a form of wave motion, and the identity of light waves and electromagnetic waves was established. After Faraday's experiments had broken the ground, Maxwell supplied the mathematical formulae which were needed. "Light consists," Maxwell concluded, "in the transverse undulations of the same medium which is the cause of electric and magnetic phenomena." The Maxwellian equations were confirmed by Hertz in a series of experiments which demonstrated the nature of the electromagnetic field and its energy. Thus it was shown that light waves and electromagnetic waves were identical, differing only in wavelength.[182]

However, the identity of speed in light waves and electromagnetic waves revealed immediately another unsolved problem, that of radiation. The transmission of light had already intrigued the older physicists and had brought forth two opposing theories: the corpuscular theory of Newton and the wave theory of Huygens. In view of Maxwell's and Hertz's findings (that light was a wave motion), physicists assumed that light needed a medium in which to travel, as sound travels in air. Consequently they postulated the existence of a substance which they named ether. This "luminiferous ether" was supposed to fill all space and to carry the light waves. Although it did not possess the characteristics of matter, inertia and gravitation, its existence seemed a necessary supposition by which alone the transmission of light could be explained. Around 1880, physical theory had reached a point where the objects of its study could be satisfactorily explained by the concepts of matter and energy.

But it soon became clear that this body of theories was insufficient to cope with the problem of radiation and the phenomena that were discovered in its pursuit. The experiments of Sir William Crookes, of Roentgen, Becquerel, and the Curies led rapidly to a revision of principles hitherto held unassailable. Since some of these experiments were based on the radioactive nature of certain elements, it became necessary to combine the branches of physics and chemistry. They merged into one enormously complicated science that, for short, is termed the "new physics." Its major object is the study of energy, and of the atom as the source of energy.

In 1900, Max Planck formulated his celebrated quantum theory which, by and large, has proved to be the most fruitful of all theories advanced by modern physics. He discovered in the phenomenon of radiation a feature of discontinuity which seemed to be linked to the existence of the atom but which could not be explained in terms of the prevailing concepts of atomic matter. Planck called the discontinuous bits or portions of radiant energy "quanta," and arrived at the conclusion that each quantum carries an amount of energy which, when divided by the frequency of the radiation, resulted always in h, the Planck constant ($E=h\nu$). Reluctantly he was forced to believe that energy must be atomic in character and that it exists in small bits or lumps, instead of in constant streams as the wave theory had assumed.[183]

Planck's quantum theory, entirely revolutionary in character, forced upon the mind of man the idea of the discontinuous exchange of energy. Light, for instance, had to be treated as a shower of energy quanta. But this was only one of the many perplexities which the quantum theory produced. Behind it lay the even more startling assumption that the elementary particles of matter, which had been considered "as solid as billiard balls," must be viewed as quanta of energy. It was Albert Einstein who carried Planck's discovery into a new domain and who postulated that all forms of radiant energy travel through space in discontinuous quanta.[184] From 1900 to 1914 the concepts of matter and energy were transformed beyond recognition. What had been considered an indivisible, invisible, and indestructible unit of matter was shown to be a complex system of electric charges.

J. J. Thomson was the first to describe the atom in terms of a nucleus positively charged, surrounded by electrons with negative charges. But "the real villain" in the great revolution in physics was Rutherford, who dissolved all that was regarded as most solid into tiny specks floating in the void.[185] Rutherford compared the structure of the atom with that of the solar system. The nucleus occupies a position comparable to that of the sun, while the electrons whirl around it in distances proportionately equal to those of the solar system. The atom was proved to be able to "exert large electrical forces, which would be impossible unless the positive charge acted as a highly concentrated source of attraction; it must be contained in a nucleus minute in comparison with the dimensions of the atom." [186]

The next step was taken by Bohr who, following Rutherford's suggestion, outlined an atomic model in which each electron is given a number of possible orbits. Radiant energy is released when an electron jumps from an outer to an inner orbit, and the amount of energy given forth is a quantum. In such manner was the quantum theory linked to atomic research.[187]

There were other implications in the quantum theory which revolutionized the traditional outlook on nature. Planck's law of radiation had set up a scale of measurements which showed that "where the encountered effects are very large, as they are for the phenomena of daily life, they behave differently from the way they do where they are of atomic size." [188] Whereas Newtonian physics had established laws equally valid for all realms of magnitude, Planck's law of radiation postulated the existence of different scales in nature. Consequently, events in different realms of magnitude need not be similar at all. One of the main stems of Newtonian physics, the law of causality, was found to be of limited use in atomic research, and Einstein suggested that certain aspects of the quantum theory had to be dealt with statistically. Gradually the idea prevailed that the "laws of nature" do not define the occurrence of an event, but the probability of the occurrence of an event.[189]

It has been noted that this approach bears a resemblance to Max

Weber's ideal type, discussed above.[190] But one must be cautious in equating the methods used by the new physics to those applied in the cultural sciences. "The crisis in causality" did furnish ammunition to those thinkers who had defended the autonomy of the Human Studies against the onslaught of the natural sciences, but it also provoked a great number of unwarranted speculations. It would seem premature to draw conclusions from a state of affairs in which only one thing would seem secure, that is, that there is no enigma in the physical world which does not point to another concealed behind it.[191] Likewise the parallel between the idea of relativity, as used by Einstein, and the relativism that we found in Dilthey and Weber is misleading. In one case the word concerns the measurements of time, space, and mass; in the other it deals with values. Relativity and relativism are two different things.[192]

When Einstein published his "Special Theory of Relativity" in 1905, he was questioning certain concepts of the Newtonian universe, especially motion, space, and time, which were used as absolute terms in the classical mechanics. Starting from the Michelson-Morley experiment of 1887, Einstein reached the conclusion that the conventional ideas of space and time were too simple. He associated time and space with an intimacy difficult for the naïve observer to conceive. In Einstein's universe they merge into a fourth dimension: the time-space continuum.[193] "The nonmathematician," said Einstein, "is seized by a mysterious shuddering when he hears of 'four-dimensional' things . . . and yet there is no more commonplace statement than that the world in which we live is a four-dimensional space-time continuum." [194] The particular nonmathematician who is the author of this book is inclined to question Mr. Einstein's observation. However, the many paradoxes which the theory of relativity pose to the student can be overcome once he realizes that the Newtonian universe took too many things for granted, especially the human idea of time. "Unless we are told the reference body to which the statement of time refers, there is no meaning in a statement of the time of an event."

Closely connected with the new concept of the time-space continuum was Einstein's revision of the idea of light. The speed of light, he contended, was not a property of a special stuff called ether, but a universal property of nature, in reality, a constant of nature, independent from the space-time system of the observer. At the time these lines are written Einstein's theory has once more been confirmed by experiment.[195] Another highly important revision of the traditional concepts of physics concerned the idea of mass. If time and distance had to be considered as relative quantities, the same may hold true for mass. In other words, the mass of a body may vary according to its state of motion. As a matter of fact, the conclusions reached from these aspects of the theory of relativity were the most incisive ones from a practical point of view.

Einstein asserted that the mass of a moving body increases with its velocity. His train of thought led to two significant consequences. The first concerns the speed of light. By simple mathematical deduction he concluded that no material body can travel with the speed of light, and consequently that the speed of light must be considered as the maximum velocity known to exist in the universe.

The second conclusion has been before the public eye since 1945. Roughly speaking, it runs as follows: since the mass of a body in motion increases as its motion increases, the increase in mass must be the result of motion. Furthermore, since motion is a form of kinetic energy, energy must have mass. In other words, mass and energy are mutually convertible. $E = mc^2$.

Einstein's discoveries led eventually to a new cosmology which revised the Newtonian concepts. The idea that the universe is a machine, regulated by gravitation and inertia, was replaced by a world-view in which gravitation is defined as part of inertia, and the movements of the stars arise from their inherent inertia. Their courses are determined by the metric properties of the space-time continuum.[196]

Although Einstein's theories were hailed by his peers, Planck, J. J. Thomson, and Eddington, their philosophical implications were not easily discernible. Only gradually did the idea prevail that they demanded a revision of many concepts to which European thinking had clung for centuries.

Dilthey might have derived comfort from the reflection that, whatever the results of the new physics, they had indeed changed the mood of scientific thinking. While the quantum theory and the theory of relativity gave no ground to general skepticism, they did knock the cockiness out of the exact sciences. The time had passed when man could think that the "Welträtsel" would soon be deciphered. It was no longer possible to pretend that science was a simple "reading" of nature. Galileo had once spoken of the great book of nature wherein God had revealed himself in numbers. Now it seemed that this book existed, so to speak, in two volumes: one was spelled in the letters of the classical mechanics; the other in those of the new physics.

Planck acknowledged that the scientist does not deal with nature itself, but with nature that had been thought through and described by man.[197] In this relationship there existed an element of irrationality that science could not shake off, even if it wished to do so. Planck, and most of the creators of the new physics, were cognizant of the gulf that separates "the present scientific world picture from the naïve world picture." The immediately-experienced sense impressions had been completely removed from the scientific world picture. The "rabble of the senses" had been overcome—at a price. The knowledge of the invisible world of the atom had been purchased at the price of "emptiness of content." If a man wished to understand these new aspects of nature, he had perforce to acquaint himself with "a skeleton structure of symbols" that had no relation to the world in which he lived.[198] Of course, one could argue that the history of the human mind has been full of such adjustments. In reality, what is common sense but the belated recognition that the average mind bestows on discoveries made long ago?

Yet something baffling remains that makes it doubtful whether the world of the new physics will ever become "common sense" as the Newtonian physics became common sense in the eighteenth and nineteenth centuries. Niels Bohr remarked once that "we are both spectators and actors in the great drama of existence." The tragic part that modern science has played in this drama consists in having shattered man's natural environment by a series of intellectual explosions which make it almost impossible to reconcile the double role we are obliged to play in life.

We would transgress the limitations imposed upon the historian, were we to imply that the crisis in the exact sciences was simply one more symptom of the underlying crisis in European civilization. But it is hard to overlook certain schizophrenic features which we have found in many other manifestations of Western culture just prior to

1914. There is a similarity between the situation in the cultural sciences and the situation in the exact sciences. At a time when the egocentricity of the Human Studies gave way to historicism, value-relativity, and sociological typology, when, in a word, the European culture had lost its naïve feeling of superiority in regard to other civilizations, a similar process broke the husk that had sheltered the exact sciences. In biology, physics, chemistry, new ideas were introduced that replaced the familiar universe of stability and unfailing forces by an amorphous continuum without any fixed architecture, constantly subject to change and distortion.[199]

Deliberately divorced from metaphysics or philosophy, science no longer furnished man with foundations on which to build or with guideposts that directed his steps. If one were to ask whether science had performed this service in other times the answer would have to be in the affirmative. Science was perhaps never a controlling force in European life, but in the long period from 1500 to 1900 it had been a compass by which the European mind had charted its course. It is worthy of note that in the decade that preceded the Great War, natural scientists and cultural scientists had abandoned the hope of retrieving their directional position in human affairs. Both Weber and Dilthey told us that historical knowledge cannot decide the struggle between conflicting values. Planck confessed that "science is not qualified to decide this question." [200]

CHAPTER V

Culture and Society

European society was, until the end of the eighteenth century, structured on aristocratic foundations. Although feudalism had been superseded in the realm of politics, and had yielded to capitalism in the economic field, society continued to show evidences of medieval privilege in many walks of life.

For centuries the bourgeoisie had made its contributions to European culture. The great names in painting and sculpture, in poetry and music, in science, philosophy, and religious thought, were mainly of bourgeois origin. "Bürgerliche" traits may be detected in Holbein and Dürer, in Molière and Pascal, in Bach, and in Goethe. But this productivity was not a class-conscious expression of the social status of the bourgeoisie. Their offerings flowed easily into the stream of European civilization which recognized the commoner's preordained place in a world of stability and imperceptible change.

The French Revolution produced an unprecedented situation. The bourgeoisie, who, as Sieyès remarked, wanted to be "something," became everything, and in short order took over the ruling power in France. The economic events that accompanied the political revolt were of even greater consequence. The land of the clergy and the fugitive aristocracy fell into the hands of the bourgeoisie. It was a decisive step toward the defeudalization of society.

The historian of the future may perhaps discern a unity of motive behind the French and the Industrial Revolutions. In any case, the mid-nineteenth century saw the merging of these two currents. A tidal wave of uprisings swept over Europe in 1848, which aimed at the restoration of liberty to a world of technical progress and industrial development.

It might be interesting to investigate the preparedness with which the bourgeoisie was able to assume the leadership of a society that

had become fluid to the point of dissolution. We shall not concern
ourselves with the political and economic thinkers of the nineteenth
century. From Guizot and Gneist to Mazzini and Mill they show
an increasing awareness of the problems that confronted liberalism
and democracy in the era, but it can hardly be said that they added
anything new to the ideas of 1789.

We have noted Comte's efforts to encompass the modern world by
the methods of modern science. Although his inspiration rose from a
justifiable desire to provide the bourgeois world with an interpretation of its own, his execution fell short of his intention. It was in
literature and art, specifically in drama, the novel, and in painting,
that the sensitivity of the bourgeoisie found its expression.

Such an assertion may provoke an immediate repudiation. The
word bourgeois has been the hallmark of the utilitarian, the pragmatic, the materialistic, and not alone in the parlance of its enemies.
Such terms seem to be in opposition to artistic sublimation; bourgeois art, then, would appear to be a contradiction in terms. It is
indeed unfortunate that the word bears connotations which are
almost exclusively derogatory, and that in English, at least, there is
no appropriate synonym. The German "bürgerlich" might fill our
needs in most cases, but for lack of an exact term we shall continue
to use the word "bourgeois."

I

The nineteenth century was the background for a movement to
liberate the individual.[1] This freedom had a special meaning for the
artist. Bourgeois society did not supply the artist with sponsors or
patrons as had the ancien régime. He was free to choose his subjects
and his means of expression; he no longer wrote or painted to satisfy
a given public, but to give vent to his own emotions or thoughts.
The public was only invited to listen to him, to understand him, and
to evalute his confessions.

Society granted the artist a right derived from its own political
premises, but reserved, in turn, the right to ignore him and to pay
him back in his own coin, that is, to let him starve. We have already
seen how this situation provoked poets like Baudelaire to accept the
rift between art and society. His work reveals a situation in modern

civilization where the artist is prone to become the martyr of society. Wagner's early years would seem a case in point.

Wagner had first concentrated on the great opera, historic in style, to which the public was accustomed. With *Rienzi* he achieved a remarkable success. Suddenly he abandoned the road to triumph and security along which Rossini and Meyerbeer were traveling. His reasons are clear. He was disgusted with the position assigned to opera in a bourgeois culture where it was taken for no more than shallow entertainment. He concluded that a revolution was necessary, and he adhered to the revolt of 1848, paying in long years of exile for his daring. He had hoped for a cultural rather than a political revolution, one that would focalize itself in the arts of a regenerated theater.

Das Gesamtkunstwerk (complete work of art), as Wagner conceived it, should combine the sensuous appeal of the theater, poetic inspiration, and symphonic music.[2] It should be a blend of music, speech, painting, and gesture, designed to fulfill all the artistic yearnings of mankind. He took it as a foregone conclusion that such an undertaking could not coincide with the frivolous taste of the upper classes. It was to serve the nation as a whole and should be produced in ideal conditions and on special occasions only. It was the conception of a musical shrine as it was later realized at Bayreuth.

For this new art a new panorama was imperative. The contemporary world which Mozart and Rossini had used was unacceptable, nor would the world of history meet his needs. Legend and myth alone could bring about the realization of the music-drama. *Tannhäuser* and *Lohengrin, Tristan, Der Ring,* and *Parsifal,* are, therefore, not only revivals of medieval legends; they are Wagner's interpretations of Celtic and Germanic lore which he evoked to express the insatiable thirst for happiness of his sensuous genius.[3]

Wagner's music dramas, from *Lohengrin* to *Parsifal,* reached an individual and remarkable position through his attempt to breathe life into the mythical haze by a psychology which was startlingly modern in texture. This approach is most obvious in *Tristan,* but scarcely less observable in *Tannhäuser, Lohengrin,* and *Parsifal.* Certainly *Der Ring* seems closer to Dostoevski than to the primeval motivations of Nordic gods. If we consider in addition Wagner's adherence to the nationalistic creed, his celebration and praise of the Germanic virtues, we need search no further for the bases of his spectacular success. This success was as passionate as the opposition which had first greeted his work, and which seemed in direct proportion to Wagner's own titanic efforts to remain faithful to his original inspiration.

Wagnerian societies began to appear, first in Germany, but soon in England and France as well. Their roster includes some of the most distinguished names: Swinburne, Beardsley, Bernard Shaw, Mallarmé, Verlaine, Claudel, Valéry, and many others. Wagner exercised over Europe a musical preeminence similar to that which Bismarck achieved in politics during the same decades. Bayreuth became, as Thomas Mann puts it, a kind of musical Lourdes, a "miraculous grotto for the voracious credulity of a decadent world." [4] It was a triumph such as no artist before Wagner had ever experienced.

What was it that brought the naïve and the sophisticated alike under his spell? His philosophy could have been more easily acquired at its source in Schopenhauer and Bakunin, and the rebirth of the myth was, at best, a pseudo renascence, the result of Wagner's own private wistful and wishful thinking. No; what gave Wagner's music the power to mesmerize a continent was its tremendous faculty for exploiting all the aspects of luxury: luxury of emotion, of sex, of lust for power.

It is impossible to deny the great musical force of Wagner's work; after a century it still enchants those who wish to surrender to its chaotic splendor. But it is equally impossible to deny the absurd and the ludicrous in his creations: the length and banality of his speculations, the cardboard gods, the unconvincing pyrotechnics.

Wagner was a bourgeois malgré lui, a fact that no Nordic "Tarn-kappe" (cloak of invisibility) can disguise. The extravagance and luxury of his private life, reveal what William Morris called his "anti-artistic traits." The whole idea of a musical shrine from which regeneration would flow to restore culture to its original purity was a false conception of contemporary life. Tremendous though Wagner's impact was on the late nineteenth century, it cannot be said that he expressed his time with the clarity attained by Mozart and Haydn.

Literature and painting performed the feat of bourgeois self-understanding on a smaller but more honest scale. The position occupied by the plastic arts during the past century reveals particularly the character of the European mind in that era. Architecture, sculpture, and painting did not follow a general trend of style in the nineteenth century.[5]

In architecture the bourgeoisie showed itself unable to cope with the tasks that the Industrial Revolution threw in its path at an ever-increasing pace. What style would be adequate for the mills and factories, railway stations and exhibition palaces, theaters and museums, that the new way of life demanded? No answer was forthcoming; only our time has worked out solutions to these problems. The age that preceded us found itself at a loss and developed in architecture and the industrial arts a "Verlegenheitsstil," a style of incertitude that marked the dilemma.[6] Romanesque churches, Gothic railway stations, Renaissance post offices appeared as bewildering solutions. Historical imitations invaded the public and private buildings, sometimes as outright copies, sometimes as hybrid blends of disparate elements. The artists in charge of constructions did not manifest the soul of their times; they suffocated it under masses of marble, granite, and steel.

Painting and sculpture, too, paid their toll to the prevailing historicism. The English Pre-Raphaelites are the most notable examples, but the German Nazarenes, Rethel and Makart, are every bit as offensive. Myth and history, the anecdotal and the picturesque were their approach to painting.

II

The French mind, to its eternal credit, met this situation squarely. An art that corresponded to the most intimate and genuine tendencies of the nineteenth century was developed. French impressionism is closely connected with the individualism of the age in the political field, and it parallels the great scientific endeavor of the century, "cette volonté de connaître les secrets de l'univers." It has been called the application of science to the domain of painting.[7]

Impressionism discovered a whole new world, precisely the one that was being built up by the Industrial Revolution: the great cities, the boulevards and squares, the factories and bridges, the bars and music halls, the racecourses and theaters, the boudoirs and parlors of bourgeois life. But this discovery did not lead to a neglect of the motives which in former times had inspired the arts: the landscape, the human body, the portrait. In each field impressionism found new beauty and taught mankind to see it. It was a revolution of the first order. Although limited to the sphere of painting and without a "literary" program, its significance surpasses the boundaries of the arts proper and must be called a revolution of the mind.

French historians like to compare its import to the development of painting during the Renaissance. Artistic progress was accompanied, just as with the Italian masters and the brothers Van Eyck, by technical innovations in the fields of light, color, form, and movement. These innovations were so bold on their first appearance that they shocked the contemporaries of the impressionists profoundly and produced angry outcries which did not abate for more than thirty years. However fundamental this transformation of the artistic technique was, it cannot be understood apart from the deeper significance of the whole movement in European culture.

The year 1874 marks the birth of impressionism. It was then that a journalist by the name of Louis Leroy lifted the title from one of Monet's paintings, "Impression," and baptized the entire group of revolutionaries, "impressionists." [8] Actually, however, the revolt against the shackles of a worn-out tradition and against the academic in painting had long been in the making.[9]

A glance at the Barbizon school, at the work of Daubigny, Rousseau, and Corot in France, at the art of Constable, Bonington, and Turner in England, will readily convince the observer that here were the forerunners of the impressionists in their study of nature and even in their techniques. But side by side with these pioneers there existed the classical tradition represented by Ingres, who believed in line as the principal means of expression, and in myth and history as the appropriate subject matters. To be sure Ingres' emphasis on the classical line had not gone unchallenged. Delacroix used color rather than design; Courbet and Daumier had discovered what Baudelaire called "the heroism of modern life," [10] but there was still a note of program and protest in the work of these masters which only the next generation was able to overcome. Although many events pointed toward impressionism as the logical fulfillment of modern art, none of the forerunners had freed his art from the remnants of a tradition grown stale; none had swept out the nymphs and the heroes of Greece and Rome who every day meant less to the modern mind; none had developed a technique which could do justice to the multiple phenomena of contemporary life. What was needed was an artistic temper untrammeled by conventions and ready to discover the bourgeois age as a subject as worthy of devotion as the "Coronation of Napoleon" or the "Death of Ophelia."

The man who brought the fight into the open was Edouard Manet. His rebellion against an exhausted inheritance took place on a strictly technical plane. The two paintings which mark the full impulse of impressionism, "Le Déjeuner sur l'herbe" and "Olympia," still follow in their composition the pattern set by the masters of the past, Giorgione and Titian, but Manet's ideal was "contemporanéité et humanité." [11] He had learned how to mold the Venetian forms to express the present by a new interpretation of light and color.

Until 1863 no one had conceived of the possibility of introducing light without the accompaniment of shadow, nor was it considered admissible to apply strong colors without intermediary half-tones.[12] Manet broke these rules. He took his models directly from life; he painted what he saw, the surface of things woven from light and color. Even the illusion of spatial depth was achieved by a careful grading of colorific values.[13]

It was this new formula that sent the official critics into an uproar and provoked scorn, hostility, and aversion among the public. At the same time, however, it deeply attracted a group of young artists who rallied around Manet. Claude Monet, Sisley, Renoir, and Bazille embraced Manet's esthetic creed. Zola became Manet's defender in the press, and Zola's friend, Cézanne, became a member of the group. In the early seventies Degas espoused the impressionist program. While the official circles continued to be unalterably hostile, the new artists decided to open an exhibition of their own. The exhibition of 1874 constitutes the public proclamation of the new school and their baptism as "impressionists."

This was a heroic generation which set itself against a blind world. Lack of understanding, lack of success, economic difficulties, even misery, did not deter these men. They were the sons of bourgeois families; some had inherited wealth, like Manet, Degas, and Cézanne; some were of modest means, like Monet, Pissaro, and Sisley; some came from humble backgrounds, like Renoir. Their characters were as diverse as their talents, but their goal was one: to restore the art of painting to its proper sphere. Manet achieved his aim by supreme craftsmanship; Monet reached his through optic sensation; Renoir through poetic sensitivity; Cézanne by trying to combine revolutionary traits with classic art; Seurat by a scientific deduction of the elementary problems of light and color.[14]

Renoir once compared the beginnings of impressionism with the advent of the French Revolution. Whereas, he said, individualism triumphed in politics in 1789, one hundred more years were required to conquer classicism and academicism in the realm of the arts.[15] There is indeed a parallel between these two events: what the revolution proclaimed in its bill of rights, the impressionists set forth on their canvasses in its consummation. The right to think freely and to speak freely led to the right to see freely and to express freely. Individualism is the foundation of all impressionist art. Already Manet was saying: one does not paint a landscape or a figure; one paints the impression of a landscape or a figure at a certain moment.[16] Hence, what counts is the sensation of the artist, his impression, and the manner in which he conveys this impression. The world is only a phenomenon, as Comte would have said; my idea, as Schopenhauer phrased it. But, although the impressionists unconsciously shared the general viewpoint of their century's philosophers, their aim was different. They did not try to reach beyond the phenomenon; on the contrary, it was sensation that enchanted them and they tried to render it in paint. They did not look for laws; they tried to arrest fleeting perceptions. The impressionists had an almost religious devotion to nature or, if the word seems too narrow, to reality. Yet reality was for them no longer the reality of fixed objects; it was the reality of the changing moment only.

This attitude had far-reaching consequences, both positive and negative, in the evolution of painting. It led the impressionists to bar all religious, mythological, or historical subjects from their paintings, all anecdotism whether sublime or trivial. It was not necessary to include nymphs and fauns in a landscape for the sake of beauty, because beauty was found in light and color. In this manner, the impressionists freed man of the ballast, whether Graeco-Roman or Christian, which was no longer needed to give meaning to an existence built on the premises of the nineteenth century. This was, after all, the world of Stephenson, Helmholtz, Darwin, Pasteur, and Koch.

Impressionism gave back to art its good conscience. I do not wish to maintain that it made art scientific (although the neoimpressionists did think so), because the communion between them is of a deeper and more intimate nature. Science and art in the late nineteenth century spring from the same fountainhead as do politics and economy.[17] In banning from art the conventional motive and the conventional form, impressionism became free to approach the contemporary world in its own perspective. Cézanne once said that what is important is to leave the school, all schools.[18] Impressionism succeeded in doing just that. With a virginal imagination it seized the world in its "charactère inédit." [19] A railway station was as much a part of reality as a flooded countryside, the Boulevard des Capucines as the coast of Normandy.

Two technical inventions contributed to the triumph of impressionist painting. One was the metal tube in which paint was now sold. This innovation made it possible for Monet and Sisley, Pissaro and Cézanne, to leave the studio and to work "sur le motif." [20] The influence of photography is more difficult to assess. The progress of photography, in particular the possibility of taking snapshots, may have proved to the artists what they already knew instinctively, that reality is eternally in motion, changing every instant, forever becoming. On the other hand, whereas photography duplicates nature, art suggests, selects, and translates into light, color, and line. It does not aim at the thing in itself, but at the effect it produces in us.[21] One has only to compare the work of two impressionist masters when they painted, as they loved to do, the same subject in the same light. Similar as their style may be, the individuality of a Monet, a Pissaro, a Sisley, a Cézanne, surges up unmistakably. In other words, whereas photography grasps the world in movement, impressionism gives us this movement as seen through the eyes of genius.

In order to conquer the elusiveness of a world in motion, painting needed a new technique, or rather a series of techniques. The impressionists realized that it is light which reveals to the painter the incessant change of things, and light, therefore, became the central theme of impressionist art. Manet was the first to recognize that the cold and unvarying light of the studio gave to reality a false appearance. It was, therefore, imperative to paint "en plein air," and to observe nature as closely as possible. But it was Monet who embodied the final deductions from Manet's discovery and who developed "pleinairism" as the fundamental tenet of the whole group. Manet, it has been said, made the painters paint; Monet made them see.[22] To paint in the open air, in full sunshine or under a clouded sky, meant to change not only the light but the colors as well.[23] Impressionism devised *la peinture claire,* the light and bright painting. It implied the discovery that the black shadows which for centuries had dominated painting were in reality an invention of the studio, that all shadows are transparent and colored, that they are filled with thousands of reflexes emanating from their clearer parts.

But pleinairism was also concerned with the form and contour of things. Here, too, the artists found that their predecessors had based their work on the abstractions of the studio. For the impressionist there could be no fixed forms. In the constantly changing light of nature, forms and colors varied incessantly. Lines became precise or dim, colors bright or mellow according to the strength of the light. These ideas are today the very fiber of painting, but in 1870 the discoveries of the impressionists were met with widespread indifference. Fortunately this apathetic attitude did not deter the pleinairists. Continuing their work in the open air, they captured the perpetual change of reflexes from one object to another, and, in the end, taught us to see. Impressionism not only altered the technical procedures of painting; it has altered our conception of the outside world to an immeasurable extent.

The principles of the new style may be summed up as follows: 1. observation of nature and honesty before the object observed; 2. expression by means of color and light. If followed to their logical conclusions, these premises might cause the painter to become indifferent to the subject matter itself, and indeed Monet seemed never to tire of painting the same object: a haystack, the cathedral of Rouen, the Thames, and, twenty times, the waterlilies.

But the technical discoveries of impressionism went still further. It was of the utmost importance for the artists to translate their new

vision of the world of light and color in pictorial values. This involved a new type of procedure which emerged only after long
experimentation. The older masters had mixed their colors on the
palette before applying them to the canvas; brilliancy and brightness
were often lost by the delay, and the colors frequently neutralized
one another.

The impressionists, relying on Chevreul's discovery of the three
primordial colors of the prism, decided to juxtapose the colors on
the canvas, instead of mixing them, a process technically known
as "division du ton." Thus the mixture of colors or tones desired by
the artist is completed on the retina of the observer's eye when the
painting is viewed from a certain distance. Pissaro gave classic expression to this experience when he remarked, "I see only spots." [24]
When viewed at close range, the pictures of the impressionists look
chaotic and dislocated. The misunderstanding and aversion which
at first greeted the new art form was largely owing to the fact that
spectators viewed the pictures with the conventional esthetics and
from the conventional distance. As we now know, it is necessary
only to retreat a few steps and apparent chaos gives way to a harmony of clear tones, delicately ordered and composed. The effect
obtained fully vindicates the overthrow of the traditional methods.
The impression of vibrating light, of an atmosphere saturated with
sunshine, or air that smells of rain or fog or snow, had never before
been achieved. Mallarmé said of Monet's landscapes that they were
as expressive as the smile of the Mona Lisa.[25] But perhaps it was
Monet himself who best interpreted the reverence and devotion that
inspired him and his friends when he remarked, "la nature sent
bon" ("nature feels good").[26]

The impressionists, in order to incarnate their new vision of the
world, had become the technicians of the fugitive moment. But
they were its poets as well.[27] Perhaps nothing would have surprised
them more than to have a philosophy attributed to them, yet there
is a philosophy behind their paintings. It is that of the world in
flux, which was so preponderant an influence in the thinking of the
nineteenth century. Nothing is; everything becomes.[28] Figures and
houses, landscapes and cities, lose their material stability; reality
becomes a succession of appearances. It was a philosophy which was
disconcerting many a man at the very time that the impressionists

were completing their work. Barrès, Bourget, Hofmannsthal, felt
deeply that such phenomenalism must logically end in relativism
and skepticism. But the impressionists seemed quite unaware of the
darker implications of their vision. With Renan they would have
said, "All is ephemeral, but sometimes the ephemeral is divine."
A special enthusiasm made them forget or overlook the vanity of
all things. For them, life, relative and fluctuating though it was,
meant not routine and servitude, but profusion, plenitude, the
power of change and renewal.[29] Their function was not to lament
the instability of things, but to seize the moment and to bestow on
it an eternal value, the value of beauty, which created out of evasive
and brittle matter something immortal. Cézanne's phrase might well
serve as the motto for the entire group: "Monet is only an eye, but,
mon Dieu, what an eye!" Their association was only a loose one
and included men of heterogeneous temperament and talent united
mainly by their opposition toward academicism. Manet himself,
who had been so admirable a pioneer of the transition, became an
impressionist only when he followed Monet's example, but in his
later paintings, such as the "Bar aux folies bergère," he shows the
traits of impressionism in their most brilliant phase: light and the
effects of light, atmosphere and modern life pulsating and rever-
berating in every inch of the splendid picture.

If anyone can be called a leader of the impressionist group it
would be Claude Monet (1840–1923). He took his start from
Manet, but his "Déjeuner sur l'herbe" showed immediately an
advance beyond Manet. A rain of rays filter through the foliage
of the trees under which a group of gentlemen and ladies take their
leisurely repast. In the delicate "Femmes dans un jardin" the same
problem is treated; the sunlight breaks in a hundred different
reflexes, dancing on the dresses and the hair of the ladies in conversation. Although Monet executed some remarkable portraits ("Ca-
mille," for instance), he soon became the painter of nature exclusively. If one sometimes feels inclined to regret his decision, one is,
nevertheless, amply rewarded by the wealth of beauty that radiates
from his landscapes and still lifes. He proved the impressionist
theory that continually new aspects are produced on immovable
objects by changing light. As we have said, this led him later to
concentrate on one object over a long period of time as he tried

desperately to captivate its variable "moods" in a series of paintings.

The most famous of these cycles are the "Vues de la Tamise" and the "Waterlilies." Enchanting as these cycles may be, one may ask whether impressionism did not reveal in them its limitations. To exhaust the infinite variety of nature produced by light changes is a work of Sisyphus. One is inclined to believe that the camera, especially the moving-picture camera, is more likely to do the trick than Monet's brush. These experiments show the extreme to which impressionism was to go, and explain why Cézanne, van Gogh, and Gauguin felt it necessary to attempt new and different approaches.

Monet was an individualist of fiery spirit, devoted to his art and the ideas he believed in and uncompromising in all matters of principle. Few words are quite so moving as the description he himself gave of painting his wife on her deathbed. He felt with horror how he had become the prisoner of his visual experience, looking for tones and colors in this figure that he adored and that had just ceased to breathe.[30] This "rustic alchemist" remains one of the greatest poets of nature. Inspired by the splendor of the world, which, as he saw it, could never last more than a moment, he succeeded in giving it permanence.[31]

Sisley (1839–1899) and Pissaro (1830–1903), though they lack Monet's passionate determination, seem closest to him as painters of landscape. Both of these men are poets of nature's moods: soft skies, roofs shining through the trees of an orchard, rivers curving lazily under the afternoon sun, frozen streets blanketed in snow.

Degas was of a different temperament and is, in reality, a borderline case in the impressionist group. He hailed from a well-to-do bourgeois family and preserved throughout his life a dislike for anarchy in all of its forms.[32] He had received his training in Ingres' school and remained devoted to the great designers of the Renaissance. He abandoned historical painting when he came over to the impressionist group, but his position remains unique. He never became a follower of pleinairism and preferred to work in the studio. Although his color is powerful, he did not abandon line and design, which were for him more important than they were for Manet, Monet, or Renoir. On the other hand, he was deeply convinced that art should present the contemporary world. He wanted to "watch life through a keyhole." [33] He realized that in the nineteenth century this could not be done by presenting life in historical or mythological disguise. "What an influence the difference of times has on us," he said—"two centuries ago I would have painted Susanna and the Elders, but I only paint women in the tub." [34]

Degas' dominating passion was the human body in motion, but he had neither the force of a Michelangelo nor Rubens' lust for life. He looked at modern life with a "frozen clairvoyance." [35] He seems close to Zola in his collection of the minutiae of life. In this manner he enriched impressionist painting by the introduction of new subjects which he presented in a new style: race tracks, jockeys, dancers, an orchestra in full swing, a circus acrobat, a nightclub singer.

What attracted his analytical eye among such miscellaneous subjects was his passion for life in motion. He was not afraid of the ugly or even appalling, and has added to our knowledge of the human body in his famous series of nudes. How far are we in these studies from the classical pose, Venus sleeping in a landscape, or Susanna emerging from her bath? Degas had indeed seen through the keyhole into the intimacy of life.

A cold and detached observer, Degas preferred to show life as he found it rather than to paint the specious lies of academic convention. Not the least of his claims to fame is his work as a portrait painter. Take, for instance, the famous canvas of the Vicomte Lepic crossing the Place de la Concorde, smoking his cigar and accompanied by his two small daughters and his dog. "Perhaps for the first time in the history of painting the portrait escapes its abstract definition . . . it enters life . . . the human being becomes part of an environment." [36] It is a precious moment preserved by the sensitivity of a great artist. Degas suffered early from an illness of the eyes that finally compelled him to take up sculpture in place of painting and design. He reached old age and could be seen wandering, completely blind, through the streets of Paris, another Lear.

Degas and Renoir are the outstanding representatives of the impressionist portrait. Beyond this, the two men are most different in character and manner: Degas, the bachelor, cold, mysogynous and hypochondriacal; Renoir, warmhearted, in love with life, and enamored of the feminine skin "that takes well the light." He painted everything of reality that he found with a sympathetic, in-gratiating tenderness, but especially "people like beautiful fruit." His painting, as full of poetry as Monet's, is perhaps less virile; it is the poetry of the adoring eye. If Renoir is not the greatest of the impressionist painters, he is, without doubt, the most lovable.

Renoir came from Limoges, and because he was poor, made his living by painting porcelain and fans. His spiritual ancestors were the masters of the eighteenth century, Watteau and Boucher. Like theirs, Renoir's art is a happy, voluptuous art, breathing a quiet paganism.[37] Pain, unhappiness, evil, are not to be found in his work. "He ignores sin as well as its brother, remorse." [38] Like Degas, he painted the life of Paris, scènes de la vie Parisienne, but his sympathies were wider than those of Degas. The lower classes had for him the same charm as the upper bourgeoisie. He was in the be-ginning a firm believer in open-air painting. The famous "Bal du Moulin de la Galette" had to be transported back and forth by his faithful friends so that Renoir might catch on the spot the laughter and light that scintillated every night over the garden. His figures were not professional models but the shopgirls and employees from Montmartre who spent their leisure time at the Moulin.[39] The same animation fills other canvases, such as the "Danse à la campagne" and the "Danse à la ville" and "Les Parapluies." But his portraits show that he was a psychologist as well. Although he knew how to represent his friends, Monet, Sisley, and others, his forte was defi-nitely in the portraiture of women and children for whom he had an innate understanding. On the whole, Renoir preferred the nude to the portrait. What I like best, he said, is "la femme nue." [40]

In his later life when he moved away from the doctrines of pleinairism and asserted himself in the great classical tradition, he sought to capture the simplicity and grandeur of the old masters. He felt he had wrung pleinairism dry and came more and more to paint his goddesses in landscapes remembered rather than ob-served, at the shores of lakes and rivers, emerging from the water resplendant in light and sunshine. His women are not like Degas' Parisiennes, caught in the elaborate processes of dressing and un-dressing, but naked Venuses in the open air. Renoir succeeded in creating a new type of feminine beauty as Giorgione and Rubens had done before him. It is a healthy, slightly heavy beauty, with a skin that seems to be permeated with light in colors of rose and mother-of-pearl.

Renoir was not spared his full share of human suffering, Arthritis crippled him until every movement was a torture, but he had the brush affixed to his hand and continued to paint, because for him, as for Monet and Degas and Cézanne, painting was his sole pleasure. He once spoke of true art as having both indescribable and inimitable qualities, and his own art supports this dictum.[41] There is a sensuous happiness, a feeling of delight and well-being in his pictures. None conveys as well as does Renoir the sensation of security and contentment, of affirmation and comfort, which characterized European civilization before 1914.

To sum up the significance of impressionism for the Western world is no easy task. That it was an artistic revolution of crowning importance is readily admitted today. That it was, furthermore, the perfect expression of bourgeois civilization may now be asserted, though it is only in retrospect that we are able to recognize this identity. The contemporary world, with few exceptions, looked upon impressionism as an uprising like the Paris Commune, as an end of culture rather than its coronation. Rossetti said, "The new French school is simple putrescence and decomposition." [42]

Impressionism was indeed revolutionary, but it did not spring up in a vacuum. We have noted its debt to Corot, Daumier, Delacroix, and Courbet, but its historical roots go even deeper. All the impressionists studied the old masters. Manet admired Velasquez and Goya, and his brush stroke can be traced back to Franz Hals. Degas was close to the classical tradition. Renoir saw his models in the school of the eighteenth century which, said he, "I love so much, which is so gentle and clear and which is such good company." [43]

In addition to this acknowledged indebtedness there are other characteristics which are paralleled in the artistic past. Canaletto and Guardi had, for instance, painted rococo Venice much as the impressionists painted their beloved Paris. Even more notable is the comparison between impressionism and the seventeenth century Dutch school. In this earlier period we find an art that also was essentially realistic, an art that combined landscape and portrait painting and that frequently represented scenes from the humdrum activities of everyday life. Yet the difference is still considerable. The Dutch painters did not practice pleinairism; most of them were subservient to their sponsors, the ruling merchant class; and the anecdotal element played a great role in Dutch art. The impressionists, on the other hand, although expressing the most characteristic trends of their time, were not subservient to it. They took advantage of the privileges which individualism had bestowed upon the artist; they worked in complete spiritual independence, in protest against the traditional clichés, revealing only what they saw.

The nineteenth century failed at first to recognize itself in the creations of its artists. Individualism, accepted so wholeheartedly in politics and economics, was unpalatable in the realm of the arts, and it was not until later that society came to perceive that a true and faithful likeness of itself, presented by keen and observant analysts, was to be found in the work of the impressionists. The intimate relationship between the impressionist painter and his society is worthy of further comment.

Let us first consider the size of impressionist pictures. In general the artists of this generation preferred the small or medium-sized canvas. There are exceptions, it is true, but if we view the bulk of impressionist painting we realize that the small-scale picture was favored by the group.[44] None of these artists painted murals; none tried his hand at the so-called "monumental" type of painting on which Menzel still wasted his talent. Of course open-air painting all but precluded the mammoth canvas, but I am inclined to believe that there were deeper reasons for the artist's choice.

The impressionists were bourgeois by birth and by the general philosophy to which they adhered, and the bourgeois mind is not given to gargantuan expression. Great though he may be as an individual, the bourgeois realizes instinctively that he is but one among millions. Self-glorification in the style commanded by Louis XIV would have appeared absurd in the bourgeois age. The artist of this period did not serve a ruler, and he would have refused to serve a class. But he did know the intimate fabric of bourgeois life because his own was woven on the same loom. He knew the houses, and the walls on which his painting might be hung. The dimensions of his work had to conform to the proportions of the bourgeois dwelling; he did not paint for the cathedral or the palace.

The impressionists demonstrated their attention to such considerations by their systematic attempts to bring their work before the public eye. Exhibition after exhibition was organized, and though the first economic returns were less than meager, the tide began to turn in 1880.[45] Manet became an accepted master; Renoir ingratiated himself with the Parisian and American public; Monet was well on his way to fame if not to fortune. But they did not, even then, obtain such commissions as Rembrandt and Franz Hals had held; neither the Crédit Lyonnaise nor the Bank of France felt impelled to have their board meetings immortalized by the masters of the time.

Another characteristic which reveals the acute response of the impressionist painter to his age is the absence of religious themes. A separation of art and church seems to parallel the separation of church and state, now well on its way in continental Europe. Religion had become a matter of private concern, cornered in the individual conscience. Even those impressionists who, like Cézanne, were believers excluded the religious motif from their work. They were in pursuit of nature, not God.

The cultural position was also indicated by the ban on philosophical or poetical subjects which had carried so much weight in preceding generations. A glance at the work of Delacroix, Kaulbach, or Böcklin gives an idea of the liberation achieved by the French masters. But, as we have noted, the poetical, the religious, the historical, were not replaced by the anecdotal or the illustrative. What impressionism tried to capture was nature itself, life itself. These artists were quite aware that painting was an interpretation of life, the only task to which the true artist might address himself, and they could, therefore, easily dispense with the knowing smile and the sentimental tear of illustrative art.

The impressionists devoted their lives to the "triomphe du vrai," as Zola expressed it.[46] And after a long struggle their efforts were rewarded. Eventually these scenes from everyday life—the crowds in the public gardens, little girls drinking chocolate or mending their clothes, men reading newspapers or listening to music—these still lifes and landscapes penetrated the obtuseness of the bourgeois mind and it came to recognize itself in this magnificent art. By 1900 the battle was all but won. There is in impressionist painting the same comfort, the same security, the same beauty that animated the best of bourgeois life. Who can look at Renoir's "The Loge," at Degas' "Carriages at the Races," at Monet's "Still Life," without feeling an intimate kinship with all that was good and decent in the life and society of 1900? It is quite true that there was much in bourgeois society that was not good, but it seemed characteristic of the impressionistic painters that they did not or would not see it. Any note of social protest is conspicuously absent. Their own rebuffs at the hands of the bourgeoisie never became the subject of artistic treatment, and if the working classes appear at all in their work, as now and again they do, they are not shown as an exploited group, but rather as part and parcel of the wonderful life that was to be enjoyed by everyone. It is also interesting to note that we find no trace of those group emotions that swept the European scene between 1870 and 1914. Neither nationalism nor militarism affected impressionist art. The majority of the impressionists—Degas is one of the exceptions—concerned themselves very little with politics. Their work has, in consequence, remained free from the blemish of ideologies rampant in their time. Thus there came to birth an art that has crossed frontiers with ease, that has attracted followers and admirers wherever it went. It is universal and supranational in character although its origin is unmistakably French. This particular form of bourgeois art was hence assured a singular triumph. In the over-all framework of the nineteenth century, impressionism became a point of concentration which represents with greater clarity what other cultural trends tried to express.

We have already said that impressionism and positivism are built on the same foundation, but what proved unsatisfactory for philosophy provided the arts with an excellent basis for the suspension of the fleeting moment in light and color. Even closer seems to be the similarity between impressionism and naturalism. It was no accident that Zola was the first to welcome Manet's painting. But again the rapprochement is but a partial one. Naturalism was bent on achieving a pseudoscientific reality by describing life as a biological function. Impressionism believed in nature, but did not study it under abstract laws; the painter strove to grasp the concrete beauty he saw in nature.

Summing up all the evidence, we may say: the many and diverse trends of the nineteenth century in philosophy, literature, and poetry are crystallized in impressionist painting with a force, clarity, and persuasion that make it the supreme artistic event in the last decades of the century, and the one that, in this writer's opinion, will be the most likely to survive.[47]

However, though we may accept impressionism as the classical expression of bourgeois culture, it was not without its limitations. We have called attention to the absence of social protest and to the satisfaction with the beautiful surface. Other critics have pointed to its lack of form and structure, of thought and ideological power. But we must likewise admit that impressionism itself produced and nurtured those minds which were to overcome it. Cézanne, Gauguin, van Gogh, Toulouse-Lautrec, all had their beginnings in impressionism. It was Cézanne who said that he wanted to make of impressionism something durable and solid like the art of the museums. Gauguin complained that the impressionists neglected the mysterious center of thought, that their art was superficial and sensual.[48] In van Gogh the turn from impressionism to a new style was even more explosive. But they, and all who followed them, retained the principle that impressionism had brought to fruition: creative subjectivity. Twentieth century art is unthinkable without impressionism.

Impressionism maintained a precarious balance between the observation of nature and the idea of self-expression. In our own century the observation of nature has gradually been discarded, and self-expression has become the prevailing trend. Thus impressionism is an end and a beginning.[49] The unique combination of creative subjectivity and closeness to nature marks impressionism as the last of those blissful moments in which great art is born. Today no one questions this claim. Museums and private collectors alike compete for the work of the impressionists. We are a long way from the day when the director of the Louvre had to be forced to accept Manet's "Olympia" as a gift. The techniques of modern reproduction have made it possible to bring the landscapes and the flowers, the still lifes and the dancers, into everyone's living room. No other school can boast of an equal dispersal of its work in the mid-twentieth century.

Impressionism also set the pace for the development of European painting outside France. The German impressionists, Liebermann, Trübner, Slevogt, and Corinth, followed up the lessons that France had taught them in their own fashion. The influence of impressionism on music and literature was likewise extraordinary. It marked, in very truth, an epoch in the sensitivity of modern man. Paul Valéry refers to a "mystique des sensations," and this phrase sums up the philosophy that impressionism imparted to the mind of Western man.

A musicologist could draw a close comparison between Debussy's compositions and the paintings of his compatriots. This music has been defined as a metamorphosis of sensations into musical values.[50] Marcel Proust's descriptions, like the celebrated vignette of the flowering lilacs, are a direct transposition of the impressionist technique into the novel.[51] Rainer Maria Rilke's poem, "The Caroussel," resembles a painting by Renoir. Thus impressionism invaded all forms of cultural endeavor, and the intensity of its impact remains a unique occurrence in the intellectual evolution of the Western world.

III

The lives of three great artists of the nineteenth century, Wagner, Manet, and Ibsen, seem strangely analogous. Each broke with tradition; each introduced new techniques and new ways of expression which met with vituperation, ridicule, and even calumny; yet each had the triumph of seeing his vision prevail. The same bourgeoisie which rejected them at the beginning, surrendered to them in the end.

For the historian who wishes to study the artistic manifestations of the bourgeoisie at the turn of the century, Ibsen has a special significance. His definition of poetry would have delighted the impressionists; "To be a poet is to see." [52] His biography gives evidence of the same movement away from the romantic and the historical toward the actual and the contemporary that we have found in impressionism. Ibsen's new technique of the drama, his relinquishment of verse as a means of dramatic expression, are comparable to the innovations that Manet and Monet introduced in painting.

Ibsen considered his development to be "absolutely consistent." [53] His biographers have accepted this view and have pointed to the ties that link his earliest attempts to the mature productions which made him the dramatic master of Europe. For our purposes it will suffice us to meet Ibsen after he had left his native Norway.

When Ibsen abandoned the Norwegian "parish Council" viewpoint for the broader stream of European culture, he obeyed an inner compulsion. Narrow-mindedness, parochialism, and prejudice had threatened to suffocate his talent. "But a man's gifts are not a property; they are a duty." [54] He chose exile, confessing that he was glad of the injustice done him. "If I am not a poet then I have nothing to lose. I shall try my luck as a photographer." [55] And he became the poet-photographer of the European bourgeoisie.

The chief result of his exile was to drive him out of estheticism which, he said, "had a great power over me—an isolated estheticism with a claim to independent existence." In other words, he gave up romanticism. The seventh decade of the century had a profound influence on Ibsen. He was a keen observer of the political events which took place in those years: the Franco-Prussian war, the unification of Italy, the Paris Commune. He noted also the momentous scientific revolt which had begun in 1859 with Darwin's *The Origin of Species*. He wrote to Georg Brandes: "I have often thought of what you once wrote, that I had not made the present scientific standpoint mine. . . . What we, the uninitiated, do not possess as knowledge, we possess, I believe, to a certain degree as intuition or instinct." [56] It was Brandes himself who made a lasting impression on Ibsen with his *Main Currents in Nineteenth Century Literature*. "No more dangerous book could have fallen into the hands of a pregnant poet. It is one of those works which place a yawning gulf between yesterday and today." [57] He was indeed at that time a pregnant poet who had already made his mark with *Brand, Peer Gynt,* and *Emperor and Galilean*, and who was ripe for new ventures. What Brandes had submitted as his principal thesis was the need for a literature "engagée." "That in our day a literature is alive is shown by its submitting problems to debate," said Brandes, and Ibsen, quite in sympathy with such a literature, became a writer who strove to be both contemporary and forward-looking.[58] At the same time, nonetheless, he asserted the principle of creative subjectivity. Everything, he said in 1880, that I have written has the closest connection with what I have lived through . . . in every new poem or play I have aimed at my own spiritual emancipation and purification—for a man shares the responsibility and guilt of the society to which he belongs. And he went on to quote his most famous stanza:

> To live is to war with fiends
> That infest the brain and the heart;
> To write is to summon one's self
> And to play the judge's part.[59]

Let us take a brief glance at this society for which Ibsen felt responsible and for whose guilt he wished to atone. Beginning with *The Pillars of Society,* all his plays take place in Norway around the year 1870, in a society which was commercial rather than industrial. Ibsen's men are bankers, judges, doctors, and architects, artists and merchants. He became the dramatic mouthpiece of the middle classes, paying little heed to the lower rungs of the social ladder, the peasantry, nor to the aristocratic few who occupied the upper reaches. "Ibsen was the first to portray the tragedies in the lives of suburban, provincial people." [60] He was not interested in the class struggle; his world is not a world of economic conflicts. He was preoccupied with the great moral principles that the bourgeoisie had raised: truth, life, freedom, responsibility, culture, and discipline. But, and herein lies Ibsen's preeminence as a moralist, he refused to be taken in by the bourgeois optimism which believed that great ideas will triumph by themselves. On the contrary, Ibsen found the way to hell paved with liberal intentions. As a criterion of evaluation he asserted the constancy of the individual in maintaining the ideals to which he professes. In order to understand Ibsen's problem we must, therefore, analyze his own interpretation of the liberal tenets, and especially the idea of freedom.

Liberty, he stated, is to me the first and highest condition.[61] But liberty had a different significance for Ibsen from that held by the majority of his European fellow men. Is it not essential, he asked, that man's mind be emancipated first of all? "Until now," he wrote, "we have been living on nothing but the crumbs from the revolutionary table of the last century, a food out of which all nutriment has been chewed. . . . Liberty, equality, and fraternity are no longer the things they were in the days of the late lamented guillotine. . . . What is all-important is the revolution of the spirit of man." [62] He was an anarchist. "The state must be abolished. In that revolution I will take part. Undermine the idea of the state; make willingness and spiritual kinship the only essentials in the case of a union—and you have the beginnings of a liberty that is of some value." [63] Together with this anarchism goes a deep-rooted skepticism and relativism. "The state has its roots in Time; it will have its culmination in Time. Greater things than it will fall; all religion will fall. Neither the conceptions of morality nor those of the arts are eternal. . . . Who will vouch for it that two and two do not make five up on Jupiter?" [64] At another time he said, I gave up universal standards long ago.

How was it then, we must ask, that he became the dramatist of a society that believed in different ideals? It was Ibsen's contention that, in the eternal flux of things, what once had been an ideal could easily become an idol or a lie; that the real slavery of his time was the submission to the idols of goodness, that these selfsame idols were threatening the evolution of human life.[65] All of Ibsen's thinking revolves around his concept of life and his concept of truth. Your marriage, your society, he told his time, should be built on freedom and truth, on independence and responsibility. But the society in which he lived did not recognize these demands, and in scrutinizing his age for its basic flaws, Ibsen became one of the most penetrating diagnosticians of the bourgeois world.

It would be a mistake, however, to consider Ibsen as first and foremost a thinker who advanced ideas from the stage, or who used actors and actresses as mouthpieces for his sermons. He was a poet. To be a poet in the bourgeois world could only mean the apprehension of the problems of the age as human problems, as conflict, passion, ambition, endeavor, and agony. "What I principally wanted to do was to depict human beings, human emotions, and human destinies upon a groundwork of the social conditions and principles of the present day." [66] Many of his contemporaries saw only the social conditions upon which he touched, and ignored the depth of the human destinies he unfolded.

Ibsen's first four social plays seem to aim exclusively at the vacuity of the society that surrounded him. In *Pillars of Society* he unmasked the idol of conventional respectability and set up against it truth and freedom as the real "pillars of society." In *A Doll's House* and *Ghosts* he turned from society to domestic life. And once more he makes life built on a lie his target. Each play is devoted to a different aspect of marital life in the bourgeois world. The bourgeoisie was touched to the quick and responded to Ibsen's exposure with a howl of offended innocence. In *Enemy of the People* he showed the tyranny which a majority of aroused citizens could exercise.

But Ibsen's quiver was not exhausted, and soon other and sharper arrows were fixed to the bow. *The Wild Duck, Rosmersholm,* and *The Master Builder* revealed that truth is a double-edged sword, and that it can bring destruction and unhappiness when wielded by some self-appointed apostle. "What is Truth? said jesting Pilate," and the question pierces the gloom at the tragic end of *The Wild Duck;* is there a truth for human beings; can they exist without illusions and lies?

In *Rosmersholm* Ibsen scrutinized another of his own beliefs. We have noted his skeptical attitude toward democratic reforms and his conviction that lasting results will come only with the liberation of the human mind. He confessed this opinion publicly when he addressed a group of artisans in Trondheim: "An aristocratic element must come into our political life. . . . I am, of course, not thinking of aristocracy of birth, emphatically not that of money, nor of the aristocracy of knowledge, nor even that of ability and talent. But I have in mind an aristocracy of character, and mind, and will. It is that alone that can make us free." [67] This is Rosmer's ideal, and he wants to make all the people of his country noblemen. But Rosmer's tragic fate shows the danger of those who form ideals for other people when they themselves are too weak to conduct their own lives by the standards of truth.

In Ibsen's later plays the dichotomy between life and the ideal is still more plangently sounded. An "October point of view" prevails. Ibsen frequently insisted that his task was to ask questions, not to answer them. The tragedy which his characters enact is likewise the tragedy of the human being who is capable of asking questions but is unable to answer them, the tragedy of man in an age of science.[68]

Today Ibsen's dramas are, in the main, outdated. The issues

which loomed so large in his day have for the most part been brought to solution, and Ibsen and Ibsenism have been the victors, most spectacularly so in the field of women's rights. If we are no longer stirred by his fight against hypocrisy in society, against the double standard in matrimony and in private ethics, we should not, however, forget that our free discussion of these problems is a direct result of his untiring efforts. Ibsen, like Tolstoi, was a reformer of the human mind, and like the great Russian he favored anarchic solutions. He reinvigorated European emotion and thought, and he also regenerated the means of expression upon which he depended, that is to say, the drama.

Ibsen abandoned entirely the mythological and historical play. He renounced verse because, he said, "we are no longer living in the days of Shakespeare," and he refused to permit his creatures to converse in "the language of the gods." [69] On this subject he was indeed quite dogmatic, and ventured to predict that verse would be abjured in the drama of the immediate future. "I have," he said, "exclusively cultivated the very much more difficult art of writing the genuine, plain language spoken in real life." [70]

This restriction in the matter of speech to "real life" applied also to his choice of subject. He gives us, says Shaw, not only ourselves, but ourselves in our own situation.[71] By such selection he rigorously circumscribed the realm of human experience, which was, after all, not limited to the perspectives of the bourgeoisie at the end of the nineteenth century. But his reformation of the drama was an act of intellectual honesty which influenced profoundly not only the theater, but the novel and the short story as well. Ibsen taught the art of understatement, of the silent implication.

He was, as we have said, more interested in human conflicts than in social problems. He portrayed *les états d'âmes* (the state of souls), not *les états des choses* (the state of things). He confined dramatic action to a minimum; in most instances it actually precedes the dramatic argument as such. Many of Ibsen's plays reveal a hidden past which ensnares the present and the future. In order to bring the past to life, Ibsen was obliged to develop a very skillful analytical and retrospective method. Donoso Cortes defined liberalism as "government by discussion"; in the light of this definition Ibsen's characters would all be good liberals, because they discuss endlessly. It could almost be asserted that discussion and play have become one in Ibsen's work.[72] Another characteristic of Ibsen's dramatic technique is his elimination of the monologue. The reasons for this omission were in part external; he wished to adhere more closely to realistic speech. But more deep-seated was his effort to avoid that self-delusion which is the greatest lie of all, since no truth is so difficult of attainment as the truth to the self.[73]

Ibsen's dual role as dramatist and social critic was frequently misunderstood by his contemporaries. He seized on ideas with an almost animal fury. "During the time I was writing *Brand*," he relates, "I had on my desk a glass with a scorpion in it. From time to time the little animal was ill. Then I used to give it a piece of soft fruit, upon which it fell furiously and emptied its poison in it— after which it was well again. Does not something of the kind happen with us poets?" [74] Time and again he had to insist that his plays preached nothing; they merely pointed to "a ferment of nihilism under the surface." A ferment of nihilism under the surface! Could Europe's situation in 1890 be more accurately characterized? Thus Ibsen found himself in close relationship to Nietzsche. Both were archindividualists; both sensed the danger to European culture that was brewing in the cauldron of time. "We are sailing with a corpse in the cargo," the young Ibsen had said. But each came to a different conclusion. Whereas Nietzsche glorifies the Will to Power, Ibsen insists on the power of the will to overcome the evils in human society.[75] He believed that he who allies himself most closely with the future is right.[76]

A full analysis of Ibsen's impact on the late nineteenth century would easily be of volume length. A German critic compared his Real-literatur to Bismarck's Real-politik. Others saw in Ibsen the most powerful exponent of their own scientific beliefs. A whole generation of European writers admired him as their liberator: Gerhart Hauptmann and Sudermann in Germany; Shaw, Galsworthy, and Joyce in England, not to mention the writers of Ibsen's own Scandinavia. Statistics on his European stage productions speak an impressive language. He had done what he had promised to do: he had attacked age-old prejudices; he had crossed many a parochial boundary line; he stepped forth as the prophet of a new gospel of nature and truth. And truth was activated by actuality.

His was an art that had the courage to deal with the problems and interests of the day. Although essentially Norwegian in his roots, his influence, like Tolstoi's, became universal, a part of that world literature that Goethe had said was bound to develop. Ibsen's naturalism was not unchallenged. The renewal of poetic impulse in England, France, Austria, Germany, and Italy restored to verse the birthright of which Ibsen had wished to deprive it, but naturalism has, nevertheless, remained a lasting feature of twentieth century art forms; our novels, our short stories, our radio and television plays, are deeply indebted to him.

Ibsen was a continuous influence until the end of World War I. The society which emerged from the great catastrophe viewed his work with indifference, and since then his fame has been eclipsed by other suns. If we revisit his dramatic opus today, we feel that we are gazing upon the tomb of the last Viking. Nora or Alving or even Hedda fail to evoke the old spell. His "message" has been dissipated in its achievement, and other ideas of his remain in the realm of Utopia side by side with the rhapsodic conceptions of Kierkegaard, of Nietzsche, of Marx, of Tolstoi.

Ibsen's lasting gift to us does not lie in his ideas, but in the defiant courage he brought to the fulfillment of duty. "So to conduct one's life," he said to Björnson, "as to realize one's self, this seems to me the highest attainment possible to a human being." [77] His other achievement was to combine the principle of self-realization with intellectual honesty and social responsibility. The dialectic process by which he constantly tested his own beliefs and ideals, the everlasting scrutiny of human motives, led Ibsen to discoveries very much akin to those of Freud and Adler, of whom he had certainly never heard. Ibsen saw man the victim of contradictory desires and feelings. "This discovery was a drama in itself." [78] The very complexity of his findings forbade him to believe blindly in the progress of civilization. But skeptic and relativist though he was, his courage did not flag. Herein he is once more akin to Nietzsche. His greatest, perhaps his only, legacy is his indomitable lust for doubt.

IV

Ibsen was a superlative dramatist, but one is inclined to question whether the drama was the best medium for portraying the human substance of the bourgeoisie. The drama demands conflict, and in obedience to this dictate, Ibsen as well as his followers, Hauptmann, Sudermann, and Shaw, chose salient situations: men and women in open dissention with their environments, classes in struggle and dispute. Dramatic production of this kind revealed the economic embroilments produced by the Industrial Revolution. Hauptmann's *Weavers* was such a play. Or they might display the bourgeois hypocrisy which widened the breach between ideal and action. But there were other considerations of equal importance to the comprehension of the bourgeoisie: the slow rhythm of work and discipline, the sedentary habits, the recurrent family traits, the gradual development of enterprises, and the establishment of fortunes from generation to generation.

It was the novel that took over the uncompleted task of portraiture, and it was in the novel that the bourgeoisie found its most striking literary expression. The novel was not burdened with the traditions that harassed the form and norm of the drama; it could embrace any subject matter, whether historical or contemporary, mythical or modern.[79]

Epic writers of the 1840's were the first to recognize the great new assignment that their century had thrust upon them. Balzac dealt with social problems, but his picture of society is still essentially aristocratic. Flaubert, in *Madame Bovary* and *Bouvard and Pecuchet,* gave a portrait of the class to which he belonged and which he hated, showing all its flaws but none of its virtues.

If one looks to Zola for the completion of this mission assigned to the novel, one finds that he undertook both more and less than the picturing of the bourgeoisie. When he first outlined the plan of the Rougon-Macquart series, he intended to disclose the whole of French society through the medium of two families. Such an undertaking, as he realized, would have been impossible before 1789: "I am basing it upon the truth of the age." [80]

His epic arose upon a foundation of preconceived ideas which he borrowed at random: from Comte, from Taine, from Claude Bernard. He brought science into the service of literature; all nature was to be his domain.[81] From Comte he acquired the technique of describing social phenomena. Human behavior followed certain laws, and he took over the laws laid down by Taine and Bernard.[82]

The human world was arranged by him under two great categories: heredity and environment, and armed with this *modus operandi,* he proceeded from the known to the unknown. The whole scheme was designed to make man the master of nature.[83] He was a self-confessed positivist, evolutionist, and materialist. But behind his naturalism still looms the idealism of the eighteenth century. Although beauty was for him no longer truth, truth was still beauty. "If my characters do not arrive at good, it is because we are only beginning in perfectibility." [84]

Today as we look back upon Zola's gigantic effort, we can only smile at his philosophy. We do not give a fig for the family tree of the Rougon-Macquarts. But we are still swept off our feet by the elementary force of *Terre,* by the vigor of portrayal in *Nana,* by the dramatic tension that penetrates *Germinal.* As far as his presentation of the bourgeoisie is concerned, Zola himself said that he utilized the class structure of the period only to have a milieu in which his characters might react to one another. The literary interpretation of the European bourgeoisie was, therefore, still to be tackled in spite of the twenty-odd volumes of the Rougon-Macquart. Nothing was done, however, until the beginning of our century when, almost simultaneously, a German and an Englishman engaged themselves in the undertaking. Thomas Mann, in *Buddenbrooks* and John Galsworthy, in *The Forsyte Saga,* captured the epic consciousness of the bourgeoisie at the moment when it had reached its greatest achievements, and when its decline was already perceptible to the sensitive observer.

Thomas Mann has called himself "a bourgeois gone astray" ("ein verirrter Bürger"). In his creative as well as his critical writings he has emphasized the significance of his social inheritance.[85] "The German bourgeois," he remarked, "was the prototype of German humanity." At another time he said, "After all, we are not gypsies living in a green wagon; we're respectable people."

Thomas Mann was born in 1875, in Lübeck, one of the three republics included in the German Empire and the old site of Hanseatic greatness. His father was a grain merchant and senator of the Free City. "But my mother saw the light in Rio de Janeiro . . . she was distinctly Latin in type . . . and extraordinarily beautiful." His father died early, but Mann had sufficient means to look about him before deciding on a career. He went to Rome where he smoked cheap cigarettes endlessly and devoured Scandinavian and Russian literature. Although he rejected the suggestion that he was indebted to Zola, he must have been impressed by the Rougon-Macquart as deeply as he was by Ibsen or Tolstoi.[86] It is true, however, that Mann and Zola are miles apart in their philosophies; Mann's foundations were not to be found in natural science, but in Schopenhauer, Wagner, and Nietzsche. His extrabourgeois experiences merged with his Hanseatic background to form a colorful but contradictory pattern. His family tradition as well as his epic gifts predestined Mann to become the chronicler of the bourgeoisie. His philosophical inclinations made him conscious of the limitations of his class. They isolated him as an artist and thinker in the midst of the bourgeois world in which he continued to live; they led him to feel deeply the forces of pain and suffering; they opened him to the sexual-musical rapture from which great art is born; they made him aware of the pathological conditions of genius. In a word, they made him familiar with the phenomenon of decadence. For Thomas Mann, disease and art are inextricably intertwined. Genius, he said in speaking of Goethe, can never be normal in the banal, narrowly bourgeois sense . . . it cannot be natural, healthy, regular.[87] This belief is Mann's leitmotif from the first to the last of his epic enterprises.

When, in his early twenties, Mann approached the problem of the bourgeois family, he gave it a singular twist from the beginning. *Buddenbrooks,* which appeared in 1901, is called the decline of a family. In this novel, Mann wrote of respectability, of wealth, of accomplishments, and of civic duties, but he also wrote of decay, of illness, of succumbing to uncontrollable urges, of music and of death. And he wrote without being aware that "in narrating the disintegration of a bourgeois family, he also told of a much greater cultural and sociological caesura." [88] Mann's claim that he had foretold the greater crisis of his class is no vain boast; the novel is, in more ways than one, a prophetic document announcing the decline of the bourgeoisie in his native Germany.

I believe *Buddenbrooks* to be Mann's greatest novel and the one that will outlive his other epic productions. After more than fifty years it still preserves its freshness and precision. His intimate knowledge of the Hanseatic society, solid, reflective, puritanically correct and with a tendency toward melancholy, allowed Mann a power and freedom of description that he later reached only sporadically. By the same token, it gave *Buddenbrooks* a historical significance equaled by few other works of the same period.

The story of *Buddenbrooks* is straightforward, and, as novels go, almost too simple to hold the reader's interest. As would seem fitting in a story of bourgeois life, the romantic element is reduced to a minimum. The rise and decline of the house of Buddenbrooks spans seventy-five years, and we accompany four generations through their prosaic, everyday life with nothing more sensational in it than business ventures, opulent meals, marriages by agreement, tedious hours at school, and occasional voyages to nearby Baltic resorts.

The historian who reads Mann's novel today can only marvel at the intuitive perception with which he grasped the changing moods of the generations that filled the nineteenth century. The oldest representative of the family, Johann Buddenbrook, lives still in Voltairean skepticism tempered by much bonhomie and an epicurean taste for the good things of life. The second generation, that of Konsul Buddenbrook, rejoices in the atmosphere of pious devotion which followed the Napoleonic wars in Germany. Thomas Buddenbrook belongs to the third generation, the generation of 1850. Louis Napoleon is its model in hair-do and general elegance; it is tense but disillusioned, and finds comfort in reading Schopenhauer in a lonely hour. There remains only Hanno, poor Hanno, Thomas's son, helpless and useless, the only child of an exhausted family.

The background of *Buddenbrooks* does not intrude on the story. It is a social rather than historical novel. The earlier years of the family are discreetly sketched in as they might appear to later Buddenbrook generations, and this continuity of effect contributes greatly to the feeling of solidarity which soon involves the reader. We learn of Napoleon and his marauding army, of Louis Philippe and the revolution of 1848, and we note the effect that German unification had on the Buddenbrooks. We also hear of business cycles, of boom and bust, of speculation and bankruptcy, which were the daily bread of the merchant class, in Lübeck as elsewhere.

Another eminently bourgeois trait is set forth in Mann's treatment of the darker side of life. There is no love story in this novel, no great passion, no adultery, such as we find in *Madame Bovary* and even in *The Forsyte Saga*. The only sins that are committed are sins against the holy ghost of capitalism, and the only crimes that are mentioned are fraud and embezzlement. There is Christian Buddenbrook, who feels a strong aversion to work and discipline and who squanders his inheritance; there is Toni Buddenbrook's first husband who manipulates his accounts to secure an heiress; there is her second husband, who shamelessly retires to live on his wife's dowry; there is the son-in-law who goes to prison for shady practices.

Whereas the older generations are drawn with loving irony, it is really the third generation of Buddenbrooks which gives direction and center to the novel. Here we have Toni, a "goose" from start to finish, a silly, amiable bourgeoise, whose life depends on the signs of outward respect that her family commands. Christian has histrionic talents and is given to the coarser pleasures of life. He suffers from "strange pains in his left side," and terminates his life in a mental institution. Thomas, the unheroic hero of the novel, is the bourgeois par excellence as Mann sees him. He is restless, tense, disciplined, and ambitious. His attire is flawless; he changes his linen twice daily and uses quantities of eau de Cologne and brilliantine to preserve his pristine appearance. He feels the lure of indolence and hedonism as much as his brother Christian, but he does not give in to these "destructive influences." He forces his nature on with relentless drive, and thus becomes self-righteous, egotistical, and impatient with those who are less gifted or less zealous. He is "without pity, without love, without humility." [89]

Thomas has married the beautiful Gerda Arnoldsen, about whom Mann tells us little except that she was somewhat exotic in appearance with bluish shadows at the corners of her closely-set eyes. The marriage has not brought happiness to Thomas; Gerda is at heart a musician and music means little to the prosaic Buddenbrooks. Their son Hanno takes after his mother—he has inherited her frail physique, her corroding love for music; the grain trade, or any kind of trade, fails to interest him. Hanno is really Thomas's hostage to a fortune which looks increasingly darker as the older man loses his self-confidence and enters into business ventures that turn out disastrously.

In hours of depression Thomas often asks: Who am I? "In the absence of any ardent objective interest, his inward impoverishment oppressed him almost without relief." He felt life running through his hands like sand, and he tells himself: I must think before it is too late. And thus it is that, very late, he begins to think.[90] Revelation comes to him on the afternoon when he discovers Schopenhauer's *The World as Will*. "It soothed him to see how a master-mind could lay hold on this strong, cruel, mocking thing called life and enforce it and condemn it. His was the gratification of the sufferer who has always had a bad conscience about his sufferings and concealed them from the gaze of a harsh, unsympathetic world, until suddenly, from the hand of an authority, he receives, as it were, justification and license for his suffering." [91] This celebrated passage has an autobiographical ring. It is the picture of the German bourgeois who was rapidly losing faith in the established protestant church and looking for solace in Schopenhauer's ascetic pessimism.

Our last picture of Thomas Buddenbrook is indeed in the grim mood of Schopenhauer. On a certain day, after a visit to his dentist, Thomas suffers a stroke and collapses in the street. "His hat rolled a little way off down the road; his fur coat was wet with mud and slush; his hands, in their white kid gloves, lay outstretched in a puddle." This death brings the story of the house of Buddenbrook to an end. What follows is but an epilogue, though a bitter and tormenting one. The old firm is liquidated with haste and at great loss; Hanno dies of typhoid fever; Gerda returns to her native Amsterdam; Christian is put away in a sanatorium. Only Toni, the goose, is left to weep over Thomas, over her father, her grandfather, over the whole prostrate house of the Buddenbrooks. In writing this story, Thomas Mann wrote the autobiography of his youth. For him the world of the middle class was both a form of life and an artistic principle. *Buddenbrooks* depicts the beauty inherent in decay where decreasing vitality produces increasing sensitivity, where the decadence of a race of merchants may give birth to a race of artists.[92] The motif is used again in Tonio Kröger which belongs to *Buddenbrooks* as *Death in Venice* belongs to *The Magic*

Mountain.[93] *Buddenbrooks* is the only great bourgeois epic in modern German literature. Mann's style, naturalism tempered by psychological irony, was admirably suited to the task. His leisurely prose, with the long and entwined sentences, has the grace of Biedermeier and the reflective dignity of *Die Meistersinger.*

Buddenbrooks appeared in 1901. It is significant that five years later John Galsworthy gave, on an even larger scale, a complete and absorbing picture of the English upper-middle class. *Man of Property* appeared in 1906, and became the organizing center for one of the most fascinating tales as yet told in modern fiction: *The Forsyte Saga.*

Galsworthy's spiritual ancestors were not the trinity of Schopenhauer, Wagner, Nietzsche, but Meredith, Maupassant, and Turgenev. No influence from the Rougon-Macquart series is recorded, though Zola's great scheme can hardly have failed to leave its mark on Galsworthy. Ibsen's social criticism was another leaven in his work. Galsworthy confessed that he was deeply intrigued by the various sections of English society with a more or less capital S.[94] He was not conscious of any desire to solve the many problems which he detected in the complicated mechanism of modern society or to provoke immediate reforms. He was an artist and set out to portray the various sections of English society: the landed gentry in *The Country House,* the ruling aristocracy in *The Patrician,* the upper-middle class in *The Forsyte Saga.* It is the last of these, however, that stands out conspicuously among Galsworthy's books as a highly representative work which pictures the English bourgeoisie at the moment of its greatest economic power, firmly holding its own against the powers from above and from below with profound complacency.

The central character of *The Forsyte Saga* is a lawyer, Soames Forsyte. Galsworthy was well acquainted with the social background which he described. His own family belonged to the upper-middle class that he had chosen as a target; his father and his grandfather had been lawyers and he himself had passed his bar examinations. *The Forsyte Saga* is the natural history of a family, representing all the virtues and the defects of a well-to-do bourgeois clan at the end of the nineteenth century. The story opens in 1886 giving a sketch of the preceding generations in retrospect. Six brothers and four sisters from the mighty trunk of the Forsytes whose fate we are to accompany over a period of three decades, are presented. Such a book, remarks a French critic, may also be classified as a zoological study.[95]

The Forsytes are a species indigenous to the British Isles, but their traits are universal and are to be seen wherever the bourgeoisie succeeded in establishing itself. This species is characterized by energy, invincible vitality, worship of health, taciturn pride, irreducible egotism, and a passion for property. Combined with these traits are other tendencies: appraisals based on money values, open contempt for ideas, superstitious respect for social taboos, and a jealous individualism strangely blended with a clannish feeling of solidarity for all that is Forsyte.[96] It is this class with its proverbial hypocrisy, its stiff upper lip, its fondness for the good things of life —furniture, food, wine, and horses—with which Galsworthy concerns himself. He gives us a picture, both ample and precise, of the British bourgeoisie and its family despotism in the Victorian age.[97] The result is a colossal tapestry of half a century of English life in which the destinies of the individual Forsytes constitute the thread from which the pattern is woven.

The Forsytes belong to the commercial or the professional groups of the bourgeoisie. Old Jolyon was a merchant in tea and has risen to be chairman of the board in several companies. Swithin is an estate and land agent, Roger a collector of urban property, Nicholas a director of mines and railways, Timothy a publisher, and James, like his son Soames, a solicitor. Galsworthy fuses the typical and the individual in an impressive manner as he unrolls the tale of these men, their wives, and their children. They are a tribe rather than a family. Neither Rothschilds nor Rockefellers, they are average bourgeois who live in an age which was the money-maker's paradise. They are smart investors and shrewd operators, but they are shown as the preservers of fortunes rather than builders of great enterprises.

Galsworthy treats them in the main with tendor irony, much as one would treat relatives of whom one does not approve but continues to visit. The Forsytes inhabit a world of their own. They have a sense of honor, of discipline, and of the certain amount of sacrifice which is essential to their survival. But although they do not lack in endearing traits, they are guided by a code of prudence that aims at the acquisition of property above all other earthly considerations. "Keep what you have—wives, money, a good address, and the blessings of a moral state." [98] "Do not offend the susceptibilities of society; do not offend the susceptibilities of the church." The sacrifice of any private feeling is to be preferred before risking the displeasure of either of these institutions. Respectability and security are the two basic social imperatives that guide Forsyte behavior. What will it profit a man if he save his soul and lose his fortune? Galsworthy presents this class with an affectionate detachment. The tone of his book, although inspired by faith and love and pity, is that of precise and deliberate serenity, of pure observation.

Yet the book is not a sociological treatise. "This long tale," says the author, "is no scientific study of a period; it is rather an intimate incarnation of the disturbance that Beauty effects in the lives of men." [99] Like Mann's Buddenbrooks, the Forsytes are very little given to religious query, nor does the lust for power tempt them, but, like their German cousins, they feel the magic attraction of beauty. Irene represents this incarnation of beauty so disturbing to a possessive world.[100] Galsworthy does not describe her directly in his effort to make us feel her influence. He chose a method at once more subtle and more persuasive. Her figure and her power are brought to us only through the senses of other characters, both men and women, who live under her spell. We are amazed to see how, one after another, she enchants the possessive Forsytes: Soames, her husband; the rough-hewn Swithin, who takes pride in the display of his horsemanship before this beautiful woman; Old Jolyon, who experiences an Indian summer of love and admiration in her company; and Young Jolyon whose second wife she becomes. Even June, whose lover she captivates, cannot help admiring her.

It is Soames, however, who suffers most deeply from the extraordinary magic which beauty casts over his possessive instincts. This man of pallor and precision, with his flat cheeks and his watchful gray eyes, as smooth and hard as the London pavement, can buy everything with his money, save Irene's love. It is Soames's tragedy that he is "unlovable without quite a thick enough skin to be thoroughly unconscious of the fact." [101] Irene is an intruder in the Forsyte universe. When she herself falls in love, it is with the only foreigner who had penetrated this hermetic world, the architect

Bosinney, June Forsyte's fiancé. Even in his description of their affair, Galsworthy continues to reveal Irene only through other characters. Through Soames's suspicion we realize that Bosinney and Irene are lovers. When finally, mad with jealousy and desire, he ravishes her, he acts according to his Forsyte nature, but in this act of possession, he degrades her to the place of a chattel, and loses Irene forever.

There are few figures in twentieth century fiction that have stirred the imagination of so many readers as have Irene and Soames. Ada Galsworthy tells of a letter that her husband received from a stranger who, walking down Haymarket, came face to face with a man "whom I instantly recognized as someone I knew . . . it was Soames Forsyte." And how many readers have been in love with Irene, or have hated her, as did D. H. Lawrence, calling her "the bitch in the manger"? [102] Lawrence's further comment is remarkable. Of Irene and her like, he says, "They are parasites upon the thoughts, the feelings, the whole body of life, of really living individuals . . . all they can do . . . is to feed upon the life that has been given by living men to mankind."

Although Irene is not possessive, she is, sociologically speaking, as much a child of the bourgeoisie as is Soames. In a bourgeois world she lives by means of her beauty as others live by means of their work or their wit. She married Soames because she was an unexperienced girl and Soames was rich. She gives him up for Bosinney because, according to Galsworthy, "sex attraction was utterly and definitely lacking" in her marriage. But Irene is spared the odium of the divorcée in the Victorian world; Old Jolyon leaves her a legacy, and her later marriage to Young Jolyon assures her of the same security that the Forsytes enjoy. One is inclined to speculate on what might have been Irene's fate in another age, but such reflections are idle and only demonstrate the vitality of Galsworthy's characters. Nor was Galsworthy himself immune to the extraordinary attraction that Irene, June, Jolyon, Timothy, James, and the others, so notably held for his readers. He became the prisoner of his own creations, and continued to be involved in their lives throughout the Edwardian period and into postwar Britain.

"The impingement of Beauty and the claims of freedom on a possessive world"—thus has Galsworthy himself defined the core of

The Forsyte Saga. It has, however, still another claim to recognition. In it we find the upper-middle class embalmed. "As the old Egyptians placed around their mummies the necessaries of a future existence, so have I endeavoured to lay beside the figures of Aunts Ann, Juley, and Hester, of Timothy and Swithin, of Old Jolyon and James, and of their sons, that which shall guarantee them a little life hereafter. If the upper middle class, with other classes, is destined to move on into amorphism, here, pickled in these pages, it lies under glass for strollers in the wide and ill-arranged museum of Letters. Here it rests, preserved in its own juice: The Sense of Property." [103]

In *Buddenbrooks* and *The Forsyte Saga* the bourgeoisie reached their highest degree of literary self-consciousness, but, as so often happens, this very self-knowledge was symptomatic of imminent decline. The parallelism between these two works is patent and has been the subject of many commentaries.[104] Both novelists picture a social and cultural process in their respective countries; both chose the rise of a family to show the driving power of the bourgeoisie. Their intuitive choice of subject matter is underlined by a sociological observation of J. Schumpeter's, according to which social classes are based on the continued and integrated work of families; the analysis of family destinies can, therefore, accomplish what the mere description of individuals could never achieve, that is, the portrait of a class.[105] Both the Buddenbrooks and the Forsytes belong to the upper-middle class; both represent financial and commercial rather than industrial interests. It is a puzzling fact that the great industrialists, the builders of economic empires, have inspired few novelists and have yet to find an adequate representation in literature. There are no really great novels that deal with the creators of steel mills, motorcar factories, or dye trusts. The Krupps, the Vicker Armstrongs, the Fords, the Bayers are still waiting for their epic. Perhaps it is because the reality of their lives is so incredible that fiction, which must give credence, is unable to deal with it.

But the analogy between *Buddenbrooks* and *The Forsyte Saga* is not confined to the sociological viewpoint. Though both deal with epic subjects, their authors treat them with "suitable irony." The more I see of people, says Galsworthy, the more I am convinced that they are never good or bad, merely comic or pathetic. And

Thomas Mann expresses himself in like manner: "What he saw, however, was that: comedy and misery." [106] Thus a basic impulse of both works is seen to be remarkably similar.

Both writers passed through the teachings of naturalism, and adopted from it what suited their purposes and their artistic temper. But they are not conditioned by positive philosophy and have indeed a deeper vision of man. The accuracy with which concrete details are reported does not aim at a surface reality, but at a deeper spiritual reality, the mystery that haunts the artist. [107]

Whereas Galsworthy is essentially visual in his descriptions, Mann is more musical. Galsworthy absorbs the world through his eyes, Mann through his ears. The difference between Irene and Gerda Buddenbrook expresses the difference in mood and genius that distinguishes the English from the German writer. Whereas Irene's beauty irradiates a magic glow that sets the Forsyte world afire, Gerda is preserved in "nervous coldness" and threatens the security of the Buddenbrook home with Wagnerian harmonies. But both novels show the bourgeois, whether he be called Thomas or Soames, as a poor wretch who tries in vain to defend himself against the greater forces of life and death behind the protective walls of property. The nemesis of the bourgeois in these books is not the class struggle or the proletarian menace, but rather beauty and love, or perhaps the atrophy of love to which the bourgeois finds himself condemned. Buddenbrooks and Forsytes alike are cursed by an inability to give themselves up, body and soul, to anything. Moved as they are by respectability and the sense of property, their emotions are attenuated by their reservations.

The world of Thomas Buddenbrook and Soames Forsyte is a world of horizontal structure, arranged in neat layers, in which all the great institutions support each other. The sanctity of the marriage tie depends on the sanctity of the family, and the sanctity of the family depends on the sanctity of property. But human beings do not live by bread alone. They thirst for metaphysical support and for a security more durable than the annual interest on investments. Both Thomas and Soames are ultimately lacking in metaphysical support. The church is for them a Sunday habit only, a guarantee against seditious thoughts from the outsiders and the have-nots. Only in Beauty do they sense this ideal world for which they secretly yearn. But the rays of beauty come from heaven and from hell, and fall only vertically into the horizontal strata of the bourgeois world.

These two great epics of bourgeois life bear out what our analysis of the European mind in other fields has taught us: that for the man of the ending century the world was justified as an esthetic phenomenon only. Such was the lesson of Schopenhauer and Nietzsche, of ars gratia artis; such was the legacy of impressionism.

It would be the presumption of hindsight to read into *Buddenbrooks* and *The Forsyte Saga* more than they contain, and to find in them the storm signals of the great hurricane that shattered Europe in 1914. Although Thomas Mann linked the life of the bourgeois with the theme of decadence, and although the Forsytes are conscious of representing "the end of the century," their perspectives do not stretch beyond the horizon of the era. Though individuals died and families became extinct, they believed that the species would prevail and that the world would be forever populated by Forsytes and Buddenbrooks.

Other authors have plowed over this same field: Duhamel's *Pasquier Chronicle,* Jules Romain's *Les Hommes de bonne volonté,* Roger Martin du Gard's novels, are similar attempts to depict the "human comedy" of bourgeois life. Whatever their literary merit, they did not achieve the symbolic density that makes *Buddenbrooks* and *The Forsyte Saga* the mirrors of an epoch.

CHAPTER VI

The Confident Years

I

Philosophical thought has always maintained its place in European civilization. Other cultures have produced reflections on man's position in the universe, but the distinguishing characteristic of the Western mind has been the integration of metaphysics and science from which formulae of systematic comprehensiveness have been framed. In the history of Western culture no period has been lacking in these daring attempts to determine where parallels meet in infinity.

The eighteenth century in particular called itself an age of philosophers, and although at its close Kant subjected this claim to a searching scrutiny and in the end denied that human reason could reach the absolute, *The Critique of Pure Reason* did not for long discourage metaphysical speculation. Fichte, Schelling, Hegel, and Schopenhauer advanced new ideas, each asserting that he had the answer to the enigmas of the cosmos and its relation with the human mind. Even Comte, who pretended to build exclusively on the results of positive science, crowned his system with a superstructure of more than "positive" validity.

About 1850, however, a situation developed which reversed the age-old alliance of philosophy and science. The empirical sciences advanced at such a rate and their findings appeared so startling that men began to entertain the idea of discarding philosophical speculation.

Historians like Ranke and Burckhardt spoke with derision of the philosophy of history. Eminent scientists like Pasteur and Koch abstained from offering speculative interpretations of nature which would go beyond the results obtained in rigorously controlled experiments. Science, though incomplete in its findings, was considered more convincing than the deductions of metaphysics. As a consequence, philosophy was severely admonished to adopt scientific proceedings and to abandon its pretension of reaching conclusive answers through the medium of the human desire for finality. It was in keeping with the spirit of the age that such trends led to a psychology essentially mechanistic and materialistic in type. But before long the speculative genius of occidental culture asserted itself anew; a French philosopher revindicated the birthright of philosophy in an age of science.

Henri Bergson was born in Paris in 1859, and lived an uneventful life, except that, as an octogenarian, he was obliged to witness the ruthless violence of the Nazis in his native city shortly before his death in 1941. When we open his books today we find ourselves far removed from the intellectual convulsions of Nietzsche and Kierkegaard, or the prophetic passion of Marx and Dostoevski. An atmosphere of pure contemplation emanates from Bergson's work, reminiscent of Spinoza. However, a world separates Spinoza's *Ethic* with its formidable array of theorems and definitions from the precise elegance in which Bergson presented his thought. His was a mind akin to Montaigne's, Pascal's, Vauvenargue's, and Chamfort's, showing beside the esprit de géometrie the esprit de finesse. While he was still teaching at Clermont Ferrand, he delivered a lecture on "Politesse," in which he described good manners as the grace of the mind. "I know no more powerful ally," he said, "in the overcoming of that intolerance which is a natural instinct than philosophical culture. . . . Dispute loses its bitterness and strife its intensity when lifted into the realm of pure thought—into the world of tranquility, measure and harmony." [1] Of such philosophical culture his writings give abundant proof.

"A philosopher worthy of the name," says Bergson in his lecture on intuition, "has never said more than a single thing; and even then it is something he has tried to say, rather than actually said. And he has said only one thing because he has seen only one point; and at that, it was not so much a vision as a contact; this contact furnished an impulse, this impulse a movement. . . . A thought which brings something new into the world is of course obliged to manifest itself through the ready-made ideas it comes across and draws into its movement; it seems thus, as it were, relative to the epoch in which the philosopher lived; but that is frequently merely an appearance. The philosopher might have come several centuries earlier; he would have had to deal with another philosophy and another science; he would have given himself other problems; he would have expressed himself by other formulas; not one chapter perhaps of the books he wrote would have been what it is; and nevertheless he would have said the same thing." [2]

What was this single thing which Bergson said in all his books? It can be stated best as the continuous creation of unforseeable novelty which takes place in the universe. Bergson says, "As far as I am concerned, I feel I am experiencing it constantly." [3] In other words, change was, for Bergson, the one single thing; actually he never did say anything else, and his philosophy might be summed up in one sentence: Je pense, donc je change. [4]

When he began to approach the problems of philosophy he was faced with a number of systems much in vogue: those of Kant, Comte, and Spencer. He compared their ideas with the "one single thing" he knew and felt obliged to reject their assertions. He said himself that it was intuition that whispered in his ear: Impossible. "Impossible even though the facts and the ideas appeared to invite you to think it possible and real and certain." What was it that he declined to accept? Contemporary philosophy maintained that we know phenomena, or the objects of the outer world, only as they present themselves to us. But, objected Bergson, we are at least assured of our existence; it is immediately given to us in our consciousness. We may deny or exclude everything else, but our relation with ourself rests upon intellectual sympathy, on intuition. [5] To these immediate data of our consciousness Bergson devoted his first book. [6] He found in man's consciousness a continuity of flow comparable to no other, a spectrum of a thousand shades, a variety of qualities, a continuity of progress and unity of direction. [7] How was it to be apprehended? What should it be called? Bergson gave it the name of duration (durée) and he was struck with the fact that previous philosophers had paid so little attention to it. He had found pure, unadulterated continuity in his consciousness; he had discovered living time, but philosophy, science, and even common sense failed to recognize it for what it was: the core of reality.

This then was Bergson's great discovery, the pivotal point around which all his thinking rotated and which crystallized in a series of meditations on body and soul, matter and memory, creative evolution, and finally society and religion. It linked his work to those who before him had seen the world in flux, in a state of becoming, notably Heraclitus, Hegel, and Schopenhauer. It also made him the representative philosopher in an age where change had become the symbol of operation for almost every aspect of life. But we would not be doing justice to this concentrated and energetic thinker were we to picture him merely as one who asserted duration, time, spontaneity, novelty, and creation in glowing terms as the essence of the universe. Bergson's stature rests upon the fact that he was bent on coming to grips with the difficulties and antinomies inherent in his intuition of time.

His experience of the immediate data of our consciousness had made him see internal duration, living time, for what it is. Here we grasp a succession, a growth from within, the uninterrupted prolongation of the past into the present which is already blending with the future. It is the direct vision of the mind by the mind.[8] In an age of materialism and determinism, in a period given to interpret man as the product of cause and effect only, this was indeed a discovery. Bergson found in his intuition the confirmation of man's spirituality and a guarantee of his freedom. It was startling to him that this basic fact had remained unknown or at least systematically obscured by the philosophical schools. Why is it, he questioned, that science, language, and the whole of intelligence seem to be on the side of determinism, eager to deny human freedom? The answer: man lives in a material world; he has a body.

The relationship of body and mind, soul and matter, presented Bergson with the greatest obstacle he had to overcome if he wished to go beyond the confines of his own consciousness. The world left to itself obeys laws; in determinate conditions matter behaves in a determinate way. Were our science complete and our calculating power infinite we could predict everything in the material universe. Consciousness, on the other hand, assures us of our freedom. Matter and mind, therefore, appear as two radically different, even antagonistic, forms in which the world presents itself, and man partakes in each. To the explanation of their coexistence Bergson devoted his second great inquiry: matter and memory.[9]

It is impossible in these pages to follow in detail Bergson's argument. Suffice it to say that he reduced the question of mind and matter to the narrower one: the relation between the brain and the mind. The life of the mind is bound to the body; there is solidarity between the two, but nothing more. Bergson compares their relation to the coat and the nail from which it hangs; the relationship is close, but the objects are not identical. Mental life transcends cerebral life.[10]

The perspectives opened up by this dissertation were significant. Without denying the importance of scientific knowledge, Bergson restored to man the legitimate right to metaphysical inquiry and the faculty to obtain knowledge of the absolute by an act of intuition. "To metaphysics, then, we assign a limited object, principally spirit, and a special method, mainly intuition. In doing this we make a clear distinction between metaphysics and science, but at the same time we attribute an equal value to both." [11]

Philosophy was thus assured of her age-old dignity. "Whence do we come? What are we doing here? Whither are we bound? If philosophy could really offer no answer to these questions of vital interest, if it were incapable of gradually elucidating them as we elucidate problems of biology and history, if it were unable to forward the study of them through an experience ever more profound and a vision of reality ever more piercing, if it were bound to be nothing better than an endless tournament between those who affirm and those who deny . . . we could well indeed say . . . that the whole of philosophy is not worth an hour's trouble." [12] Thus did Bergson defend philosophy's claim to be the lighthouse of human knowledge. It was not competing with science, but complementing it.

Bergson's next endeavor established his name as the most representative thinker of his time. We speak, of course, of the *Creative Evolution,* his most important work. "It is a sign of the times," said H. Höffding, "that nowadays every philosopher has to take up a position with respect to the concept of evolution. . . ." [13] It is indeed a characteristic of modern thought to see the world in this perspective, and the nineteenth century had already brought forth a number of systems which tried to incorporate the idea of evolution into the disciplines of philosophy. Bergson in particular had reason to accord a preponderant role to this concept. He had stated that the immediate data of our consciousness and the intuition which captures it display a continual movement, a fluid and a current in which forever new properties appear and unfold.

Was there a bridge from this discovery to a deeper penetration of evolution as observed in history and biology, that is, to a deeper penetration of life itself? Through a criticism of the human intellect Bergson hoped to prove that the idea of evolution, as science had so far applied it, was insufficient to enter the perpetual flux of life; Darwin and Spencer had accorded too much importance to circumstances, and had overlooked life's own impulse. In this manner Bergson showed the theory of knowledge and the theory of life to be interdependent. To understand life, we must first understand ourselves, especially the human intellect which guides our action and determines our outlook on the world. "The history of the evolution of life . . . reveals to us how the intellect has been formed by an uninterrupted progress, a long line which ascends through the vertebrate series up to man." [14]

The human intellect is not designed for disinterested contemplation; it is an appendage to our faculty for action. It is intended to secure the perfect orientation of body and environment; in brief, it is structured to think matter. But from this it follows also that our intellect is incapable of presenting to us the true nature of life and the full meaning of the evolutionary movement. We have only to compare the human intellect with other forms of consciousness, divergent from our own, that life has developed, to realize the limitations of our own understanding. We grasp this difference if we compare animal instinct with human intellect. But if these other forms of consciousness were brought together with the human intellect, might it not be possible to obtain a consciousness as wide as life itself? To achieve such a consciousness, even though the vision were fleeting, is Bergson's ambition in *Creative Evolution;* he undertook to picture the process of life's becoming by means of an intuition in which, he hoped, intellect and instinct had been blended.[15]

As we have noted, Bergson counted himself among those philosophers who had but one thing to say. His one thing was the discovery of change. "To exist is to change, to change is to mature, to mature is to go on creating oneself endlessly." And, he asked, should the same be said of existence in general, not only of man but of the universe? He comes to the conclusion that the universe endures as man endures.[16] Life is like a current passing from germ to germ through the medium of developed organisms. Organic evolution is thus interpreted in analogy to the evolution of our consciousness in which the past presses against the present and produces the up-springing of new forms of consciousness.[17] In other words, life is irreducible and irreversible. It is Bergson's contention that, life being a process in time, eludes science which can think and conceive only in spatial terms.

Two conflicting views have been advanced to explain life: the mechanistic thesis and the teleological conception. The first considers the organism and the whole of life to be in the nature of a machine the parts of which may be isolated and analyzed. It operates on the supposition that the totality of the real is postulated completely for all eternity; creation is merely an illusion, taking its rise in the infirmity and limitation of the human mind which can neither know nor foresee all things.[18] In opposition to this idea Bergson maintained his view of creative evolution with the accent on creative. But the other doctrine, which finds purpose and plan in the universe, is equally unacceptable to Bergson. Because the teleological concept also aims at the realization of a program previously arranged, it likewise denies time, creation, and invention. It it only mechanism inverted. Bergson said that his own doctrine transcended both mechanism and finalism. Against the hostile school of Darwinism and Lamarckism Bergson proclaimed an original impetus of life, his famous "élan vital."

The élan vital is the life force that passes from one generation to the following, producing in its course the variations that constitute the species.[19] The vital impulse is really what makes evolution creative and not simply recurrent.

The evolutionary movement in which the vital impulse manifests itself would be a simple one if life adhered to a single course like that of a cannon ball. But life proceeds more like a shell bursting suddenly into fragments, which, in turn, burst into further fragments, ad infinitum. Life has split into individuals and species; it does not reveal itself as a river gushing forward and onward; it is conditioned by the resistance of matter which it meets at every step. To overcome this resistance of matter is the greatest obstacle that life has to conquer.[20]

But the resistance of matter is not the only cause of division which life bears within its bosom. Life is scattered in manifestations which are incompatible and often antagonistic. There is discord among the species; there are species which are arrested in their development, and others which are in retrogression. No doubt there is also progress to be found, but this progress is accomplished only on two or three great lines of the evolutionary movement. It is in this part of his meditation on life that Bergson admits that not all of these directions have the same interest to him. "What concerns us particularly is the path that leads to man." [21] It is this human perspective that has made *Creative Evolution* more than just one more treatise on the mysteries of life and has raised it to the level of those philosophies which endeavor to make man see his own fate in the looking glass of unifying thought.

In its unrelenting fight with matter, life unfolds and expands in different directions. The greatest division is that between vegetable and animal life, the one fixed in place and deprived of consciousness, the other mobile and conscious. In the animal kingdom Bergson stresses the separation between the insects and the vertebrate animals which reach their culmination in man. They are characterized by different and even opposed ways of solving the struggle for survival, instinct and intellect, divergent solutions which are equally adequate for the same purpose. The insects use instinct, the faculty of employing and constructing organic instruments; man uses intelligence, the faculty of making and employing instruments. It is here that Bergson introduces his definition of man. "If we could rid ourselves of all pride, if, to define our species, we kept strictly to what the historic and prehistoric period shows us to be constant characteristics of man and of intelligence, we should say, not Homo sapiens, but Homo faber." [22] For Bergson, son of the nineteenth century, man is the intelligent animal, who has the ability of manufacturing artificial objects, especially tools to make more and better tools, and thus of indefinitely varying the output. Who can fail to discern in this definition the stamp of the age?

Intelligence has as its chief object the unorganized solid, the discontinuous and immobile; it has unlimited power to decompose matter and recompose it into new systems. In its sphere it works wonders, but it is marked by a natural inability to comprehend life. Instinct, on the other hand, is sympathy. If this sympathy could extend its object and also reflect upon itself, it would give us the key to vital operations. Thus Bergson reverts once more to his concept of intuition. Intuition is instinct that has gone through the purgatory of thought and has become disinterested, self-conscious, and capable of reflecting upon its object. Intuition will give us a sympathetic communication between ourselves and the rest of the living; it introduces us into life's own domain which is endless continuous creation.

It is obvious that Bergson is as critical of man's intellect as Kant, Schopenhauer, Kierkegaard, and Nietzsche had been. But he has always defended himself against the accusation of being anti-intellectual or antiscientific.[23] Intelligence and science aim above all at making us masters of matter; before we speculate, we must live, and life demands that we make use of matter. Beyond the immediate necessities of our existence, however, there is a realm of truth to which we are admitted by methods different from those that help us to survive. "In the absolute we live and move and have our being." The knowledge we may gain of the absolute is incomplete, no doubt, but it is neither external nor relative.

In Bergson's view life is of the psychological order. He states, and sometimes overstates, a cleavage between the organic and the inorganic, or between mind and matter. The vital impulse, in need of creation, cannot act or manifest itself absolutely, because it is confronted with matter. But it seizes upon matter, which is necessity itself, and strives to introduce into the material universe the largest possible amount of indetermination and liberty. Thus optimism triumphs once more over determinism.[24]

Bergson believed, as did so many of his fellow Europeans, that it is man who justifies the universe because he reveals the victory of mind over matter, that is, freedom. Bergson's optimism is less naïve and more circumspect than that of the rationalism preceding him, but it is optimism just the same.

In the animal world invention is never anything but a variation on the theme of routine; by pulling at its chains it succeeds only in stretching them. "With man, consciousness breaks the chain. In man, and in man alone, it sets itself free. . . . Everywhere but in man consciousness has had to come to a standstill; in man alone it has kept on its way." [25] On flows the current, running through human generations. The meaning of evolution was summed up by Bergson in unforgettable words: "As the smallest grain of dust is bound up with our entire solar system . . . so all organized beings, from the humblest to the highest, from the first origins of life to the time in which we are, and in all places as in all times, do but evidence a single impulsion. . . . All the living hold together, and all yield to the same tremendous push. The animal takes its stand on the plant, man bestrides animality, and the whole of humanity, in space and in time, is one immense army galloping beside and before and behind each of us in an overwhelming charge able to beat down every resistance and clear the most formidable obstacle, perhaps even death." [26]

Such was the view of life that Bergson presented to his time in 1907. Its impact was instantaneous. Although Bergson had not touched upon the problems of ethics, and though it took him twenty-five more years to draw the religious conclusions implied in his premises, he had opened an outlook for which his age had been thirsting. Bergson took the interpenetrating flow of time and pictured it as an emanation of the Godhead.[27] God is conceived as pure creativity, not as a fountain but as a flowing, and man's mind is made in his image. Bergson himself believed he had established "creation as a fact." Needless to say, his was no longer the Hebrew-Christian idea of creation, but one that had survived the onslaught of Darwinism, though the scars of the encounter were there. Bergson's God is the generator of both matter and spirit, an idea which involves considerable difficulty. God had given the original impulse, the élan vital, and his work is continued on the side of life by the evolution of the species and the building of human personalities. "I

speak of God," he explained to a Jesuit father, "I speak of God as
the source whence issue successively by an effect of his freedom, the
'currents' or 'impulses' each of which will make a world." [28]

It seems clear that this vindication of the divine origin of life, of
spirit and individuality, more than anything else, produced Bergsonism, a phenomenon strongest in France, but spreading all
through the Western world in the years before the Great War.
Librarians have estimated that in a brief time no less than four
hundred and seventeen books and articles on Bergson appeared.
In 1911 alone there were seventy-nine; in 1912 one hundred and
twenty-six dealt with him and his metaphysics, not all of them with
sympathy, of course. Translations of his works appeared in all European languages.

While Bergson touched a tender chord in the heart of his time
when he declared that the essence of life was spirit, he was also
close to the revolutionary ideas that were revamping physics in this
decade. His view of reality as movement and nothing but movement
was akin to atomic science which in the same years began to penetrate the mysteries of the atom. From Roentgen to J. J. Thompson,
Rutherford, and Niels Bohr, modern physics gradually abandoned
the idea of the atom as an irreducible material unit and replaced
it with the concept of a center of electric discharges. It was reserved
for a later time, however, to apply the lessons of atomic physics to
the problem of life itself and to look for an explanation of the élan
vital compatible with nuclear theories.[29] Bergson had insisted that
life was a spiritual force, and modern biologists are not content
to accept such an answer lest it close the door to further inquiry
into the question: What is life?

Another critical stand is taken by those who object to Bergson's
use of intuition, to his claim to have resolved the antinomies which
Kant had analyzed in so masterly a manner. Bergson asserted that
intuition could do what reason could not do and could assure man
of freedom, spirit, and even of the immortality of his soul. His opponents contend that intuition appears in Bergson's philosophy as a
deus ex machina who terminates the conflict when all other attempts
have failed.

It must be admitted that Bergson had been no more successful
in assuaging the uncertanities which beset the human mind than

any previous philosopher. The impact that a philosophy has on its time, however, depends in but small degree on its logical consistency. In commenting on the sudden rise of Bergsonism, Réné Gillouin wrote in 1911, "The enormous and very rapid success of Bergson's philosophy is the result of many causes, but to my mind the most important is this. Toward 1880 philosophy was about fifty years behind the stage of advance reached by the physical sciences. In . . . Bergson it suddenly recovered all the ground it had lost. Bergsonism was vaguely anticipated in the minds of men; in the measure in which it took shape we recognized it. It offers an open way when all other roads are closed." [30] Indeed Bergsonism did open a new road. It explained evolution without denying God; it acknowledged the gradual development of man without lowering the individual to a mere accidental position in the greater accident of the species. "This vague and formless being, may he be called man or superman" felt assured of his individuality, of his freedom, and of his spiritual spontaneity.

Though Bergson had not yet approached the world of human society in his meditations, the socialist movement hailed both his interpretation of evolution as an upward movement and his anti-intellectualism as kindred to the realism of Marx and Proudhon. George Sorel wrote a penetrating essay on *Creative Evolution*. From a different camp, Catholic writers like Péguy found in Bergson a source of inspiration. So also did Marcel Proust, who encountered in *Matière et mémoire* the speculative expression for the experience of duration and time lived which formed the wellspring of his artistic productivity. *A la Recherche du temps perdu* is the epic which corresponds to Bergson's thought as Schiller's work corresponds to Kantian philosophy. Bergson himself recognized their spiritual consanguinity.[31]

In philosophy proper the effect of his thought was extraordinary; it is sufficient to mention only a few of the great ones who confessed their indebtedness: Dilthey, William James, Scheler, Ortega y Gasset, and lately Arnold Toynbee.

There may be still another explanation for the impact that Bergson had on his time. It was an age of assured security and unperturbed progress. To many, Bergson's vital impulse seemed the magic catchword for the titanic drive which impelled Western civilization toward shores yet unexplored. Viewed from this angle, Bergsonism was a misunderstanding. Bergson's criticism of "Homo Faber," of man's intelligence primarily concerned with material things, was not understood by his contemporaries in its full implication. Bergson himself was, as we know, aware that, had he been born centuries earlier, his whole outlook might have been different. From his later work we can judge that he might have joined the choir of the great Christian mystics, such as Meister Eckhardt, Tauler, and St. John of the Cross. As early as 1907 his thinking pointed in the direction of religion. But these were consequences from which the prosperous optimism of his period shrank. As Bergson later expressed it, the European body had expanded out of all proportion, while the soul remained what it had been, too small to fill it, and too weak to guide it.[32] What Bergson recommended was the mystic joy which might engender spiritual reform, and this was obtainable only by the very few. Europe yearned for confirmation of its impulses and activities in speculative thought, but refused to be deterred by warnings which might spring from the same source. Thus Europe settled for the counterfeits of religion, for nationalism, imperialism, and estheticism.

II

Benedetto Croce would not have agreed with Bergson's theory of the philosopher as a man "who knows only one thing." Rather would he have concurred with Bacon: "I take all knowledge to be my province." It was his desire to comprehend many things. Although his mind was focused from the beginning on history, art, and literature rather than on nature, he aimed, beyond reality, at systematic coherence without which no philosophy is authentic. His work, produced over a long and diligently applied life, is impressive in size and scope. It generated a new intellectual climate in Italy, far removed from the morbid splendor of d'Annunzio's verbal cascades, and it assured Croce of a European reputation. The adjective "Crocian," says an English critic, will stand in Italian dictionaries as "Shavian" does in ours.[33]

Although Croce's production is not confined to the period before 1914, it is nevertheless true that the most significant aspects of his variegated writing were present before that date. We shall not, therefore, be guilty of violating the rules of historical chronology by placing him in this part of our studies.

"Anyone," says Croce, "who . . . was born and grew up in the early years of the unity and liberty of Italy must proclaim in every company and against all opponents that he knows what it is to have lived the greater and better part of his life in a sublime spiritual atmosphere." [34] According to him it was a period of full and fruitful expansion of energies and of noble cooperation of man with man. Europe had reached a more reflective self-consciousness, coherence, and harmony than ever before. To this self-consciousness, coherence, and harmony Croce himself was one of the chief contributors. The generation which came to maturity after 1918, viewed him with measured admiration. Thus we may approach this eminent figure with an attitude not unlike the one he adopted for himself when he began the study of Hegel; we may ask, what is living and what is dead in the thought of Benedetto Croce.

For a man to whom the world of the mind appeared essentially as history, the historical approach would seem appropriate. Croce himself takes us by the hand. His autobiography, though neither recollections nor confessions, opens the door to an intimate understanding of his mind. It bears the characteristic title: *Contribution to the Criticism of Myself.*[35]

Croce was born in 1866 in southern Italy, one more example of the speculative genius of this part of his country, after the fashion of St. Thomas, Bruno, Campanella, and Vico. Croce's parents were wealthy landowners in the Abruzzi region, but Croce spent most of his youth, and indeed most of his life, in Naples. Here he went to a Catholic school run by priests for the nobility and the gentry. A religious conflict soon cast its shadow over his awakening consciousness. He realized "his inability fully to obey the commands of religion." "I found the idea of a loveable God too abstract to grasp." The day was not far off when he was obliged to admit to himself: I am done with my religious belief.[36]

After losing his parents in an earthquake, he came to live in Rome in the house of his cousin, Silvio Spaventa, one of the luminaries of liberal Italy. But life in Rome was far from pleasant for the boy; he found it indeed more in the nature of a bad dream, and afterward recollected these years as the darkest and bitterest of his life. But he did meet in Spaventa's house Antonio Labriola whose Socialist ideas became later the springboard for Croce's own thought. At the time, however, Croce was by no means aware of his philosophical calling, and gave himself up to antiquarian studies and to wide travel in Germany, Spain, France, and England. He became deeply steeped in historical and philological research and acquired therefrom the discipline inherent in this kind of scholarship. Much as he liked these studies, they remained to him "something external," and more and more he felt the necessity of doing "something inward." The reading of Vico and de Sanctis strengthened a growing conviction that a synthesis between history and philosophy, history as the essence of philosophy, philosophy as the core of history, was by no means impossible. But it was Labriola's essay on the Communist Manifesto that sent his mind into a spin from which he emerged tonified and determined to work out his own solutions.[37] "I felt my whole mind burst into flame. New thoughts and problems took root in my spirit and so overran it that I was powerless to free myself from them."

For several months he threw himself into the study of economics. He participated in the discussions of socialist circles and exchanged letters with George Sorel. He even experienced a yearning to give up his privileged position, to renounce economic and social advantages, and to enter the crusade for the oppressed. In the end an intellectual catharsis cleared his mind and found expression in his first important work on historical materialism and the economics of Karl Marx.[38]

Croce's infatuation with Marxism was only a phase in his development, but, one would like to think, an indispensable one. He had no great difficulty in finding the loopholes in Marxian doctrine, the labor theory of value and its derivative, the surplus value theory. It was easy to show that these were merely economic suppositions, and that the conclusion to which Marx had arrived would not stand the test of thorough scrutiny. Although Croce acknowledged the insight to be gained from economic materialism toward a deeper understanding of historical processes, he was disappointed with the general picture of the evolution of mankind that resulted from the Marxian dialectic. History appeared in it simply as "a kind of anthology of all proletarian rebellions." [39]

Croce could not accept the Marxian equation of matter equals reality equals economics, nor would he for a moment admit to the assumption that man could be defined by his economic condition. He looked for help and turned to the great Italian sociologist, Pareto.[40] In their correspondence Croce tried to ascertain what part of man's being could be defined by economic activity. No agreement was reached by them, yet the feeling grew in Croce that the Marxian answer was no answer at all. The goal of life could not be the Utopia of a classless society because "the end of life is simply life in its fullness, the sacred mystery of existence which we must worship." [41]

Perhaps the most important effect that Marx had on Croce was to ready his mind for the contact with Hegel; only in Marx and his school was Hegel at this time still a living force.[42] Croce's beginnings, his thorough immersion in historical scholarship, had much in common with Hegel's own youth as we have come to know it. To outline a philosophy that would do justice to history, to becoming and evolution, nay, that would be in itself history, becoming, and evolution, was a goal to which both men were committed. Small wonder then that Croce discovered the Hegelian dialectic anew, and praised it for having established the truth that reality is "not static but living, not fixed but changing," and that it, therefore, demands the explanatory principle of the dialectic. "Modern thought cannot do without this force of contrariety, nor the synthesis which at once retains and overcomes the opposing elements." [43] Thus did Croce hail Hegel's dialectic as the philosophical method for the comprehension of "die Welt in Werden" (the becoming world).

But Croce's essay on Hegel is not merely an acclamation. It is a piece of criticism, discerning and surgical, which separates the living tissue from the dead. It shows how Hegel's genuine inspiration became encumbered and overburdened by his typically German reverence for authority, by his panlogism and by an outworn theological attire which Hegel refused to discard.[44] Croce said of his relation to Hegel that it resembled Catullus' love for Lesbia; he could neither live with him nor without him. But by praising Hegel as the last great speculative genius of the Occident, Croce ushered in a Hegel renaissance of vast significance for the intellectual and political history of the twentieth century.

It was more than a coincidence that Dilthey at this same time published his *Jugendgeschichte Hegels* which revealed for the first time the emotional wellsprings that had nourished Hegel's thought before it froze into the majestic grandeur of the concluded system. Neo-Hegelianism became indeed one of the most influential trends of the early twentieth century. Hegel had defined the goal of history as "the progress in the consciousness of liberty." Whereas this was, as we have seen, a highly ambiguous definition that could mean different things to different men, Croce interpreted it in the way the liberals of the nineteenth century would have understood it. His own historical enterprises, *The History of Italy Since Her Unification* and *The History of Europe During the Nineteenth Century,* follow Hegel closely and are geared to show the evolution of Western mankind as evidence of constant "progress in the consciousness of liberty." In his history of Europe, completed in 1932, he gave a classical exposition of the liberal creed which he called the religion of liberty. "He calls it so," we read, "because he looks for what is essential and intrinsic in every religion." Every religion, then, has at its core the belief in freedom which is for Croce the highest religious tenet of our occidental world. Liberty is a continual reacquisition, a continual liberation, a continual battle, one in which a last and final victory is impossible and which will go on as long as the human spirit knows its birthright. Socrates as well as Jesus Christ, Augustine as well as Luther and Calvin, are among the saints of this religion of liberty. And Croce was convinced that it would prevail in spite of all obstacles. Not only has it the future for its domain; it has something better still; it has eternity.[45] These words were written while Italy was smarting under Mussolini's rule, but they express what Croce had said and felt since he began to take issue with the great questions of his time. *The History of Europe in the Nineteenth Century,* dedicated to Thomas Mann, may rightly be called the testament of classical liberalism.

In the best of liberal traditions were also other of Croce's enterprises, especially the foundation and publication of the famous *Critica*. This bimonthly review, established in 1902 and continued without interruption into the days of World War II, was one of the great European publications, like the *Neue Deutsche Rundschau,* the *Revista del Occidente,* or the *Nouvelle Revue Française*. *Critica* was meant to bring national and European culture together. In its opening number Croce proclaimed as his aim a general awakening of the philosophical spirit in Italy. As the enemies of such a revival, he lists the positivists, the pseudo-naturalistic detractors of thought and freedom, and the mystic reactionaries. In other words, *Critica* was a tool of polemics and reconstruction.

The work on *Critica* gave Croce "the calm conviction" that he had found his place in life; through it he became the master and spiritual guide of the younger generation. It was the most immediate service which he could render Italian culture at that time. The review was accompanied by collections such as *Classics of Modern Philosophy, Writers of Italy,* and *The Library of Modern Culture*. Croce did not do this large amount of editorial work single-handed. He had the help and advice of a young philosopher, Giovanni Gentile, whose friendship and good offices he was fortunate enough to engage. Both men were admirers of Hegel, and for a short time this bond held them together, but by 1913 their friendship had ended. Later Gentile became the official apologist of the Fascist regime.

But to return to *Critica;* it was in this review that Croce published his criticism of literati like d'Annunzio, in addition to a good number of literary essays. The range of these essays is extraordinary, and I should judge that they will always occupy a high place in literary criticism. Those on Ariosto and Corneille, the larger treatises on Dante and Goethe, have a freshness of judgment, a directness of expression and opinion, and, last but not least, a grain of common sense and humor which makes their reading a salutary experience.

Of course it must be admitted that Croce, like other literary popes, shows a tendency to be dogmatic and opinionated (witness his essay on Proust), and to condemn any approach opposed to his own. In his esthetic theory Croce equated art with expression, and refused to be attracted by what may lie behind or beneath a given work. His treatment of poetry is, therefore, often formalistic, and in any case opposed to the modern tendency to look for psychological or biological revelation in a work of art. Just as he refused in his autobiography to follow the model of Jean Jacques Rousseau, so he refrains in his criticism from looking for psychological motivation. It was this particular restraint and aloofness that caused a critic to ask whether there might not be a fundamental aridity in Croce's mind.[46]

Alas! the question recurs when one opens Croce's four-volume work, *The Philosophy of the Spirit or Mind*. A philosopher, Croce once said, is by his calling consumed with "the passion for clear thinking." [47] There is too much of the passion for clear thinking in these volumes, and the reader's interest flags, at least this reader's interest. As an early critic of Croce comments, "There seems nothing to inspire, nothing to thrill the imagination; there are no bold speculations or brilliant hypotheses of cosmological origins of destinies." [48] Croce's philosophy is first and foremost an inquiry into thinking and not into being, or, to use his own words, philosophy is methodology, not ontology. This paradox stands in need of explanation. Like all true philosophers, Croce wished to understand reality, more specifically the concrete, but for him reality was the mind, and philosophy the science of the mind. "All philosophy . . . shows that there is nothing outside the mind." [49]

We shall not trouble the reader with an explanation of the manner by which Croce arrived at this conclusion. The student of philosophy knows that the dispute about the reality of reality is as endless as it is meaningless; the opposing schools will never become reconciled. Suffice it to say that Croce occupies a position technically termed objective idealism. Mind is reality and there is no reality which is not mind.[50] This mind which is reality shows activity, and it is with the activity of the mind that Croce concerns himself. We find in the mind order and the relation of forms. In other words, reality is a system, and it is the task of philosophy to present these forms of activity and to show how they unite to form the concrete world of our human experience. In this manner everything is neatly classified into categories of theoretical activity and practical activity, and they in turn are subdivided into four pure concepts: beauty, truth, usefulness, and goodness. It is of course the business of philosophy to shed light on a chaotic world and on ourselves in this world. But Croce, like his model, Hegel, belongs to that class of thinkers who would willingly sacrifice the concrete, which he wants to understand, if it does not fit into the strait jacket of his thought pattern. Croce's critics objected to his denial of the reality of the objective world, and reproached his "unscrupulous genius" for logical coherence. There is indeed a great deal of scholastic hair-splitting in Croce's *Philosophy of the Mind* which does not become any more convincing because it is presented with a boastful logic. Even Croce's esthetic—called the expressionist theory by the textbooks—that beauty is expression, leaves us unmoved today.

There is, however, a part of Croce's systematic effort which is still fresh and stimulating after forty years. It is his interpretation of life as history and history as life. From the beginning, Croce, very much like Bergson, had striven to overcome the panscientific claims of positivism. In words which remind us of his French peer, Croce denied the pretention of the natural sciences that they alone could give us an adequate picture of reality. Said he, "They calculate, measure, posit equations, establish regularities, fashion classes and types, formulate laws, show in a method of their own how one fact is derived from other facts." They increase our control over nature, but, he maintained, they are turned away from reality and not toward the individual, the concrete which alone is real. Croce was much like Bergson in his insistence on the reality of mind, but whereas Bergson discovered the true nature of the mind in listening to what is immediately given to us in our consciousness, time and duration, Croce turned his attention to the historical world. Life for Croce is not the élan vital but reality manifesting itself in ceaseless activity. The interpretation of this action is history. Thus philosophy becomes one with history, and history is identical with philosophy. It was a renovation of Hegel's famous saying that the rational is real and the real is rational.

At first thought, the identification of life with history, and of history with philosophy, seems paradoxical. Croce qualified his statement by making clear what kind of historical writing could be considered as history. A narrative of events, arbitrarily selected, or dryly recorded, he considered to be neither history nor philosophy. History, he contends, is a judgment of events, and this judgment derives its strength, impulse, and truthfulness directly from the pres-

ent, that is, from life itself. In order to support his first paradox
Croce advances a second and more daring one. It is his idea that all
history is contemporary history. "Only an interest in the life of the
present can move one to investigate past facts." [51] This is the meaning of the old saying historia magister vitae. Dead history revives,
and past history again becomes present, as the development of life
demands them. Says Croce, we know at every moment all the history
that we need to know, and since what remains over does not matter
to us, we need not possess the means of knowing it, or if we do,
we shall possess those means when the need arises.

Thus Croce adhered to the growing fold of thinkers who define
man as a historical animal. He would have agreed with Ortega y
Gasset, who said that man does not have a nature, man has a
history, and his nature will be revealed in all its potentialities only
during the historical process. From Montesquieu to Herder and
Hegel, from Ranke to Burckhardt, Tocqueville and Dilthey, this
creed had gradually gained depth and perspective until it developed
into one of the most influential trends of the early twentieth century: historicism. Croce's panhistoricism is one of the most provocative expressions of this way of looking at the world.

Croce's radical formula, that all history is contemporary history,
seems to place him on the extreme wing among those who emphasized the subjective character of all historical knowledge. But he
did not mean to preach subjectivism. "Document and criticism, life
and thought," he states, "are the true sources of history." He did
wish, however, to distinguish between history that is life and history
that is a mere recording of dead facts which he calls chronicle. He
also takes the field against the pseudo histories, the philosophy of
history that speculates on the course of events rather than comprehends it, and against poetical or fictionalized history where the
interest of sentiment takes the place of the interest of thought.
Croce's theory that all history is contemporary history was a reaction against the naïveté of certain historians who believed that they
could tell the story "wie es eigentlich gewesen" or those who sub-
scribed to Taine's "collection des faits." The twentieth century has
come to accept Croce's viewpoint. We believe in the dignity of
history; we believe in history as an indispensable way to learn about
human nature, but we no longer hold its reconstructions to be

infallible. Further, we know that historical reconstructions must of necessity be transitory. They deal with temporal matters, and, as Croce says, they have their origin and impetus in time. History could be infallible only if it had reached its end. Obviously such a history could be written only on doomsday, and who would then care?

But history never dies, says Croce; she always joins her beginnings with her ends. These ideas to which we have become quite accustomed, were daring when Croce published them in 1916. Living as we do in a time when official and unofficial history is constantly rewritten, we would not object to Croce's paradox that all history is contemporary. We would only demand a criterion that would salvage historical objectivity from irresponsible fancy or wishful myths. It was in Germany that Croce's idea found the most resounding echo. Ernst Troeltsch and Friedrich Meinecke pursued and improved Croce's teaching and developed it into the philosophy of historicism.

The significance of Croce's evaluation of history is not confined to the academic world, however. His was an interpretation of history that was both humane and humanistic. "Enfranchising itself from servitude to extra-mundane caprice and to blind necessity . . . thought conceives history as the work of man, as the product of human will and the intellect, and in this manner enters that form of history which we shall call humanistic." [52] Croce believed that true history is the history of the individual in so far as he is universal, and of the universal in so far as it becomes individual.

From here then stems Croce's belief in the "religion of liberty" that would ultimately supersede the church religions in their present form. But it was not only in the churches that Croce found the obstacles to human history humanly conceived. Mankind in general has a tendency to bow to idols and images which have been raised to the rank of deities. Croce's concept of history and of "true modern thought" is both amythical and antimythical. To him modern thought is "thought uncontaminated by myth." [53] This myth may be religious or political, philosophical or economic—Croce rejects them all. He sees in them merely excuses for circumscribing the labor of the rational mind which is endless.

He failed to see that the rational mind, just as well as his religion of liberty, could be elevated to a myth among the many that have blinded or inspired mankind. Hence it would be a relatively simple task to point to the limitations of Croce's philosophy. Its foundation was rational humanism; as such it was antimythical and antiutopian. Catholic writers find Croce wanting in a sense of drama and deprived of respect for the mystery of human life. Marxian theorists, as one would expect, accuse him of formalism, and of being unrelated to "the preponderant activity of the popular classes." [54]

Croce was a liberal thinker who worked energetically to restore the human mind to a place of preeminence, a philosopher who saw in the pursuit of liberty the best of human endeavor, and in history the great unfolding of reason which gives significance to mankind.

Alacrity, alertness, elasticity, and common sense are the weapons with which Croce's critical genius approached the work of humanity. We are inclined to believe that these are qualities by which Croce himself would wish to be judged. He condemned despair and confusion just as he condemned oppression. The picture that he gives us of humanity resembles a self-portrait; it is colored by overoptimism and the belief in the predestined victory of reason over the forces of tragedy and darkness.

But withal, he was one of the principal agents of transition who saved and gave as a bequest to our time the legacy of the liberal thinking of the past. He was convinced that the nineteenth century would one day be recognized for its true greatness and would then be compared to the Athens of Pericles and the France of Descartes.[55] He was a good European, steeped in humanistic tradition and at home in the poetry and thought of all Western nations in whose treasuries he wandered about at ease. European as he was, he nevertheless felt a sense of commitment toward his native Italy, and he did not hide in an ivory tower when his services were demanded. He was made Senator for life in 1910 and became Minister for Education in 1920. His writing had assumed public character and significance. Croce became the symbol of the opposition against Mussolini, and in 1943 one of the focal points for Italy's resurrection. But that is another story.

III

The reader may, at first glance, feel a certain surprise to find Bernard Shaw brought into line with Bergson and Croce. Nonetheless, it is here that "the most challenging and disruptive of European writers" must take his stand.[56] Although George Bernard Shaw lived to a greater age than any other modern writer, the essence of his thought emanates from the late Victorian and, even more, the Edwardian eras. By 1960 it has become quite clear that when Shaw speaks of "today" he refers to the years between 1890 and 1910.[57]

Shaw was born in Dublin in 1856, and spent his youth in the household of an alcoholic father. The poverty which surrounded his early years, though not abysmal, produced a deep-seated fear that the penury of his childhood might one day become "the real thing," the degrading misery which held the proletarian masses in its grip. From these first experiences, more than from Marx, Shaw acquired the emotional impetus which drove him on to the road of socialism. "The greatest of our evils and the worst of our crimes is poverty." [58]

In his early days he lived in a world of his own making, full of fantasy and imagination, amply fed by reading and music. On leaving this world, however, he found himself confronted with a society in which he had no standing, and as a result, he became excessively shy and sensitive. Success came to him only with winning the race in spite of his many handicaps.

The answer to the baffling questions that arise from Shaw's contradictory attitudes and poses may well be found in the complexities of his youth. An immense ambition drove him to overcome external obstacles as well as internal difficulties which might endanger his ascent. Thus he came to view emotion objectively, to decry romanticism, and to explode the codes of society as hypocrisy and snobbery. But the fight left its scars on his soul, and he was never really free from snobbism and romanticism himself. We are not here concerned with the mysteries of Shaw's erotic life—his late maturity, his unconsummated marriage, his "affairs" which seem to have been ignited by a desire "to tease" rather than to find fulfillment.[59] His craving for tenderness and passion was satisfied by listening to Mozart and Wagner rather than by surrender to the living charms of living beings. Like Nietzsche, he was enamored of disguises and was a man of many masks.

That there was much of the poet in Shaw can easily be seen through such works as *Candida* and *St. Joan,* but it is equally clear that this side of his genius never reached fruition. Was it stillborn, as T. S. Eliot assumes, or conscientiously smothered? Shaw's anti-romanticism, fashioned on personal grounds and for personal reasons, was further strengthened by his fear of becoming contaminated with Irish excitability. "I am a typical Irishman; my family came from Yorkshire," he used to say, expressing in one sentence his fear of what he might be and what he wanted to be. Common sense and sanity became his guides when he set out for London. He entered England an alien and a stranger, but he was also naturally endowed with certain very English qualities; there was much in him of the puritan, the moralist, the radical, and the reformer. Though he liked to think of himself as unique, he fitted perfectly into the tradition of radical thought of the 1880's.[60]

After working for a real-estate agent and for the Edison telephone company, he turned to writing novels, which were rejected by some sixty publishers. At the age of forty he had earned no more than six pounds by his pen. Yet these were the most important years of his life, veritable *Lehrjahre*, during which he taught himself short-hand, bookkeeping, public speaking, and many other skills which he thought might become useful.

He grasped the political ideas of his age, albeit in a typical British perspective, and made industrialism, democracy, agnosticism, and feminism the basic categories in which this world should be discussed. And discussion, or rather debate, became his chosen medium, mastered with brilliance, whether as pamphleteer, critic, or dramatist. He called himself an original thinker whose business it was to question and test all established creeds and codes to see how far they still are valid and how far worn out or superseded, and even to draft new creeds and codes.[61] He made it his business to blast old beliefs; he caught the unconventional in conventional poses and vice versa; and he did outmarch, outmaneuver, and out-debate everybody in the process. Since he was not linked to any tradition or institution, he was in a splendid position to call anyone's bluff. The whole world became one enormous debating society and Shaw was its favorite speaker. To his natural gifts of superb wit, unrelenting probity, and powerful imagination, he added information and scholarly perception. He accepted what more tutored intellects had to offer. He was not finical, and borrowed equally from the Webbs and from Henry George, from Samuel Butler as well as from Theodore Mommsen.

But inseparably woven into this process of intellectual development was a desire for self-assertion which made use of debate and entertainment in performances where showmanship and Shawmanship became one. When success finally came to Shaw, it found him more than prepared. He fell easily into the role of the last of the G. O. M. of Victorian literature. Actually he asserted his right to be great old man and enfant terrible at the same time. Jaeger suit, knickerbockers, and the famous beard became the trappings by which even the newsboys of Fleet Street could recognize G. B. S.

Shaw's rise to literary prestige coincided with the appearance of the great urban newspapers catering to mass audiences, and he was keenly aware of their potentialities. He played alternately the jester, the crank, and the heresiarch to satisfy his need for publicity. Iconoclast by birth, Anglo-Irish puritan by background, eighteenth century rationalist by temperament, he undertook to forge a philosophy from such heterogeneous components. But one must distinguish between primary ideas which sprang from Shaw's very vitals and secondary ideas which he embraced only in moments as jeux d'esprit. To the first group belong his social convictions. Beginning with Henry George, he moved on to Marx, who, he said, made a man of him. But he also said that while *Das Kapital* had made man ashamed of capitalism, it contained not a word on socialism.[62] He joined the Fabians. The first Fabian manifesto he drew up, in 1884, is to the Communist manifesto as a cup of tea to a vial of prussic acid. He refused to believe that "millions of our fellow-creatures must be left to sweat and suffer in hopeless toil and degradation" and suggested equal income and status for all as the remedy. To achieve this aim he advocated the transitional approach of social democracy. He gave up, not without regret, the idea that "an army of light" might at one great stroke set Justice on her rightful throne. With the Webbs and H. G. Wells he adhered to constitutional gradualism.

Counter to Fabian convictions, Shaw took a dim view of the democratic process as such, especially in its British form, and scorned it for being slow, muddle-headed, and cowardly. He believed in the necessity for prompt action which could be expected only from superior leaders. His classless society presupposes a strata of charismatic men. It is modeled on Plato's *Republic*. How planned economy could be reconciled with freedom of criticism, and how powerful authority could exist side by side with a bill of rights freely enjoyed by free citizens, was a problem that Shaw could solve by sophistry only. (This may explain, though it will not excuse, the position he took during the 1930's when he lauded Fascist and Communist dictators alike, discounting their cruelty and persecution as mere holes in their armor.) Shaw's insuperable gift of exposition aided the Fabian Society in its long struggle to win public approval of its aims, but the victories of the labor movement were indebted to stronger forces than the arguments presented in Shaw's economic pamphlets, which combined a sense of missionary zeal with the license of the professional jester.

There is, however, a final point which must not be overlooked if one is to understand the significance of Shaw's economic views. Marxism had revealed to him the importance of economics as a motivating force in history. He was the first artist to apply this lesson to the drama. The conflicts with which he dealt stemmed more often than not from economic roots: *Mrs. Warren's Profession, Major Barbara, Widower's House,* even *Pygmalion.* Just as Marx added new dimensions to our understanding of mankind, just so did Shaw's plays bring to light the economic motivations in human behavior.

Shaw once said that the study of economics had served his dramatic art as the study of anatomy had served Michelangelo. This typical Shavian modesty does not even cover the case. It is characteristic of contemporary literature to look for a fourth dimension in the delineation of human beings, the hidden complex of motives that might explain the unexplainable. Marxism and Freudianism alike have become keys to decode human conduct. To an age which had lost its faith in transcendental values, there was a special incentive to relegate heaven and hell to a habitation in the human heart alone.

There was one point, however, where Shaw refused to subscribe to the tenets of Marxism. He found it impossible to adhere to the underlying thesis of materialism. Instead, he superimposed his own view of Life on his economic interpretation of man. The timbers of this edifice were freely borrowed from Schopenhauer and Nietzsche, from Samuel Butler, and especially from Henri Bergson. The final achievement was unorthodox by any philosophical standards. That he sometimes pooh-poohed his own ideas must not discourage us from taking them seriously. The stature to which he aspired was that of the "philosopher-artist." "I rail at the theistic credulity of Voltaire, the amoristic superstition of Shelley, the revival of tribal soothsaying and idolatrous rites which Huxley called Science." [63] Against them Shaw proclaims his view of Creative Evolution, to use Bergson's term. Shaw called it the divine Life-Force.

The divine Life-Force is "vitality with a direction"; it moves onward and upward. "Imagination is the beginning of creation. You imagine what you desire; you will what you imagine, and at last you create what you will." Everything must have been created out of nothing. For Shaw, the universe was not a "gigantic clock" in which matter had at one point become conscious of itself by some rare condition and thus produced life and consciousness. Against the Darwinian scheme of a universe that is thrown into operation under the two laws, natural selection and the survival of the fittest, Shaw, like Bergson, postulates a world made up of two components, Life and Matter. Originally Life was a whirlpool of pure force; it entered Matter and compelled Matter to obey it. "I brought Life into the whirlpool of pure force and compelled my enemy, Matter, to obey a living soul," says Lilith.

But by so doing Life became Matter's slave. The process of evolution takes as its aim the termination of this slavery and the conquest of Matter. "After passing a million goals they [the living beings] press on to the goal of redemption from the flesh, to the vortex freed from matter." One day Life will be set free; it will cross the last stream that lies between flesh and spirit; it will be pure thought and will conquer death. Our destiny is to be immortal. "The day will come when there will be no people, only thought . . . and that will be life eternal." [64]

The religious overtone in this tirade will not be wasted on the reader. Shaw was, to quote Chesterton, a heathen mystic, an agnostic who hoped for salvation by doing the work which God could not do himself. "This," says a famous passage, "is the true joy in life, the being used for a purpose recognized by yourself as a mighty one; the being thoroughly worn out before you are thrown on the scrap heap; the being a force of nature instead of a feverish, selfish little clod of ailments and grievances complaining that the world will not devote itself to making you happy." [65] This was Shaw's religion, a faith that coexisted with his socialism, superseding it as a metaphysical creed. It is the faith of a puritan agnostic, the belief of a tragic optimist who "took life for something too glorious to be enjoyed." [66] Small wonder then, that when in his old age he became a friend of the Abbess of Stanbrook, he asked to be included in her prayers and signed his letters to her as Brother Bernard. "When I play with my wireless set, I realize that all the sounds of the world are in my room. . . . The ether is full of prayers, too. . . . It would be shockingly unscientific to doubt it." [67]

Bernard Shaw crowned the bizarre edifice of his philosophy with a very personal interpretation of civilization; it was, he maintained, a result of the interplay and struggle of the sexes. Feminism, the New Woman, the battle of the sexes, were, of course, topics much in vogue around 1890. Shaw did not discover them; he inherited them from Hebbel, Ibsen, and Strindberg. But he gave them a personal twist and a cosmic significance.

Shaw gives us to understand that we are instruments of life, created by life for its own purposes. Our fulfillment can never be our own selfish satisfaction, but only the furtherance of life's great design. "Happiness and Beauty are by-products," and the direct pursuit of happiness and beauty is folly.[68]

Woman is life's greatest invention. "Sexually, Woman is Nature's greatest contrivance for perpetuating Nature's highest achievement. Sexually, Man is Woman's contrivance for fulfilling Nature's behest in the most economical way. She knows by instinct that far back in the evolutionary process she invented him, differentiated him, created him in order to produce something better than the single-sexed process can produce." But, Shaw continues, it proved dangerous to invent a separate creature whose sole function was woman's own impregnation, because man became too imaginative and mentally vigorous to be content with mere self-reproduction. Man has created civilization without consulting Woman, taking her domestic labor for granted as the foundation of it. Civilization is thus essentially the work of the male spirit. It has diverted energies away from the perennial labor of the life-force. Woman lets man play at civilization, at his dreams, his follies, his ideals, his heroism, provided that the keystone of all is the worship of womanhood, of the family, of the hearth. And this is the real meaning of the struggle between the sexes. Man is fatally attracted by beauty and knowledge, by visions of God and glory, but woman will pull him back to his biological functions: the siring of children and the protection of the home.

Shaw believes that there is but one type of man who is able to shed the biological shackles: the man of genius. For him, marriage is apostasy, a profanation of the sanctity of his soul, an acceptance of defeat. "Woman must marry because the race must perish without her travail," but genius is as ruthless in pursuing its affairs as woman.[69] Genius will sacrifice anything and anyone to its purpose because it recognizes but one necessity: response to the demand of his calling. There are hints of Shaw's own struggle in these declarations which give them a peculiarly persuasive ring. "Finding one's place," he wrote in his later days, "may be made very puzzling by the fact that there is no place in ordinary society for extraordinary individuals." Ordinary society is the work of woman, but genius is assigned to challenge the existing order and to make it advance. "The superior man is chosen by nature to carry on the work of building up an intellectual consciousness of her own instinctive purposes." [70] The masculine element in history is the revolutionary and progressive, the feminine the conservative and societal one; between them they weave the fabric of human life.

There can be little doubt as to where Shaw's sympathies lay. He was convinced of his own genius, yet at one time or another he must have felt the temptation to surrender to the warmth and routine of instinctual life. Deliberately, however, he chose intellectual pursuit rather than the pursuit of happiness. His contention that through the work of genius we may eventually progress from man to superman remains as unconvincing as Nietzsche's, from whom he borrowed it.

His idea of genius is found in various sketches dispersed throughout his opus. Probably his portrait of Caesar expresses his conception most clearly. Shaw's Caesar is a "somewhat chilly type of superman," one of the elect whose intelligence guides his mercy, who shrinks from human frailty and from small sin, not because it is sin, but because it is small.[71] His magnanimity is glacial and may inspire admiration but hardly love. But then, it may be that love will become extinct among a race of supermen. Shaw was intrigued by the great heroes and men of action, and was led into the belief that Mussolini and Stalin were the equals of Caesar and Napoleon. In this world, he thought, genius must either conquer humanity or be crucified by it.

Looking back on Shaw's artist-philosophy, one feels a sense of disappointment. He is not only contradictory; he is confused, a fact which is just barely disguised by the surface logic of his prose. "Shavian" may mean many things to many men, but hardly a doctrine on which to build. Paradox that he was, he carried his rationalism right into the irrationalism of his life-force. "A chaos of clear opinions" sums up his situation.[72]

Much of the confusion is, of course, the result of Shaw's use of the drama to convey his convictions. He was, above all, a dramatist and he considered the theater his best medium. "I am," he said, "no ordinary playwright. I am a specialist in immoral and heretical plays. My reputation was gained by my persistent struggle to force the public to reconsider its morals. I write plays with the deliberate object of converting the nation to my opinion on sexual and social matters. I have no other incentive to write plays." In view of such a statement one might expect to find Shaw's ideas clearly manifest in his plays; but this does not follow. He reasons every case, every doctrine, and every predicament from several different angles; he hobnobs simultaneously with the pros and the cons. In the end we are back where we started, and we leave the theater with a feeling of amused bewilderment.[73] Critics and laymen alike have pondered the question as to where Shaw really stood, what was pose and what was belief in this inveterate showman, what was mask and what the face behind it? The answer has never been given. It may even be wrong to ask it, because Shaw's weakness as a philosopher turned out to be his strength as a dramatist. Despite his own claims, therefore, he should not be called a writer of problem plays. The Irishman in him conceived the conflicts of his age not as problems but as paradoxes, that is, as collisions between apparent and inherent truth.[74]

His own struggle for success and his socialism made him look at society as one great conspiracy in which exploitation and hypocrisy had joined forces. His alienation from ancient tradition made it easy for him to come out with extravagant statements, baffling suggestions, startling vistas, and sudden denouements which seemed to stand the world on its head. But at its best his was a comic rather than a tragic genius. Shaw was much more concerned with exposing Victorian pomposity, vanity of all shades and varieties, cant and humbug in private and public life, than with evoking a vision of the future in which humanity would be cured of the ills that capitalism had inflicted on its soul. And Shaw the artist was most himself when he could explode the lies in which his society abounded. Rarely, however, does he probe to the root of a problem. His mind, shifting from one viewpoint to another, could advocate incompatible ideas without a trace of embarrassment for their evident contradictions. Was it a universal, intellectual sympathy which caused him to present with equal force those ideas he opposed and those he embraced? Or was it merely superficial dialectic? This enigma, too, defies solution. Only a writer who fancied himself above human reality could have adopted this procedure.

Because of Shaw's adherence to and defense of Ibsen, people thought that he followed the Norwegian's example. The resemblance is a surface one only. When Shaw defined the essence of Ibsenism as Drama by Discussion he spoke for himself first and foremost; his plays debate problems rather than reveal them. Had he been a propagandist, he would have insisted on driving home his "solutions." Had he been a tragic dramatist, he would have shown the conflicts as irremediable, but his was a comic genius; his polemical mind ran the gamut of reason.

The social situations of his time furnished him the material for most of his plays. They are conceived around ideas, but since he was a dramatist, he caused ideas to perform like human beings. His characters do not behave like ideas with uncontrollable logic, rather do his ideas behave like characters with all their inherent contradictions. And the propagandist's loss is the artist's gain. In his own day he was called "our greatest polemicist," but posterity will very likely award him another crown, as one of the greatest of English playwrights. The debates, the socialist confessions, the moral tirades, the philosophical digressions are hopelessly dated, but some of his characters, Candida, Higgins, Undershaft, Major Barbara, St. Joan, are still alive with generative vitality.

Like many great writers, he was deeply mistaken about his own gifts. He confused what he could accomplish with what he wanted to accomplish. If it was his aim to make an analysis of contemporary society and to save civilization, he failed. As Hegel pointed out, essence of lavender will not remove gangrene. Thus, if Shaw admitted resignedly, "I have produced no permanent impression because nobody has ever believed me," he was both right and wrong.[75] He could not produce lasting impressions because it takes more than a playwright's argument to make man change his ways. There is a tragic undertone in his statement: "The real joke is that I am in earnest."

He did not want to be the court jester of a civilization which he had challenged at every turn, but he was too much of an individualist, and an Irish individualist at that, ever to control the caprice of his epigram or the whimsical attitudes of his exhibitionism. He was impermeable to the idea that an irresponsible showmanship such as his, with its whirlwind of iconoclastic contradictions, might eventually jeopardize the social foundations of every free mind. Viewing man as a walking idea, and drama as a conflict of ideas, his art never reaches the depth of human agony. It is a vegetarian's art.

The public was often puzzled by his pronouncements, but rarely misled in its reactions to them. Shaw might coat his pills with whatever sugar he had at hand; the public was not fooled, and, as Egon Friedell has observed, they licked off the sweet and left the medicament alone. This was one way of paying Shaw back in his own coin, allowing him to understand that his very existence was based on the orderly functioning of the society which he so ruthlessly criticized. Writers like Shaw are possible only within the framework of a social order; they may ridicule it, they may execrate it, at their will; but their words are directed to a contemporary audience which speaks the same language. Absolute monarchs have tolerated the writers of comedy such as Molière, but the socialist states that Shaw admired and envisioned have not yet produced a Bernard Shaw, nor have they granted license to publicists and pamphleteers to vent their grievances with impunity.[76] The world for which Shaw wrote was the world before 1914, and although he took great joy in lampooning the British, he was himself quite British in judgment and prejudice.

Shaw belonged to the era of transition in which one could hold antibourgeois views and still live a bourgeois life, with a large income, a Victorian house, and plenty of servants. One could fight against a fossilized tradition, maintain that military heroism was but a civilian invention, that parental authority was a superannuated fiction, that marriage was neither a reality nor an ideal but a pis aller. Bernard Shaw's theses were in reality neither destructive nor anarchic; they were part of a spiritual slum clearance of European society to the which Shaw's heart belonged. And he won his victories. People listened to him, with indignation at first, but they did listen. But as Kenneth Tynan observed, a slum cleaner is not a city planner.[77] Shaw's irony, his furious exposures, could point out the cracks in the walls, but it took the steam-roller of the Great War to shatter the old building. The demolition accomplished, it was another story to think in terms of reconstruction, and here certainly Shaw failed. "A world made up of Bernard Shaws," wrote Beatrice Webb in her diary, "would be a world in moral dissolution." [78] But, for better or worse, the world is not made up of Bernard Shaws. A figure like his is indeed conceivable only against the background of a society which was confirmed rather than destroyed in its tenets by Shaw's paradoxes.

Looking back over the long sweep of Shaw's life, one is obliged to admire the sheer output of his work: the plays, the pamphlets, the articles and essays, and last but not least, the wealth of personal revelation poured out in thousands of letters and notes which may one day well outrank his theoretical writings. What a genial atmosphere they convey, how much friendship, generosity, even magnanimity, they show in the midst of his fierce polemics. They make us forget his boyish pranks and clownish escapades. It must have been a delight to live in this London where H. G. Wells, the Webbs, Somerset Maugham, Arthur Balfour, and Winston Churchill might meet at the same dinner table. The optimism that filled the air of Shaw's London was as little justified as that of Croce's Naples or Bergson's Paris. It was the dusk of a civilization which they mistook for the dawn of a new era. But who would have refused to share their company?

A Note on Autobiography

The cultural history of the nineteenth and twentieth centuries would be incomplete without some mention of the autobiographical works of this period. Autobiography has a long and glorious history in our Western world unparalleled in any other culture. This tradition was maintained by philosophers and poets—Renan, Newman, Mill, Chateaubriand; by statesmen and soldiers—Napoleon, Talleyrand, Metternich, Guizot, Garibaldi, and Bismarck.[79]

On the period preceding World War I we have a wealth of autobiographical information. From the protagonists down to the last stagehand everyone connected with the tragedy of 1914 has left us his side of the story. The first concern of each, as might be expected, is with his own political responsibility, and yields little to the intellectual understanding of our period.

When we turn to some of the great writers of the age, we find a similar disappointment. Tolstoi's *Childhood Memories* is a minor work giving little hint of his epic power.[80] Maxim Gorky's autobiography reveals the poverty of the Russian proletarian, but it, too, seems an inferior production.[81] Kipling's account of himself is of interest to admirers of Kipling only.[82] Strindberg's confessions, it is true, give us some impression of contemporary society. This greatest neurotic of the nineteenth century, born out of wedlock, was extremely conscious of his precarious standing in Swedish upper circles. More than his Russian fellow writers, he concerns himself in his autobiography with social problems; family, marriage, education, and sex are discussed at considerable length, as is also the cleavage between Christianity and science. However, an overpowering ego prevails throughout his account and awakens little sympathy for its fruitless rebellion.[83]

There are certain autobiographies of the period, however, which present a more revealing picture of the fission in European society. For our purpose we have chosen four writers from different European countries and from different strata of society who have distinct and often opposed viewpoints. At the time they were setting down their recollections, the prewar world was already in ruin. These writers indulge in hindsight and nostalgic reflection, but there is sufficient sincerity in their work to lend it an exegetical value.

IV

H. G. Wells's "experiment in autobiography" carries the subtitle, "discoveries and conclusions of a very ordinary brain since 1866." [84] Wells stemmed from the lower middle class, which still accepted with phlegmatic acquiescence its dreary fate. His mother took the social order as the work of Divine Providence; "over it all ruled God the Father, in whose natural kindness my mother had great confidence." [85] Of his father, Wells states that he grew up to gardening and cricket. "They were both economic innocents made by and for a social order . . . that was falling to pieces all about them." Thus Wells was reared in an atmosphere of piety, respectability, and thinly concealed poverty.

Even after he broke with his parents' way of life he continued to bear the stamp of his origin. Lenin said of him that he was "incurably middle class." Yet his was a "sample life," typical of the break with religious dogma and social doctrine that led to the emergence of the English Labour movement. When he discovered Plato's *Republic,* he found "the amazing and heartening suggestion that the whole fabric of law, custom and worship which seemed so invincibly established, might be cast into the melting pot and made anew." [86] His first efforts to support himself met with small success. He became a draper's apprentice and failed; he tried his hand as a pharmaceutical chemist, and failed. Finally he went into teaching.

Wells remarks that a large part of his life was concerned with trying to make history and sociology fit into the category of practical applicable sciences. He did not, however, take his start with the social sciences. He had the good fortune to win a scholarship which brought him under the direction of Thomas Huxley. In this manner he acquired a working knowledge of natural science which included biology, physics, geology, and chemistry. He gained an advantage over the average historian of his day, but his judgment and the perspectives in which he chose to see the historical world were thereby conditioned. He became an evolutionist and an agnostic. He believed human progress to be a certainty. "Never did anyone believe more firmly in the promptitude of progress than I." [87]

This attitude opened the avenues to socialism. Like Bernard Shaw he fell under the spell of Henry George, but, unlike Shaw, he recoiled from Marxism. He combined religious skepticism, socialism, and an enlightened attitude toward sexual problems, a synthesis very characteristic of the atmosphere of late Victorian England. But though Wells may have had theories about the recasting of society, he was still blissfully ignorant of the actual conditions that surrounded him. By his own admission he was totally unaware of the intricacies of international relations. He believed that, as a species, we are caught in an irreversible process of ascent and that such a process would, in all probability preserve the Empire which the British had laid possession to by means of "sheer native superiority." He had the feeling of living in "an absolutely fixed world" which might be improved but would never be destroyed.

His attitude is quite understandable. Though he was obliged to fight against economic difficulties and a whole host of infirmities, his ambition prevailed and he became one of the most successful writers of his age. He had the flair for problems that interested his contemporaries and a facility of expression which allowed him to toss off one book after another. The majority of them fail to hold our interest today, but in Edwardian society he had his place and mingled freely with the great and near-great. He gives us perceptive and amusing profiles of Frank Harris, Henley, Henry James, Bernard Shaw, Arnold Bennett, Joseph Conrad, and Stephen Crane.

If his was not the best of all possible worlds, it was well on its way to becoming so. If only the lessons of enlightened Darwinism could be properly understood, mankind would mend its ways and a benign evolution would take care of the rest.

When the war finally came, he slipped rather badly. He became nationalistic and readmitted "God" into his writings. He frankly confessed later that "the great war was an all-fools' war." "To me, as to most people, it was a revelation of the profound instability of the social order." [88] This seems a rather naïve admission for a Fabian. "It was also a revelation of the possibilities of fundamental reorganizations that were now open to mankind." He became a champion of the new international order which would eventually overcome the anarchy that had caused the war. He claimed a great deal of credit for having started the discussion about a League of Nations in British circles, and, tongue in cheek, he might have said: the world state, c'est moi.[89]

The picture that emerges is a highly representative one: a radical and noncomformist turned socialist and internationalist. His attitude always preserved the confidence that animated the world before 1914. Nothing really obstructed the establishment of freedom in a world of abundance for all. The obstacles to man's betterment were not to be found in human nature, but in the egocentric obsessions of a few men, in intellectual tangles, in misconceived phrases, which the advancement in enlightenment and general education would finally cure.

V

Children of the same era, Wells and Stefan Zweig shared many illusions, but they occupied different spheres in life. Zweig's autobiography, *The World of Yesterday,* is one of the outstanding books of this genre in our period. Few works convey with the same sensitivity of mind and nerves the picture of a golden age. We do not use the words, golden age, inadvertantly; gold and money play a large role in the reminiscences of this writer, and disclose, if nothing else, his bourgeois origin.[90]

Zweig was born in 1881 in "a great and mighty empire, the Habsburg Monarchy," and he grew up in Vienna. His father, a Moravian, was a Jewish textile manufacturer who had risen to considerable wealth. This good fortune allowed Zweig to devote himself entirely to his passion for literature. He calls the years of his youth "the golden age of security." [91] He identified his own privileged position with the political stability of the Austrian Empire, which Napoleon III had already termed "un cadavre." Everything in our Austrian monarchy, writes Zweig, seemed to be based on stability, and the state itself the highest warrant of it. He goes on to describe how all groups in society were guided by this longing for security, and adds, "Finally even the labourers organized themselves." [92] The idea that his carefree existence might have been bought at a price never seemed to disturb Zweig's satisfaction with the *status quo*.

He sums up the belief in progress and humanitarian endeavor as an illusion of the generation that preceded his own, but he calls it "an admirable and noble illusion." The Viennese bourgeoisie had many excellent traits, but political foresight was not one of them. The Boer War and the Russo-Japanese War were to them no more interesting than the sports page of the daily paper.[93]

Zweig was conscious and, I would judge, proud of his Jewish blood. And well he might be. Many of the leading names of intellectual Vienna in 1900 were Jewish: Freud, Schnitzler, Kraus, Mahler, and scores of others. There are few, if any, indications in Zweig's autobiography that he suffered in his youth from anti-Semitism. He even speaks in an apologetic vein of the famous Karl Lueger, the mayor of Vienna, who was one of the first to make political hay under the hot rays of anti-Semitic propaganda. Yet this was the same Vienna where the young Hitler peddled his postcards.

In like manner, Zweig refused to be alarmed over the rising tide of nationalism in the Dual Monarchy. "We young people . . . completely wrapped up in our literary ambitions, noticed little of the dangerous changes in our country; we looked only at books and paintings. We did not have the slightest interest in political and social reforms; what did these squabbles mean in our lives?" One of the finest pages in Zweig's autobiography is entitled *Eros Matutinus* and pictures the rebellion of his generation against Victorian morals. His analysis of the hypocrisy that shrouded all manifestations of sex except the recognized ones of marriage and prostitution is one of the best commentaries on the subject.

As soon as he had finished the Gymnasium, Zweig embarked upon a literary career. He had the genius of friendship and an uncanny desire to complete his education in personal contacts with the constructive minds of his age. He befriended Herzl, the prophet of Zionism, and Steiner, the founder of anthroposophy. But his first and foremost love was poetry. He met and translated Verhaeren and Yeats; he was close to Rilke and intimate with Romain Rolland. Without a care in the world, he journeyed to Brussels, to Paris, to Florence. Walther Rathenau advised him to take a look at the non-European world, and Zweig started off on a tour to the Far East and the United States. In the latter place he was allowed to enter the country without a passport! The outbreak of the Great War found him in Belgium. He had never heard of the Schlieffen Plan and was willing to stake his life on Germany's respect for Belgian neutrality; treaties were, after all, sacred instruments! When he learned that they were but "scraps of paper," he returned to his beloved Austria. What followed lies ouside the limits of these studies. Zweig rose to popular fame after the storm had blown over. His historical biographies were among the best-sellers of the twenties and thirties, but they do not equal his autobiography in sincerity and intimate knowledge.

This expansive mind, tender and amorous of cultural values, could never comprehend that humanity is moved by other forces than love for peace, friendship, and human brotherhood. Following the example of Romain Rolland, he embraced an uncompromising pacifism. His voluntary death in 1942 was his final admission that the World of Yesterday was, in very truth, the world of yesterday.[94] It is difficult to do justice to his type of mind. There was something of a parasitic nature in his existence, which he failed to realize: his dependence on a social structure which was already doomed, his willingness to rely on a political framework which could provide but deceptive stability. Zweig mistook the Austrian dusk for a new dawn in European civilization. When he became aware of his illusion, there was little he could do beyond allowing the growing shadows of the night to allure him into their embrace.

VI

The scene shifts to Germany. The writer selected to shed some light on the Second German Empire is less distinguished than either Wells or Zweig, but chance brought him near the nerve center of action in Germany which was still the Hohenzollern dynasty. Though Gustav Hillard never played an important role himself, he occupied a vantage point for observation and analysis. His autobiography is entitled *Lords and Fools of the World*.[95]

Hillard was born in Rotterdam in 1881, the son of a German industrialist who was working for the house of Krupp in Holland. After the early death of his father, Hillard's mother returned to her native Lübeck, where the son attended the famous Katharineum, of which Thomas Mann has given such an acid picture in *Buddenbrooks*. Hillard's description of German education around 1890 is very much like Mann's. The Gymnasium still pretended to maintain the ideals of Goethe's humanism as the foundation of all true culture, but it gave lip service only; the belief in the binding force of ideas had long since yielded to practical realism. Most of the teachers were educated philistines.

Financial difficulties moved his family to enroll the boy in one of the military institutes, the notorious Kadetten-korps, where the majority of the future officers of the imperial army were prepared. These institutions were remnants of the aristocratic schools of the eighteenth century and combined a semifeudal outlook with modern military skills. The Prussian Minister of War, von Roon, defined their purpose thus: "Not universality, but specialists make for fitness." [96] German history is replete with the products of these schools where political and human problems were measured in terms of military expediency. By accident Hillard was chosen to become one of the three student-companions of the Crown Prince, who was then entering the Kadetten-korps to complete his military instruction. The others were the son of a Silesian Magnate, and the son of a Junker.[97] The selection is representative of the social hierarchy that ruled imperial Germany. Instruction was imparted to this group of four, occasionally glorified by visits from the Kaiser.

The Crown Prince is a minor figure in European history, and would have fared better as an actor in his favorite genre, musical comedy. Hillard's memoirs of the period give a good account of this representative of a failing dynasty. Hillard advanced from classmate of the Prince to courtier in a milieu which had become an anachronism in the twentieth century.

Hillard was only an underling at the court, biding his time until the Crown Prince should become Emperor. In the meantime he enjoyed life to the fullest. The chapter in which he tells of his officership carries the title, "Lord of the World." Such a caption might have provoked consternation in any country but Germany. In Prussia, where the officer was accorded an attention out of all proportion to his social usefulness, it seemed a natural eminence for the young lieutenant. The officer corps was a closely knit unit; it had its code of honor; it decided which social contacts were suitable, which marriages were advantageous or at least permissible. Religious differences between Protestants and Catholics no longer played an important role in prewar Germany. They had been replaced by differences in wealth and influence.[98] Again we encounter the strange confidence that this ephemeral world would last forever. "The past appeared simply as condition, preparation and evolution pointing to the German unification. Nobody doubted that what the generation of our fathers had finally obtained would last forever." [99]

Slowly the young officer rose to membership on the General Staff. He was not, however, entirely happy in the circle of his highly trained companions. He began to read Schopenhauer; he visited the Nietzsche archives in Weimar, and soon found himself between Mars and Minerva. His personal charm made him attractive to many people. Hillard's autobiography contains many vignettes of these acquaintances: the generals Schleicher and Groener; the industrialist, Rathenau; painters like Liebermann; the poets, Hofmannsthal and Rilke; and many others. Nor was his horizon a narrowly German one; he spoke French and English with elegance, and met at one time or another, Balfour, Lyautey, and André Gide. There is much that is various and interesting in this life, but here too the class barriers remain unscaled. After the First World War, when Hillard was obliged to live on half pay, he turned to contemplation. But what in reality he sought was an escape and a substitute. With many of his caste, such as Moeller van den Bruck and Heinrich von Gleichen, he became a conservative and played a minor part in what Germany called "the conservative revolution." Its spawn was Hitler. Although Hillard did not pay as high a price as Stefan Zweig, he too became a victim of the great cataclysm. His illusory world was in ashes, and there was no escape and there was no substitute.

VII

"If our life had not been uprooted, we would preserve only paradisiac images in our memory." [100] With these words Fedor Stepun introduces us to the blissful days of his childhood. His lament for a paradise lost is more despairing than the recollections of the other writers we have considered.

Stepun's father managed one of the greatest paper mills in Tzarist Russia. It was located in a rural district, and Fedor grew up in a Russian manor house of classical style. He early began to reflect on the relationship between upper and lower classes. He noted that even the most liberal estate owners had no close feeling for their workers, considering them necessary figures in an enjoyable social landscape.[101] Of the many episodes of his childhood, one was deeply etched on his memory: "A former servant of ours, a sickly, quiet, man with dark and tired eyes . . . whose duty it was to drive a paralyzed lady in a wheelchair, one good and beautiful morning drew his razor from his pocket and cut his moody mistress' withered throat."[102]

Stepun's father belonged to a Baltic family, and his mother was of Finnish-Swedish descent, yet Fedor identified himself completely with Russia. In his description of his school days in Moscow the element of discontent, so characteristic of Zweig and Hillard, is entirely missing, but he did recognize very early those "natural chaotic forces" in the Russian soul which, in his opinion, brought about the later triumph of the Bolshevic Revolution. "The last roots of our revolution should not be looked for in theories; they are to be found in fundamental beliefs." After he obtained his high school diploma, he entered the army in compliance with the universal military training law. He became a declared enemy of war. War was "madness," an attitude clearly reminiscent of Zweig.

With a confused desire to understand the world and find his way among conflicting theories, Stepun entered Heidelberg University. He became acquainted with the University's luminaries: the art historian, Thode; the philosopher, Windelband; the law professor, Jellinek. More revealing were his contacts with the socialist movement in Germany; he met Ludwig Frank and Clara Zetkin. In 1905 he gave a lecture before his compatriots on the poverty of ideas in the Russian Revolution.

The story of his first marriage reads like a page from Dostoevski. His wife, the widow of a student friend who had died of typhus, introduced him to a Russia that was new to him. "I made the observation that at the end of the nineteenth and even more at the beginning of the twentieth century every Russian family, the imperial not excepted . . . had a radical member, its own home-grown revolutionary." [103] His honeymoon was spent in endless political and philosophical discussions. When his wife was drowned in an attempt to save the life of her first husband's brother, Stepun interpreted her death as a sacrificial one, a voluntary return to her earlier love.

Despite his many problems, the young man finally passed his Ph.D. examinations, and soon after he engaged himself, with other Russian expatriates, in founding the review *Logos*. The desire to gain collaborators led Stepun to Italy. On his visit to Croce in Naples, a doorman in livery complete with stick and three-cornered hat ushered him in to the great man's study.[104]

He returned to Moscow a few years before the outbreak of the war and was immediately impressed by a change in mood among the revolutionary groups. "The hatred against the government had not abated," he notes, but the revolutionary fervor among the bourgeoisie had diminished. Only the orthodox Marxists were steadfast in their belief in the coming of the revolution and were waiting patiently for a new tidal wave.[105]

Stepun's description of changing conditions in urban and rural Russia is full of interesting reflections on the general rise in the standard of living that had come with Stolypin's reforms. Revolutions triumph when their victory is no longer needed, he remarks.[106]

His work in adult education, which he took up at this time, was concerned mainly with the working class. In this manner he felt himself a part of the great cultural flowering that Russia experienced before 1914. Stepun speaks of Moscow's international fame in music, ballet, the theater, with the same pride that Zweig felt in writing of Vienna, and he may well have rejoiced in such names as Rachmaninov, Chaliapin, Diaghilev, and Stanislavski. Nor was Moscow excluded from the generous give and take through which the Europeans came to know each other in those years; Stepun speaks of the visits of Verhaeren, Marinetti, Matisse, Werner Sombart, and many others.

"The misfortune of the prewar period lay in the following: there was a spring in societal and cultural life, while the political life hastened toward a fateful autumn. The government was shaken by fevers; soon they let the reins slide without determination; soon they tightened them, whipped by fear, . . . it was obvious that the cadaverous smell of this rotting body-politic . . . would finally poison the culture of the age." [107] The cleavage in European civilization, which we have so often encountered in our studies, becomes apparent even when seen from the easternmost bastions.

Stepun's autobiography gives us some snapshots of the intellectual life of Moscow, that life which the Communist fury was later to disperse in many directions. Berdyaev, Andrei Bely, A. Tolstoi, and Blok were there, to mention but a few. In April of 1912 Blok wrote in his diary, "The sinking of the Titanic has made me indescribably happy; after all, there is an ocean." [108] Soon rivers of blood would float the foundations of European society, and Russia would turn her face to the East.

Stepun indulged the hope that his hazy idealism would act as a tranquilizer on the tense nerves of the Russian body. As he looks back upon this period, he is quite aware that the intelligentsia shared with the Tzarist regime the responsibility in making Lenin's victory possible. "We have lived well in old Russia, but sinfully. The government and the reactionary groups backing it were autocratic; the liberal and socialist circles showed an empty oratory behind which were concealed laziness and lack of courage." They feared the catastrophe, but they did not believe in it.

When the war broke out, it was not even discussed around the family samovar. Stepun explains "this incredible fact" as evidence of the traditional lack of interest in international affairs. The words are almost the same that Wells and Zweig use: "The war surprised us more as a natural catastrophe than as a historical event." [109]

Our study in autobiography lays no claim to comprehensiveness. We have considered four members of the bourgeoisie whose lives were devoted to the world of letters. Research that would include entrepreneurs, merchants, and manufacturers could add significant details to the picture. Likewise the autobiographies of members of the working class, like Bebel, should be considered. One of them, written in novel form, by the Italian poetess, Ada Negri, is full of moving details. And, of course, the European aristocracy should be heard. But the impression we have gained would not, I believe, be substantially altered.

What conclusions may be drawn? The aristocratic strata of European society were still in control of the mechanism of international politics in all the great powers except France. Although the motivating forces sprang from overheated nationalism and economic rivalry, the management of international politics was left to those who for centuries had been trained for the diplomatic service. They proved to be incapable of controlling the energies which they pretended to guide, and for the fundamental reason, I believe, that they were out of touch with the powers that move an industrial society. Count Harry Kessler remarks in his memoirs: "Parallel with the intellectual revolution of the cultured middle classes through the devaluation of moral values went the technological revolution of life through new and always more startling inventions and the political revolution of the masses through the spreading and organization of Marxism. Something very great—the ancient, cosmopolitan, agrarian and feudal Europe—had grown old and sick and was ready to die." [110] Yet no new élite had emerged to cope successfully with this triple revolution.

It cannot even be said of the world before 1914 that it felt itself to be dancing on the verge of a volcano. Those who had premonitions that the same forces which had built the house of Western society were now corroding its foundations were rare. The thin wreath of smoke curling above the crater went unobserved or was thought to lend variety to the summer sky.

CHAPTER VII

The Search for the Lost Dimension

I

The philosophical climate of the last quarter of the nineteenth century was heavily charged with materialistic thinking. The converging influences of the earlier years had produced a negation of everything that transcended material life. Schopenhauer's system had been the first to promulgate the new revolt, and Comte's theories were in parturition.[1] Positivism was accompanied by a staunch denial of supranatural and suprahuman values. There is nothing in the essence and consciousness of religion, said Feuerbach, that is not already implied in the essence and consciousness of Man. Transcendence gave way to immanence.

Of the various attempts to define man in a strictly immanent way made between 1890 and 1914, none surpasses that of Sigmund Freud in significance and result. It is an interesting phenomenon that the founder of psychoanalysis first saw the world in the declining light of the Austro-Hungarian Empire. His love-hate for his native land was deep and strong and must be recognized as one of the powerful influences in the formation of his mind.

Freud was by no means the only genius that Old Austria produced. How may one explain the appearance of so many significant figures against a background of lassitude and disintegration? There were Hugo von Hofmannsthal, Rilke, Schnitzler, and Karl Kraus in literature; Husserl and Freud in philosophy; Max Reinhardt in the theater; Hugo Wolff and Mahler in music; there was Kafka. Cultural fatigue is sometimes preceded by a kind of euphoria, a last flare-up, which forecasts the impending collapse. One is tempted to apply this idea to the Austrian Empire.[2]

It was, we suppose, inevitable that Freud should one day become the victim of his own invention. The light of his teaching has been turned on him, and his ideas have been interpreted as the projection of his own ego.[3] However, we must not try to explain Freud by psychoanalyzing the psychoanalyst.[4] He must first be understood in the context of his time and evaluated by his contributions to our civilization.

Sigmund Freud was born on May 15, 1856, in Freiberg, Moravia, a region fertile in talents of many kinds. He was Jewish and clung to his origins with a mixture of stubborn pride and cynical resignation. There are traces of Talmudic sophistry in his writings, but it is more enlightening to note the Jewish resentment in his thought. The desire to unveil and unmask, the urge to reveal the hypocritical lie in the cultural environment in which he lived but to which he did not belong, was as strong an impulse in Freud as it was in Marx. He was overconscious of his heritage, hypersensitive to any criticism of it, and he cherished Jewish lore and Jewish wit. Devoid of religious feeling, he adhered to the common Jewish fate with tribalistic devotion.

Freud had a passionate love for his mother, and wrote, "a man who has been the indisputable favourite of his mother keeps for life the feeling of a conqueror, that confidence of success that often induces real success." [5] He was a precocious child, showing symptoms of an unwonted sexual curiosity; he tried to explore the secrets of the parental bedroom; at the age of two he became enamoured of his mother upon seeing her naked body. Quite understandably these aberrations incurred his father's ire. At the age of seven he urinated deliberately in his parents' room and his despairing father prophesied that the boy would never amount to anything. "This [reprimand] must have been a terrible affront to my ambition, for allusions to this scene occur again and again in my dreams, and are constantly coupled with enumerations of my accomplishments and successes, as if I wanted to say, 'you see, I have amounted to something after all.' " [6]

It is obvious that these experiences constitute the basis for the notorious Oedipus complex, but it would seem equally obvious that they are of such a personal nature that no sweeping generalizations should have been drawn from them.

We have spoken of Freud's ambition, and here we encounter

one of his fundamental emotions. When he was only eleven years old, some jester prophesied that he would one day become a cabinet minister. Young Sigmund was so impressed by this remark that in his later life he still dreamed that he had arrived at such a post of honor. At twenty-nine, he speaks to his bride of "my biographer." "I have," he wrote, "destroyed all my diaries of the past fourteen years, with letters, scientific notes and the manuscripts of my publications. . . . Let the biographers chafe; we won't make it too easy for them." [7] He had a great admiration for military genius and loved to think of himself as a Semitic conqueror like Hannibal or Massena. At the height of his maturity he described himself as follows: "I am really not a man of science, not an observer, not an experimenter, not a thinker. I am by temperament nothing but a conquistador,—an adventurer . . . with the curiosity, the boldness, the tenacity that belongs to that type of being." [8] Circumstances closed to him the avenues of power and made him look for intellectual rather than political or military conquests. A Jew could not easily become either cabinet minister or general in imperial Austria. But was not the power over the mind of man the greatest power of all?

When the time came for Freud to choose a profession, he settled on medicine. "Neither at that time, nor indeed in my later life, did I feel any predilection for the career of a physician. I was moved, rather, by a sort of curiosity, which was, however, directed more toward human concerns than toward natural objects." [9] It would seem that admiration for Darwin and for Goethe's "beautiful essay" on Nature had something to do with his choice.

"When, in 1873, I first joined the University [of Vienna], I experienced some appreciable disappointments. Above all, I found that I was expected to feel inferior and an alien, because I was a Jew. I refused absolutely to do the first of these two things. I have never been able to see why I should feel ashamed of my descent . . . Without much regret, I put up with my non-acceptance into the community." [10]

After some hesitation he concentrated on physiology and found in Ernst Brücke a respected teacher. Brücke represented Helmholtz' school of thought which held that no other forces than the physical-chemical ones are active in the human organism, and that hence no others should be used to explain its functioning.[11] The principle of the conservation of energy, discovered first by Robert Mayer in 1842 and popularized afterward by Helmholtz, was the philosophical foundation of Brücke's lectures on physiology. It was from Brücke that Freud first learned what later became known as the "dynamic aspects" of psychoanalysis. Brücke's laboratory was the scene of Freud's efforts from 1876 until 1882. He notes that, "the various branches of medicine proper, apart from psychiatry, had no attraction for me."[12] He took his examination in 1881, but because of his very restricted material circumstances he was unable to consider a career devoted to research.

With a heavy heart Freud turned to the practice of medicine, selecting neuropathology as his chosen field. In 1885 he became Privatdozent at the University of Vienna. However, his academic career was stifled first by anti-Semitism and later by the hostility that his theories provoked. It was hence of the greatest importance to him that he was able to obtain a government grant to continue his studies in Paris at the Salpetrière under the direction of the great Charcot. French medicine was at that time much more advanced than that of Germany or Austria in the study of nervous diseases. Freud began to interest himself in the phenomenon of hysteria, which eventually led him into the psychology of neuroses.[13] One day, while discussing the issues involved in the explanation and cure of hysteria, Charcot chanced to remark: There is always "la chose génitale."

Before we approach Freud's scientific discoveries, a word should be said about his marriage. The emotional character of his childhood reveals to us an individual who was open to passion. "An intimate friend," he confessed, "and a hated enemy have always been indispensable to my emotional life. I have always been able to create them anew, and not infrequently my infantile ideal has been so closely approached that friend and enemy have coincided in the same person."[14] In his marriage he found another outlet for his volcanic nature.

In the early eighteen eighties Freud had met Martha Bernays, a girl of Jewish extraction, and had fallen in love with her. His economic situation made an immediate marriage impossible. A long betrothal ensued, complicated by separations, family interference,

and a disparity of character between the two young people themselves. Freud wrote more than nine hundred letters to his fiancée.
His biographer writes: ". . . there we are confronted with a tremendous and complicated passion, one in which the whole gamut
of the emotions was evoked in turn, from the heights of bliss
to the depths of despair, with every grade of happiness and misery
being felt with unsparing intensity." [15]

Freud was a domineering and distrustful lover, fiercely jealous
not only of real and imaginary rivals, but also of Martha's relatives.
However, by autumn of 1886, when he had settled in Vienna and
had married Martha, his violent feelings had been brought under
some control, at least to the point of his being a companionable and
compatible husband. His marriage was, to all appearances, quite
successful. But God, and perhaps the psychoanalyst, alone knows
the heart of man. The same Freud wrote: ". . . in most men love
remains torn in two directions; where they love they cannot desire,
and where they desire they cannot love." And again: "The sexual
life of civilized man has been . . . badly injured." [16]

As a young doctor, Freud concentrated on the treatment of nervous ailments. [17] He soon found that the textbooks and the standard
treatments had been able to effect no real cure. Freud fared better
with hypnosis. He studied the method used by Bernheim, a French
doctor from Nancy. "I received the profoundest impression of the
possibility that there could be powerful mental processes which,
nevertheless, remained hidden from the consciousness of men." [18]
How was he to gain access to these hidden processes? Here he received help from an older colleague, Joseph Breuer, who had long
been his friend and protector.

Breuer had at his hands a case of hysteria, the by-now famous
case of Fräulein Anna O. Breuer observed that his patient could
be relieved when induced to express in words the phantasy by which
she was at the moment dominated. Breuer used deep hypnosis on
the girl and in this state she was made to relate the cause of her
oppression. "In her waking [she] . . . could no more describe than
any other patient how her symptoms had arisen . . . in hypnosis
she immediately revealed the missing connections." [19] This was a
single case and Freud was aware of the hazards of generalization.
However, he decided to investigate for himself. Although he later

broke with Breuer, Freud has always acknowledged that it was Breuer's "cathartic method" that started him on the path to psychoanalysis.[20]

Freud's approach to his problem proved him to be a true investigator; his research was deliberate and exhaustive.[21] It involved the advancement of daring hypotheses, which had to be tested, general concepts on the relations between body and mind, and deep-reaching changes in therapeutic methods. In every case, Freud took the offensive.

His patients, he discovered, suffered from reminiscences. He found that the essence of their illness lay in the fact that their emotions had become imprisoned and, in consequence, had undergone a series of abnormal changes.[22] For what reasons had the patients forgotten so many of the facts of their external and internal lives? Whatever was forgotten had been in some way painful, had been either alarming, or disagreeable, or shameful. Freud came to an immediate and spontaneous conclusion: what was painful to the patient had retreated to the obscurity of the unconscious, and this was precisely why it had been forgotten. "I was thus led into regarding the neurosis as being without exception disturbances of the sexual function." [23] Freud had set foot on a continent the existence of which had always been know but never openly admitted. Medical authorities had spoken of it *sub rosa:* ". . . actually they had told me more than they knew themselves, or were prepared to defend." [24] Freud had the courage to break through the intellectual and social tabus which impeded comprehension of so fundamental a drive in human existence. It cost him his popularity as a doctor and brought him an ostracism which overshadowed his existence for many years. He did not bear his burden lightly, but neither was he intimidated by the derision and hatred that his discoveries encountered.

He gave up hypnotism and replaced it with the method of "free association." He became convinced that from the surface memories revealed to him, he might gradually descend to the repressed complex. With this belief in mind, he allowed the patient to speak freely and associatively, feeling certain that he would bring forth only what bore on the buried enigma. "If this method of discovering seems too circumstantial, I can at least assure . . . that it is the only available one." [25] His technique has become so widely known that we do not need to enlarge upon it. It was by no means, however, the only method which Freud tried in his effort to widen our knowledge of the unconscious. [26]

By the turn of the century Freud had achieved full maturity. He submitted himself to an autoanalysis from which he derived insights that he considered basic to the understanding of human behavior in general. Four different aspects of his work began to crystallize. There was first the cathartic or therapeutic one, dealing with the actual treatment of neuroses; second, the theory of the subconscious and its relations to the conscious; third, his theory of sexual life; and finally a metapsychology based on a new understanding of man. [27] Little need be said about the first issue; psychoanalytical treatment is now generally accepted. Even where Freud's tenets are disputed, the pioneering qualities of his work are unquestioned. His influence in this field belongs, however, to the history of medicine rather than to the history of culture.

It is quite a different affair when we turn to the theoretical suppositions on which his method is built. We have seen that Freud found the key to the understanding of neurotic phenomena in the process he called repression. "The theory of repression became the foundation stone of our understanding of neuroses." [28] He reached the conclusion that neuroses have no specific content which cannot be found in normal minds. In other words, the study of the neurotic mind served to establish a pattern for the understanding of the mind in general.

Freud abandoned the method, then in general use by scientific psychology, which believed the last word to have been found in the laws of association. He came out with the statement that everything mental is, in the first instance, unconscious. Glimpses of this notion can be found in the work of the great poets; Nietzsche had expressed it frequently, as had also the German romanticists. Yet the gap between Freud and his predecessors remains wide. No one before Freud had used this insight systematically, nor had anyone ever attempted to draw a map of the territory that encompasses consciousness and unconsciousness. [29]

According to Freud the mind operates on three levels: the unconscious, the preconscious, and the conscious. The unconscious i the true psychic reality; in its inner nature it is just as unknown to us as is the reality of the outer world, and it is just as imperfectly communicated to us by the data of our consciousness as is the outer world through the information reaching us from the sense organs.[30] The motivating force in our mental apparatus is the wish, the aim of which is to avoid displeasure and to attain pleasure. All that is connected with wish-fulfillment belongs to the primary processes of the psyche, which are unchecked by logical contradictions or causal associations, and have no sense of time or outward reality. But the wish is not always fulfilled nor the pleasure always granted. Reality opposes the free-flowing energy of the wish. Thus Freud sets up two antagonistic principles which determine human life: the pleasure principle and the reality principle. When pleasure principle and reality principle meet, inhibitions are created and thought develops. The vital needs (*die Not des Lebens*) in their clash with wish and desire bring about mental development. "It is from the contrast between reality and wish-fulfillment that our psychical life grows." All thinking is a complicated and circuitous path toward the goal of wish-fulfillment.[31] The discovery of these primary irrational processes will remain Freud's heroic deed. Whereas others, especially Nietzsche, had been aware of man's irrational nature, it was Freud who succeeded in eliciting an answer from this irrational nature.

In his early research Freud had found that the underlying causes of the neuroses were conflicts between the individual's sexual impulse and his resistance to sexuality. He now arrived at the conclusion that man's basic wish is sexual. The unconscious is not only shot through with sexual desire; it is ultimately identical with it. Libido was the term Freud gave to the energy of sexual instinct. His whole theory has, therefore, been called pansexualism or monism of sexuality.[32] Man is an animal, said Freud, and the principles of the animal world furnish a satisfactory explanation for his development. He never veered from this opinion which completed the deposition of man from his throne in the center of the universe which Darwin and Nietzsche had initiated.

One of the revolutionary aspects of Freud's psychology was its dynamism: the discovery of the functional interconnection between the unconscious and the conscious. This dynamic principle, in its

specific coloring by libidinous wishes, was now applied to the individual soul and its history. "In my search . . . I was carried further
and further back into the patient's life and ended by reaching the
first years of his childhood. What students of human nature and
poets had always asserted turned out to be true: the impressions of
that remote period of life . . . left ineradicable traces upon the
individual's growth. But since the experiences of childhood were
always concerned with sexual excitations . . . I found myself faced
with the fact of infantile sexuality—once again a novelty and a
contradiction of one of the strongest human prejudices." [33] We will
dispense with any detailed picture of Freud's outline of infantile
sexuality. In its first stage he sets autoeroticism, which is, however,
soon overcome. In the second stage, the mother becomes the first
love-object and a relationship known as the Oedipus complex is
established. A period of latent sexuality follows, which in turn ends
in the full awakening of the sexual impulse at the age of puberty.

Freud included within the realm of the sexual impulse all the
merely friendly and affectionate emotions "to which usage applies
the exceedingly ambiguous word love." [34] According to him all
these emotions were originally of a sexual nature and have become
inhibited in their aim or sublimated. The manner in which the
sexual instinct can be influenced and diverted in human beings
enables them to be employed for cultural activities of various kinds. [35]

Before we consider how Freud linked childhood experiences with
cultural activities and the universal fate of mankind, we are justified
in asking for the evidence on which his theories were based. We
have already noted that he did not depend exclusively on the
method of "free association." He had discovered another procedure
pregnant with exegetical possibilities: the interpretation of dreams.
The book which carries this title has been called his magnum opus. [3]

Freud fulfilled one of the oldest aspirations of mankind; he
brought proof for the belief that dreams have a meaning. "But
modern science would have nothing to do with them; it handed
them over to superstition." Freud arrived at a different conclusion.
He discovered a mental structure in dreams which revealed them as
analogous to any other product of the mind. A dream is, he says,
"the disguised fulfillment of a repressed wish." Dreams are compromises between the demands of repressed impulses and the resistance

of a censoring force in our ego. But the impulse is the actual architect of the dream; it provides the energy for its production and makes use of the day's residues as materials of construction. Freud later defended himself against the accusation that he had asserted the sexual content of all dreams. Be that as it may, dreams provided him with very efficacious material for tracing the processes of the unconscious. Dreams likewise revealed the specific dynamic of the human mind by means of which component parts become condensed, displaced, dramatized, and elaborated. To be understood a dream had to be interpreted.[37]

At this point we come to one of the greatest difficulties in psychoanalytical thought. It demands "an art of interpretation"; it employs admittedly "the instrument of suggestion." [38] Inevitably the interpreter will many times reach a priori conclusions; he has then only to select the particular Freudian complex that most comfortably accommodates the case. In other words, the interpretation of dreams, together with the whole body of psychoanalysis, proceeds along preestablished lines; it presupposes the Freudian creed, the validity of which it strives to prove in each individual instance. Furthermore, it is by its very nature, subjective; an "art," as Freud calls it, rather than a science. No evidence can ever be given that the picture of a personality arrived at through analysis is more than conjecture. The pieces of the puzzle may call for a completely different pattern. From this insurmountable dilemma stem the multiple schisms from which the psychoanalytical school has suffered.

The same objections hold for another attempt of Freud's to unveil the dark workings of the unconscious. *The Psychopathology of Every-day Life* (1904) is his most popular book.[39] Freud's study of the slips which we make in our daily lives, our failures of memory, the miscarriage of actions for unknown reasons, proved beyond doubt that these occurrences are not always accidental. They often have a significance which justifies us in assuming the interference of restrained or repressed impulses which may block the successful completion of the act.[40] Freud's demonstration was so conclusive that it has entered the realm of the cliché; it is his great contribution to the common sense of the twentieth century. Nevertheless, though the phenomenon has been assigned a basis in truth, there still remains the subjective interpretation which makes it fallible.

Freud's own evaluation of these two books may furnish us with further understanding. "If dreams turned out to be constructed like symptoms, if their explanation required the same assumptions—the repression of impulses, substitute formation, the dividing of the conscious and the unconscious into various psychical systems—then psychoanalysis was no longer a substitute science in the field of psychopathology; it was rather the foundation for a new and deep science of the mind which would be equally indispensable for the understanding of the normal. . . . A path lay open to it that led far afield, into spheres of universal interest." [41] Thus Freud came to develop a metapsychology, which we may call his anthropology.

Freud's picture of man lays stress upon the emotional life and upon the division between those acts which are unconscious and those which are conscious. He introduced a dynamic element into psychology by showing the interaction between the unconscious and the conscious; he pointed to an "economic factor" which explained human acts as the products of the libidinous energy which would otherwise have been employed in a completely different way.[42] But there are concepts in this anthropology that were never scrutinized by Freud.

However content Freud may have been, certain questions are bound to arise. If man is basically driven by instinct, what explanation is forthcoming for the world of consciousness? A better name for psychoanalysis would seem to be "psychogenesis"; it had led to the discovery of the unconscious, but this in turn had induced an underrating of the conscious functioning of man's mind, a tendency to reduce man's consciousness to a mere by-product of his all-powerful libido.

According to Freud, conscious life is only possible at the expense of the unconscious, in most instances by repression, or, as in the artist, by sublimation. The artist is for Freud a man who refuses to accept the necessary privations of life and turns from reality to the world of phantasy where his unsatisfied wishes can receive imaginative fulfillment. He uses his "special gift" to find a way back to reality by creating works that appeal to similar dissatisfactions in other people.[43] Obviously this is a fallacious argument. Not only does Freud presuppose the "special gift" which stands in need of psychological explanation, but the whole process of sublimation demands an answer that Freud cannot supply. Why do we sublimate? asked Max Scheler; why do we repress, why do we have guilt feelings? To reduce the world of the spirit to a conscious superstructure of the unconscious infrastructure is as hopeless an attempt as is the analogous undertaking of Karl Marx in the realm of economics.

Freud's own life refutes his arguments. He was guided by the categoric imperative of scientific truth; but where is scientific truth if man is nothing but the result of instinctive forces? The same consideration holds true for his attempt to convert religious conscience, knowledge, and art, in other words, man's spiritual creativity, into a mirage arising from man's sexual appetite.

No one will be surprised to encounter the same dilemma in Freud's attempt to describe the evolution of mankind in psychoanalytical terms. He asserts that the sexual experiences of childhood reflect the primeval experiences of the species. Were it true that the individual relives the common fate of man in his childhood, it should be possible to reconstruct the history of mankind in Freudian terms.

Once more Freud starts with the dangerous premise of equating obsessive acts with cultural manifestations. Religion is for him "a kind of universal obsessional neurosis." In *Totem and Tabu* he endeavored to deduce the origins of religion, morality, and social life from the Oedipus complex.[44] His thesis was based on *The Golden Bough* of J. G. Frazer and on W. Robertson Smith's *The Religion of the Semites*. "When I further took into account Darwin's conjecture that man had originally lived in hordes, each under the domination of a single powerful, violent and jealous male, there rose before me . . . the following hypothesis, or I would say, vision [*sic!*]. The father of the primal horde, since he was an unlimited despot, had seized all the women for himself; his sons being dangerous to him as rivals, had been killed or driven away. One day, however, the sons came together and united to overwhelm, kill, and devour their father, who had been their enemy but also their ideal. After the deed they were unable to take over their heritage since they stood in one another's way. Under the influence of failure and regret [*sic!*] they learned to come to an agreement among themselves; they banded themselves into a clan of brothers

by the help of the ordinances of totemism, which aimed at prevent-
ing a repetition of such a deed, and they jointly undertook to forego
the possession of the women on whose account they had killed their
father. They were driven to finding strange women and this was
the origin of exogamy." Freud goes on to say: ". . . whether we
suppose that such a possibility was an historical event or not, it
brings the formation of religion within the formation of the father-
complex and bases it upon the ambivalence which dominates that
complex." [45]

We have quoted Freud here at length because the passage
shows very distinctly how his mind worked and how he jumped
from a vision to a conclusion which, to him at least, affirmed the
tenets of psychoanalysis. Social science would find such a procedure
quite inadmissable. Freud's theory has not been confirmed by an-
thropological research, nor, on the other hand, will it ever be refuted, since it delves into the shadows of prehistoric events where
"all cats are gray."

Freud has frequently, and with great modesty, spoken of the
limited value of psychoanalysis. "By itself," he says, "this science
is seldom able to deal with a problem completely, but it seems
destined to give valuable contributory help in a large number of
regions of knowledge." [46] Such reservations are speedily canceled by
the tendency of Freud and his school to award psychoanalysis the
position of a key science the findings of which have an all-encompassing validity.

The desire for a key science is highly symptomatic of the situation
in which the European mind found itself at the end of the nineteenth century. We have noted the attempts of philosophy to understand the world in material terms only. It was accompanied by the
illusion of a stable social order brimming with harmony, steadfastly
moving toward an ever greater degree of coherence and integration.

The illusionary nature of this idea was exposed by many of the
independent minds of the nineteenth century, such as Baudelaire,
Kierkegaard, and Dostoevski. But Marx, Nietzsche, and Freud were
not content merely to map out the shallows in the legend of bourgeois order and harmony. They tried to restore to the world the
dimension which had been lost with the renunciation of transcendence. The term "depth psychology," though not coined by

Freud himself, is characteristic of this attitude. "The discovery of the neuroses did not occur accidentally at the end of the bourgeois period; it was just about that time that the neuroses increased and demanded an explanation of their nature." [47]

Marx had provided the great masses of the working people with a philosophy of history which defined their place in the evolution of mankind and illuminated the future with the rosy glow of hope for a classless society. Freud's message was not directed to the economically dispossessed. On the contrary, he strongly advised that psychoanalytical treatment be limited to persons of means and a certain standard of education. Not that the poor were lacking in neuroses, but their strained economic situation made it impossible for them to sublimate their difficulties and hence reach a cure. [48]

In this manner psychoanalysis became one of the substitute religions for the disillusioned middle class. Analysis is accompanied by ceremonies and rituals that resemble a religious rite. Its concepts, at best debatable, are repeated as articles of the faith. Schools have developed which define, combat, and evaluate Freud's ideas with an ardor that makes the disputations of scholasticism look pale. Magazines and drawing rooms echo the magic formulae of the Ego, the Id, and the Superego. They have obtained a degree of imaginary reality which bears out Freud's observation that "belief in the omnipotence of thought" is in itself a neurotic symptom. Karl Kraus defined this attitude deftly when he said that psychoanalysis is itself the illness it pretends to cure.

Freud realized that psychoanalysis was in need of a system of human instincts to support the daring assumptions that had been thrown out in all directions. The older he grew the more his own thinking moved toward a metapsychology. But he failed to reconcile the dualism of his theories. Throughout his work we find a dualistic tendency to base theories on "the interaction of two opposite powers": conscious-unconscious, love-hate, eros-thanatos. [49] Very likely this dualism reflects an inner conflict in Freud's own mind which he was never able to overcome and of which he seemed unaware. He left a jungle of concepts which make it unlikely that a consistent anthropology can ever be derived from it.

The most gifted of his disciples have early felt this shortage. Jung, for instance, realized that the overexpansion of Freud's concept of libido entailed the loss of any specific content, and he decided to redefine it as a general biological drive similar to Bergson's élan vital. Jung was also aware of the destructive, not to say nihilistic, consequences of Freud's theories.[50] Adler in turn felt that Freud's model of the ego could not explain one of the most basic human drives, that is, the will to power. But Freud refused to recognize the importance of Adler's contribution and made the acid comment, ". . . presumably the object is to save the world from sexuality and base it on aggression." [51]

The dissentions and desertions which Freud suffered throughout a long life are ironical confirmations of the rebellion of beloved sons against an overpowering father who threatened to crush them. Jung and Adler were the outstanding examples, but minor voices soon swelled the chorus. Freud's own attitude toward the continuous schism among his followers was ambiguous. He showed an apparent willingness to discuss controversial topics, but there was never a doubt in his mind that only the founder of psychoanalysis could be right. When in 1914 he wrote the history of the psychoanalytical movement he stated flatly that he had a better right than anyone else to know what psychoanalysis was. "La psychoanalyse, c'est moi." [52]

There was without doubt a dictator's ambition in Freud and he has frequently been censured for his dogmatism. His desire for power was no less strong because it aimed at man's mind rather than at his activities. Nor was he lacking in cunning when international recognition seemed to be within his reach. One reads with surprise of the political finagling, the struggles for prestige, the will to power and the self-assertion that permeated the meetings of the International Psychoanalytical Association. It would seem that these gentlemen had not really benefited from their knowledge of the unconscious motivations of human action.

We note this propensity in Freud even more clearly when we learn of the organization of a secret council of trustworthy analysts who were to surround Freud in the capacity of "an old guard." It was a kind of psychoanalyst's politburo, and Freud gave it his blessing: "I dare say it would make living and dying easier for me if I knew such an association existed to watch over my creation . . . this committee would have to be secret in its existence and its actions." [53] It remains a characteristic detail in the picture of the man who called himself first and foremost a conqueror.

After the experience of the First World War, Freud engaged more and more in speculations for which he did not claim the same validity as for his earlier investigations. These speculations nevertheless round out his philosophy in a significant manner. *The Future of an Illusion* and *Civilization and Its Discontent* disclose the ultimate consequences of his premises.[54]

It was a deeply pessimistic outlook to which Freud confessed. "Life . . . is too hard for us; it entails too much pain, too many disappointments, impossible tasks." Our possibilities of happiness are limited from the start. Suffering comes to us from three quarters: from our bodies, which are destined to decay and dissolution; from the outer world, which can rage against us with the most powerful and pitiless forces of destruction; and finally from our relations with other men. What then is the purpose of life? A religious answer to this question would have been to the mind of Freud both infantile and archaic. In its place he offers the hedonistic one: man seeks happiness. Freud, however, gives a tragic addendum: happiness is denied to man. The "Plan of Creation" has not provided for human happiness. In other words, the purpose of life, as conceived by human beings, runs counter to its existential conditions.[55] We live in a no man's land where pleasure principle and reality principle fight for the possession of our souls. Happiness, which he conceives as sexual happiness, is only an episodic phenomenon. Conscious that we play a losing game, we grasp whatever comfort we may: intoxication, libido-displacement, sublimation.[56] Science and art rank highest among these substitute-solutions, since they at least cannot be frustrated by the outer world. "Yet art affects us but as a mild narcotic and can provide no more than a temporary refuge from the hardship of life." [57] The esthetic attitude which looks for happiness in beauty also produces only "a mild intoxicating kind of sensation."

A large part of man's suffering is inherent in his destiny: the superior force of nature and the disposition of the body to decay. We may learn to mitigate these detrimental conditions, but we can never conquer them. However, the world of culture presents a different aspect. "We cannot see why the systems we have ourselves

created should not . . . ensure protection and well being for us all."
For Freud culture is the sum of the achievements and institutions
which differentiate our lives from those of our animal forbears. It
serves two purposes: it protects humanity against nature, and it
regulates the relations of human beings among themselves. The
evolution of culture is a process which accomplishes modifications
in our instinctual dispositions. Civilization is based on repression and
sublimation. Man is the animal that represses. The history of man
is the history of repressions. A nonrepressive civilization is impossible.[58] "Civilization is built up on renunciation of instinctual gratification." It starves the sexual instinct into monogamic submission.
Love opposes the interest of culture and, on the other hand, culture
menaces love with grievous restrictions. So far the whole discourse
on civilizations and their discontent seems to be a lament for the
lost paradise where man could give vent to his libido with impunity.

The older Freud had come to assume, however, that man is
not only possessed by the sexual instinct. Besides the instinct that
helps to preserve the organic substance, he said, there must exist
another, a desire to reinstate the inorganic origins of life, a desire
to return to nirvana. This constitutes the famous death-wish.

Life oscillates between Eros and Thanatos, and Freud rooted
the human tendency toward aggression in this death-wish. Culture
reflects the struggle between eros and death as it works itself out
in the human species. Freud is in line with Machiavelli and Hobbes
in his attempt to explain the sinister aspects of human civilization
which the eighteenth century and the Hegelian school had all too
often overlooked. A theory of cultural retrogression based on Freud's
death-wish and its manifestations of aggressiveness could be easily
developed. Many of the phenomena of the twentieth century could
be explained in this manner. Freud himself called attention to the
collective neuroses, but he remained skeptical on the subject of
correct diagnosis and cure. His closing words, written in 1929, have
lost none of their impressive tone: "The fateful question of the
human species seems to me, whether and to what extent the cultural
process developed in it will succeed in mastering the derangement
of communal life caused by the human instinct of aggression and
self-destruction. . . . Men have brought their powers of subduing
the forces of nature to such a pitch that by using them they could

now very easily exterminate one another to the last man. Men are aware of this possibility, and it is responsible for a great part of their current unrest, their dejection, their moral apprehension. And now it may be expected that the other of the two 'heavenly forces,' eternal Eros, will put forth his strength so as to maintain himself alongside of his equally immortal adversary." There is grandeur in this view which has not received the attention it deserves from historians.[59]

Yet, when we lay *Civilization and Its Discontent* aside, our minds are assailed by many questions. Our first impulse is to prepare a refutation entitled *Civilization and Its Contentments*. Is it really predominantly discontent which is experienced as part of the cultural process? Is the human condition truthfully defined by repression and frustration? Are cultural values understandable in terms of sublimation alone?

It is the weakness of all psychology, but especially that of Freud, to believe that genetic explanations can ever do justice to the works of the human mind. Culture is not only repression or sublimation; it is creation. If we listen to Bach, or Mozart, or Beethoven, we do not think primarily of the repressed or sublimated emotions from which their works may have arisen. We have witnessed acts of creation which can never be explained in Freudian terms. Freud may help us to understand the artist but never his art. The world of objective form, of harmony and style cannot be successfully compressed within genetic categories, nor can it be reduced to the dynamics of the unconscious.[60] Freud was by no means impermeable to artistic or poetic experience, but his attempts to deal with Leonardo, Michelangelo, or Goethe in psychoanalytical terms border on the ludicrous. He was obliged to admit that "unfortunately psychoanalysis has less to say about beauty than about most things." But this admission should include almost all forms of cultural endeavor. Poetry, music, the plastic arts, can never be measured by their biological usefulness, because, biologically speaking, their value is zero. To say that architecture sprang from man's desire to create an edifice in which human beings would be as protected as they were in the womb does not add one iota to our comprehension of architecture. And so we could go on ad infinitum, or rather *ad nauseam*.

Freud's attempts to explain human consciousness and its gradual emergence in the history of mankind as an evolution of repressed or sublimated instincts is likewise unsatisfactory. Again we must ask: if man is the animal that represses, why does he repress? Whence comes this feeling of guilt that propels him toward repression? Freud has no answer to our question. "Many of us," he states, "will find it hard to abandon our belief that in man himself there dwells an impulse toward perfection. . . . But I do not believe in the existence of such an inner impulse, and I see no way of preserving this pleasing illusion. The development of man up to now does not seem to me to need any explanation different from that of animal development, and the restless striving toward perfection . . . is easily explicable as the result of that repression of instinct upon which what is most valuable in human culture is built." [61]

But even a deeply disillusioned observer of mankind would have to admit that such a view fails to cope with the most intrinsic problems of the cultural processes. One of the significant oversights in Freud's work concerns, for example, the appearance of language as a cultural tool. Does either repression or sublimation offer an explanation? In its intricate logical structure does it not rather reveal that man is to a higher degree determined by Logos than the prophets of the unconscious will allow? Our very questions bring us to the obvious conclusion: the mind can be understood only by the mind. If man is nothing but a higher mammal, one still must admit that somewhere along the line a mutation has occurred. But the concept of mutation only indicates the jump from one species to another; it clarifies but it does not explain. [62]

We come finally to a much discussed question: how consistent was the discoverer of the unconscious in his attitude toward reason? Obviously Freud was not a romantic who gloried in throwing himself into the fathomless abyss of irrational forces. He blended the most naïve belief in scientific truth with the conviction that blind uncontrollable forces guide our actions and thoughts. He spoke once of an ideal state in which the human community would submit its instincts to the "dictatorship of reason." [63] At another time he remarked that the primacy of the intellect may be far away, but not altogether unattainable. He never questioned the right to rational pursuit, nor did he seem to understand that scientific investigations like his own entail of necessity value judgments. Freud's faith in scientific truth and his stubborn courage in upholding it are the most telling arguments against his underrating of man's consciousness. If guilt, repentance, and conscience are illusions, it is imperative to ask, why are illusions necessary to man's existence and what role do they play in our psychological economy?

Without choice, responsibility, and values, man ceases to be man. Jung was right to sense the danger that pschoanalysis may saw off the branch on which sits our whole civilization. Such remarks do not lessen Freud's significance for his time or for our own. He was both influence and symptom; in him the two are inextricably intertwined. His discoveries were momentous because he touched his time to the quick. It is for this reason that Freudian terms became a part of our daily language, and the therapeutic couch became the altar on which are daily offered in sacrifice the many souls who prostrate themselves before the unknown deity of the unconscious.

Freud's impact on literature defies description, at least in the framework of these studies. Among certain authors, Thomas Mann, Kafka, Virginia Woolf, T. S. Eliot, a direct dependence can be asserted. More astonishing and revealing are the cases of independent and parallel development, such as we note in Joyce, Marcel Proust, and Faulkner.[64]

Freud's influence ran along lines which had first been traced by Schopenhauer, Darwin, and Nietzsche, though his work is completely devoid of that note of suffering so characteristic of Nietzsche.

Freud's personality vanishes behind his findings. When Marie Bonaparte likened him to Kant and Pasteur, he politely declined the compliment: "I have," he said, " a high opinion of what I have discovered, but not of myself. Great discoverers are not necessarily great men. Who changed the world more than Columbus? What was he? An adventurer . . . so you see that one may find great things without it meaning that one is really great." [65]

II

It is the task of cultural history to call attention to the affinities which may be found in the expressions of the human mind during a certain period. These affinities are responsible for the mysterious coincidences which we call "Zeitgeist."

The relationship between Freud and the stream-of-consciousness literature is clear, but there are other trends in the nineteenth century which reveal less readily their link to the discovery of the unconscious. They too, however, share with Freud the anxiety to restore a lost dimension to human life. This aspiration is found to be particularly strong in the arts, especially in the painting called postimpressionism.

Vincent van Gogh is one of the best known artistic personalities of modern times. Biographies of him are abundant; books of all kinds—scholarly, fictional, and semifictional—have been devoted to his life and his work. He has been made the subject of plays and films, and reproductions of his paintings may be found in any dime store.[66] Yet during the short span of his days he lived and worked in complete obscurity; only one of his pictures was sold. In the thirty-seven years that were his before he decided to take his own life, he experienced a degree of torment, privation, and agony inflicted on few others. But his sufferings have been raised above the purely personal level through their sublimation in some of the most representative works of contemporary art.

Vincent van Gogh was born in a small village in Brabant, in 1853, the son of a minister. The family was deeply rooted in the Dutch soil. The Calvinist faith of his father became an integral part of his life, and in his early manhood filled him with a burning desire to do good, to preach God's word on earth, and to share the burden of the downtrodden. Long after he had lost his faith, he was still consumed by the zeal to do his duty regardless of the sacrifices it might entail, to fulfill his mission, and to offer himself up *in majorem gloriam Dei*. And like a true Calvinist, he was never to know whether his place was among the elect or the condemned, since he was not permitted to see the final and overwhelming triumph of his art. The asceticism of the Calvinist religion combined in him with an inherent morbid tendency, producing a drift toward self-immolation and self-destruction which made him one of the great martyrs in the history of European art.

Of art itself, there was plenty in van Gogh's early environment Three of his uncles were art dealers and one of them was the manager of the famous Goupil Galleries in The Hague. At the age of sixteen Vincent became an apprentice in his uncle's store.

He was a lonely youth, and confided in only one human being, his brother, Theo. Theo, too, was preparing to enter the art trade. The two boys had great plans, and during their evening strolls they discussed the problems that assailed humanity. One day they walked to the old mill of Ryswick, and in a moment of religious enthusiasm, pledged themselves to strive for good as long as they lived.[67]

From The Hague Vincent moved to London, still as an employee of his uncle trying to learn how to sell pictures. It is in London that some of his most intimate character traits are revealed to us for the first time. He conceived a deep attachment for the daughter of his landlady. Both mother and daughter had taken pity on the solitary youth and had been kind to him on many occasions, but the daughter's heart was elsewhere engaged. When, eventually, Vincent realized the hopelessness of his love, a tragic pattern seems to have established itself that held control throughout his life. It must be admitted that he was a thoroughly unlovable person, who at the same time was consumed with a desire to be loved. Even those who felt affection or admiration for him, like Theo, could not endure living with him for long. It is difficult to say whether Vincent's loneliness was the result of childhood longings that had remained unanswered or had been thwarted, but it is certain that from the age of twenty he lived in the prison of his own solitude.[68] Every attempt to escape from his cell seemed only to strengthen and heighten the walls.

He was not prepossessing in appearance, and he did affect a complete disregard for the care of his person, but it was not because of this that women recoiled from his declaration of love. It was the fierce demon of his self-centeredness which caused them to turn away from him in terror. Even prostitutes preferred a return to the brothel rather than become the companion of this inscrutable eccentric. Because he not only accepted but actually welcomed hardships and privations as the deserved punishment for his sins, he never implored a woman's pity. Neither does it seem that he ever appealed to the maternal instinct in women. It is indeed curious that this lost soul, so obviously incapable of coping with the simplest tasks, could never find any loving or protecting heart except Theo's. He would, it is true, have rejected pity; what he wanted, obstinately and passionately, was love, and he considered it rightfully his in spite of his physical handicaps of which he was all too conscious. Was not the sacred flame which consumed his heart something higher and worthier than the vile body in which it was arrested? But time and time again he heard the cruel answer: No! No! Never! Each rejection produced a masochistic desire for self-immolation. The notorious encounter with Gauguin at Arles is only the last of a series of similar affairs. Whether he burned his hand over a blazing lamp or cut off his ear, his motive was always the same: to find relief from the intolerable suffering that was destroying him by inflicting physical pain on himself. Those who did not flee from him in horror were driven away by his obstinacy or his aggressiveness, or by the squalor in which he lived. Very late he came to know that there was but one medium which allowed him communication with the world: his art. With deep melancholy he repeated the French saying: "L'amour de l'art fait perdre l'amour vrai." [69]

Another trait that emerges from his London experience is the conviction that he had a mission to fulfill in life. It was first revealed in contacts with his uncle's customers; he thought it his duty to direct their purchases. This was a fatal beginning, and he was soon dismissed from the store. After a brief try at teaching, he turned to preaching. He had always been a great reader of the Bible, and his urge to become an evangelist had been spurred even by such worldly writers as Renan and Michelet. In Renan he had found the words: "pour agir dans le monde, il faut mourir à soi-même." [70] But he did not find it easy to overcome himself. Unrest, melancholy, and listlessness drove him hither and yon. His religious fervor could not wholly restrain the perpetual storm in his heart. Moreover, he was quite incapable of mastering the studies which were indispensable to the career of a divine. When he realized that he could never learn the ancient languages, he resorted to ascetic mortification, sleeping on the bare floor during the winter and beating his back with a cane.[71] Vincent's love of God was, like everything else he felt, a glowing furnace. He rebelled against the sterile intellectual pursuit that was demanded of him, and decided to become a lay preacher. To prove his calling, he chose one of the mining districts of Belgium, the Borinage. The Borinage was one of the infernos of European industrialism, plagued by low wages, slum conditions, and frequent explosions, but for van Gogh it was the promised land. He remained in the Borinage from November of 1878 to September of 1880, holding Bible classes, visiting the sick, comforting the poor and the oppressed. He was always at home with simple people, now as later in Arles, and he preferred the worker, the peasant, the postman, or the whore, to the bourgeois friends of his family. In reality he was a man born out of caste and class. When Theo ventured to reproach him for the company he chose, he replied, "I am a passionate creature . . . the thing is to derive advantage from my passion . . . instead of giving myself up to passive melancholy, I have chosen active despair. . . . You will ask what my real aim is. Well, my aim will assume a more definite shape just as a drawing becomes a sketch, and a sketch a picture . . . my inner self has not changed." And he goes on to say, "Many a man has a bonfire in his heart, and no one comes to warm himself before it . . . I am drawn more and more to the conclusion that to love much is the best means of approaching God." [72] He compares himself to a prisoner: "Do you know what would make the prison disappear? To have friends, brothers, to love—that opens the prison as if by a charm." [73]

This was his eternal longing, and at that time he still hoped to assuage it by becoming a socially useful being. But, as we have said, van Gogh was really an outsider and looked at the social order of his day with deep misgivings. "We are in the last quarter of a century that will end with a colossal revolution . . . we shall not know the better times of fresh air and rejuvenated society which will come after the great storm." [74]

Van Gogh, though sometimes the despair of the grammarian, was a prolific correspondent, and he poured out his extraordinary confessions and prophecies in his letters to Theo. To the very last, he felt a need to alleviate the turmoil within his soul by unburdening himself to "une âme sœur," and he was on much safer ground when he wrote than when he talked. In conversation he refused to be interrupted or contradicted, and was very apt to fly into a rage if his utterances were attacked. His letters are the soliloquies of one of the loneliest souls who ever walked the earth, and his emotions would have choked him to death, had he not been able to set them forth on paper.

Only slowly did it dawn on him that he was not to find his destiny as an apostle of the Lord. At the end of two years in the Borinage, he returned to the parental home. He was twenty-seven years old, and in the eyes of his family a failure, a tramp, and a wastrel. His kind-hearted father might have forgiven all and clasped the prodigal son to his breast, but Vincent was by no means willing to accept absolution. He had left the underground world of the mines for one purpose only—to pursue his perennial goal, love, in a new world, the world of art. This time it was not in the picture mart, however, but in the studio. He was well aware that he had everything to learn.

In the years that followed he taught himself to draw, trying with uncertain, almost childish strokes, to depict the reality of peasants and workmen. With the hindsight that is now ours, we are able to see that his "gawky scrawls" contained even then the seeds of a painter's style.[75] He asked the advice of artists who had already left their mark and he attended academies, but his seditious temperament always got in his way, and most of these contacts ended in disaster. His taste was untrained and undisciplined. He admired Rembrandt and Franz Hals together with such second-rate painters as Millet and Meissonier.

His erotic life was as unstable as ever, his economic basis the narrowest on which a man could survive. Only the small remittances which Theo could spare him kept his head above water. Few other cases in European society show the rift between the artist and society as does that of van Gogh. Wishing desperately to become a useful member of society, he came to realize that the consumer value of revolutionary art is nil. He accepted his lot without much complaint since there was no other road to his goal, but in spite of Theo's generosity and tact, it must have been deeply humiliating for Vincent to find himself entirely dependent on his brother's bounty. During his entire life he was one of those who are enrolled in "the free courses of the great university of misery." [76] His models too were drawn from the sump of society. Unable to pay for expensive models, he relied on those who were willing to oblige him: the poor, the old, the peasant, the prostitute.

For six years he concentrated on drawing; only occasionally did he dare to paint, feeling that "the depth of color" still evaded him.[77] He conceived the idea of working for the people only, and planned a series of lithographs which he wanted to call "heads of the people" and which might be bought for a few centimes. In this manner he thought to bring a note of beauty into the homes of the disinherited.[78] It is part of the irony of his life that he never knew to what an extent his dream was to be fulfilled. He thought of artists as the ameliorists of life. Painters, he said to Theo, are in modern society what Puritans used to to be . . . art is the America of the modern pilgrim, a promised land of freedom.

Little by little he advanced himself in this promised land. The influence of admired masters was still great, but he began to divine that the real aim of modern art was to produce what no past had ever produced. He became increasingly intrigued with colors; they had, he thought, a life of their own. Color had its own message which surpassed the trivial communications of a slavishly copied reality. "There is something infinite in painting that I cannot explain . . . in the colors there are concealed things of harmony and contrast which work by themselves." [79] And at another time he said, "In all of nature I see expression and, so to speak, soul." [80]

Throughout this period he was, nevertheless, completely ignorant of the great revolution in painting which was then taking place in Paris. In spite of the information furnished him from time to time by Theo from the French capital, van Gogh knew next to nothing of the aims and the techniques of the impressionists. "Il y a, je crois, une école d'impressionists. . . . Mais je n'en connais pas grand chose." [81]

However, with one of those inexplicable decisions so characteristic of him, he suddenly arrived in Paris. It was February of 1886, and van Gogh made his home there for two full years. The impressionist school was at its height: pleinairism, the light palette, the ever-changing world revealed through light and color, all this was laid before him. Van Gogh absorbed it with a ravishing thirst, like one who has traveled for days through a desert waste and suddenly finds a well of fresh water.

In place of weavers and plowmen, he began to paint flowers, street corners such as the famous Moulin de la Galette, or restaurants. The influence of Monet and Pissaro is apparent, yet it is equally clear that van Gogh has now the power to hold his own, or, even better, to come into his own. His brushwork attains for the first time the fierce stroke so indelibly his, which cuts through the lines like a sword thrust or rips through the colors like a whip.[82] He tried his hand at portraits, and could at one sitting complete a masterpiece such as the one of Père Tanguy. In Paris he also turned increasingly to self-portraits. His lack of commissions together with his urge for introspection are poignantly expressed in his letters. One of his self-portraits shows him standing before the easel, palette and brushes in his right hand. There is no trace of vanity or pose in this study, only the desire to reveal the essence of his grim and tortured self. The combination of composition and color values—blue, red, and yellow—is of the highest order and proves that van Gogh was already leaving the newly learned technique far behind.[83]

Nor did the many conversations on art in which he took part deflect him from his goal. The impressionist school was already breaking up and the Parisian air was fermenting with new theories: neoimpressionism, Cloisonnism, pointillism, and so forth. By that mysterious chemistry, characteristic of genius, van Gogh digested them all in a manner that only helped to free his own gifts.

Human encounters were less easy to manage. Toulouse-Lautrec, Signac, Seurat, Bernard, and many others whom he met, perturbed or delighted him as the case might be. But one man well-nigh overwhelmed him with his self-assurance, his sarcasm, and his determination: Paul Gauguin. There was a strange parallel in the lives of these two: the one a former bank clerk who had severed ties with the bourgeois life and was now scanning the horizon for new adventures in which the imperishable dream of mankind could be rediscovered; the other a pilgrim who had set forth on an uncertain quest and who had fought his way onward through humiliation and privation. Yet van Gogh did not dare to place himself side by side with the French corsair. That he singled out Gauguin from among the hundreds of painters whom he saw in Paris to become his idol was one more of those tragic errors with which his life overflowed.

The longer he stayed in Paris the more he became convinced that his idea of color was not identical with that of the impressionists. He was not yet able to demonstrate on canvas *his* orange, *his* blue, *his* yellow, *his* green, but he talked of them with a veritable obsession. He could not find the colors he dreamed of in Paris, and longed for a different sky, another sunlight, for the sight of the earth, and the breath of a new wind on his face. He thought of going to Marseilles but finally settled on Arles. Theo agreed to let him go. Life with Vincent had been at times unbearable, but when he had gone, Theo wrote: It seems so strange to be without him. He meant so much to me.

The ten months van Gogh spent in Arles will always be thought of as a miracle and a mystery. Everything in his life that had preceded this period—his religious fervor, his long apprenticeship in Holland, his stay in Paris—came to fruition during this brief season in which the bulk of his work was produced and in which he conquered the style adequate for his explosive personality. It is a unique case of accumulation which made this eruption possible, though by no means does this explain it. The landscape of the Provence in which he found himself cast overwhelmed him by "a riot of colors," an outburst of growth and force, such as he had never known.[84]

But was it really the potentials of nature which he felt, or was it the pressure within his own soul so rapidly approaching the point where its volcanic energies could no longer be housed within a human body? Van Gogh was quite conscious that he was walking very close to the abyss of madness.[85] He speaks of his "lucidité terrible," of moments in which he completely lost himself and in which the picture came to him as a dream.[86] In one of the most moving confessions ever to burst forth from an artist, he wrote: "I can, in life and in painting, do without the good God (le bon Dieu), but I cannot, suffering as I am, do without something greater than I, that is my life, the power to create."[87] The power to create! It was in him and it was in the universe outside of him, and in his trancelike state he could hardly tell them apart. But have not many of the greatest revelations been captured on the threshold of insanity where man is lifted beyond the borders of the temporal and is allowed to behold the essence of things?[88] He began a race with time. He painted spring as if the almond and peach trees would never flower again; ten pictures in as many days. He defended himself against the reproach that he was working too fast. It was emotion, intensity, and sincerity that drove him on in his "frantic labor." [89] Already summer was coming; there would be fields of corn to paint and the flowers, sunflowers and roses; there was the beach that he longed to see, and there was the sun itself and the starry sky. He conceived of paintings that no other artist had dared to envisage. More and more color became the symbol of things. It was suggestive, expressive, and the manifestation of a burning temperament, a simile of human passion. Yellow expressed light and, consequently, love; blue the infinite; and red and green "the terrible human passions." The colors are juxtaposed without any particular system, without mysterious or artistic tricks, and their harmony results simply from the connection between the colored masses in each picture. "Je cherche maintenant à exagérer l'essentiel." [90] How well he succeeded.

It was the same when he turned from nature to portrait, still life, or inanimate objects. When he painted the railroad viaduct near his house, he conveyed the impression of the absolute loneliness of contemporary man in a technological world. F. Novotny has given a technical analysis of this picture. [91] Van Gogh deliberately violated the laws of perspective in order to produce an impression of depth that would engulf the spectator and draw him into the unknown space. "Exagérer l'essentiel." He does it in his portraits of those few souls who befriended him in Arles. There was the postman, Rollin, and the kindhearted Madame Ginoux. Whoever sees these portraits for the first time feels a magic hand grip his heart and hold it in a vise. The portraits are more democratic than those of the impressionists, or perhaps it would be more accurate to say, they are less determined by class, and consequently are more human. As Meyer Schapiro expresses it, there is a deeply moving exchange between the character represented and the predominant color in the portrait, strikingly strong, for instance, in the blue and gold of M. Rollin.

"Gauguin's Chair" is perhaps the best example of this extraordinary power by which van Gogh wrung from material objects an energetic force. When we behold his pictures we are tempted to cry out as did Goethe once: "Wie wahr, wie seiend" ("How true, how being"). These simple things, an armchair, two books and a candle, pulsate with life and the overflow of power. And this miracle is accomplished in the most dismal objects: the pots and chairs and beds that his poverty allowed him to buy. Likewise in his landscapes and flower pieces, organic function takes the place of organic being. "He ceased to paint trees, but growth . . . not blossoms, but bloom." [92] The inner drama of his soul overflowed into the world. But his paintings, needless to say, are not the projections of a madman; in them are discovered the pulse of fire in the fields blazing under the sun, the weight of stone and those crevices he beheld, the struggle and the peace of cosmic life in the sunflowers.

This art is dramatic, and it revealed more than any other drama written in Europe at the time, the convulsions which were soon to wreck the Old World. One of the first to sense the prophetic character of van Gogh's art was the poet Hofmannsthal, who was an excellent seismograph for the European terrain. We can do no better than repeat the words which he wrote in 1901.

At first sight these [paintings] seemed to me loud and restless, quite crude, quite strange . . . in order to see the first of them as pictures at all, as a unity, I had to prepare myself—but then I saw, then I saw them all thus, each single one and all together, and Nature in them, and the strength of the human soul which had transformed Nature, and tree and bush and field and slope which were painted here, and also that other strength, that which was behind the paint, the essence, that indescribable sense of fate. . . . There is an incredible blue, most powerful of blues, which constantly reappears, a green like that of molten emeralds, a yellow that deepens into orange. But what are colours if the innermost life of objects doesn't break through them? And this innermost life was there, tree and stone and wall and gorge gave of themselves their innermost, almost casting it at me . . . the impact of its existence, the ferocious wonder of its existence surrounded by incredibility, made a dead set at my soul. How can I make it clear . . . that here each Being—the Being of each tree, each strip of yellow or greenish field, each fence, each gorge cut into the stony hill, the Being of the pewter jug, the earthenware bowl, the table, the clumsy armchair lifted itself toward me as though newly born from the frightful chaos of Non-living, from the abyss of Non-Being, so that I felt—nay, that I knew—how each of these objects, these creatures, was born from a terrible doubting of the world, and how with its existence it now covered over forever the dreadful chasm of yawning nothingness. . . . And now I could, from picture to picture, feel a something, could feel the mingling, the merging of formation, how the innermost life broke forth into colour and how the colours live one for the sake of the others, and how one, mysteriously, powerfully, carried all the others; and in all this I could sense a heart, the soul of the man who had created it, who with his vision did himself answer the spasms of his own most dreadful doubts.[93]

It would be useless to pretend that van Gogh attained such extraordinary heights in all his paintings. There is a wide margin between the best of his work and those pictures which show us only the wild routine of his brush stroke. (It is this latter part of his work that permitted skillful forgers in the 1930's to circulate great numbers of imitations.) Whether this oscillation between mastery and weakness was due to the haste in which he painted or whether it was a foretaste of his illness is well-nigh impossible to establish. Regardless of these reservations, however, van Gogh at his best brought about exactly the experience that Hofmannsthal has described: he makes us feel the Being of things, their very essence wrung from the abyss of nothingness.

It was through such vision, and not by any technical improvement that van Gogh forged ahead of the impressionist school. The impressionists had converted the world into a veil of beautiful appearances, where the substance of things evaporated behind a mist of color and light. Magnificent as their achievement had been, it was inevitable that man would, sooner or later, tire of an art which could only show the phenomenal aspects of reality. Van Gogh retained from his masters the subjective approach, the emphasis on the power of the artistic self. But he was not only a mirror that threw back the image of the world. He deliberately changed contour and color until his objects breathed a life of their own: the essence of reality which he had all his life been pursuing.

Of course, van Gogh could not permanently restore to painting the lost dimension which the European mind had forfeited in the nineteenth century. He could brush aside the ephemeral beauty that impressionism had woven and point to the fierce force of life in field and star, in house and chair, in strangers and in himself. But this was accomplished only through the symbolism of color, and remained an accomplishment in the world of art, or to put it bluntly, an esthetic accomplishment. Van Gogh's own development from evangelist to painter symbolizes the metaphysical situation in which Europe found itself around 1890. All that an artist could do was to point to the lost dimension, to disclose in lightning flashes of blue, green, orange, and yellow, the "essence of things." But if the truth must be told, they remained fleeting visions, after which we feel even more strongly the utter loneliness of man in a universe where to his deepest question he hears only his own answer.

The impressionist school had been the last to show a homogeneous style in the history of the arts. As European society gave way to the tensions that were tearing its body asunder, no new style could emerge. From then on only subjective interpretations were possible. In the market place one artistic fad after another might be displayed: cubism, expressionism, and a cartload of other isms, but these have little to do with real artistic values. After the impressionist school, Europe has produced, in painting at least, not art but artists. As Maurice Denis said, "La nature peut donc n'être pour l'artiste qu'un état de sa propre subjectivité. Et ce que nous appelons la déformation subjective n'est practiquement que le style." [94]

Thus van Gogh, like Freud, is both a symptom and an influence. The solipsism of the European mind was expressed by him with a power equaled only by Nietzsche who collapsed even as van Gogh was approaching his tragic end. By the same token the loneliness and the subjectivity of the artist were strongly accentuated by his art, to the point where the individuality of the artist became all but supreme.

The cleavage between the world and the self spread with incredible speed through all spheres of European culture, with the result that the Western world finally produced the schizophrenic civilization in which we now live. A contemporary of Freud, Van Gogh made the amazing prophecy that one day perhaps everyone would have his own neurosis.

One more observation may be added. Van Gogh's art followed the impressionist tradition in that it avoided the religious theme as carefully as it eluded the historical or the mythological. But there are themes in Renoir and Monet to which van Gogh either had no access or felt no attraction. The beauty of the human body, "the female form divine," had no magic for him. How strange that this tireless hunter after love was never fascinated by the great illusion that makes us search for love in beautiful forms. Perhaps his disappointments had been too numerous or too deep for him to believe in what Stendhal called, *une promesse de bonheur.*

Van Gogh's sympathies belonged to those artists and poets in whom he felt the soul most powerfully expressed. He too wanted to manifest joy and peace, sadness and utter loneliness, in his paintings. What a contrast to "art for art's sake." Art was for van Gogh a destiny in the strictest sense of the word, and his artistic career became quite logically a great drama with ethical and religious overtones.[95] But the revolution that he accomplished was in the field of the arts and specifically in color and design. His own criticism in evaluating his work was always the same: had he been able to transpose his subject in lines and colors "as I feel them"? It is an anarchic soul that speaks in his pictures. Van Gogh said once that he hoped to save all the fundamental qualities of the Old Masters in this radical transformation that he brought to European painting, but all he could save was his own powerful message.[96] Obviously it is close to that of other tormented souls of the nineteenth century; Nietzsche we have spoken of, but there are also Kierkegaard and Dostoevski. But Vincent van Gogh can be described only as he once described Rembrandt: he had "a hand of fire."

III

Paul Gauguin's encounter with van Gogh in Arles brought the accumulated pressures in the Dutch artist's life to the point of explosion. Van Gogh's subsequent illness, his desperate attempts to elude his doom, his harrowing days in Saint-Rémy and Auvers sur Oise make a moving story which has received its full due of notoriety and needs no further word from us.

The man who unwittingly set the spark to van Gogh's pathological outburst, Paul Gauguin, is interesting to us not so much as a rival but as a parallel. In their lives and in their work both men defied the culture from which they sprang. Paul Gauguin especially is an example of *Civilization and Its Discontent*. The challenge which he flung in the face of Western culture became a myth during his own lifetime—the self-exile to those exotic isles of a distant ocean whence he sent his disconcerting and inimitable pictures of an existence both savage and beautiful to disturb the placidity of his homeland.[97] His legend grew, nor has he escaped the frivolous twist of the novelist or the rapacious hand of the script-writer. This is in no way surprising; his life pulsated to a dramatic beat. But the world of make-believe pales before the drama of his actual existence

Gifted with an imagination that recognized no limits to his desires, eager for independence, master of his thoughts and slave of his temperament, he suffered from an incurable illness which a French critic diagnosed as l'anxiété du beau.[98] Thus he had all the essentials for a profound unhappiness and became the architect of his own misfortune. But from the fire that consumed him, he wrested a world of beauty that bears the imprint of his soul and the fate it chose to embrace.

Gauguin maintained that on his mother's side he was descended from the Borgias of Aragon and that he had Inca blood in his veins. These claims, though exaggerated, are not entirely fantastic. Born in Paris in 1848, he spent part of his early life in Lima, Peru, "the fortunate land where it never rains." [99] What remained with him from such childhood impressions was the recollection of tropical exuberance for which he yearned throughout his life. Was he perhaps searching for it when at seventeen he enrolled in the merchant marine? He went to South America, and it may well be that on one of these voyages he heard for the first time of the Polynesian Islands.[100]

In 1871, after six years at sea, he left abruptly to enter an exchange bank in Paris. In 1875 he married a Danish girl who saw in him the fulfillment of her bourgeois aspirations, and settled down to a peaceful and monotonous existence. For ten years he acted the part of a model husband, a model father, and a model clerk who speculated successfully on the stock exchange. But those biographers who present Gauguin's decision to throw off the burden of a well regulated life as a sudden coup de théâtre neglect the imperceptible changes which prompted his resolve. There was a constant ground swell in Gauguin's life which finally made him take the fateful step. Gauguin himself uses the word "incubation," saying, "Wherever I go I need a certain period of incubation, so that I may learn every time the essence of the plants and trees, of all nature, in short, which never wishes to be understood or to yield herself." [101]

He took up painting first as a pastime, devoting to it his Sundays and holidays. Mme. Gauguin, at a much later date, remarked, "I had no idea that he had any artistic inclinations." But Gauguin himself must have been certain of his vocation long before he decided to break with his bourgeois existence. What he was not so certain about was his talent. Was he perhaps not just another amateur? Manet assured him that he was a painter, making the observation, "The only amateurs are those who make bad pictures."

Gauguin made a friend of Pissaro who taught him much of the impressionist technique, and even though his coloring was at first drab and clumsy, he made genuine progress. He was invited to participate in the sixth exhibition of the Impressionists and sent the picture of a nude which Huysmans applauded as "la femme de nos jours." In the meantime, still hesitant, he collected the work of his confreres: Manet, Monet, Pissaro, Sisley, and especially Cézanne, for whom he had an admiration that was not reciprocated. By 1882 he was convinced of his calling and was ready to make the inevitable decision. He had been a banker by profession and a painter in his spare time; henceforward he would be a painter by profession and an amateur as a provider.[102] At least he would be free "to paint every day."

It is an error to think that he took his resolution with cold-hearted cynicism. He had been a good husband and a devoted father, but from now on he lived under a law which overruled all other demands: la légitime férocité d'un égoism productif.[103] It is probable that he did not foresee the tragic estrangement from his family which his decision entailed, but it is very certain that he never regretted it. His pride, which was ultimately faith in his genius, bore him up through all the disappointments and difficulties that life held in store for him.

The break with his bourgeois existence was only the first of several acts which converted Gauguin's life into a sustained protest against the world of the late nineteenth century. His next step was in the world of the arts proper. "En art," said Gauguin, "il n'y a que révolutionaires ou plagiaires." There can be little doubt in which category he belongs.[104]

He had begun as a disciple of the Impressionists, and by 1883, had mastered their techniques. He always retained from this mode of art the basic principle of creative subjectivity. But like van Gogh, he believed that the inner meaning of things is mysteriously grasped by the artist's self and that both are manifested to the impressions of the eye.[105] "Les impressionists," he remarked, "cherchèrent autour de l'œil, et non au centre mystérieux de la pensée. . . . Quand ils parlent de leur art, quel est-il? Un art de superficie tout de coquet-terie, purement matériel; la pensée n'y reside pas." [106] It was from this "mysterious center of thought" that Gauguin endeavored to renovate the arts. His art should express sentiment and ideas. Lines and colors, he discovered, could be noble or deceitful; they could convey quiet harmonies that lend comfort, and others that excite by their daring.

But how was he to prevail in a world that accepted only the traditional or the manifestly real? The only answer was to work freely and frantically (travailler librement et follement). Gauguin did not limit his activities to painting; he tried his hand at sculpture, woodcuts, and ceramics. He felt that he was about to evolve a new system, a new way of seeing and expressing himself; he was working at the creation of a plastic world.[107] It is in his painting, however, that he will endure.

His intention to root art in the mysterious center of thought was the creative nucleus from which flows all Gauguin's mature art. Faced with a hostile world, however, he was obliged to seek out an environment that would not blight his impetus at the outset. This was no easy matter and he was forced to improvise, but it was only in his external life that he improvised. Whatever disorder or incoherence may be noted in his life were never tolerated in his art.[108]

"I always had a fancy for running away," he once confessed, and he thus retreated from Paris to Pont Aven in Brittany.[109] A variety of reasons conspired to make this part of France attractive to him; living was cheap there, a cogent consideration for a penniless man with pressing obligations. In addition, he was seeking a country of archaic customs far removed from the overcivilized and sophisticated atmosphere of Paris, a place free from sham, hypocrisy, and re-straint, where he might give form to the melancholy that had in-vaded him.

In Pont Aven he would moreover, meet kindred souls who were working and exploring along the same lines as Gauguin himself. We have spoken of the schools of Cloisonnism, synthetism or sym-bolism. The painter, Emile Bernard, has claimed to be the inventor of the new technique which emphasized the line of objects rather than the juxtaposed colors of the Impressionists.[110] The rivalries of

these schools and cliques are today forgotten, and indeed should not
be denied their well deserved *pax perpetua*. As for Gauguin, he was
utterly indifferent to schools and their various claims to priority
and vainglory. "What does it matter if I am the pupil of Bernard
or Sérusier? If I have made good things, nothing will blemish them;
if I have made rubbish (de la merde), why try to gild it?" [111] As
Gauguin's fame has grown, his work in Brittany has come into focus.
"For me," he wrote to his friend, Schuffenecker, "the artist is a
formulation of the greatest intelligence; he is the recipient of sensations which are the most delicate and consequently the most invisible expressions of the brain." Gauguin's work of this period shows
that he had already overcome "the abominable error of naturalism."
The still lifes and flower pieces painted during his three sojourns at
Pont Aven, the "Calvary," "La Belle Angèle," and above all the
famous "Christ Jaune," prove him to have been in full command
of his faculties. "His insatiable eye" had found in Brittany for the
first time the primitive violence, the unexpected harmonies that
alone could satisfy him. "I find here," he wrote, "the savage, the
primitive. When my sabots echo on the granite, I hear the sound
dull and strong that I am looking for in painting." [112] His pictures
became exceedingly daring and showed already the synthesis of
harmonies and contrasts which made his later work famous. The
paintings from Brittany are perhaps more somber than those from
the South Sea islands, but both are marked by austerity and splendor. Gauguin had learned to simplify the lines and volume of his
models, thus achieving a maximum effect of color. "Paul Gauguin
had become Paul Gauguin." [113]

The most sensitive of Gauguin's contemporaries were aware that
here was an artist who had struck a new chord in the emotions of
his time. Mallarmé and Verlaine discovered a hidden sympathy
between their poetic efforts and Gauguin's new synthetism. Gauguin,
though he lent himself to the game of esthetic discussion, cast a
cold eye on any attempt to classify his art under the heading of
symbolism, which for him was only another form of sentimentalism.
However, in contrast to the complete solitude that surrounded van
Gogh, Gauguin found understanding in *avant-garde* circles. Octave
Mirbeau published in *Echo de Paris* an appreciation which over a
period of sixty years has lost little of its original value.

"Paul Gauguin," wrote Mirbeau, "is a very exceptional and disturbing artist. . . . He is a restless spirit, tormented by the infinite; never satisfied with what he has accomplished, but ever searching beyond. He feels that he has not given all that he is able to give of himself. The dream of this active mind is never at rest." Mirbeau goes on to say that Gauguin's art is "strangely cerebral and impassioned, uneven but always poignant and impressive, the work of one who has known sorrow and the irony which leads to the mystical. Sometimes, indeed, it rises to the mystical act of faith; at other times it grins in the darkness of doubt." [114]

Mirbeau's article caused quite a stir in Paris, and served as an introduction to the catalogue listing some thirty pictures which Gauguin had arranged for an exhibition. The result was by no means negligible. Gauguin sold all his paintings for a total of ten thousand francs, enough to realize his dream of turning his back on Europe and retreating to a world of tropical splendor.

As early as 1887 Gauguin had made an attempt to settle in one of the French colonies, but he got stranded in Panama, where for some time he maintained a wretched existence digging ditches. Eventually he arrived in Martinique where he was plagued by lack of money and an attack of tropical dysentery. His experience in Martinique was, however, decisive. "Only there," he told Charles Morice, "could I be myself," and on another occasion he said, "Never has my painting been so light in color, so lucid (though with plenty of fantasy)."

But the image of the Caribbean islands was replaced by an even more enticing one, and in 1891 he arrived in Tahiti determined on isolating himself from civilization, voluntarily seeking oblivion and silence. It was not long before the troubled life of Europe took on the aspect of a forgotten dream, and the silence and oblivion he had sought set him free for his real purpose. Here, at last, he found those deeper colors, those greater contrasts and wilder harmonies which *la douce France* had failed to supply. The man Gauguin yearned for the savage embrace which neither his wife nor his mistress had been able to give him, and he cherished the illusion that his passionate nature would find its counterpart in his *vahine,* the native girl, Tehura, who shared his hut and his bed. "I am no more conscious of days and hours, of good and evil . . . I know only that everything is good, because everything is beautiful." It might have seemed that he had given himself over to the powers of Eros.[115] But it was not libido alone that stirred Gauguin; in reality it was something far beyond the "pleasure principle." It was a fierce determination to seize "all this gold and all this joy of the sun" so suddenly discovered and make it flow across his canvases. It was not life for lust but lust for life that was finally to crystallize in the transcendent dream. In *Noa, Noa,* from which we have quoted, there is the following confession: "In man's soul are innate feelings which will never be satisfied by real objects, and it is to these feelings that the painter and the poet can, by his imagination, give form and life. . . . An impression results from a certain arrangement of colors, light and shade. . . . One might call this the music of painting. This emotion appeals directly to the intimate part of the soul and it arouses feelings which words can only express in the vaguest way." When Mme. Gauguin reproached him for deserting the center of the artistic world, he answered: "My artistic center is in my own brain and nowhere else . . . there are changes in my work each year, it is true, but it always follows the same road." [116]

Gauguin has given an idyllic description of his life in Tahiti in *Noa, Noa* and in *Avant et après.* When we read his letters we come upon a different story, a story of sickness, lack of money, and surprisingly enough, a fear of premature old age. However, he still could say, "Avec beaucoup d'orgueil, j'ai fini par avoir beaucoup d'énergie, et j'ai voulu vouloir." [117] He was immersed in his painting, and was entitled to assert, "I am sure no one else has ever done anything like this before." [118]

Gauguin's art is an extraordinary phenomenon in European culture. True enough, he was not the first to raise his voice against our old civilization; such protests had been heard many times since the days of Jean Jacques Rousseau. Nor was he the first "to go native"; many an adventurer had disappeared in the jungle of the colonial world. Neither was he the only one to fall under the spell of the tropical world. Loti and Conrad felt the same allure. But for Gauguin was reserved the power to combine the qualities of reckless adventurer and creative genius in such a fashion that his singular magic is preserved to this very day.

When Gauguin set sail for Tahiti, he was neither primitive nor savage; he was the representative of an overripe civilization intent on reminding the arts of their origins and principles. "In our present misery," he wrote, "there is no salvation except through a reasoned and frank return to the beginning, that is to say, to primitive art." But even though he decided to live like a native, he did not become one, and he was entirely conscious of this fact. The miracle that he expected from the tropical, primitive world was rejuvenation. It was the ancient dream of the fountain of youth, and he hoped to find it in Tahiti. Its charmed waters might give him a comprehension of himself and might teach him the art of living and the secret of happiness.[119]

If this was indeed his goal, his life in Tahiti was a failure; his letters give abundant proof that the adaptation to primitive life was never complete or successful. The list of illnesses which beset Gauguin is long and heartbreaking. He suffered from eczema, his heart was weak, he vomited blood, and, most tragic of all, his eyes became infected. It would seem that the fountain of youth did not flow for Gauguin. The estrangement from his children and his friends troubled him deeply; with what eagerness he waited for the arrival of mail from Paris and Copenhagen, where the family now lived. With what bitter disappointment did he turn away each time at the words: "Nothing for you, Monsieur Gauguin."

Did a realization of the inner contradictions of his existence ever come to him? He had risen in rebellion against an old civilization, but it was to Europe that he was obliged to appeal for his very livelihood. He could not have remained in Tahiti had it not been for the ties which bound the islands to France.

In order to support himself he was obliged to sell his pictures. Although the results fell short of his expectations, he dispatched crates of his work to his dealers every year. And the connection is not one of expediency alone. Gauguin's art was directed toward Europe, or perhaps we should say, to the Western world. He did not paint for the Tahitians; these innocents had no possible comprehension of the impulse of his work. It was to France, to the Old World, that he addressed himself; and it was Europe that should be reawakened to the true principles of great art. His Tahitian captions and his use of native legends and religion in his creations have little to do with his art. These matters were his private mythology. But his attempts to revive the arts by a return to primitive myth is indicative of the situation which the European mind had reached by 1900.

The great artistic imaginations of the nineteenth century were no longer in thrall to Christian mythology, but no new provocative legend had arisen to take its place. Gauguin sought to fill the vacuum with a myth of his own making, the primitive pantheon of the Tahitian people as interpreted by himself. He failed to realize that savage and alien conceptions could never, for the European, replace the age-old and deeply enshrined symbols of Christianity. They might captivate the imagination momentarily, but they were lacking in binding power. Gauguin's pictures are great in artistic value, but their metaphysical significance is limited. From a religious point of view they will remain strange, irrelevant, subjective, and personal.

Even where Gauguin endeavored to meet the problem head-on, as in his greatest canvas, "Whence do we come, who are we, where are we going?"—even there we feel that he is overreaching himself. He was not a primitive, but a highly cultivated mind who sought in the primitive a means to retrieve the lost dimension, to resurrect for himself and for Europe the dying impulses of the imagination. He was a skeptic who longed for oblivion in those dark recesses whence mystical feelings arise. His religiosity is akin to "the second religiosity" which Spengler refers to in *The Decline of the West* as a phenomenon characteristic of a decaying civilization.

Whereon then, we may ask, does Gauguin's claim to greatness rest? Even more than van Gogh, he realized in his art a dream born from "the mysterious center of thought." He was essentially a poet and the poems that filled his soul were recorded on canvas with new lines and in colors which have no parallel in European art.[12]

In these dreams women play a predominant role. They are there in all attitudes, standing, walking, crouching, reclining. They represent desire, tenderness, jealousy, fear. In the picture, "L'Or de leur corps," the golden bodies breathe a gentle seduction. Other works such as "The Seed of the Areois" or "Tahitian Women with Red Mangoes," suggest a dream of pleasure rather than pleasure itself.

Gauguin's nudes do not have the sovereignty that ennobles Greek art, nor do they have the sensual directness of Titian or Rubens. They have innocence, or should we say, a second innocence, acquired rather than innate, which sometimes comes as the fruit of love. The world which Gauguin paints is a world where shame was unknown, but it was captured by one who knew well "the old routine of Europe," and who longed for his Eden. Gauguin's art is paradise regained, replete with joy and the assuagement of desire.

It seems a remarkable coincidence that Freud was writing *The Interpretation of Dreams* at the same time that an art analogous to his discovery of the unconscious was born. Gauguin painted a people who appear to be moved by the same force in which Freud found the root of human happiness.

Gauguin's art would not, of course, attain greatness merely as the manifestation of dreams. He once said of himself, "I am two things . . . a child and a savage," but he was also an artist of discerning taste, deeply conscious of the means he had to employ to reveal his dreams.[121] Besides being a poet, he had the genius of decoration. In representing the golden bodies of the Tahitians or the exuberance of tropical nature, he introduced a statuesque element in his painting, emphasizing line and contour in a manner all but banned by the Impressionists. The magic of his art, however, rests on color rather than on line. "He was," says Cogniat, "a prodigious inventor of . . . colors, for whom reality did not matter any more. For he created for his own purpose another reality. His roads are red, the fields violet, the trunks of trees green, and the foliage yellow."[122] As in van Gogh's art, the intensity and exaltation of his pictures grasp something that photographic realism could never have arrested: the soul, the essence of the luminescent world in which he lived.[123] He, too, ignored deliberately the laws of scientific perspective in favor of a poetic dream world. Here, too, the colors have a life of their own; they are saturated with an immaterial power: this flaming red, this deep blue, this cool green, this tender purple.

Fate denied Gauguin a final fulfillment in murals to which in other times he would surely have turned. The world of the twentieth century has no place for the magnificent wall paintings that are to be found in Santa Maria Novella or the Sistine Chapel. Even so, for his own age, he came as close to "the mysterious center of thought" as was possible.

From Gauguin's own pen there are two moving confessions that define his place in our Western culture. One was addressed to his friend, Daniel de Montfreid, in October of 1902 shortly before his death: "You have known for a long time what has been my aim to vindicate: the right to dare anything. My capacities (and the pecuniary difficulties in my life have greatly interfered with the carrying out of my task) have not allowed me to achieve a great result, but the mechanism has been set in motion nevertheless. The public owes me nothing, since my pictorial œuvre is only relatively good, but the painters of today who are benefiting from this new-won freedom do owe me something. True, many of them imagine that it has happened all by itself. However, I expect no recognition from them and I can find my reward in my own conscience." [124] Gauguin underestimated his work on both counts. The artists who followed him were quite conscious of the debt they owed him: his revolutionary vision, his creative dreams, and his courage to "dare everything." And if one observes in the museums of Paris, London, New York, or Boston, the figures that linger, enchanted, before the paintings of Gauguin, one is assured that his dream has not perished.

In these pictures one senses the soul of the artist who wrote: "I believe in the saintliness of the spirit and in the truth of the arts, one and indivisible. I believe that art is of divine origin and that it lives in the heart of all men enlightened by the heavenly light. I believe that if one has once tasted the sublime joy of this great art, one is vowed to it fatally and forever. . . . I believe . . . that the faithful disciples of great art will be glorified and that they, wrapped in heavenly tissue, made of rays of perfume, melodious chords, will return to lose themselves in all eternity in the divine origin of all harmony." [125]

The search for the lost dimension did not end here. Whereas Freud attempted to find it in the depth of the unconscious, and van Gogh and Gauguin looked for it in the "mysterious center of thought" to be reflected in their art, one thinker placed himself intrepidly in the no man's land between transcendence and immanence. It is a Spaniard, Miguel de Unamuno who, together with other Spaniards of his generation, led Spain back into active participation in European culture.

IV

Spain's long-overdue awakening came at the close of the nineteenth century, and came, as is well known, in response to the final disappearance of the ruins of her imperial greatness during the Spanish-American war.[126] After 1898 her goal could no longer be "a Dios infinitas almas, al rey infinitas tierras" ("for God an infinitude of souls, for the king an infinitude of lands"). After almost two hundreds years of intellectual hibernation, Spain awoke to regain a cultural position which had been rightfully hers in the times of the Renaissance and the Counterreformation. The men who accepted the challenge thrust upon them have been called "the generation of 1898." These men comprised the artistic and intellectual nucleus of contemporary Spain.

The generation of 1898 embraces personalities whose date of birth falls within the decades between 1860 and 1890. Unamuno was born in 1864, Ganivet in 1865, Picasso in 1881, and Ortega in 1883.[127] The inheritance of the past which overshadowed the youth of the Spanish writers and thinkers of 1898 was the long struggle between liberals and traditionalists which had filled the greater part of the nineteenth century.

In spite of the fact that the two parties stem from opposite philosophical roots, both were engaged in grappling with the same problem: Spain and her attitude toward the European civilization of the nineteenth century. And this is where Unamuno takes his start. He was born in Bilbao, capital of the Basque country. "I am a Basque, " he loved to say with a certain truculence, "which means I am even more of a Spaniard than the other Spaniards." With Ignatio de Loyola he represents the mystical toughness of this unique little country.[128]

When he was nine years of age Bilbao was besieged by the Carlistas, one of the factions in Spain's perpetual civil war, and Unamuno never forgot the smell of gunpowder and the terrifying sound of shells and bullets. Perhaps he realized, as he inhaled the clouds of smoke, that it might become his destiny too, to fight men, though not with material weapons. And in very truth he was all his life to be both besieger and besieged, both liberal and traditionalist, like those who fought for the possession of Bilbao.[129] Otherwise his childhood offers but few clues to a deeper understanding.

In 1891 he became professor of Greek at the university of Salamanca, after having tried in vain to obtain a chair in philosophy or psychology. Salamanca became more to Unamuno than a teaching position. It was a profound experience, one of the most deepreaching of his life, through which he became absorbed in the spirit of Castile. His life became identified with Salamanca because he found there the landmarks and the silence of history, Spanish history of course, which nourished his soul. In 1900 he was appointed rector of the university, a position which he held in spite of temporary demotions to his last lecture in 1934.[130] Although his interest in Greek was nothing peripheral to this great lover of words, he steadfastly refused to become a specialist in Greek or in any other branch of the humanities, because, as he expressed it, Spain needed something very different from experts in Greek, or as Ortega y Gasset would later put it, because he abhorred the idiocy of the specialist.[131] It was in Salamanca that he reached the youth of Spain, however, and it was there that he became the legendary "Don Miguel" to whom his compatriots referred with intimate pride. Indeed Don Miguel never was, nor did he aspire to become, a specialist. He tried his hand at philology, philosophy, poetry, and the novel. The metaphysical inquiry and the sonnet, the literary and the descriptive essay all attracted him at different times, though with varying degrees of success.

His critics have judged his versatility variously. Some accuse him of having dispersed his energies, while others praise him as being head and shoulders above all his Spanish contemporaries, the greatest genius which Spain has produced since the days of Cervantes.[132] But almost everyone admits that the picture which emerges from so many diversified undertakings shows "grandeza de conjunto," a greatness of the whole, even if the parts are sometimes disappointing.[133]

One of Unamuno's volumes is entitled *Contra Esto y Aquello, (Against This and That),* and to the superficial observer Unamuno presents himself as the perpetual rebel who always had a desire, and moreover a need, to be in opposition. Certainly the spirit of protest was strong in his veins; nevertheless, there is a coherent though dialectic structure in his work which cannot be explained in terms of opposition.

In reality what Unamuno was striving for all his life was precisely the reconciliation of contradictions, the *coincidentia oppositorum*. In words which strongly evoke the memory of Faust, he says in one of his sonnets:

> Busco guerra en la paz, paz en la guerra,
> El sosiego en la acción y en el sosiego
> la acción . . .
> ni martir quiero ser ni ser verdugo.[134]

("I search for war in peace, for peace in war,/repose in action, in action repose . . ./Neither martyr nor hangman am I.")

In 1895 Unamuno addressed Spain for the first time in a series of essays which were later published under the title, *En Torno al Casticismo (The Essence of Spain)*. It was Unamuno's first attempt to define Spain's greatness and misery, her historical achievements and her isolation in the midst of European civilization.[135] Unamuno struck in these essays one of the dominant chords of his entire work, which, through his influence, became an important leitmotiv for the generation of 1898.

"Castizo," or "casticismo," is a Spanish word of untranslatable meaning. Its original sense points to what is racially pure, but it has gradually been taken to represent the ideal of pure Castillian expression, the spiritual concept of an incorruptible tradition.[136] To Unamuno tradition does not and cannot mean the backwash of Spain's entire history. Against an attitude of indiscriminate conservatism he set the eternal tradition of Spain. Unamuno's polemic against the historical-minded Spaniards of his time resembles in many aspects Nietzsche's ideas. Only that which is more than historical makes history important, the suprahistorical essence, or as Unamuno puts it in happy coinage, "lo intrahistorico," the essence of history, as opposed to the merely temporary and transitory.[137] The eternal tradition is what the seers of every people should search for, because it is this eternal tradition that makes mankind what it is.[138] His fight is for a living scholarship against a senile and sterile erudition. "Los mejores libros de la historia son aquellos en que vive lo presente" ("The best books of history are those in which the present lives") sounds like a sentence by Croce.[139]

In applying these ideas to Spain, Unamuno endeavored to ascertain what her share of this tradition might be. And indeed Spain had produced eternal values which were supranational and by the same token suprahistorical. Other people have left books, says Unamuno; we have left souls. But he was also aware that the contemporary Spain which he was addressing had all but forgotten her mission, that she had been hiding behind the protective walls which the Inquisition had once constructed around her to prevent the free commerce of ideas. Stagnation had been the result. But the Spanish soul was great only when it opened itself to the four winds and poured itself out into the world. When the valves were throttled Spain sank into slumber. "We have not yet awakened." [140] Unamuno's message to Spain was, therefore, to open her windows to the currents of Europe and to reject the fear of losing her personality, for only thus might they "regenerate this moral steppe." [141] To Europeanize became the watchword. Let us lock the tomb of the Cid with seven keys.

However, so complex and paradoxical a thinker was Unamuno that we have to be on our guard lest we interpret his ideas too much from a liberal viewpoint. In truth, Unamuno never quite accepted the tenets of our technological society, and very soon came to reverse his opinion about the true nature of the relationship between Spain and the rest of Europe. Although he was fully cognizant of the advancement of the sciences, both theoretical and applied, he had no great faith in the idols of the nineteenth century—reason, progress, and civilization. He summarily cursed the progress that obliges us to get drunk with business, work, and science, and that does not hear the voice of eternal wisdom which murmurs its *vanitas vanitatum*.[142] From there it was only a step to defend the technological backwardness of Spain and even the ignorance of her people; not as ignorance and backwardness, of course, but as the complement of a higher form of knowledge. Eleven years after Unamuno had admonished the Spanish people to Europeanize themselves, he confessed, "Alone with my conscience I ask myself: Am I European; am I modern? And my conscience answers: No, you

are not European, what is called European; no, you are not modern
either, what is called modern." [143]

And his reason for this strange admission? It was not simply that
Unamuno wished to take advantage of his "inalienable right to
contradict himself" that he reversed his previous stand. Of all tyrannies, the most hateful to him was the tyranny of ideas, the
"ideocracia" which carries with it the "ideophobia" as an inevitable
consequence. And he wanted to be an "ideoclasta," a "rompe ideas,"
a destroyer of ideas. [144] Again the similarity to Nietzsche seems significant. And like Nietzsche he wished to destroy ideas for the sake
of a deeper understanding of life, which does not surrender to
abstract concepts.

Truth, says Unamuno, is something more intimate than the con-
cordance of two concepts, something closer (entrañable) than the
equation of intellect and things; it is the consortium of my spirit
with the spirit of the universe. [145] Such statements are not in harmony with the predilection for the Europeanization of Spain. Rather
than Europeanize Spain, Unamuno would now like to "hispanizar"
Europe. The order seems reversed, and so are the moral values. Our
flaws, he now declares, are the roots of our excellencies. And the
result of his reflections was a new affirmation of Spain and her
intrinsic values: the exaggerated individualism, the excessive imagination, the temperament and language of passion. [146]

It is not surprising to learn that this new position led Unamuno
to a revaluation of the classical ideals of Spanish literature. Among
the many aspects of Spanish literature which may attract the
student is its singular capacity in the creation of great human types.
Actually there is no other European literature which equals the
Spanish in this respect. Of the great prototypes which Spanish poets
have begotten, only two exercised a deep fascination over Unamuno's mind: Don Quixote and Segismundo, and it can be said
that the second phase of his work is dedicated to an interpretation
of Spain through the looking glass of two classical works: *La Vida
es Sueño* and *Don Quixote.*

Segismundo, the hero of *Life is a Dream*, becomes for Unamuno
the true symbol of Spain. [147] Calderón's wisdom, so strangely resem-
bling that of Prospero, that life is a dream and that dreams are but

dreams, becomes the expression of all the illusions in which the
Spanish soul was and is steeped. Now Unamuno praises the Middle
Ages, for which he found inherent and ample sympathy in his mind,
and he expresses a desire for the return of this golden age in which
the people worked, prayed, believed, hoped, and dreamed.[148] But
Cervantes' Quixote comes even closer to the core of the Spanish
soul. Unamuno does not hesitate to call it a Spanish Bible. As such
it deserves a mystical interpretation. And this is exactly what Unamuno intends in his commentary on the life of Don Quixote.[149]
Therefore, Unamuno feels free to interpret Cervantes' hero in the
way medieval theologians interpreted religious texts. He acknowledges little of the ironic outlook that Cervantes maintained throughout his work. Instead he makes it a legend and almost a scripture.
It is the paraphrase of the life of "Our Lord, Don Quixote," and
the similes to Christ are abundant throughout the whole book.[150]

To call Unamuno's interpretation of Quixote lopsided would be
an understatement. He confessed that he himself had little humor.
He therefore misses completely the atmosphere of serene and smiling
depth which enabled Cervantes to show greatness in ridicule and
ridicule in greatness. Don Quixote takes on the traits of a saviour
and his madness is the madness of the Cross. He becomes for
Unamuno the champion of all spiritual values against the utilitarian
and pragmatic outlook of the twentieth century.

Yet toward the end of this strange treatise, Unamuno touches a
chord which explains what he was trying to find in Cervantes' epic.
Don Quixote's madness is the madness not to die, *la locura de no
morir*. "Intercede then for me, O my lord and patron, so that you,
Dulcinea del Toboso . . . may take my hand and lead me to the
immortality of name and fame. . . . And if life is a dream, let me
dream it without end." [151] Cervantes' wisdom merges thus with
Calderón's in this craving to circumvent death, this desire to survive
through all eternity, to be immortal. "Creer es crear," to believe is
to create; with this guidon we have already crossed the bridge which
leads to Unamuno's greatest undertaking, his inquiry into the tragic
sense of life.

We cannot, however, depart from Unamuno's comments on
Cervantes and Calderón without a final word about his personality
as revealed in them. Although reared in Spain, and rarely out of the

country except for the years of his exile, his horizon was universal and his concern was that of his own convulsed and perturbed age. But while he was a citizen of the world, he remained patriotic and even provincial. There are traces of parochialism in Unamuno which have, we believe, prevented him from becoming as widely known as his originality and his sincerity would seem to merit.

One other characteristic of Unamuno's personality should be mentioned. His ideas, though vital for our time, were few. They are always expressed with vigor, but they are burdened by the attenuating monotony of repetition. He was quite aware that the core of his intellectual concept was limited, and he spoke of his habitual reiteration with a mixture of irony and arrogance.

Because the few basic ideas around which Unamuno's work revolves are deeply rooted in the Spanish heritage of mysticism and saintliness, he has frequently been linked, and indeed linked himself, with the great Spanish saints, St. Ignatio, St. Teresa de Avila, and Fray Luis de León. Unamuno was a mystic and a moralist who wanted to foment "el culto a las almas no a las letras," the cult of souls not of books, but he was a moralist *sui generis,* and certainly *Hispaniae generis.*[152]

As a Spanish moralist he was an individualist in outlook and judgment, both on himself and on the world around him. Unamuno's end as well as his beginning is the self, or to use the Spanish pronoun, "el Yo." [153] It is the individual that counts, but the individual as a complete and concrete human being, the whole man, the man of flesh and bone, not simply the concept of the individual. This is the axis around which all of Unamuno's philosophy rotates. But this concept of the self—"este terrible Yo"—did it not cut Unamuno off from his fellow men? He was conscious that it might make him the "prisoner of himself," and with a daring somersault, he decided that it was precisely this principle that united him with all men. He rings a change on an epigram of the ancients to make this clear: " 'Homo Sum; nihil humani a me alienum puto,' said the Latin playwright. And I would rather say, 'Nullum hominem a me alienum puto': I am a man; no other do I deem a stranger." [154] In this manner he establishes the principle that the self, or the man of flesh and bone, is the one experience which all human beings share. This is a truism, and to this length everyone is constrained to agree with Unamuno. His real philosophy begins only when he advances toward the interpretation of the self. Man is an end in himself, not a means; man should not be sacrificed to humanity; in reality, man should not be sacrificed to anything since his highest desire is to survive. But man is not assured of survival, and this is the question that disturbs him more than any other. The uncertainty of his survival makes man tragic and gives him "The Tragic Sense of Life."

Unamuno lists a large group of thinkers and poets who have been typical examples of this tragic sense of life: Marcus Aurelius, St. Augustine, Pascal, Chateaubriand, Sénancour, Leopardi, Vigny, Lenau, Kleist, Amiel, Quental—and Kierkegaard. When Unamuno, in 1912, undertook to circumscribe man's position in the universe, he belonged to the few who were then cognizant of the solitary depth of the Danish philosopher. His own position as well as his philosophical affinity made Unamuno a godfather of twentieth century existentialism.

"Whence do I come, and whence comes the world in which and by which I live? Whither do I go and whither goes everything that environs me? . . . Such are the questions that man asks. . . . And if we look closely, we shall see that beneath these questions lies the wish to know, not so much the 'why' as the 'wherefore,' not the cause but the end." [155] Such was, of course, the quest of all the saints, but Unamuno, son and saint of the twentieth century, had lost the firm metaphysical ground on which the saints could build their visions and their hopes. The old Christian business of saving one's soul was still his, but the answers once given could no longer satisfy him. He lived in a world of scientific truth which did not admit of any proof but factual evidence. But what proof could there be of immortality, and what basis could there be for man's hope of survival? The fact that science refused to recognize man's urge to be immortal as anything but wishful thinking, "the future of an illusion" as Freud put it, led Unamuno to take a new position. "For living is one thing and knowing is another; and . . . perhaps there is such an opposition between the two that we may say that everything vital is antirational, not merely irrational, and that everything rational is antivital. And this is the basis of the tragic sense of life." [156]

The old conflict between faith and reason is thus converted into a conflict between life and reason. But Unamuno was not simply a vitalist like Nietzsche, Bergson, or Dilthey. Life does more than supersede reason; the conflict between the two forms the basis for Unamuno's tragic sense wherein he finds the true status of human beings. Life and reason are compelled to seek mutual support and this involves struggle.[157] I will not make peace between my head and my heart, cries Unamuno; rather let the one affirm what the other denies. . . . I shall live by contradiction. Unamuno erects himself on the ground, if ground it may be called, of uncertainty, doubt, perpetual wrestling with the mystery of our final destiny, mental despair, and the lack of any stable foundation. If it is a solution, it is the solution of despair.[158] Unamuno's hope against hope, his belief against belief, is, in more than one way, a representative position of our time. His *credo quia absurdum est* states the troubled feeling of the age. Unamuno expressed the loneliness of Western man as like that of the firstborn son who trembles at having lost his birthright. Constantly torn between rational pride and cosmic submissiveness, his importance in the universe has diminished in direct proportion to his knowledge of its laws. He can no longer believe himself to be God's favorite son, and even less the lord of creation; he is only an apparently meaningless by-product of cosmic forces which have initiated his life and will in turn destroy it. Pascal expressed a similar feeling when he spoke of being terrified by the silence of infinite space, and Kierkegaard went so far as to say that the rational interpretation of life would of necessity lead to suicide. Unamuno frequently quotes Sénancour's Oberman, who observed, "Man is perishable, but if we have to perish, if nothingness awaits us, let us not act as if that were justice." [159]

In so openly and desperately stating the metaphysical deadlock into which man has maneuvered himself, Unamuno touched our time to the quick. It is my task to plunge all life into unquiet and longing, he is quoted as saying, and in *The Tragic Sense of Life* he has gone a long way toward his goal. He was one of the first to point to the insoluble antinomies of life which later in Jaspers' work achieved such significance. The final objective, then, was unattainable according to Unamuno, yet man could not give up the pursuit. Here again his Spanish background breaks into his philosophy; Unamuno feels that, though he speaks for all mankind, he expresses essentially the philosophy of his own people, the philosophy of Don Quixote.[160] "My religion is to seek truth in life and life in truth, even though knowing full well that I shall never find them as long as I live; my religion is to wrestle with mystery; my religion is to wrestle with God from nightfall until the breaking of the day . . . and at all hazards I seek to scale the unattainable." [161]

Unamuno's comprehension and appreciation of man's tragic position were more responsible for making him one of the first of the existentialists than the solution he proposed for man's escape from his dilemma, since his solution will inevitably strike many as obsolete. For Unamuno, the longing not to die, the hunger for personal immortality, the effort whereby we tend to persist indefinitely in our own being, is the effective basis of all knowledge. He therefore remains a prisoner of the self. " 'I, I, always I,' some reader will exclaim, 'and who are you?' I might reply in the words of Oberman . . . 'For the universe, nothing,—for myself, everything.' " [162] The salvation of man thus becomes the center of Unamuno's emotions and thoughts, but a salvation not so much from sin as from death. His philosophy remains steeped in Catholicism, but it is heretical, not dogmatic, Catholicism. From his agnostic preoccupation with death he appeals to Christianity, but his Christian faith is vacillating and heterodox.[163] His imaginative anticipation of death, his desire to get, so to speak, a preview of it already here in life, seems yet another eminently Spanish trait. Just as the Spanish soul can never resign itself to the finality of death, just so does Unamuno rebel against it. Despair, "the master of impossibility," becomes the instrument, not so much for a sacrifice of the intellect as for an intellectual *volte-face*. Love is the answer, Unamuno's answer. "Love is the child of illusion and the parent of disillusion: love is consolation and desolation; it is the sole medicine against death for it is death's brother," God, who is love, the Father of love, is the son of love in us. For thinking believers today faith is before all and above all wishing that God may exist and acting and feeling as if he did exist. "And desiring God's existence . . . is the means whereby we create God, that is, whereby God creates Himself in us, manifests Himself to us, opens and reveals Himself to us." [164]

The tragic sense of life, then, is the foundation and the only proof of God's existence. To many, Unamuno's speculation will seem inadmissible; his insistence on the survival of the ego may appear almost childish. Yet many also will admire and uphold the courage that caused Unamuno to become a witness to man's desire to be immortal, to eternalize himself, a desire which is so deeply rooted in Man's mind that, once exiled from its religious abode, it takes refuge in substitutes such as fame, family, humane efforts, or patriotic acts. At least Don Miguel would not settle for ersatz solutions, and he will be remembered, if for nothing else, as having voiced man's yearning for immortality with the true ring of a heretic who would not renounce hope and a mystic who was not willing to decry reason.

It would seem appropriate here to mention Unamuno's last book, separated by twelve years from *The Tragic Sense of Life, La Agonia del Chritianismo, (The Agony of Christianity)*.[165] Although it is less coherent and less convincing in its argument, it reveals a position similar to the one taken in his previous book. The agony of Christianity represents the agony of Unamuno's own perturbed soul where he found no simple or clear-cut alternative, but where he did discover faith in the midst of doubt, struggle in the midst of peace, life in the midst of death. But a final consequence of his position is revealed to the observer in this book. The tragic sense of life does not cause him to become pessimistic or resigned. On the contrary, the feeling of uncertainty that overcasts life produces a spirit of desperate combat and heroic activity. To believe is to create, and it is in the process of human life that this creativity unfolds itself. Man is not born with a soul; he dies having one if he has made himself a soul. The goal of life is to give oneself a soul, a soul that is one's own work.[166]

Thus we have come full circle, and return to Unamuno's initial effort—to arouse Spain. His audience had grown to include the whole of the Occident, but he remained what Giordano Bruno had wished to be, an awakener of sleeping souls, a man who continued to comfort the restless and provoke the indolent.[167]

> Cuando me creais más muerto,
> retemblaré en vuestras manos.
> Aqui os dejo mi almo-libro,
> hombre-mundo verdadero.
> Cuando vibres todo entero,
> soy yo, lector, que en ti vibro.[168]

("When you think me most dead,/I shall tremble again in your hands./Here I leave you in my soul—the book,/the man, a world in truth./And if you vibrate in all your being,/it is I, O reader, who vibrates in you.")

CHAPTER VIII

The Social Fabric

The Youth Movement

The first chapter of these studies called attention to the prevailing political trends of the opening century. We found elements of deceptive stability, together with evidences of growing unrest and agitation. We are now approaching the end of our journey and it would seem fitting to glance at those tendencies in which cultural and social components compounded to announce a new society. I believe there are four trends which indicate with special clarity the social revolution of the twentieth century: the youth movement, feminism, the advance of socialism, and the introduction of scientific management in industry. I am conscious that such a selection may seem arbitrary. I have not, however, aimed at encyclopedic comprehensiveness in this book, and I leave to the scholars of the future the task of presenting a more comprehensive view.

In the mid-1890's a perplexing phenomenon appeared in certain countries of the Western world. This was the Youth Movement, and it reached its climax shortly before 1914. He who today returns to the yellowed pamphlets, the magazines, the leaflets, wherein young men and women of the antebellum generation poured their hearts will experience a feeling of nostalgia mixed with impatience.[1] How much good will, and how much misguided idealism was theirs! How little they realized their own limitations; how much they underrated the strictures of economic and social reality!

Each new generation views the work of its predecessors with critical eyes and thinks of itself as the dynamometer of a new regime wherein the old idols will be destroyed and the ancient wrongs will be righted. Moreover it is true that there have been several instances in European history where revolutionary changes in thought and action have been brought on by new generations determined to wipe the slate clean and to take a fresh start. However, powerful forces guaranteeing stability and tradition had always counterbalanced the power of youthful enthusiasm. The rhythm of European culture had been that of daring innovation checked and tempered by social institutions and intellectual habits.

The Youth Movement proper did not appear before the end of the eighteenth century.[2] At that time the influences of the Enlightenment, of Rousseau, and of Pre-Romanticism blended with the first consequences of industrialization. The French Revolution, Napoleon, and the wars of liberation increased these energies. In a society in flux, youth seemed called upon to play a decisive role. *Sturm und Drang,* English and French Romanticism, the Burschenschaften at the German universities, and Mazzini's Young Europe, came along in rapid succession. Even Russian Nihilism has been called a youth movement.[3] The Youth Movement of 1895 owes something to all of them, but it differs from them in scope and magnitude.

What is youth? asked La Rochefoucauld, and he answered: a perpetual intoxication, reason in a state of fever. The youth that became aware of its intoxication was the German youth of 1895–1905, and it carried its frenzy like a torch. Finding no environmental response to its desires and dreams, it withdrew into a world of its own.

The German Youth Movement began as a protest against the bourgeois world as it was before 1914 and it never outgrew the behavior pattern of the protest. At the beginning its revolt against a stereotyped society which refused to recognize that childhood and youth are autonomous stages in the development of mankind was fully justified. The German child of 1900 was not allowed to dwell in its own house of fragmentary experience and overflowing imagination. Instead it was expected to ape the grownups, to become a replica of the conventional adult.[4] This was not a new procedure. Adults have always, and often justly, considered themselves the prototypes which their children should emulate. But the Germany of 1900 was a country satiated with material success. Military power had brought unification, and unification had produced wealth and a prosperity to which the German middle class was unaccustomed. They accepted the new comforts, the respectability, the upholstered stuffiness, as God's gift to the German middle class, and it was their wish to pass these new acquisitions on to their children.

The German state was basically authoritarian and bureaucratic. The personality of the Kaiser was emulated by some and criticized by others, but rule by an enlightened bureaucracy was accepted by all. The people had long been in the habit of leaving crucial decisions to experts "who knew best," and they took pride in the smooth running of an administrative machine whose personnel was, on the whole, efficient, honest, and discourteous.[5] Religion, too, had become a social rather than a personal matter. In most German states the church was a state-church. Hypocrisy was, therefore, profitable, because religion offered an insurance for personal welfare and was, at the same time, considered a bulwark against atheistic doctrines.

This position was untenable because the people were already contaminated by certain new ideas which they professed to abhor. Darwin's theories were spreading by leaps and bounds. E. Haeckel, a popularizer of evolutionism, wrote his *Welträtsel* in 1900 and sold hundreds of thousands of copies. Nietzsche was widely read, and he had thrown it into their faces that the Germans were drowning in philistine complacency, in soulless materialism, accepting the rule of the heartless monster, the State, as their God.[6] Other writers, like the lonely Paul de Lagarde, had written in 1885, "I do not complain because our youth is lacking in idealism, but I do make the accusation that adults, especially those in control, do not offer youth the genuine ideals out of which alone the latent idealism of youth can grow. Germany is hypnotized by the belief that the State is the highest form of human living . . . I believe in the youth; I believe in the future of our country, but I do not believe in the right of the ruling system, nor in the capacities of the men who want to satisfy the longing and needs of their sons and grandsons with the rubbish that has remained theirs as the leftover from bygone days." [7]

The young people of the day were not widely conversant with the criticism that was leveled against the older generation, but they did know enough of it to feel confirmed in their own revolt against the system. As was natural, they attacked the two institutions which weighed most oppressively on their own impulses and desires: school and family. The German high school has often been slandered. As an institution transmitting a treasure of knowledge, it was still very much to the fore. It failed abysmally, however, as an educational institution to form young minds. The reason for this is clear: the school, like the church, was a state institution. The teachers, the notorious Oberlehrer, were civil servants. They were forced to impart, along with their subject matter, the rampant nationalism and militarism that dominated public opinion. Free minds were the exception. Religious indoctrination, too, was tainted by routine and tradition. Early morning prayers, attendance at chapel, were thought by most students to be a dull routine. The teachers who supervised religious instruction considered the young skeptics and rebels to be cranks or ill-tempered *Einzelgänger*. Even the honestly inquiring youth was given short shrift.

Family life was scarcely less suffocating. The week's routine was crowned on Sunday with the family promenade on which each member displayed his best regalia. The day ended with tedious calls on relatives. Again the child found himself imprisoned in a world of grownups whose pomposity and serious behavior either frightened or wearied him.

There is in children a merciless talent to see through sham and hypocrisy. Oscar Wilde remarked that as children mature they begin to criticize their parents; eventually, he added, they may even pardon them. But these German youths were far from the state of forgiveness. "They thought that parental religion was largely sham: politics boastful and trivial; economics unscrupulous; education stereotyped and lifeless; art trashy and sentimental." [8] To be sure, there were thousands of middle-class children who felt nothing of all this. This writer, for one, was blessed with understanding teachers and with parents who endured his antics with patience and humor. But among those who were less fortunate, the revolt of youth was seething.

When the German Youth Movement finally broke through to the surface, it seems to have chosen a most unlikely stage. Steglitz is a suburb of Berlin, inhabited in unequal proportions by well-to-do patricians and a great number of white-collar workers, civil servants, and merchants. The type of locality where the German Youth Movement first saw the light of day reveals one of its characteristic traits, its reaction against the urbanization brought forth by the industrial process, against the crowded apartment houses and the niggardly squares of grass where a single tree was considered a luxury.

The middle-class youth was free from the economic want that drove the proletarian boy into the factory or workshop at the age of fourteen. And thus it was that the Youth Movement was born into an environment of prosperity and ease. The Mark Brandenburg was the scene of its inception, and it became a fact when a university student named Karl Fischer first outlined a new way of living in 1896.[9] This boy appears to have made an immediate impression on his fellows. "Everyone who had any dealings with Karl Fischer, or who enjoyed his friendship, invariably had this experience: here stands someone who has greater capacity than yourself." [10] Fischer, quite naturally, considered himself a Promethean character, a Karl Moor of the twentieth century. He had no program; he did have some notions of what sane and sound living should consist of, and he had the determination to win disciples to his way of thought. Essentially, his desire was to return to nature. He yearned to rediscover the fields and forests, the brooks and meadows, from which the urban- and suburbanites had become alienated. He wanted to feel sun and rain, wind and snow on his skin, to walk rather than be carried on a train, to sleep in haystacks, to cook his own meager food, to forego the stimulants, alcohol and nicotine, with which the bourgeoisie maintained its flagging vitality. In a word, he wanted to live like the first man. This program of life was, quite obviously, antibourgeois, and Fischer clothed it with antibourgeois forms and rituals. In the place of the conventional stiff greeting, the bow from the waist, the click of heels, these youngsters inaugurated the shouted "Heil!" and the uplifted right arm. They chose a garb that was well suited to their country tramps, but that looked rakish and eccentric in Wilhelminian Berlin. Their outfits consisted of shorts and dark-colored shirts, gay neck-scarfs, heavy boots, knapsacks, and the indispensable waterproof woolen cape. And they dubbed themselves *Wandervögel*.

It was not long before the weekend hike failed to satisfy them. They wanted a place of their own, a home away from home, or perhaps we should say, an antihome. They rented a room where they gathered once a week to chat, to drink chocolate, and to sing.

This retreat they called the "Nest." The trend that German Romanticism had started one hundred years earlier when Arnim and Brentano had collected *Volkslieder* and published them under the title *Des Knaben Wunderhorn* was thus given continuity. The musical instruments cultivated in their parents' homes, piano and violin, were discarded in favor of the guitar, the mandolin, or the lute, and these they played to accompany their songs. Their romantic admiration for forgotten poetry was enhanced by the new element of music. In their wanderings through the countryside and in their grubbings through tales of bygone romance and adventure, they unearthed a vast treasure of folk music, and they made these melodies their own, singing them on the road, and in the "Nest," over and over again. Finally Hans Breuer, a friend of Fischer's, transcribed them, fitted music and lyrics together, and published them under the title, *Der Zupfgeigenhansl*.[11] "Pluck Fiddle Jack," as it may be translated, became the Book of Common Prayer for the German Youth Movement. It ran to hundreds of editions, and is one of the lasting contributions of this movement to German culture. It offers, as Howard Becker has said, "a true cross-section of the dear dead days," in its love songs and ballads, its sailors' chants and spinning room melodies, its marital tunes and country dances.[12]

This renaissance of the German folk song had, moreover, a definite sociological significance; it was a deliberate rejection of the *Schlager*, the hit tune so beloved by the adults and so characteristic of the type of entertainment that delighted the age. The slang, or secret language, restricted to the initiated and understood only by them, was another kind of rejection, and one more expression of their determination to set themselves apart from the sedate world of their elders.

It should be clear by now that the Youth Movement was in its essence a voice of dissent, dissent from the life into which urbanization and industrialization had forced mankind. It was a protest against mechanization and its calculated virtues, against softness brought on by technical devices; it proclaimed instinct, the world of nature, and primitive habits as the remedies for a sick civilization.

It is an amazing fact that the Youth Movement with so little to offer, spread like a brush fire. No better proof can be offered that it was more than a passing fad, or that it manifested, in a hazy and aimless fashion, the urge of German youth to sunder the shackles of threadbare culture and to cure the age by a panacea of its own devising. One of the advocates of the Youth Movement, Gustaf Wynneken, coined the term, *Jugendkultur* (Youth culture).[13] "A synthesis must be found, a reconciliation of youth and culture . . . but this reconciliation cannot consist in the return of youth to the family circle, nor in the submission to the conventional style of life of the old ones." [14] Wynneken was one of the most influential leaders of the educational reform which had been sparked by the Youth Movement. Radical and vociferous in his ideas, he put forth a plan to take the children out of their homes and place them in a community of their own, the Schulgemeinde. We are inclined to believe that he would have done no more than replace the despotism of parental authority with the tyranny of fanatical educators.[15] Be that as it may, it cannot be denied that the Youth Movement presented the child clearly as a being in his own right who was not to be molded after shopworn bourgeois models. This was, after all, the "century of the child," and this slogan of Ellen Keys echoed throughout the dispersed groups of German boys who roamed the Fatherland from the North Sea to the Alps. What Marie Montessori had preached, what John Dewey was later to instill into American education, found here a genuine, though chaotic, expression.

The original impetus of the movement gained speed. Karl Fischer's Wandervögel soon split, one group remaining faithful to Fischer, calling itself the Altwandervögel, and the dissenters setting up their own organization.[16] Soon new formations sprang up at every turn, differing from each other in details only. Certain questions, however, such as the admission of Jewish boys, foreshadowed problems of nightmarish proportions.

The period of the *Bünde* began. Each of these groups chose a minor question and made it the crucial basis of a separate association. Sometimes it was the question of the use of alcohol and nicotine; sometimes it was nudism; sometimes the attitude toward girls, for they too had become infected with the desire to escape the family yoke. Should the girls tramp over the countryside with the boys or should they take to the road by themselves? Should they adhere to the same principle of leadership? Should they learn to rough it as the boys did? Eventually the girls developed their own organizations and their own garb, the dirndl. The dance became the outstanding form of their artistic self-expression. They, too, had their meeting places where they practiced virtues which would make their adult lives "gemütlich und behaglich." [17]

Underneath such harmless considerations, however, loomed many more serious problems. The break with family conventions meant not only the escape from parental authority; it involved the sex taboos of the era. The return to nature was not alone the rediscovery of the beauties of the countryside; it was perhaps even more a growing awareness of the beauty of the body which had for so long been decried as sinful, or, as the Victorians said, unspeakable. There developed in this new generation a physical joy, a delight in their own bodies which they felt to be one with the brooks in which they swam or the sun to which they exposed themselves.[18] They knew little of Freud's concurrent discoveries, but they paralleled his findings by an attitude which was in no need of theory. The new paganism so characteristic of the twentieth century was first experienced among the boys and girls of the German Youth Movement. Hans Blüher developed the thesis that it was, in essence, a homoerotic movement. Others, less lenient, called it a club for pederasty.[19] It is difficult to give conclusive evidence for either assertion. Those who participated in the trips and gatherings of the Youth Movement will undoubtedly remember that the air was heavily charged with erotic tension. The homosexual proclivities of the German youth became, at a later date, one of the ingredients of the witches' brew mixed by Hitler and his cronies.

But if we follow the situation to its sources, we are still faced with the fact that the Youth Movement was again protesting, this time against the one outlet for sexual urges which bourgeois society admitted. Confronted with the prostitution in the great metropolitan areas, both the professional and the free-lance type, with its mire of ugliness, venereal disease, and perversion, these boys and girls sought less squalid encounters. Their solutions were not the best; they were still in the realm of escape and protest; but at least they were sanitary. Many of these relationships ended in tragedy, as protest and escape so often do, and it is not mere accident that so great a number of German writers of the day concerned themselves with the problem of adolescent love, trying to make the bourgeoisie aware of their sins of omission and blindness toward their children. Frank Wedekind's *Frühlingserwachen,* written in 1891, posed the question that the young generation endeavored to answer by trial and error. For a proper evaluation of the German Youth Movement, it is, however, not enough merely to observe its iconoclastic attitude toward old institutions, such as the school and the family, or its boldness in meeting eternal problems like sex. The most convincing proof of its sway lies in the force by means of which it bent other social strata to its ideals. In this connection, we should mention first the proletarian Youth Movement, where we find that the problems are of a quite different nature from those of the original Wandervögel. The proletarians hated the bourgeoisie, not as an age group, but as a class. They hated industrialization, mechanization, and the rationalization of everyday life, but they, nonetheless, considered these to be inescapable stages in the dialectic process which would one day end with the victory of the disinherited. The working-class movement had its own eschatology: the day of victory would soon break. In the meantime it was essential to preserve the fighting force. Organization, solidarity, discipline, were the watchwords of the workers before 1914. Leadership was in the hands of the trained unionists who formed the political élite in the national and regional parliaments of Germany.[20]

In these circumstances, the dilemma of the laboring youth was, if not discounted, at least neglected; it was considered as part of the general misery which the proletarians must endure until the great day of reckoning. But the proletarian youth was in dire need of spiritual and material help. His schooling was, as a rule, ended at fourteen, and he then entered a factory or workshop. At that time there were no provisions for professional or cultural improvement among the young laborers or apprentices, although a few members of the middle class did volunteer work in this field. Finally, in 1904, an association of apprentices and young laborers was founded in Berlin, the purpose of which was the "economic, legal, and intellectual advancement of its members." [21] Since political activity was prohibited to persons under eighteen years of age by Prussian law, the association was nonpolitical. Other cities fell in line, and in 1906 Ludwig Frank founded the Young German Workers in southern

Germany. Similar organizations already existed in Belgium, Denmark, Norway, Holland, and Spain.[22]

Their differences from the middle-class Youth Movement are apparent. The laboring-class youth did not oppose the elders of its own class; instead, it fought in discipline and solidarity with the more mature members of its class against the "doomed capitalistic order." They copied the Wandervögel in their excursions and in the setting up of "homes," also in giving certain evenings over to discussion, and in renouncing alcohol and nicotine. But their purposes were of another kind. The proletarian Youth Movement wanted to indoctrinate the young with socialist ideas.

An indirect result of the proletarian Youth Movement was the decision of the German government to pay closer attention to the unrest among juveniles. To be sure, the deeper historical significance of the movement escaped them, but new legislation was prepared and the first institution dedicated to the care of youth appeared in 1908. Its activities do not fall within the orbit of these studies. Without doubt the Youth Movement must be given the credit for having opened the eyes of recalcitrant adults to the problems that the younger generation faced.

The militarist, too, tried to make hay while the sun shone upon the Youth Movement. Although they approved of the hardy training that the Wandervögel offered, they thought its activities were aimless and without discipline, and they called attention instead to the virtues of daily drill on the Prussian barrack grounds.[23] More far-reaching than these attempts of the military were the efforts of the Christian churches to hitch their wagons to the dynamic force of the German youth. The Catholic Church had always known that the rising generation cannot be neglected with impunity. The Catholic Youth Movement was, therefore, a deliberate attempt to offer to Catholic boys and girls the same satisfactions that the Wandervögel promised, but under the authority of the Church. The Catholic youth was free as long as his actions were compatible with Church doctrine and teaching. The outward manifestations of the Catholic and the secular youth movements were much the same. There was the excursion, the return to nature, the songfests, and the "Nest" meetings, but under the Church, all was guided and disciplined. The *Quickborn* separated boys and girls rigorously; it insisted on abstinence and temperance; its motto was "To live in God for others." The Catholic Youth Movement revived some of the most beautiful of the medieval hymns and found in morality plays a welcome outlet for religious ardor. But, on the whole, it was an example of pouring new wine into old skins.[24]

The Protestant Youth Movement, like the Catholic, had strong international affiliations, but it was more of a revival movement, and concentrated heavily on the reading of the Bible and on prayer meetings. Protestantism proved itself less able to integrate the impulses of youth into its own framework. The external forms were taken over, but the substance remained alien to the spirit of Lutheranism.[25] With few exceptions the Youth Movement stood outside the Lutheran Church.[26]

So far we have touched only on the salient characteristics of the Youth Movement. A bewildering variety of youth groups sprang up in Germany between 1900 and 1910. The Boy Scout Organization made its appearance and competed steadily with the Wandervögel; there were young merchant leagues, associations for sport, hiking, and so on.[27] It is interesting to note that only the Socialists among the political parties deemed it worth their while to woo the youth. Wilhelminian Germany was led by old men who had little or no understanding for the changing world around them. Out of their lack of concern grew the Youth Movement; the young men and women were determined to make their voices heard in society. These young insurgents were not, however, clear as to the exact nature of their demands. The movement had started as a protest against a superannuated way of life; its formulae had the imprint of escapism. The distinctive features of its program were negative and evasive. Its basic impulse was to free youth from the bourgeois world, but their goals were vague and impractical; with characteristic irrationality, they even boasted of their lack of program. Many of them cherished the illusion that youth was of value for itself alone and that it might be perpetuated at will. There was the "Ewige Wandervogel" who refused to mature, and there were many others who held to the conviction that the old world on which they heaped their scorn and contempt could be rejuvenated by the merest touch of their inexperienced hands.

We have noted that the political parties took no interest in the

Youth Movement. The movement, likewise (with the exception of the proletarian youth), had no political affiliations, nor was it eager to make its debut on the stage of politics. Knowledge and conviction about economic and social problems were both lacking. Here and there an anticapitalistic bias was voiced together with a general aversion toward the mechanization which the ever-growing industrialization forced upon the German people. Their attitude was, however, resentful rather than constructive. They remained blissfully unaware of the fact that their own existences depended upon the economic order which they affected to despise.[28] The more thoughtful among them felt that the return to nature should find its complement in a forward-to-culture attitude. But here, too, the solutions offered suffered from confusion and fragmentation. They took their ideas wherever they found them: from Fichte, Nietzsche, Schopenhauer, Hegel, Bergson, even from Hindu philosophy. Anti-intellectualism is the only common denominator of this mental hodgepodge.

They also maintained an ambiguous position in regard to the fundamental problems of human ethics. Their original impulse had been to rebel against a soulless society. Quite naturally they emphasized the rights of the individual, but they also felt impelled to seek a new type of community in which the individual would feel a sense of solidarity with others whose lives moved in the same rhythm. The "Bund" was the name they gave to these tightly-knit associations, but "sect" would be a more exact term. "Our happiest hours were those in which there was nothing planned beforehand, nothing argued out and finally fixed . . . there is nothing more wonderful and fruitful than the communion in a small circle of confidence . . . every day is begun with eagerness and hope, and every hour brings forth our wondering gratitude for rich overflowing experience." [29] Such anxiety to sidestep order, clarity, and discipline easily explains the ability of the Youth Movement to embrace contradictory and even mutually exclusive ideas. Their "nostalgic traditionalism" placed them close to an affirmation of nationhood. From there it was one step only to the acceptance of racist principles, or, as the expression went, *völkische* ideas. Other groups, however, proclaimed lofty humanitarian ideals and addressed themselves to the youth of all nations.

Atomized and disunited as it was, the Youth Movement did not withdraw its demand for a hearing, and its opportunity arose in 1913. Official Germany was then celebrating the centenary of the battle of Leipzig. The Kaiser was to unveil a monster-monument on the eighteenth of October, and the leaders of the Youth Movement believed the propitious moment had arrived for the proclamation of their faith. A rally took place on October 11–12 on the Hohe Meissener in the vicinity of Kassel.[30] Sundry manifestoes had paved the way for the affair. Borrowing from Ibsen, they called the occasion, "Das Fest der Jugend" ("The Festival of Youth"). Free development of the self, truthfulness, sincerity, and responsibility, were proclaimed, "Beyond all things, we hate sterile patriotism which indulges in words and emotions," a patriotism which looks to the past rather than setting itself new aims.[31]

Thirteen groups participated in the rally. There were campfires, communal singing, and community dancing, but there were also a few thoughtful speeches which revealed a good deal of soul-searching. The opening address, delivered by a student from the University of Marburg, stated that the principal goal of the Youth Movement was self-education. Other speakers emphasized the necessity of social awareness in a period when work had converted human beings into "tools of tools." Wynneken warned against the cheap hypnosis of nationalistic slogans, and stressed the cosmopolitan inheritance of German culture. "May the day never come when war hordes devastate [our country], and may the day never appear when we would be forced into waging a war in the valleys of foreign nations." [32] The final resolution that summed up the rally reads: "The free German youth is determined to fashion its life on its own initiative, on its own repsonsibility, and in inner sincerity." [33]

The words just quoted were spoken in 1913, one year before the great avalanche all but destroyed the original Youth Movement. In the grim years following 1914, thousands joined the army and died on the battlefield; others returned to their homes wounded and crippled; still others had lost their enthusiasm. The resurgence of the Youth Movement after 1919 does not concern us here.

The German Youth Movement was "a symptom of crisis," rather than a crisis; it aimed at curing symptoms and ignored the disease.[34] Plans to reform the schools, the family, or to alleviate the humdrum of everyday life were scarcely enough to arrest the steam roller of advancing mechanization. The German writer, Frank Thiess, has called the rebellion of youth, "the invisible revolution," [35] and it has remained just that; an invisible, or rather, an abortive revolution. No one can deny that it had an appreciable effect on the old institutions of bourgeois life which it wanted to supersede. It loosened them up to a considerable degree, but it was unable to replace them with any creation of its own. More important still, it failed completely in the realm of politics. Searching for an ideal society, it scorned parties and parliaments, and left the dirty work to the professional politician. Its criticism of the old social order remained nebulous, the expression of a stricken conscience.

In the final analysis one may well agree with Von Klemperer's statement: the Youth Movement "contributed to undermining the middle classes from within rather than rejuvenating them." [36] In the realm of culture, too, its contributions were sparse. The tradition to which it had linked itself, medieval folklore, remained a dream world; one might take refuge in it for an evening, but in the cold morning light, the familiar ugliness of chimneys and factories, of railway stations and post offices, were there to greet the disillusioned eye with their customary solidity. Not a single great book emerged from the Youth Movement.[37]

One more question presents itself: was the Youth Movement an exclusively German occurrence, or did it reach European proportions? It is obvious that the conditions against which it revolted were those of the Western world in general. Why, then, should Germany be the only country to provoke such a protest? It is true that in England and in the United States there were powerful movements whose aim was to give youth the objectives of the Wandervögel, but there was no Youth Movement in England or America, in France or in Italy, that parallels the German phenomenon. The Boy Scouts, the Girl Scouts, the Brigades, the YMCA and the YWCA, were organized by adults to protect and to guide youth. In Germany there was a genuine movement *of* youth instead of organizations *for* youth.[38] In countries where democracy had already made substantial strides, youth did not feel the same urge to rebel as they did in authoritarian countries. Even the change brought forth by industrialization could not shake the conviction that youth would find its place in society. True, there was no lack of criticism, but there was no outright revolt. Furthermore, an interest in sports and club life absorbed a great deal of energy in Anglo-Saxon schools.[39] And finally, coeducation in America encouraged a more natural approach to the sex problem.

In France we find the inevitable change from the old to the new generation, with its concomitants of criticism and revolt. The youth of 1912 looked to Gide, Rolland, Bergson, Claudel, Péguy, and Maurras. They rejected rationalism; they were optimistic, they emphasized action; they favored nationalism. Without doubt, one finds analogies to the principles of the German Youth Movement; but *Les Jeunes Gens d'Aujourd'hui* instinctively found their place in the traditional society of France.[40] Little or no criticism of school, family life, or industrialization was voiced. A conservative attitude prevailed. French and German youth might have agreed on the motto, "Jeunesse oblige," but the idea of placing any responsibility for the culture of its nation in the hands of youth was alien to the French mind.

The observation has been made that whereas youth movements are typical twentieth century phenomena, their impact has been stronger in authoritarian societies such as Germany, Russia, and China. Democratic societies are obviously better equipped to integrate the young into the body politic, and to use their enthusiasm and even their rebellion to change petrified patterns. The industrialization of life, the loosening of family ties, confronts every country with the same problems (witness the incidence of juvenile delinquency in the United States), but the solutions will differ widely in accordance with the social structure.[41]

The German Youth Movement was admittedly a failure, but one should not judge it too harshly. It wished to bring a new life to a society whose existence had reached such a danger point that the good will of isolated individuals or groups could not rescue it. Youth could not understand that institutions may be transformed only when the reforming process takes place within the confines of the institutions themselves. The Youth Movement shied away from such imperatives. It was afraid to lose what it considered its finest quality: the spirit of youth. But the spirit that fails to prove its fruitfulness produces no more than the idle dream.

After 1919 the militant dictatorships in Russia, Italy, and Germany built up youth organizations of their own. The Hitler Youth took over many of the symbols and rituals of the original Youth Movement, but it was no more than a caricature of the associations of young men who aspired to act on their own initiative and under their own responsibility. In very truth, the totalitarian youth organizations are quite the opposite of genuine youth movements; they abuse youth for the purpose of political indoctrination.[42]

Thus we come to the end of another chapter in the history of European civilization before 1914. Once more we observe that the tensions in society had reached such a pitch that palliative measures were impotent. The "invisible revolution" of the Youth Movement was a futile experiment; injections of youthful idealism could not revitalize the body of European society; la calentura no es in las sabanas, as the Spanish proverb puts it ("The fever is not in the blankets").

Feminism

The Youth Movement was an abortive rebellion, but feminism was a successful revolution. It engulfed all of society and affected in its course some of the oldest institutions of mankind. At the time these lines are written, women have been elected to England's peerage and may now enter the floor of the House of Lords. Feminism has altered the structure of both family life and politics; it has produced a new code of sexual ethics; it has made its influence felt in literature, art, the theater, and on the screen. Bertrand Russell has called it one of the most important transformations of society in his lifetime. It is one more triumph of the European mind; beginning as a demand from Western womanhood, it has now reached universal proportions. Its origins are easily traceable, but its implications are not yet wholly within the grasp of the historian.

Today's student of feminism is confronted with a staggering amount of literature which is violently partisan from the first page. Sibyls with visions of glory vie with prophets who anticipate doom. A multiplicity of hopeful predictions, heralding the millennium of woman's victory, alternate with virulent denunciations of feminism as the most patent symptom of the decline of the West. Everyone who took up the subject aired his preconceived ideas with heartfelt abandon.[43] It is indeed difficult to avoid pitfalls of prejudice and prejudication, and to recognize that historical changes are not necessarily for better or for worse, but simply modifications of societal patterns.

Nearly everyone who has written on the feminist movement has felt constrained to begin with the Stone Age and follow its course through history. We will not here repeat the journey from matriarchy and the neolithic age to the present day.

Feminism, like so many trends of our time, is the child of two revolutions which occurred at the end of the eighteenth century: the political and the industrial revolutions. Woman's earlier position in society had been one of subjection; her problem had been essentially personal.[44] Her task had been that of producing and protecting life and of passing on to new generations the accepted behavior patterns of her time.[45] She dealt with individuals: her parents, her husband, her children, her relatives, her neighbors. Her circle was narrow and its center was the family. The insignia of her civilization was the seal of the dominant male. When women rose to eminent position as queens, abbesses, or princesses, they provided the exception that proved the rule. It is true that women had a share in the promotion of the Reformation and that they were treated as man's equal during the Renaissance.[46] They could be landed proprietors, governors of schools, guardians of the poor, poetesses, even statesmen. But only the exceptional woman whose genius refused to be crushed was able to defy the rules of convention laid down for her sex.[47]

Woman's economic possibilities were likewise limited. Domestic service, work in the household, and work in the fields were, generally speaking, her only means of livelihood. Her economic dependence on the male, whether father or husband, was almost complete. She contributed to the family income by doing her share of spinning, household chores, or farm work, but her labor was cooperative and participating, rather than independent. The "domestic system" which preceded the Industrial Revolution is an evidence of the subordinate position of women.

As we have noted, the break occurred simultaneously on two fronts, the economic and the ideological. The first voices clamoring for women's rights were heard during the American Revolution. When the Continental Congress convened in 1776, Abigail Adams wrote her husband, John, that women were determined to rise if the representatives of the nation should neglect their interests.[48] She also demanded that women be admitted to the schools of higher learning. Her words, however, were given little heed.

The situation in revolutionary France was much the same. When the National Assembly met in 1789, it was showered with petitions demanding the recognition of women's rights. If Liberty, Fraternity, and Equality were to be the guiding stars of public and private life, they asked, how was it possible to exclude one half of humanity from the enjoyment of its rights? Some of the members of the National Assembly, Talleyrand for instance, frankly admitted to the contradiction, but the majority were not willing to take any definite stand. Not even in the realm of education were men and women placed on an equal footing.

On the other hand, women in great numbers participated in the drama of the Revolution. Women entered the political clubs; feminine associations for the debate of political issues made their appearance. *Femmes républicaines et révolutionaires* in Paris counted six thousand members. Madame Roland influenced the policies of the Girondists, and Olympe de Gouges became the most eloquent defender of women's rights, publishing in 1791 her *Déclaration des droits de la femme*. "Women are born free and men's equal ... if women have the right to ascend the scaffold, they must have the right to ascend the Tribune." [49] One of these privileges was granted her: the right to end her life on the guillotine. The Convention adopted an antifeminist attitude and dissolved all political women's clubs in 1793.

Certain isolated individuals, like Condorcet, had asked for complete equality of the sexes. Women, he said, should be enfranchised and should not be excluded from public office. In 1789 he published an article demanding that the Bill of Rights be extended to women. The natural rights of mankind, he asserted, called for no less.[50] But Condorcet remained a lonely pioneer in a country whose political outlook was soon to be determined by Napoleon.

Even though the first attempts to gain women's rights by assault had failed, one thing had become clear: the idea of equality could not henceforth be considered a monopoly of the human male. Equality, this strange amalgam of Christian thought and natural law, would be applied to all barriers that prejudice and selfishness had erected. The fight for women's rights is only a subheading in the evolution of this idea as it works its way through modern history.

Meanwhile the cause began to gain momentum. On the continent the German, Von Hippel, wrote a book called *The Civic Improvement of Women*,[51] and in England Mary Wollstonecraft published her *Vindication of Women's Rights*.[52] The latter had herself experienced the difficulties which women faced in eighteenth century England. She had begun her adult life as a teacher and had given much thought to the education of her sex. Thomas Paine drew her into the maelstrom of revolutionary agitation, and she defended the French Declaration of Rights against Edmund Burke. These activities were, however, only a prelude to *The Vindication of Women's Rights*. Mary Wollstonecraft did not assert that women were the intellectual equals of men. She said that circumstances had forced them into subjection and inferiority. She compared women to those trees that bear flowers but no fruit. Education for women was directed toward the production of ladies who were instructed in manners, not morals; in the art of entertainment, but not in the value of work. These weak and empty-headed creatures should not be surprised when men threw their faults in their faces. "Only that education deserves emphatically to be termed cultivating which teaches young people how to think."

What Mary Wollstonecraft outlined was in many ways more conservative than the program set forth by Condorcet. The first step was to give women the chance to become rational beings. After they had been educated, men could no longer treat them as their slaves. In other words, reform of education must precede reform of the law. Like many revolutionists, Mary Wollstonecraft thought poverty was the result of vice and crime. Women must, therefore, try to become economically independent. Only when education and women's own labor had wiped out the servitude of her sex would she be able to stand side by side with man, like him a free citizen.[53]

Mary Wollstonecraft was the pioneer of a great movement. Her

book shows her to be a wise and sensible woman who could discuss
the problems of her sex with probity and moderation.[54] What she
devised became the program of the more alert women of the middle
class.

Liberal theorists of the nineteenth century, with few exceptions,
looked upon the emancipation of women as a minor problem, but
the movement nevertheless received support from many sources.
Saint-Simon preached "la réhabilitation de la chair," a doctrine
which led logically to the recognition of women's rights.[55] George
Sand was a brilliant exponent of the new revolutionary ideas.
Through her temperament and her attitude, George Sand set an
example of emancipated womanhood. Many women shuddered at
her exhibitionism; few were ready to emulate her daring, but nearly
all envied her courage.[56] As liberalism advanced, magazines that
championed women's interests began to appear: *La Femme Nouvelle* (1832–1834), *La Gazette des Femmes* (1836–1838). They
agitated for the opening of the professions to women. The year
1848 brought further advances. A Frenchwoman, Jeanne Derain,
ran for the Legislative Assembly in 1849; a young German woman,
Louise Otto, fought for the right of women to participate in the
unification of Germany. There were parallel activities in Denmark,
Poland, and Hungary.

Although the feminist movement still met with opposition and
derision in the field of politics, it scored remarkable triumphs in
the realm of education. Schools for girls were established in England
and on the Continent. North America founded seminaries for girls,
and at the same time set up experiments in coeducation, such as
Oberlin College.

The feminist movement was furthered in a singular way through
another great reform movement, the emancipation of the slaves.
Lucretia Mott, a Quaker, opened a campaign to liberate the colored
slaves, and conducted it, as such causes were usually conducted in
the United States, by holding meetings, writing to newspapers, and
swamping the country with propaganda material. For the first time
women were demonstrating their power to intervene in matters of
public interest. It was not long before they began to draw the
parallel between their own state and that of the slaves. A feminist
association was founded. In 1848 it held its first convention and

issued a manifesto that echoes the spirit of 1776: men and women are created free and equal with inalienable human rights; governments exist only to protect these rights. Since men have monopolized and usurped these rights, women must reject their laws and fight for justice.[57] The immediate fruit of their defiance was a bill passed in New York state which gave a wife full control of her own property.[58]

The Civil War relegated women's problems to a secondary place, but after the war the feminist agitation reappeared with increased intensity. Susan Anthony went to the polls in 1872 and asked to be registered. In court she lost her case, but not her cause.

It was at this time that the most articulate apostle of democracy, John Stuart Mill, published his treatise on the subjection of women (1867). Mill's thesis is simple. Under the law, women should be entitled to do everything of which, by their natures, they are capable.[59] Probably no other written work has done so much toward the creation of an enlightened public opinion on the question of women's rights. In 1867 Mill proposed to the House of Commons an amendment to the electoral bill that would have enfranchised women. The amendment was defeated, but only by a vote of seventy-three against one hundred and eighty-six, a result far in advance of Mill's expectations.

Other tendencies in the feminist movement had in a way more important aspects than the fight for political equality. These were found in the struggles for legal equality and economic opportunity, and it was here that the nineteenth century saw women's greatest advances. Until this time the only profession open to middle-class women was the teaching profession; nursing and domestic service were considered below middle-class dignity. Thousands of women gave music lessons, taught school, or acted as governesses in well-to-do families. Gradually other professions yielded to feminine pressure. It was a heroic struggle against prejudice, competition, and outright stupidity. The "right to work" brought with it a transformation of home and family life, of social and state institutions. Once more the Anglo-Saxon countries took the lead. In 1872 Illinois passed a law declaring that no person should be debarred from any occupation or profession on account of sex.[60] Little by little the door to man's world was forced open; women were admitted as physicians, lawyers, superintendents of schools, factory inspectors, librarians, archivists, and eventually they were allowed to enter the higher echelons of the teaching profession. In every field they proved their talents.

England fell into line and the colonies followed the example of the mother country. Universities in India and Australia were opened to girl students. Other occupations were added to those listed above. Nursing became an honorable profession through the efforts of Florence Nightingale; prisons and poorhouses were placed under women's supervision. The opportunities provided by telephone and telegraph swelled the ranks of the working women of the middle class.

The reasons for the steady penetration of the bourgeois world by working women were not only ideological. Need was a most efficient teacher. Women outnumbered men in the nineteenth century, as they continue to do today. E. von Hartmann called the woman problem, quite accurately, the spinster problem. Many families considered it sound economic policy to make greater allowances for the professional training of their sons than for that of their daughters. Girls who did not marry were confronted with the alternative of withering away in the parental home or choosing an occupation that would permit them a minimum of economic independence. As the scope of women's labor expanded, there came to be many occupations which could be filled with these refugees from domestic boredom: photography, the industrial arts, accounting, commercial responsibilities of various types.

It is as this juncture that our rapid survey must take into consideration the other great wing of the movement for women's rights, the proletarian. The working class accepted the introduction of women's labor not from any enthusiasm for human dignity or political equality, but from necessity. The history of proletarian women's labor is almost identical with the history of machines in industrial production.[61] Before the machine age women had worked in the home for the simple reason that they did not possess the physical strength to wield hammer and tongs, saws and planes. Only the introduction of machines made it possible for women to replace the hitherto predominant male in industrial work. The incipient industry of the late eighteenth century accepted women and children for a strictly economic reason: their work was cheaper than the work of men.[62] The discovery of mechanical appliances, such as the spinning jenny, the weaving machines, and the printing machines, had led to a breakdown of the "domestic system." The cheapening of production in the textile industry, where one machine could now do a hundred times as much work as one man had done before, brought about a state of starvation and misery.[63] The machines forced previously self-reliant workers into dependence on the owners of the new "means of production." These were large and expensive and the worker was obliged to go to the places where the machines were installed. Thus the factory system began to edge out the domestic system.

The capitalistic bosses preferred women for all jobs which did not require special skill because women were willing to accept lower pay. Woman labor was particularly prevalent in the textile industry, but it could be found in many other places, even in the mines. The male worker found himself suddenly confronted with a new competition. Women, who had been his helpers in the home, threatened to replace him at his work. The workingman's reaction to this aspect of the Industrial Revolution was like his initial reaction to the introduction of machinery. In rage the workers had smashed the insensate objects which seemed to them the causes of all their troubles. They looked upon the competition of their womenfolk with equal hatred and suspicion. The unions tried to exclude women from factory work because they undercut the male laborer, and because they did not adhere to the principle of class solidarity when they acted as strikebreakers, as they often did.

Ironically enough, the machine eventually superseded women just as it had superseded men. As more and more machines came into use, women's labor also became expendable. A case in point is the invention of the sewing machine, which left innumerable seamstresses without work.

The Industrial Revolution not only destroyed the domestic system and women's place in it; it also produced changes in occupations which had formerly been held by women, notably in agriculture and domestic service. In agriculture, machines again tended to replace the farm hands. As for domestic service, the statistics of the period show a steady decline in this branch of feminine labor. The use of gas and electricity, community services, such as a more efficient water supply and modern sewer systems, made households less dependent on domestic help.

To these changes was added a psychological one: many women preferred factory work to work in the house. It was not alone the question of better wages, but of personal independence. Domestic service was the one profession still close to servitude; the worker sold not only her labor but her spare time besides. If proletarian women spurned domestic service, they could still enter many other occupations which demanded a minimum of education. The tremendous increase in goods produced by the Industrial Revolution demanded larger and better shops. The department store came into existence, and women of the laboring class were particularly attracted to these opportunities since they did not require long and expensive training. The more ambitious girls began to invade the clerical positions in industry, commerce, and banking, previously a monopoly of the middle-class women.

It is at this point that the feminist movement of middle-class origin and that of the proletarian class began to merge. In many cases the working woman of either class might still preserve her social outlook; that is to say, she might feel herself a part of the bourgeoisie or the proletariat. Unconsciously, however, she had become a member of the great army of women which was marching inexorably onward toward the ultimate goal of economic independence and political equality.

With these facts in mind, it is not surprising to find that the advocates of socialism became the most ardent defenders of feminism. Just as in the United States women had identified their lot with that of the Negro slaves, the Socialists now came to identify the cause of the exploited classes with that of the oppressed sex. In the old bourgeois order there was no hope for the working class except in overthrowing the capitalistic system. In the same manner, women could hope to come into their own only in a classless society. In the meantime, however, the enfranchisement of women would swell the ranks of the working-class voters, thus hastening the day of reckoning.

August Bebel's *Die Frau und der Socialismus* is the classical expression of this profeminist ideology held by many socialists before

1914.[64] Its impact was extraordinary; in a few decades it ran into
fifty-one editions. Bebel's argument is couched in strictly Marxian
terms. He begins with a description of the position of women in
primitive society and ends with a statement of her future in a
Communist world. Paradise lost and paradise regained! In between
lies the fall, women's subjection by man and his evil capitalistic
habits. Needless to say, the bourgeoisie is held responsible for every
degrading feature in women's life, from the decay of the family to
prostitution.[65]

Bebel does not deny that women have benefited from the process
of industrialization. They have, he says, become freer and more
independent.[66] They can now form associations, hold conventions,
and join the male under the benefits of union labor. A radical
change in women's position, however, could take place only in a
socialist society. When the expropriation of the expropriators has
been accomplished, woman will return to the freedom which she
had enjoyed in the primitive state, enhanced, of course, by the
advantages of socialism. She will continue to work, since work will
be a privilege in the new society; life will have become peaceful
and stabilized, and the state will have withered away.[67] Many of
the chores that have been women's lot since time immemorial will,
he says, be taken over by society. Community kitchens will take
care of the cooking, and everyone will dine in cafeterias. Laundering
will be done in centralized establishments, and a progressive industrialization will take care of such drudgeries as dusting and clean-
ing. Bebel defies Treitschke, who had coined the phrase, "No culture
without servants." [68]

Continuing with his list of socialist advantages, Bebel states that
women will have complete freedom of sexual choice, since the
satisfaction of natural urges is a matter of private concern.[69] Over-
population will be avoided. In the new society humanity will plan
with foresight and sagacity its own evolution.[70] The end of the book
constitutes an appeal to women to do their share in the approaching
fight for liberation and salvation. "She must prove that she has
understood her position in the movement and in the struggle of the
present for a better future. . . . The future belongs to socialism,
id est, to the worker and to women." [71]

We have noted that Bebel's work had an astonishing impact in the years before 1914, and not in Germany alone. It was clear that the fight for women's rights had reached the political stage. By 1900 the integration of women into the industrial economy was an established fact. Women were not yet admitted to key positions in industry, banking, or commerce, but they were an auxiliary force without which the industrial apparatus could no longer function, let alone be extended. The argument over her creative capabilities still raged, but it was difficult to deny women's potentialities in the light of such eminent figures as Marie Curie.[72] The decisive battle was now the political one; the integration of women in the constitutional life of the Western world could be accomplished only by making them full-time partners in the democratic process.

The contest over women's right to vote extended over a period of fifty years. Antifeminists predicted the ruin of all social institutions if women were given the vote. Ellen Key answered by saying, "A ballot paper in itself no more injures the delicacy of a woman's hand than a cooking recipe." [73] The protagonists of the feminist movement ranged from such sober figures as Lili Braun and Helene Lange to the exhibitionistic Miss Pankhurst, who said that votes for women "mean a new heaven and a new earth." (That a new hell for women might also be included, seems to have escaped her.) The fight for women's rights became one of the great issues of the first decade of the twentieth century. It was discussed in parlors and in beerhalls, in public meetings and in university classrooms. Some of the literary leaders of Europe sided with the emancipation group: Ibsen, Shaw, Gerhard Hauptmann. Others, such as Strindberg and George, opposed it. And women naturally bore the brunt of the struggle.

In England the clash of arms was particularly loud and violent. The suffragette movement hardened in a rigid routine and became an "organized method of creating disorder for the purpose of advertising a grievance in season and out of season." [74] The suffragettes were a mixed lot. Some of them belonged to the well-to-do class with no outlet for their vitality; these became suffragettes from a desire for notoriety and sensationalism. There was also a rowdy element which embraced the end because they enjoyed the means, that is, behaving in a scandalous manner and getting themselves looked upon as public nuisances. And finally there were such distinguished champions as Beatrice Webb and Ethel Snowden, both women of great intelligence and character.[75]

Before long a national league for opposing woman's suffrage was formed, but the avalanche had started, and all efforts to block it were futile. Today's reader finds it strange that the modest demands made by the feminists produced so great a storm. By the middle of the twentieth century not only had all their claims been allowed, but they had made advances which the noisy Mrs. Pankhurst could never have envisaged.

Let us note briefly the stages by which the women's movement reached success. New Zealand's women were enfranchised in 1893; Australia's in 1902. In 1910 the Parliament of Australia expressed the opinion that the reform had brought nothing but good, and it urged all nations enjoying representative government to follow Australia's example.[76] Among European countries, it was Finland, still under Russian rule, that granted women full citizenship. Norway followed Finland's lead in 1907, and Denmark did likewise in 1912.

In the great continental nations recognition came more slowly. Not until after the Great War did Germany, Russia, and Great Britain surrender to the feminist claims. Throughout the war women's labor had been indispensable in maintaining the industrial effort at the home front. At the close of the conflict, women outnumbered men by millions as the result of war losses. Parliamentary interests of all shades saw the potentials of this voting force. Women's vote did not in every case prove to be sound or even constructive. Prohibition in the United States, the rise of Hitler, the downfall of the Spanish Republic, were, in some measure, attributable to women's votes. A probable explanation is that women were inclined to vote, not along carefully considered lines, true to their own type or reasoning, but in the pattern of an existing social fabric which they accepted without substantial change.

This same reasoning seems applicable to other aspects of the feminist movement. The code of sexual ethics changed profoundly in the twentieth century. It was first set forth by Ellen Key in a series of books: *Love and Marriage, The Century of the Child,* and *The Women's Movement.* She believed in a new ethic, a synthesis growing out of the nature of man and the nature of women, out of the demands of the individual and the demands of society, out of the resolve to mold the future and out of piety toward the past. Other writers concerned themselves with more tangible problems of sexual ethics: protection of the mother, divorce laws, the defense of illegitimate children, and so forth.[77]

Although the change in sexual ethics is the result of a variety of influences, it would seem certain that the decisive elements were brought about by women themselves. Women's rights were implemented by women's needs. Having been left at the close of the war in a position of numerical superiority, a far from enjoyable situation, they reached out for a greater freedom in the pursuit of their normal satisfactions. And the arguments of the feminists allowed women to make a virtue out of necessity.

A final assessment of the feminist movement is not yet possible. The participation of women in all spheres of life is an acknowledged fact; to what extent it has brought and will bring deep transformations is a question that only the future can answer. Like the absorption of the working class into the body politic of modern democracy, the feminist movement has given women freedom and equality without producing any disruption of society. Women have not taken over men's world; the family has not disappeared, nor does it seem to be seriously jeopardized, but women's former subjection has been replaced by cooperation. Though the final results of this great revolution may be still unpredictable, its influence in twentieth century life cannot be denied.

Taylorism

Among the ranks of the American feminists was a young woman from New England by the name of Emily Winslow. Her marriage to Franklin Taylor, a wealthy Philadelphia Quaker, was productive of three children. One of them was Frederick Winslow Taylor, who introduced scientific management to the world and whose ideas have become a ferment in the development of our century.[78]

Frederick Taylor was an amiable, obedient, and vivacious child. He received an excellent education, and after a visit to Europe with his parents, returned to his country with a more than ordinary knowledge of foreign languages, a love for France, and an intense dislike for Germany. From Exeter he entered Harvard with the intention of becoming a lawyer, but soon realized that his eyes could not stand the strain of prolonged reading. He abandoned academic pursuits for a career in industry and became an engineer.[79]

From early childhood he had displayed an inventive spirit. His boyhood companions even thought him a bit of a crank. When he played croquet, he made the game a source of study, working out the angles of every stroke. At the age of twelve, when he suffered from terrifying nightmares, he constructed for himself a sort of harness made of straps and wooden points, so arranged that when in his sleep he turned on his back the points would press on the dorsal muscle and awaken him.[80] He learned engineering the hard way, from the bottom up, and in later years confessed, "The very best training I had was in the early years of apprenticeship . . . when I was under a workman of extraordinary ability coupled with fine character. I there learned appreciation, respect, and admiration for the everyday working mechanic." [81] His career as an engineer was a distinguished one, but our own purposes will best be served if we concentrate on what at first seemed a by-product of his profession: the system of scientific management. As an inventor he revolutionized the process of high-speed steel cutting, making observations and drawing conclusions that led him to become the prophet of a new approach to industrial production.[82]

"When the intellectual history of this period comes to be written," said H. G. Wells, "nothing . . . will stand out more strikingly than the empty gulf . . . between the superb and richly fruitful scientific investigations that are going on and the general thought of other educated sections of the community." Taylor's work furnishes ample proof of his statement. Taylor based his ideas on the most painstaking observations, assembling great amounts of information before venturing to formulate rules. If Herbert Spencer's idea of tragedy was, as George Eliot said, a theory killed by a fact, Taylor's idea of tragedy was a fact killed by a theory. Taylor would not deserve a place in the history of Western culture, however, had he done nothing more than introduce certain time-saving devices in the processes of production. Behind his innovations is his moral outlook on man and man's labor, and his optimistic belief in the future of mankind.

In studying the origins of Taylor's thinking one cannot escape the conclusion that here is another striking example of the interac-

tion of capitalism and Puritanism.[83] Taylor's Quaker background
has been mentioned, and he had many of the negative virtues that
characterize the Puritan. He did not drink nor would he permit
the serving of alcohol in his home. He struck tea and coffee from
his fare and eschewed tobacco in any form. His attire was markedly
simple, and, in a word, he would have been the exemplar of Quaker
virtues had he not been a past master in the use of profanity and
had his opinions on the church been something less than unprintable.

Obviously Taylor was a Puritan of the nineteenth century, or,
let us say, a secularized Puritan. The psychological pattern developed by his forebears under the influence of Calvin's idea of predestination served him in worldly pursuits. His inspirations were not
theological but moral; his aims were not otherworldly but earthly.
But who can fail to note that behind his theory and practice stand
three hundred years of Calvinistic discipline.[84] "Character," he
wrote in a lecture on success, "is the ability to control yourself,
body and mind; the ability to do things which your common sense
tells you you ought to do; the ability above all to do things which
are disagreeable, which you do not like . . . It takes a lot of character to do things which are tiresome, monotonous, and unpleas-
ant." [85]

Taylor was extraordinarily conscious that "scientific management" was based on ideas which were nothing short of revolutionary. When a committee of the United States Congress asked him to
explain his methods, he answered, "Scientific management is not
any efficiency device. . . . It is not a new system of figuring costs
. . . it is not holding a stop watch on a man and writing things
down about it; it is not time study; it is not motion study . . . in
essence, scientific management involves a complete revolution on
the part of the working man . . . and it involves the equally complete mental revolution on the part of those on the management's
side." [86]

Frederick Taylor's inauguration of this mental revolution was
his great accomplishment. But, "Taylor or no Taylor," says Stuart
Chase, "scientific management would have come." [87] Industry had
grown by leaps and bounds during the nineteenth century. The
number of wage-earners, the gain in capital, the expansion of manufacturing, all pointed to the second phase of the Industrial Revo-

lution: large-scale production which would lead eventually to mass production.[88] From 1780 to 1880, however, industry had proceeded by trial and error; management had been geared by experience only. The Industrial Revolution—the result of scientific knowledge applied to manufacturing—had moved forward in a very unscientific manner. Taylor recast it by the introduction of scientific methodology; one could almost say that through the medium of Taylor's mind industry took a good look at itself and found itself wanting, wanting not only in the methods it used, but also in the general philosophy by which it had been guided.

The principles which Taylor outlined are as follows: "The great revolution that takes place in the mental attitude of the two parties under scientific management is that both sides take their eyes off the division of the surplus as the all-important matter, and turn their attention toward *increasing the size of the surplus* [the italics are mine]. They both realize that when they substitute friendly cooperation and mutual helpfulness for antagonism and strife they are . . . able to make this surplus so enormously greater than it was in the past that there is ample room for a large increase in wages for the workmen and an equally great increase in profit for the manufacturer. . . . Both sides must recognize as essential the substitution of exact scientific investigation and knowledge for the old individual judgment or opinion, either of the workmen or the boss." [89]

One of Taylor's associates summed up the intellectual revolution that occurred in industry in the following words: "We are passing from a stage in which there was a simple and unconscious following of tradition into a stage of self-consciousness in which we are moved to subject our habits and our motives to severe self-scrutiny." And with a sigh he added, "It is a very painful stage to have arrived at." [90]

A large number of misconceptions have grown up around the term Taylorism, such as the use of the slide rule, time study, piecework, and the use of efficiency devices. Definitions of this type neglect the point that these are elements of an integral system which must be understood and judged as a whole. Taylor's own explication of the principles of scientific management is more comprehensive: first, the development of a science for all implements used in industrial production; second, the development of a science for each element of a man's work. Using such studies as a basis, workmen would be selected and trained for the job which best suited their abilities. They would be expected to work to capacity and to perform a standardized amount of labor.

Thus both machines and men were subjected to standardization in order to obtain a maximum of standardized products in the shortest time possible. Taylor realized that his plans could not be put into effect without offering the workers special incentives. Therefore, higher wages should be paid to the workmen who approached the highest performance, and to those who took more than the standard time only their nominal wages would be paid. Last, but not least, management and workers would share the responsibility for obtaining the largest surplus or output. Responsibility was to be divided between management and workers on the basis of scientifically determined functions.[91]

The shift to scientific management, then, would embrace two complementary innovations: control and operation of machines would be transferred from pragmatic experience to a veritable science, and labor would be standardized to reach a goal of maximum efficiency and maximum speed.[92]

The first of these projected alterations in the manufacturing process demanded the conscious use of the most advanced technology. Innumerable laboratory experiments had to be conducted and their results analyzed and coordinated, before the best evaluations could be made. In certain respects, all tools that man's ingenuity have produced, from the wheel to the steam engine, are labor-saving devices. But only since the introduction of Taylor's ideas has industry been bent on systematically bringing out such devices in order to speed up the output and increase its volume.

The application of the same ideas to human labor proved to be most difficult. Although Taylor had complete confidence in his methods, he was aware that the introduction of scientific management in a shop might not always produce the anticipated result, and in his quandary he often resorted to bluff. What exactly was a day's work and what was the maximum result to be obtained? [93] His dilemma led him to develop a system of measurements previously unknown in industry. To circumvent the waste of time, he clocked the worker with a stop watch. "All the operations . . . which were performed while putting work into and taking it out from the machines were analyzed and timed," he wrote.[94] But the study of the time actually consumed had to be complemented by study of the time required for a specific operation, and here Taylor ran into heavy opposition from labor. The workmen considered these time studies to be an infringement on their right to decide for themselves how much work they could do in a given time.[95]

But Taylor persisted. He introduced a planning department which analyzed the job in advance for the workmen, gave him written orders, and told him in the most minute detail each motion he was to make and the time which he might spend in performing it. In the face of continued criticism from the workmen, Taylor maintained that all modern labor-saving devices necessitated the sacrifice of individual opinion in the interest of scientific accuracy.

One of the most significant aspects of Taylor's system lay in the fact that it depersonalized and dehumanized labor even more than the introduction of machinery had done one hundred years before.[96] For instance, the instructions which Taylor outlined for a certain company in 1896 read as follows:

> The hours of work shall be from 8:00 A.M. till 5:00 P.M.
> No talking above a whisper during working hours.
> No smoking during working hours.
> Each clerk shall be allowed to go home at any time during the day when his work is done.
> Each man must finish his work properly belonging to that day, even if he has to stay all night to do it.[97]

Quite understandably, workers and employees became enraged at such hard-and-fast rules, especially when they had reason to doubt whether management would live up to its part of the bargain. It is amusing to note that Taylor was confronted with equally stiff opposition when he tried to convince business leaders of the efficiency of his ideas. They, too, were loath to submit to rigorous discipline or to relinquish part of their authority, and it demanded considerable vision on the part of management for them to give Taylor a free hand in their plants. Even after they had decided to try his system, they more often than not turned him out again.[98]

Moreover, Taylor was no easy man to deal with. He demanded

that his suggestions should be accepted beforehand and he brooked no interference. To the directors of a factory who had called him in for consultation he said, "These workmen will show you . . . that . . . I know nothing about my business and that . . . I am a liar and you are being fooled. . . . The only thing I ask of you, and I must have your firm promise, is that when I say a thing is so, you will take my word against the word of any twenty or any fifty men in the shop." [99]

Gradually he overcame ill will, sabotage, dismissal, and failure from whatever side it might come. At the end of his life he abandoned all practical considerations and devoted his whole energy to the propagation of his ideas. Was his crusade simply for the material benefit of industry, or was there more to it? Was there in Taylor a vision of a new era in human progress? The answers must be in the affirmative. A Puritan, Taylor believed deeply in the ethical value of human labor. Son of the nineteenth century, he affirmed that man was entitled to enjoy the fruits of his work. He embraced the hope that all human and social problems created by industry could be solved by industry, that the spear that had injured could likewise heal the wounds. Industry would make this earth into a world of plenty. Like Coudenhove-Kalergi, he might have said, "The inventor and the engineer are fighting want and poverty; they are not fighting wealth. They are fighting slavery; they are not fighting rules. Their object is to universalize wealth, power, leisure, beauty, happiness. . . . Ethics and techniques are sisters; ethics rule the natural forces within us. Techniques rule the natural forces without us." [100]

Very likely Taylor had never heard of the Communist Manifesto with its assertion that all history is the history of class struggle. In any case, his own belief was diametrically opposed to that of Marx. His "mental revolution" consisted in substituting industrial peace for class war, and cooperation for contention and strife. Scientific management, he believed, would replace suspicious watchfulness by mutual confidence. Management and labor would pull together in the same direction instead of heading for opposite poles. This may sound like a lot of wishful thinking, or worse, ideological bilge introduced to disguise the cruel features of the Taylor system. In reality, however, it was the prophecy of a new period in industrial relations.

Taylor's philosophy conceived of management and labor as indispensable and consequently complementary parts of the industrial process. The introduction of exact measurements for labor actually performed, the speed-up devices that his ingenuity invented, the search for better and faster machines, were paralleled on the side of management by a stricter accounting system and by elaborate planning. Both sides would be obliged to make sacrifices in order to overcome superannuated habits. Taylor predicted that labor would at first find piecework and gauged wages distasteful, but that in the long run they would appreciate its benefits: shorter hours, higher incomes, and better standards of living. Management would have to forego short-time gains for long-term advantages. The solution for the many human problems that the Industrial Revolution had created would be found in an ever-increasing and expanding industrialization. The growing output would be geared to include all classes and not those alone who in former times had been the principal consumers.

The political consequences of the Taylor system are manifest. Whereas in Europe the working class had to fight for shorter hours and social legislation, in America capitalism was beginning to comprehend that concessions to labor would ultimately benefit society as a whole. This does not mean that such results were immediately forthcoming or that the managerial class embraced labor as its long-lost twin. Far from it; Taylor himself was guilty of animosity and even outright hostility toward labor unions. In his opinion they misrepresented his ideas. For decades unions had taught their members to restrict the output, and to look at the boss as an enemy.[101] It was not easy for them to revise their attitude and to admit that great progress could be made under a new system.[102] "I think," Taylor said, "that the time will come when the trade-unionist will realize that the true and permanent road to prosperity lies in so educating themselves that they will be able and willing to do more work in return for larger pay, rather than to do less work for the same pay, or the same work for larger pay. . . . I have a very great confidence in the common sense of the American citizen." [103]

Developments in the United States have borne out Taylor's predictions. Labor has not constituted itself as a fighting group with definite party affiliations, as was the case in Europe. Nor has it adhered to the idea of class struggle or revolution. It has been integrated in the body politic, conscious and sometimes overconscious of its particular interests, but also willing to recognize the larger interests of the nation. Thus one can say that Taylor is among the leaders of industrial democracy and a champion of the nebulous creed that we call "the American way of life."

As we have noted, scientific management would have moved into the act even without its protagonist, Taylor. Henry Ford introduced the assembly line in the production of motorcars in the same year that Taylor's *Principles* appeared.[104] Obviously Ford used a new approach: he eliminated manpower as much as possible and replaced it by automatic or semiautomatic machines.[105] Whereas Taylor had only tried to reduce laziness and waste and reach a point of greatest efficiency, Ford was contemplating the possibilities of machines. But the underlying reasoning is the same in both cases. Ford and Taylor held the same economic creed. Ford stated his goals as follows: "To make an ever-increasing large quantity of goods of the best possible quality, to make them in the best and most economical fashion, and to force them on the market. To strive always for higher quality and lower prices as well as lower costs. To raise wages gradually but continually and never to cut them." [106] For both men the ultimate aim of the industrial process was to abolish poverty. "The abolishing of poverty is the only legitimate purpose of business, not selfish competition or the profit motive," [107] wrote Ford. He also shared Taylor's conviction that industrial progress was no progress if it benefited only a restricted group. "Prosperity cannot be considered as achieved unless it reaches to all parts of this country and to all classes. And we shall not be able to raise our own prosperity to that point without also raising that of the world." [108] This is the American Utopia: an earthly paradise built by technical ingenuity.

There are certain other aspects of Taylorism to consider. The idea of scientific management made its appearance at a time when large-scale production came to the fore. Taylor was not satisfied with the mere control of the production process; he wanted to plan it.

"The shop, and indeed the whole work, should be managed not by the manager, superintendent, or foreman, but by the planning department." [109] It was Taylor's conviction that only if industry would adhere to the functional principle could it yield its utmost.[110] Big business was at this same time abandoning its old practice of depending on a balance sheet of assets and losses and developing a budget of the type that previously had been used by states and nations, a budget that planned ahead. At the beginning of the twentieth century planning was rapidly becoming an essential part of large-scale production.

In Taylor's thinking, planning was still limited to the individual enterprise, but there was no reason why it could not be applied to the whole economy. With the advent of World War I Germany found herself blockaded and was thus obliged to apply planning on a nation-wide scale. With imports of raw material and machinery suspended, the resultant industrial standstill would have brought military collapse. Walther Rathenau was the first to sense this danger, and assisted by Wichard von Möllendorf, an electrical engineer, he developed the idea of *Planwirtschaft*, an emergency economy in operation for the duration of the war.[111] The *Planwirtschaft* included rigorous allotment of raw material, the setting up of production goals, the rationing of consumer goods, and so forth. It is certain that Lenin, then in exile in Switzerland, followed the German experiment with keen interest. When he came to power in 1917, he applied the principles of planned economy in Bolshevist Russia. On April 18, 1918, he published an article in *Pravda* called "Problems of the Soviet Rule." Under the heading of "Higher Productivity of Labor" he wrote, "We should immediately introduce piecework and try it out in practice. We should try out every scientific and progressive suggestion of the Taylor System. . . . The Russian is a poor worker in comparison with the advanced nations, and this could not be otherwise under the regime of the Tzar and other remnants of feudalism. To learn how to work—this problem the Soviet authority should present to the people in all its comprehensiveness. The last word of capitalism in this respect, the Taylor System, as well as all progressive measures of capitalism, combined the refined cruelty of bourgeois exploitation and a number of most valuable scientific attainments in the analysis of mechanical motions in determining the most correct methods of work, the best system of accounting and control. . . . The Soviet Republic must adopt valuable and scientific advances in this field. The possibility of socialism will be determined by our success in combining the Soviet Rule and the Soviet organization of management with the latest progressive measures of capitalism. We must introduce in Russia the study and teaching of the new Taylor System and its systematic trial and adaptation." [112]

With his customary clairvoyance Lenin realized that Taylorism was not a technical monopoly of the capitalistic world and that it could be used by an economy aiming at large-scale production. In reality, Taylorism is neither more nor less than the systematization of the engineering spirit applied to the economy. Since Taylor's day it has invaded agriculture, the wholesale and retail trade, and other areas, and many European countries have followed Taylor's lead.[113] Some of his all too harsh advice has been softened; industrial psychology has taken the venom out of the control measures which made them hateful to labor, but his basic ideas continue to make headway.

In the perspective of intellectual history Taylorism would seem one more step toward the ever-growing rationalization of the world. This process, begun in Greece and renewed by the Renaissance, had reached universal proportions at the beginning of the twentieth century. With it came what Max Weber called the progressive disenchantment of the world (*die Entzauberung der Welt*).[114] Taylor, as well as Lenin or Ford, perceived only the positive results of this process. Not only did they think its coming inevitable; they welcomed it and minimized its human and cultural repercussions. However, these cannot be passed over lightly. Taylor thought that maximum production demanded the standardization of labor. It did not escape him that standardization meant mechanization and that mechanization meant depersonalization. He believed that while work may lose some of its significance for the individual, this will be compensated for by higher wages and long hours of leisure. He further believed that freedom from drudgery, want, and famine would increase the sum total of human happiness. Certainly, few would deny that the advances in medicine, industry, communication, and food production have lifted from man's shoulders burdens under which he anguished for thousands of years. Only a complete retrogression in civilization would cause man to relinquish these achievements. But these manifest advantages have furnished man with only a negative happiness. Taylor and his followers were prone to close their eyes to the dreary side of industrialization and technocracy.

The mechanization of life has liberated us from many of the scourges which have previously afflicted human existence. But in all too many instances men and women have been converted into the cogs and wheels of a machinery which they neither understand nor control. From a work that has lost its meaning and offers no other compensation than the weekly pay check, man plunges into an equally meaningless leisure. His moral and esthetic development have not kept pace with his intellectual evolution, thus producing an unprofitable, not to say pernicious, vacuum.

It is a fallacy in Taylor's thinking that greater output in industrial goods is inevitably followed by a rise in cultural standards, just as, in Hegel's dialectic, that at a certain moment quantity becomes quality. There are, of course, obvious exceptions; the paperback classic, the recording of musical masterpieces, the reproductions of great paintings, have put cultural treasures within the reach of all. But, by and large, Taylor's hopes have not been fulfilled. The concentration on material goods has unleashed a greed for more material goods. Meaningless work is not conducive to meaningful leisure. It voids the human personality; it forces it into a rigid frame where only a small part of the human potential can come into play; in a word, it dwarfs and cripples the human mind.

Perhaps the fundamental error in Taylorism is the belief that the greatest happiness of the greatest number can be obtained by producing the greatest amount of goods. There are imponderabilia in human life which escape the engineering mind. There is one part of man which will always resist scientific management, and it will either dwindle or rise in rebellion when its existence is threatened by an excess of rationalization. From a human point of view, Taylorism can lead to Huxley's *Brave New World* or George Orwell's *1984,* as easily as it can lead to Henry Ford. Though Taylor believed sincerely in the moral implications of mechanization and rationalization, they are really neutral forces and constructive only if they are made to serve human values.

Socialism

We have been engaged in observing certain momentous trends which were influential in structuring the European society of the twentieth century, but the one which was most pregnant for the future of Europe still remains to be discussed. European socialism, says H. S. Hughes, witnessed its greatest expansion in the decade of the 1890's.[115] Its development was accompanied, colored, and determined by the intellectual labor of a group of men who held that the advance of the working class was the decisive factor in the history of the century. No other significant political ideology developed between 1890 and 1914. Conservatism, which defended the stabilizing forces in European society, was barely holding its own; liberalism was in retreat, and democratic thought had already found its classical expression in the writings of J. S. Mill.

Certainly there could be no doubt that labor was here to stay. Even the most enraged opponents of modern industrialism were obliged to admit its survival; its very numbers spoke an all too eloquent language. The growth of trade-union membership, discussed in another part of these studies, showed the increasing power of the labor movement. The social-democratic parties of Germany, Austria, and the Scandinavian countries were constantly gaining in strength. In Italy and Spain the movement had associated itself with syndicalism.[116] Moreover, social legislation had been introduced in many countries to mitigate the worst of the hardships produced by the Industrial Revolution.

But the fate of the working class was still in debate. Their successes, significant though they were, had by no means laid a solid foundation for the socialist concept of a future society. The ambiguous situation which developed within the socialist ranks was deeply rooted in the history of the movement. Insurgent labor had not been content with gaining for its members a place in the sun; its goal was the annihilation of the existing social order and the creation of a new society untainted by power, greed, and self-aggrandizement. This focal principle of the socialist movement was something new to Western thought.

The class struggles which had preceded the socialist movement, though not unheard, were less articulate. The rise of the bourgeoisie in the Middle Ages, the revolt of the peasants, the triumph of the English gentry, had not been accompanied by such excessive hopes. It was the lunatic fringe of European society, the Anabaptists, the Levellers and Diggers, who alone looked forward to a society ordered by divine justice. The socialist writers of the nineteenth century, however, though varied in methods and aims, envisaged labor in the role of a Messiah, whose coming would presage the millennium. With this in mind they set about tracing the architecture of the New Jerusalem in their blueprints of a new society.

Karl Marx was no exception. It is true that he had turned his wrath on the "Utopians" and had asserted the validity of his own scientific findings, but his tenets—the classless society, the withering away of the state, the belief in the eventual compatibility between man's needs and his abilities—these were likewise Utopian auguries which history has steadfastly refused to consummate.

In the 1890's these predictions were contested by non-Marxians as being inconsistent with human nature, but the Marxians countered this argument by asserting that the new society would change everything, even human nature. No such facile answer could be given to another question, however: how was socialism to account for the steady upswing of the capitalist economy which showed no signs of the "impending collapse" prophesied by the Marxians? Here lay a most serious dilemma: if capitalism did not rush from crisis to crisis, inevitably approaching its own destruction, then the Marxian premises would stand in grave need of reexamination. Should socialism adhere to its revolutionary principle of the total disruption of existing society, or should it modify its methods and work out an evolutionary solution? There was a still deeper problem. Should the working class persist in its allegation that history had chosen it to replace all other classes, or should it be content to stand beside the older classes which had built the Western world?

The intellectual eminence of Karl Marx was responsible for the fact that this great debate, more often than not, took the form of a critical discussion of his basic tenets. However, the real issues would be obscured were we to see in the development of socialist thought from 1890 to 1914 nothing more than an intellectual attempt to correct certain mistakes of the Marxian doctrine. The future of European society was involved and, if Marx was right, the future of mankind. The body of Marx's writings became the testing ground only because he had more deeply and more passionately than anyone else attempted to envisage this future and to spell it out for his fellow men.

Marx himself had invited controversy when he said, "Moi, je ne suis pas marxiste," and Engels had freely admitted that the Communist Manifesto had been colored by revolutionary hopes. History, acknowledged the latter, proved us in the wrong, and revealed our opinions of that day as an illusion. History went even further; not only did it destroy our former error, but also transformed the conditions under which the proletariat will have to battle. The fighting methods of 1848 are today [1895] obsolete in every respect.[117] But the followers of Marx paid scant heed to Engels' candid assessment of the situation. They maintained their conviction that the foundations of Marxian theory were indestructible, and that the economic interpretation of history, the doctrine of class struggle, and the concept of the surplus value were irrefutable. These three basic beliefs were all to come under heavy fire during the twenty-five years that concern us here.

When the academicians trained their guns on Marx, they were confronted with a barricade of amalgamated theories, facts, suppositions, and prophecies. After reading *Das Kapital,* Emile Durkheim commented, "What a lot of statistical data, of historical comparisons, of studies, would be indispensable to settle a single one of the innumerable questions it treats." [118] "The research," he adds ". . . was undertaken to establish the doctrine . . . far from the doctrine resulting from the research." It became clear that the arguments would have to be tested in order to learn whether the doctrine would hold.

The first dogma to come under attack was Marx's theory of surplus value. Marx asserted that the common substance of all commodities was labor, and that the general tendency of the capitalist system was to hold the value of labor toward the minimum limit in order to guarantee a maximum profit to the capitalist entrepreneur. This theory was exploded by a number of Austrian economists, notably by Böhm-Bawerk, who replaced the surplus value theory by the theory of marginal utility to which many English economists adhered, Jevons and Shaw, for example.

Another bastion in the Marxian line was opened to barrage when Pareto examined Marx's dictum that all history is the history of class struggle. Here the position was reversed. Pareto accepted Marx's thesis (he called it Marx's "one clear idea"),[119] but he refused to entertain his conclusion, that socialism in the fullness of time would end class antagonism. He maintained, on the contrary, that the proletariat was only fighting for its own cause. Eventually, he said, a new élite would emerge which would continue the class struggle just as the bourgeoisie was doing under the capitalistic system. With extraordinary perspicacity he predicted that in a collectivistic society conflicts were bound to arise between the different classes of workers, between intellectuals and nonintellectuals, between innovators and conservatives.[120]

We have taken note that Pareto's compatriot, Croce, had also come under the spell of Marx, but his orderly mind was quick to disperse the Utopian fog that swirled around the analysis of the industrial processes. He accepted the economic interpretation of history as a heuristic method whereby the maze of historical data might be illuminated, as a new procedure which complemented the older ones rather than supplanted them. Croce's contribution to Marxism was strictly theoretical, or, as one of his critics has said, "literary and intellectual." Max Weber's strictures likewise remained in the realm of historical scholarship.

Popular Marxism asserted that the economic infrastructure determines everything, including religion, and in his attempt to refute this claim, Weber undertook to trace the forces which had contributed to the qualitative formation and the quantitative expansion of capitalism.[121] It was not his aim to substitute a lopsided spiritualistic interpretation for a lopsided materialistic interpretation.[122] Few historical studies of this period have made a deeper impact on the thinking of the age. But Weber's efforts, like those of Durkheim, Croce, and Pareto, were directed to the intelligentsia who were interested in sociology rather than in socialism.[123] The masses and their leaders were little affected by the academic criticism of Marx.

To them he continued to be the compass which pointed them to their place in history.

Most of the Socialist leaders of the period 1890 to 1914 were well aware that revolutionary action, the immediate seizure of power, was out of question. Except for the Russian Revolution of 1905, the European scene was conspicuously lacking in revolutionary upheaval. This discrepancy between theory and practice, between the dream of a new social order and the drab reality of everyday life, created tensions that compelled the leaders of socialism to review the tenets of their belief. The result of their scrutiny was Revisionism.

Revisionism is generally considered to be a modification and a moderation of orthodox Marxism, but the movement proceeded from the left as well as from the right. The main feature of the intellectual position of socialism before 1914 was the acknowledgment of a need to reconsider its place in the light of the uninterrupted prosperity of the European countries.

As we have noticed, Marx's following was particularly thin in England. The British tradition of practical solutions for pressing problems was hostile to an all-embracing dogmatism. Logically British socialism moved farthest away from the Marxian prescriptions. No political party displaying the banner of socialism developed in England before 1906. Liberals and conservatives, concentrated on the advancement of democratic practices by enfranchising all except the poorest, but shied away from any direct interference in economic problems.

However, there had been a predisposition toward progressive political thinking, especially in the writings of Mill, which demanded open-mindedness in social questions. We are, said Mill as early as 1850, too ignorant, either of what individual agency in its best form or socialism in its best form can accomplish, to be qualified to decide which of the two will be the ultimate form of human society. Other exponents of advanced social thought, such as Kingsley, Henry George, and Hyndman, were likewise influential. The offspring of this intellectual fermentation was the founding of the Fabian Society, established in 1883 under the name of The Society for the New Life, with the avowed purpose of reconstructing society and securing the general welfare and happiness. Like so many socialist movements, this too had a solid middle-class background. Its core was composed of writers, artists, civil servants, bank clerks, and intelligent women whose consciences were moved by the discrepancy between the idleness of the Victorian leisure class and the drudgery to which the working class was condemned.[124]

The roster of the Fabian Society included the names of William Morris, George Bernard Shaw, H. G. Wells, Havelock Ellis, J. Ramsay MacDonald, Beatrice and Sidney Webb, and many lesser lights. As befitted the individualism of its illustrious members, it was a loose association, half debating society and half club, and was in no way a conspiratorial gathering. Its discussions were carried on in the bright light that Victorian society accorded even its dissenters. And they were quite conscious that socialism would have to wait; they chose for their hero Fabius Cunctator. "For the right moment you must wait, as Fabius did most patiently when warring against Hannibal . . . but when the time comes, you must strike hard." [125] It may be questioned whether the Fabians ever did strike hard, but no one would deny their influence.

At first this group dealt in the main with abstract generalizations, Land and Capital, Industry and Competition, the Individual and the State. They had the "invaluable habit of freely laughing" at themselves, of considering each other as equals, and they did not indulge in denouncing their opponents as enemies of the human race. They felt scant sympathy for the "Social Democratic Federation" which professed an unqualified belief in every dogma uttered by or attributed to Marx. "By 1886," says G. B. Shaw, "we had already found that we were of one mind as to the advisability of setting to work by the ordinary political methods." To them socialism did not mean the control of all industry by a centralized state, nor did it require a revolution; it could be brought about piecemeal, by vote and by progressive legislation. In other words, socialism could be built on the foundation of existing institutions. It was simply one more step which followed logically from the Industrial Revolution. It was inevitable, said Sidney Webb, that democracy should learn this lesson. Socialism would come in a democratic fashion, when it was acceptable to the majority of voters, and thus cause no dislocation in society. The recommendations of the Fabians were, therefore, couched in practical terms, and the group was, for the most part, content with correcting existing legislation rather than conjuring up dreams of a perfect society.[126]

The Fabians reserved for themselves the role of the general staff in relation to the great army of the industrial workers who had found organizational support in the trade unions. They admitted that they had, in the early days of the Fabian Society, been inclined to neglect the trade union movement, an omission rectified later by Sidney Webb's exhaustive study of trade unions.[127] Another omission, frankly confessed by the Fabians, concerned the cooperative movement. But these were minor mistakes which could be easily redressed because recognition of cooperatives and trade unions did not contradict their central thesis, that socialism would come peacefully and within the framework of democratic institutions. Sidney Webb developed his famous theory of penetration, by which he meant that the Fabians would find their place in Parliament and in the national and municipal councils, ready to take over should they receive a mandate from the people.

The history of the labor movement confirmed the wisdom of their strategy. The Fabians soon outdistanced the Marxians in the favor of the working class. They did not claim to be the voice of the English people nor even of the Socialist party. Public opinion in Great Britain was not slow to respond to Fabian ideas. The Local Government Act of 1894, the Workmen's Compensation Acts of 1897, were early fruits of their agitation. By the turn of the century Labour candidates began to score victories over competing Liberals and Tories. In 1906 twenty-nine members were elected to the House of Commons.[128]

Among the continental nations the problem of democratic socialism was presented in a different manner. In France it had merged easily with the revolutionary tradition of 1792. However, the French socialists had before their eyes the memento of the bloody holocaust of the Commune, which was no invitation to direct action. The more radical-minded set their hopes on the syndicates. We will speak of them when we discuss Georges Sorel. A group of independent Socialists realized that reform and not revolution would carry the day, and the Dreyfus affair worked as a catalyst, drawing radicals, republicans, and Socialists together against monarchists, nationalists, and anti-Semites. Waldeck-Rousseau set up a cabinet for the defense of the republic in which he offered a post to one of the Socialist leaders, Millerand, who accepted it and in 1899 became the first Socialist since Louis Blanc to hold such a position. In defense of his action he said, "It is not only the right but the imperative duty of social democracy in France to adapt its methods to the condition of the political regime in which it moves. . . . Let us then have the courage . . . to call ourselves by our name, 'reformists,' since reformists we are." [129] One might say that from the point of view of the Third Republic the socialist movement had become house-broken. Viviani, Briand, and many others marched through the breach that Millerand had opened.

The situation in Germany was essentially different. The German Empire was based on an alliance between the agrarian aristocracy and the bourgeoisie, with the bourgeoisie in the role of a junior partner. The working class had not been a contributing factor to Bismarck's Reich. After the Chancellor's brief flirtation with Lassalle, he had to face the unflinching opposition of the social-democratic party, which made full use of the universal manhood suffrage that Bismarck himself had adopted by 1867. The leaders of the party, Bebel and the older Liebknecht, were orthodox Marxists, and in 1875 the party drew up the Gotha program which called for the establishment of a socialist society. Two years later the party became the fourth strongest group in the Reichstag. Bismarck's anti-Socialist laws failed to curb its advances, just as the system of social security, introduced in 1881, left the working class unimpressed.[130] Neither repression nor paternalism seemed able to stem the Socialist tide.

It was from the rank and file of the German Social Democratic party that the most penetrating criticism of orthodox Marxism was raised. Its author, Eduard Bernstein, remained a professed Socialist to his death, but he did not shy away from a constructive scrutiny of Marx which he thought had become imperative. Bernstein was born in Berlin, of a poor Jewish family "blessed" with fifteen children. He made his livelihood as a bank clerk until 1878, when he left for Switzerland. From then on he worked as a journalist, first in Zurich and later in London where he was in close contact with the aging Engels. This association did not, however, prevent him from studying closely the *Fabian Essays on Socialism* or from discussing mutual problems with leaders of the British labor movement. He was deeply impressed with British methods, and after much soul-searching he decided to find out for himself where Marx had been right and where he had been wrong.[131] The fruit of this investigation was his book, *Die Voraussetzungen des Sozialismus und die Aufgaben der Sozialdemokratie,* published in 1899 and known in English as *Evolutionary Socialism.*[132] When Bernstein returned to his native Germany in 1901, he realized, to his chagrin, that he had become the storm center of a bitter controversy. His book was the revisionists' bible and a target for all those who clung to the idea of a revolutionary uprising.

Bernstein was not a systematic thinker. His criticism came from an unfailing intellectual honesty. How could anyone, he asked, escape the conclusion that Marx's prediction about the future of capitalism had been proved wrong? "Peasants do not sink, the middle class does not disappear, crises do not grow ever larger: misery and serfdom do not increase." [133] Each of these observations flatly contradicted a favorite notion of Marx, and Bernstein could support each with facts and figures. The workers, he maintained, not only grow in numbers, but in economic, ethical, and political ability as well, and thus become one of the governing factors in state and national economy. It is important to note that Bernstein says *one* factor and not *the* factor.[134] He discarded the idea of the dictatorship of the proletariat as "barbaric" and replaced it by the conviction of the slow but inevitable advent of a Socialist society.[135] No one, he continues, has any idea of destroying bourgeois society as a civilized, orderly, social system. On the contrary, social democracy does not wish to dissolve this society and to make proletarians of all its members. Rather, it labors incessantly at lifting the worker from the social position of a proletarian to that of a "bourgeois" thus making the bourgeoisie universal.[136] Consequently, argued Bernstein, the Social Democratic party did not aim at the complete and exclusive domination of the state; it was willing to enter into alliances and to compromise. This was a far cry from Marx. Bernstein declared the theory that a general strike could force capitalism to its knees to be arrant nonsense. For him, socialism was the legitimate heir of the great liberal movements and would inevitably triumph by democratic means.[137]

The effect of Bernstein's critique was considerable. This was due,

I think, less to his theoretical intrepidity than to the fact that even his opponents acknowledged the necessity of readjusting their general frame of reference. Bernstein's honesty had simply exposed an untenable position. Not everyone, however, was willing to admit the facts. The pope of Marxism, Karl Kautsky, saw in Bernstein an apostate who had forsaken the true belief for the British heresy of gradualism. Left wingers, like Rosa Luxemburg and Hilferding, were dismayed at the blight that Bernstein's thought was spreading over the revolutionary determination of the proletarians. On the other hand, party leaders who had risen from the trade union movement looked askance at whatever traces of revolutionary thinking might still be found in Bernstein, and condemned him with being out of touch with the masses.[138] Such criticism, of course, implied that the masses didn't give a fig about the final triumph of socialism and were interested only in the palpable results which accrued to them in their everyday economic struggle. We shall see that Lenin made use of the same argument for his own purposes.

Bernstein's revisionism entered the solid block of the German Social Democratic party like a wedge. Although his theories were officially denounced as an "accommodation to the existing order," they were instrumental in bringing about the final split in the party which occurred during World War. I.[139] It is not our task to trace the great schism from the level of ideology to the final institutional division.

On the plane of ideas there are still two other "mutations" of orthodox Marxism to consider, both as different from Bernstein's evolutionary socialism as surgical operations are from homeopathic cures. We refer to the encyclicals of Lenin and Sorel. Obviously Lenin's contribution to the momentous question was no academic exercise. He was concerned with problems of party strategy and party tactics first and foremost. Yet in tackling in the boldest fashion one of the basic questions that troubled socialism in the prewar period he made an indelible mark on socialist thought.

We have seen that all the thinkers who concerned themselves with the future of the working class were disturbed by the relationship between political action directed toward the Socialist Utopia and the economic immediacy of the day-to-day gains. In the English labor movement the two sides had become reconciled at an early date. In Germany and Austria a stalemate developed; the party pinned its hopes on the suicide of the ruling class and the consequent assumption of authority by the workers.

It was clear that the problem was essentially different in Russia. This country had entered the Industrial Revolution several decades later than England, France, or Germany.[140] Thus the dilemma of revolutionary socialism showed another face. Whereas Bernstein had been obliged to deal with a collapsing capitalism which failed to collapse, a disappearing middle class which did not disappear, and economic crises which did not go from bad to worse, the Russian revolutionary was confronted with a much greater enigma. The latter had to explain how revolutionary activities could be justified in a country that had not yet gone through all the stages of capitalistic development. Had not Marx himself said that no society could "clear by bold leaps, nor remove by legal enactments, the obstacles offered by the successive phases of its normal development."?[141] But Lenin's revolutionary temperament was not to be daunted by such scruples. He was, after all, a visionary thirsting to get his hands on reality. He wanted revolution; one might almost say that he wanted revolution for the sake of revolution—and he wanted it soon. How it could be achieved was the question.

For Lenin, the problem centered around the necessity to instill a revolutionary spirit in the working class. How could the masses be made "class conscious"? The relationship between party and trade union became the touchstone. Marx had defined the trade unions as "the schools of socialism"; through them the workers are educated to become Socialists by witnessing the daily struggle against capital.[142]

This dictum of Marx's was interpreted by Lenin in his own manner. Since trade unions were not legalized in Tzarist Russia until 1906, their existence was at best precarious, and their activities were restricted to local underground operations. In addition, the situation had been further impaired when the government in its effort to check the spread of the genuine trade-union movement had established trade unions which were organized and controlled by the police.[143]

Lenin's early exertions in the League for the Emancipation of the Working Class had brought him in touch with the struggling underground unions, but his exile to Siberia had changed his outlook. To be sure, he continued to emphasize the importance of unions in strikes, but he also recognized that "as capitalism grows and strikes become more frequent, strikes become inadequate. . . . It is no longer a single employer that confronts the worker in a particular factory, but the whole capitalist class." And it is then, he concludes, that "it becomes absolutely necessary to exert the joint efforts of the whole of the working class."

What Lenin meant by a "joint effort of the whole of the working class" was clarified in his controversy with the "Economists." There existed in the Russian Social Democratic party a group of men who believed that a raise in wages today was worth more than all the dreams of a Socialist society in the future. In 1899 a letter, called the Credo, was circulated which stated that the Russian proletariat was moving away from its hope of seizing political power; instead it would concentrate on peaceful reforms.[144] Lenin fought this deviation bitterly, and he made trade unionism the pivot of his critique.

Trade unions, he argued, were admissible as "schools of war" in which the worker learned to understand the evils of capitalism, but the party should not overemphasize their importance, since they could achieve only economic gains. Lenin's final answer to the economists is contained in his famous pamphlet "What Is to Be Done?"[145] He insisted that his opponents were only deceiving themselves if they thought they could limit the fight of the working class to economic goals. The struggle was political; its aims were the abolition of a social system which compelled the poor to sell themselves to the rich.[146] Obviously a bouleversement on such a scale could not be expected from peaceful reforms. Lenin did not oppose trade unions, nor did he belittle their importance, but he knew that by themselves they could never develop a political consciousness, which was a *sine qua non* for the overthrow of the existing order. Lenin asserted that a social democratic consciousness among the workers was as yet nonexistent, and could only be brought to them from without.[147] The creation of such a consciousness had been the work of Marx and Engels, and intellectuals would continue to be the leaders of the working class. Anyone who thought that the labor movement "pure and simple" would achieve consciousness spontaneously was profoundly mistaken. A spontaneous response, said Lenin, would do no more than bring the workers a petty bourgeois ideology. The political struggle was more extensive and more complex than the economic fight. The trade union organization should be as broad and as public as possible. The political organization, on the other hand, which aimed at revolution, must be small and secret. "A dozen experienced revolutionists no less professionally trained than the police, will concentrate all the secret side of the work in their hands—prepare leaflets, work out approximate plans and appoint bodies of leaders for each town district, for each factory district, and for all educational institutions." [148] A new Archimedes, Lenin said, Give us an organization of revolutionists and we shall overturn the whole of Russia.[149]

Secrecy was a very important element in this conspiratorial organization, second only to the question of membership. Leadership, selectivity, and secrecy were to be imposed on the labor movement from without by the revolutionary intelligentsia, a self-appointed élite who knew what the proletarian struggle was about, who were the guardians of the socialist dogma and its authentic interpreters. That democratic considerations were thrown to the winds can surprise no one. Lenin wanted the Russian Revolution to take place during his own lifetime, and he thought he had found the means to hasten its coming. It disturbed him but little that his device implied contempt for the masses who, if left to themselves, could not be counted on to find the straight and narrow gate to their emancipation. Nor was he perturbed by the flagrant contradictions between Marxian determinism and his own voluntarism. The hard core of "professional revolutionaries" that developed in the Bolshevik and eventually in the Communist party would exercise the dictatorship of the proletariat. He recognized that the time for the onslaught had to be right, as it was in 1917, when, according to Lenin, power was lying in the streets. All that was necessary was to stoop and gather it up. Thus one of the most important political institutions of the twentieth century was conceived during the ideological struggle which centered around the best method for conducting the Socialist movement. The Gordian knot—how could a revolution take place in a country lagging in capitalistic development—was cut by the fiat of Lenin's fierce determination.

In this manner the Marxian doctrine had acquired another contradiction, which the Russian Communists would explain as they saw fit. Lenin's voluntaristic addition could serve as an inspiration for the fanatics in their ranks, while economic determinism was useful in convincing the more reluctant of the inevitable triumph of the Socialist cause. It was not to be feared that such conflicting viewpoints might jeopardize the movement. As the greatest of all Communist heretics, Trotsky, put it, "The party in the last analysis is always right, because the party is the single historic instrument given to the proletariat for the solutions of its fundamental problems. . . . I know that one must not be right against the party. One can only be right with the party and through the party, for history has created no other road for the realization of what is right." [150]

No such certainty was to be derived from the work of Georges Sorel. It has been hailed by Fascist and Communist alike as one of the fountainheads of the monolytic state. But those who are acquainted with the many contradictions of Sorel will be reminded of Rilke's remark: "What is glory but the sum of misunderstandings gathered around a great name?"

Sorel was certainly not without responsibility for these misunderstandings; his life and his thoughts show a profound ambiguity.[151] A retired railroad engineer, he spent the latter part of his life in a continuous discussion of the future of European society. What brought this man, who to all appearances lived a thoroughly bourgeois life, to Marx and socialism was less a sympathy for the worker than a profound disgust for the democratic practices which he witnessed in the Third Republic. His writings overflow with invectives against the stupidity, the cowardice, and the inertia of the "politicians." His innermost preoccupation was with problems of ethics rather than with social reality, and it is as a moralist that he should be understood and judged.[152] Croce has called Sorel the only original thinker that socialism produced after Marx. This seems hyperbolic praise for one whose following was never great.

Sorel was not a systematic thinker. Deeply influenced by Henri Bergson and William James, he despised ready-made knowledge. He preferred to put before his readers "the working of a mental effort which is continually endeavoring to break through the bonds of what had been previously constructed for the common use, in

order to discover that which is truly personal and individual." [153]
The egotistic overtones in this statement will not be lost on the
reader.

Sorel's original quest was for freedom and grandeur. His disappointment with the bourgeois world resulted from his belief that
modern man is condemned to impotence. Man can overcome this
emasculation only by participating in a movement that promised
both fervor and glory. On the contemporary scene, the struggle of
the proletariat alone held out such promise.[154] Sorel identified democracy with mediocrity, as did Nietzsche. But unlike Nietzsche,
who hoped to overcome mediocrity by evoking a new type of higher
beings, Sorel thought that the syndicates of the labor movement
offered a source of social authority on which to build a moral regeneration. From such considerations emanated his famous work,
Reflections on Violence.

In his introduction, a letter to Daniel Halévy, Sorel confesses
himself to be a pessimist. Pessimism, he says, is a philosophy of conduct rather than a theory of the world.[155] It assures man of his "will
to deliverance," which for the courageous is sufficient to preserve
his ardor. What Sorel meant by pessimism was the determination
to remain untempted by bourgeois slogans such as "progress" and
"the triumph of reason." Whereas the politicians condemned the use
of violence a priori as a barbaric relic, Sorel set out to investigate
"the functions of violence in actual social conditions." [156]

Sorel was a Marxist in so far as he accepted socialism as the
philosophy of history in regard to contemporary institutions. But,
like Lenin, he replaced Hegelian determinism by voluntarism and
activism. The class war offered to him those elements of "revolutionary and direct method" by which the proletariat would eventually impose its will on middle-class cowardice.[157]

He brushes aside the hope for a democratic triumph of socialism,
because "this dictatorship of incapacity" would soon become as stupid as the whole middle class.[158] Proletarian violence, on the other
hand, not only makes the future revolution certain; it is also the
only means by which the European nations can recover their former
energy.[159] Sorel does not wish his plea for violence to be confused
with the bloodshed of the bourgeois "terreur." For him the whole
of the Socialist drama will be concentrated in the final act of the

general strike. In order to do justice to Sorel's concept of the general strike, one must remember the atmosphere of the world before 1914. A large sector of the Socialist leadership considered the general strike as "general nonsense." Sorel was less concerned with the question of whether the Socialist battle would be won by a single stroke or by a number of successive engagements; he tried to establish a new proletarian belief at the center of which was the idea of the general strike.

We now approach Sorel's famous concept of the myth. "The myth," he says, "is a body of images capable of evoking instinctively all the sentiments which correspond to the various manifestations of the war undertaken by socialism . . . strikes have engendered in the proletariat the noblest, deepest and most moving sentiments that they possess." [160] The myth must be taken as an individual whole; it cannot be analyzed or refuted. "People who are living in this world of myths are secure from all refutation." [161] Whereas Lenin had emphasized the necessity of an intelligentsia at the service of socialism, Sorel expected the intellectuals to disappear in the maelstrom of the revolution together with other "fashionable people." His position is arational and antirational at the same time and has been well defined as "sociological mysticism." [162]

Hostile as he was to all middle-class concepts, he also held that science—the science of the nineteenth century—was little more than a bourgeois prejudice. "For the middle class, science is a mill which produces solutions to all the problems with which we are faced." But for Sorel science was only a recipe to procure certain advantages. He asserted that the revolution would come not from the politicians nor from the intellectuals, but from the syndicates, and that it would take the form of the general strike. "It awakens in the depth of the soul a sentiment proportionate to the conditions of a gigantic struggle." [163] "It will place the forces of production in the hands of free man, i.e., of men who will be capable of running the workshop created by capitalism without any need of masters." Thus once more ethical preoccupation supersedes economic or political thinking. Under what conditions, asks Sorel, is regeneration possible? Do there exist among the workmen forces capable of producing enthusiasm? His answer defies logical scrutiny: "There is only one force which can produce today that enthusiasm without whose cooperation no morality is possible, and that is the force resulting from the propaganda in favor of a general strike." It produces an epic state of mind conducive to a new ethic; the ethic of the producers. "It is to violence that socialism owes those high ethical values by means of which it brings salvation to the world." [164]

An evaluation of Sorel's contribution to socialism is a difficult enterprise, and not only because he abandoned his own syndicalist affiliation early to enter a tenuous alliance with the French Royalist movement, but also because the true effect of his work is hard to gauge. It is easy to point to his mistakes. The general strike has never fulfilled the hopes that Sorel pinned on it. It was not tried in 1914 when it might have halted the war machines. The only time when a general strike was called to challenge a capitalist economy, that is, in Great Britain in 1926, it proved a failure. Nor did the myth of the general strike set the proletarian imagination on fire. When violence came to Europe in 1914, it was not of the kind that Sorel had envisaged. In 1908 he predicted that only two accidents would have the power to halt political socialism: a great foreign war or a great expansion of proletarian violence.[165] The Bolshevik triumph was the fruit of both, but it was far removed from the moral regeneration that Sorel had expected. If one adds to these considerations his verbose and often confused argumentation, one must feel obliged to ask what foundation there may be for his extraordinary reputation.

In the first place, the very title of his book shocked the prewar European. Secondly, his idea of the myth as a social force was a new and compelling thought. Ironically enough, the idea of the myth became a weapon which could be used against the proletarians as well as by them. Sorel's irrationalism blended with Fascist and Communist ideology alike. In his later years he hailed Lenin as he had prophesied Mussolini's rise to power in 1912.[166] However, neither of these men was his disciple, and it would be erroneous to credit Sorel with their achievements or blame him for their misdeeds. It would seem that Sorel, like Nietzsche, whom he admired and to whom he bears a resemblance, was an excellent observer, a perspicacious analyst of the forces of social unrest that were brewing in the European cauldron. And like Nietzsche, Sorel failed signally in his hopes for the future. Both men declared their contempt for the intellectuals, yet both were guilty of the most objectionable habit of that group, namely, experimentation with ideas regardless of their social consequences.

Nietzsche's ideas of superman and superrace fell into the hands of the Nazi gangsters. Sorel's myth might seem harmless as a topic of conversation in cafés and parlors, but after the theorist had explained his ideas of violence, the practitioners took over, the chauvinists, the Jew-baiters, the black knights of Mussolini's street fighters and the malign passions of Hitler's S.S. They had no need to be told that violence was permissible; they practiced it with delight. To be sure, Sorel had never said that violence should be used for its own sake, but it makes small difference to the half-educated or the uneducated that they are unable to comprehend their masters and prophets. Had Sorel been a dispassionate observer of the contemporary scene, he would not have cloaked his ideas in so controversial a vernacular, but he was passionate, contemptuous, eager to criticize and even to destroy a society to which, malgré lui, he belonged.[167] He demolished positions only to replace them with irrational tenets which, as he said, could not be refuted. This was exactly what the mob-intellectuals like Rosenberg and Goebbels were looking for. It is debatable whether a man is responsible for the misunderstandings provoked by his teachings, but in Sorel's case, as in Nietzsche's, the culpability cannot be denied. Sorel was, however, a symptom of disintegration rather than its cause. He, too, sowed the wind and was perplexed at the end of his life that he must reap the whirlwind.

The results of this rapid survey are indicative of the roads over which European society was to move forward. When the great crisis of our civilization burst into the open, the forces of national cohesion proved to be much stronger than those of international solidarity. In every country the working class fought the war shoulder to shoulder with the bourgeoisie; their leaders voted the war budgets and were easily contaminated by the nationalistic furor that swept the European scene. Only in Russia, where the bourgeoisie was less deeply rooted, did socialism succeed in erecting over the ruins of the old regime the foundations of a society conceived in Marxian terms. In Germany and Austria, Bernstein's revisionism paved the way for the coalition governments of the postwar period. All European countries went ahead with enlarging the democratic bases of the nation-state, either by extending universal manhood suffrage or by granting suffrage to men and women alike. "Industrial democracy," advocated by the Webbs, became the characteristic trait of most of the countries of Europe proper. The prophecies of Marx were not fulfilled, and even less were those of Sorel, who ultimately was only a sport in the Socialist movement.

CHAPTER IX

Conclusion

The historian has sometimes been called a prophet in retrospect. Surveying the past from the vantage point of the present, he may indeed find little difficulty in fitting together the scattered pieces of his puzzle in such a form that they give a rational picture of time past and time present. Is this, however, the end of his task? He tells us what happened, even why it happened, but if asked for the underlying significance of events, the historian who is only a "prophet in retrospect" will be unable or unwilling to answer.

Without doubt, the historian who searches for meaning in history is conditioned by his own position in space and time. His efforts to ascertain the sense of past events will include value-judgments. The closer the event, the truer this becomes. But the historian should not be intimidated by these considerations. If his search for the meaning of historical events leads him beyond the confines of objective evidence, he must accept the challenge, unless he is content to be a mere chronicler in the Crocean sense.

I do not imply that the historian has a passkey to history, or that his judgment should be guided by his own hopes or fears. I mean only that, speaking for myself, I have tried to ascertain the significance of the events forming the background of this book by taking into consideration the implications that were present, albeit obscured, in the cultural history of the period.

From this perspective, what was the meaning of the great change that came over the world in 1914? Obviously the war was more than a diplomatic accident of gigantic proportions. No one can believe that the handful of old men who controlled Europe's foreign affairs were ultimately responsible for the holocaust, or that the mechanics of a superannuated alliance system dragged the Old World against its will into the war. Few of the leaders welcomed the conflict. Some, like Sir Edward Grey, had a foreboding of the darkness that was settling over the Continent. But the number of those who contemplated the dimensions the war might assume or had any idea of its length or its consequences was small.

If we review the interpretations of the war put forth while the conflict was still in progress, we meet likewise with an astonishing myopia. The nationalistic aims of France, Germany, Italy, or Russia, which were served up as justifications, may be passed over in silence. Some, like Bernard Shaw, maintained that the war was only another example of the struggle that had been carried on for so long under the balance-of-power system. And there were the idealists, like H. G. Wells and Woodrow Wilson, who proclaimed that this was the war to end international anarchy, a hope that was recognized as futile even while the war was raging. Finally, there was Lenin's interpretation of the war as the end-phase of imperialism which would open the gate to world revolution. This vision, too, was soon scorned by everyone who did not wear the blinkers of dialectic materialism.

Contemporary historians, like Hajo Holborn, have maintained that the First World War initiated the political collapse of Europe which the Second World War consummated. In our perspective, it would seem that the First World War did something more and something less than usher in the political collapse of Europe. Stated positively, it generated an awareness of the global interdependence of all countries and all nations. Lest this be construed as a voice for One World, let me add that no such hopes are implied by recognizing that World War I demolished some of the barriers which have, in the past, separated one civilization from another.

From inside Europe the war looked like collective suicide; from outside it took on a different aspect. Like many that preceded it, this war was "an express train of history." It speeded up developments already envisaged by prewar writers. Europe's triumph over the world had been, as we stated earlier, the result of an ecumenic civilization. Nineteenth century Europe continued to believe that the fruits of such a civilization would remain the privilege of Western man. His political and economic position before 1914 was indeed unique, but ultimately untenable.

Positions of power, however, are not lightly surrendered. The

First World War exposed the inherent contradiction in the European situation. By an ironic dialectic, it encouraged the non-European to adopt the ideals which Europe had for many years claimed as her own, but which she seemed to have forsaken during the carnage. Dostoevski prophesied that "we arrive all or none," and had proclaimed the coming of a pan-human consciousness. It is my belief that the twentieth century is on the way to an acknowledgment of pan-humanism as one of its important commitments.

The term "pan-humanism" stands in need of clarification. It is both a fact and an assignment still to be realized. It implies a recognition of universal interdependence, and it is by no means limited to the fields of politics or economics. In the arts, Malraux has described its significance in the phrase, "museum without walls." It can be noted in religion, in philosophy, literature, anthropology, and last but not least, in history. Those who assert that in a world torn by strife and global competition there seems little room for pan-human consciousness, must still admit that it is already used as a potent weapon for propaganda. Even where it is employed only as an ideological decoy to conceal the struggle for power, it bespeaks a new stage of global awareness.

The European preeminence that drew to a close in 1914 prepared the world for this new consciousness; herein lies the greatness and the tragedy of this phase of European history. To give it birth, the shell that had enclosed nineteenth century European civilization had to be shattered. It was in this perspective that the war of 1914 became a World War.

Let us summarize briefly the contributions to this process made by philosophers, scientists, and artists. First, there were the efforts of those who wanted to understand the world exclusively in terms of immanence or, as we might also say, in materialistic terms. From Marx to Darwin, from Nietzsche to Freud, man had been deprived of his claim to appraise human existence in terms of values. The new vistas did not replace the old transcendental ones outright, nor did they necessarily make them obsolete. But they did create tensions that ranged all the way from nature to history and from society to the individual. The Europeans who were exposed to these ideas became involved in conflicting arguments and antinomic motivations which deprived them of the naïve confidence that had once guided their lives. As a result, the belief in European superiority was gradually impaired in religion, in race, and in culture.

The human personality had not been spared in this process of reevaluation, or devaluation. This great force, which since the days of the Renaissance and the Reformation, had supplied so many of the creative impulses by which European civilization had advanced, seemed now reduced to a shadow of its former self. Remote indeed were the days when Locke and Adam Smith had seen in the competitive power of the individual a fertile source for harmonic progress. Even the individualism of Goethe, the ideal of personal fulfillment, seemed no longer achievable in the societal setting of an industrial age. All that was left was the esthetic individualism which replaced the categorical imperative of Kant by an esthetic imperative. But the esthetic attitude was reserved for "the happy few," for the privileged members of the bourgeoisie. It would have been ludicrous to recommend it to the working class. Moreover, it left a large part of human existence unfulfilled; it did not quench the longing to be a sharer in the human community. In this way, it led some leaders, such as George, d'Annunzio, and Barrès, to embrace nationalism as a remedy for loneliness and isolation.

As we have seen, the idea of the free and self-determining national community appeared on the European scene at the same time that political individualism scored its first great triumphs in 1789. However, at the end of the nineteenth century the national community, with its ideological corollary, nationalism, had all but overpowered individualism.

By and large, it may be said that in 1914 the Europeans considered the nation-state to be the highest and most desirable form of communal living. Consequently it should command the greatest sacrifices. And the war surpassed all expectations as to the sacrifices that could be demanded. Of course, competition and strife between political communities were nothing new. They had existed in all times and had often led to merciless action. But the scale on which the Europeans were fighting from 1914 to 1918 was novel. Whereas populations had been enslaved and cities erased during the period of antiquity and in the Middle Ages, it was now the fate of an entire civilization that lay in the balance. The ferocity with which the Europeans threw themselves into the struggle, the fact that peace by compromise was ruled out, seems to prove the point.

But while Europe bled white, the majority of non-Europeans looked on. Realizing that the power of Western man was crumbling as a result of his own acts, they nevertheless did not hesitate to take into their own hands the tools of his fate: industrialism for one, nationalism for another. Here, then, is the legacy that Europe bequeathed to the world at the very moment when the days of her supremacy were numbered. From the disintegration of colonial empires in Asia and Africa (begun in 1914), an amazing array of nationalities has arisen, each claiming the right of self-determination. Even the Russian Revolution, marching behind the shield of international solidarity, has drawn its real strength from national forces and from the desire of its leaders to make Russia the most powerful nation. Hence, it may be argued that the world took up Europe's battle. If history is, as Hegel says, the progress in the consciousness of liberty, a new phase of this development began in 1914. If Europe was forced to relinquish her eminence, it was by means of weapons forged in her own arsenal, and the white man may derive what comfort he can from such reflections.

The change in class and society that came after 1914 is not limited to the Western world, but few would deny that it originated here. The battlefields of the Great War produced a democracy of death, and from it the survivors should have learned a single lesson: the democracy of the living. But they were slow to see the light. The war brought dynastic rule to an end in the four great Eastern empires: Russia, Austria, Germany, and Turkey. In turn, the removal of dynasties brought about the elimination of feudal remnants in central and eastern Europe, although the liquidation of the landholding class and its influence on the government was, in some instances, delayed until 1945.

Wherever dynastic rule was preserved, it was stripped of its quasi-religious splendor, of the belief in the magic qualities inherent in royal blood, a relic of medievalism. In general, one might say that the old horizontal order of society gave way to a vertical structure. A hierarchy of talent and work replaced the old hierarchy of blood, property, and church membership. The integration of the working class into the body politic, well under way by 1914, was greatly speeded up by the war. In Western Europe the teachings of evolutionary socialism were adopted in large measure. In Russia the "fourth estate" took over and destroyed the older classes. But if we examine the picture a little more closely, we must admit that the shaping of society was not determined by one theory or another, nor by the dynamics of the masses themselves, but by the process of rationalization in its multifaceted aspects. In this respect Max Weber has proved most clairvoyant.

Weber's formula, "the disenchantment of the world," would, however, seem too simple to describe the complicated process of rationalization. The rationalism of the twentieth century bears little resemblance to that of the Enlightenment. It knows its own limitations; it knows that man is only partially susceptible to rational analysis. It is, therefore, much less confident of its potentialities.

In the realm of history and of sociology Western man has lost the feeling of superiority, the narcissistic concern with Europe. As other civilizations came within the range of his curiosity, he admitted, not without regret, to historicism and relativism. The impact of these theories, esoteric as they were, on the masses may have been negligible, but it did influence the outlook of the European intelligentsia, and contributed in large measure to the new awareness of which I have spoken.

The natural sciences, on the other hand, found themselves in their spectacular advances confronted with revolutionary aspects of the universe which resisted a unifying explanation. The world of science, which had for so long inspired the European claim to superiority, was without a common bond. Where once a great cognitive effort had spread out fanwise, there were now only divergent labors lacking a common philosophical foundation. The antimetaphysical attitude of Marx and Darwin found its consummation in Weber, Dilthey, and Freud, and the countercurrents of Bergson and Croce were not strong enough to turn the tide. By 1914 an impasse had been reached which had important consequences. Since man cannot long survive in an atmosphere of general skepticism, the European turned to other sources for justification. If science could no longer furnish the support needed, and if religion had lost its unifying power, there seemed nothing to do but look for an ersatz solution. Of such, Europe produced a large supply after 1914. The manufacturers of myths had a field day; state, class, race, and sex were set up on the altars to which man brought the sacrifice of his intellect and often of his conscience.

Strangely enough, the process of rationalization was not thereby deprived of its momentum. The impact of technology on European life continued. Throughout the nineteenth century there had been an expansion of the practical intellect at the expense of creativity and moral consciousness which had produced an undisciplined monster groping blindly in all directions. Premonitions of this state of affairs can be noted in Kierkegaard, Baudelaire, Burckhardt, and Bergson, but it was left for the Great War to drive the lesson home.

Obviously the war itself was an irrational happening which seemed to refute all the claims of the rationalists. Nevertheless, it was conducted by the most advanced technology: poison gas, airplanes, tanks, submarines. An irrational undertaking was carried out by rational means. The war was ultimately decided by the industrial potential of the United States. We have seen Lenin's grasp of the lessons to be drawn from scientific management, and his advocacy of their application in the new Soviet society. If I may be forgiven an overstatement, I would say that he and his successor followed Taylor's advice in their deliberate effort to industrialize Russia.

We are led logically into another aspect of the problem of rationalization and its impact on the European scene. To what extent did Europe try to rebuild society according to rational principles? Here we must depend on the answer to a second question. Does Russia belong to Europe, to the West? Only in Russia was society reconstructed according to preconceived notions and blueprints. Lenin erased the old society and erected a new one. It has often been said that in doing so he turned Russia's face away from the West. Yet the inspiration for this experiment came from Karl Marx and his belief that the age of social justice was about to begin. That this appeal has inflamed the imagination of millions of non-Europeans is, therefore, one more triumph of the European mind. One is inclined to think that Khrushchev is closer to Western leaders than to Ivan the Terrible.

In the meantime, the West followed its old habit of counterbalancing revolutionary principles by evoking traditions and customs heavily weighted with emotional appeal. In other words, the progress of rationalism was not unconditional. The institutions with which Europe emerged from the First World War were substantially the same as those by which the Old World had lived before the cataclysm. This fact in itself should caution us against too far-reaching an interpretation of the effects that the war had on Europe. However, there can be no hesitation in asserting that Europe had lost her supremacy. Her own self-confidence was shaken and the world had learned that the principles on which the European position rested could be emulated without great difficulty.

The consequences of Europe's deposition were not well understood by the Europeans; it took the Second World War to make the meaning of the first apparent. However, the joint result has been the advent of a new consciousness, though its manifestations may be dim, confused, misguided, and often contradictory. Submerged as we are in the day-to-day struggle between two competing ideologies and systems of power, we often fail to see the similarity between the leading figures of the twentieth century, regardless of the camp to which they belong. I feel certain that future historians will, however, discern this resemblance. Such an assertion returns us to our original thesis: that the meaning of the First World War lies in the destruction of European supremacy and the consequent dawn of an era of global awareness and interdependence.

It would be folly to pretend that the whole of European culture before 1914 had pointed toward such a transformation. There were broad strata that were not at all affected by the schismatic trends we have found it necessary to stress. In the novel, the drama, the opera, there is much that should warn us against hasty generalizations. The names of Arnold Bennett, Yeats, Puccini, Chekov, come to mind. There is always more in any given era that a schematically constructed Zeitgeist is able to account for. I neither wish to belittle the importance of these men, nor do I claim that the picture of European culture given in these pages is all-encompassing. Yet the conclusion remains that the European mind had reached a deadlock, that its most representative productions had become schizophrenic and self-contradictory.

Such an observation should not, however, lead us to adopt catchwords like "decline of the West." The decline of the West became a certainty only in the fields of politics and economics. In the realm of culture the seeds sown by Western man have survived. There was in 1914 no other literature, no other art, science, or philosophy that was comparable to the European production in those fields. And when the world adopted Europe's legacy it naturally fell under its spell and continued to interpret human existence in terms derived from Darwin and Marx, from Nietzsche and Freud, from Einstein and Planck.

That the "world of yesterday" in its particular form was destined to vanish was a foregone conclusion. Europe has never tried to fossilize its own creations; it has always allowed new impulses to assert themselves. That these impulses in 1914 broke through barriers and frontiers which had until then checked their force, would seem preordained.

Historical consciousness, as the West developed it, implies the knowledge that all forms and structures built by the human mind are finite and destined to be superseded. Yet this same resignation to which modern man is constrained assures him of an asset of which he cannot be deprived, his spiritual self-determination. Einstein said once that the most incomprehensible thing about the universe was the fact that it is comprehensible. In regard to man, one is tempted to rephrase this comment by saying that the most incomprehensible thing about him is his determination to comprehend himself. Born with the sickness unto death, victim of folly and pride, he maintains the single distinction to dare fate by his thought.

Of such daring there is ample evidence in the period that has occupied our minds. To many, the age that preceded the First World War is remote and clouded. For some it was a fool's paradise maintained by prejudice and self-indulgence. For others it was an Eden of security. Neither interpretation does justice to its particular importance at the threshold of a new era. The words "progress" and "decline" have meaning only for those who belong to a given society, to a given civilization. The transformation of European culture which took place between 1890 and 1914 makes it apparent that historical developments do not lose their significance once we realize that mankind does not move upward, but onward.

Notes

CHAPTER I: THE STRESS OF TRIUMPH

1. Arnold Toynbee, *The World and the West* (New York, 1953), p. v.
2. Leopold von Ranke, *Sämtliche Werke* (Leipzig, 1899), XXXXIII, XXXXIV, 518. See also Gerhard Masur, *Ranke's Begriff der Weltgeschichte* (München, 1926), p. 72.
3. H. Plessner, *Das Schicksal des deutschen Geistes in seiner spätbürgerlichen Epoche* (Zürich, 1935), p. 14.
4. *Ibid.,* p. 72; Hajo Holborn, *The Political Collapse of Europe* (New York, 1951).
5. A. J. P. Taylor, *The Struggle for Mastery in Europe 1848–1918* (New York, 1955), pp. 201–227.
6. Otto Hintze, *Gesammelte Abhandlungen* (Leipzig, 1941), I, 133.
7. Barbara Ward, "Asia's Need and Western Policy," *Atlantic Monthly,* February, 1956, p. 45.
8. Gerhard Masur, *Friedrich Julius Stahl* (Berlin, 1930), p. 207.
9. W. Hallgarten, *Vorkriegsimperialismus* (Paris, 1935), p. 298.
10. Louis L. Snyder, *The Meaning of Nationalism* (Rutgers University Press, 1955); Boyd C. Shafer, *Nationalism* (New York, 1955).
11. Carlton J. H. Hayes, *Essays on Nationalism* (New York, 1926), p. 26; Carlton J. H. Hayes, *The Historical Evolution of Modern Nationalism* (New York, 1931).
12. Hayes, *Essays on Nationalism,* p. 6; see also Hans Kohn, *The Idea of Nationalism* (New York, 1944), and Hans Kohn, *Nationalism: Its Meaning and History* (New York, 1957).
13. L. Gottschalk and D. Lach, *Europe and the Modern World* (Chicago, 1955), II, 11.
14. A. Fischel, *Der Panslavismus bis zum Weltkrieg* (Stuttgart, 1919); Hans Kohn, *Panslavism* (Notre Dame Press, 1953).
15. *Ibid.,* p. 491.
16. M. J. Bonn, *The Crumbling of Empire* (London, 1938), p. 128.

17. Hayes, *Essays on Nationalism,* p. 258.

18. *Nationalism,* The Royal Institute of International Affairs (London, 1939), pp. 170 ff.; A. Cobban, *National Self-Determination* (London, 1945).

19. A. Vagt, *A History of Militarism* (London, 1938), p. 11; H. Fick, *Der deutsche Militarismus der Vorkriegszeit* (Potsdam, 1932); R. Girardet, *La Société militaire dans la France contemporaine* (Paris, 1953); Gordon A. Craig, *The Politics of the Prussian Army* (Oxford, 1955); Hans Rosenberg, *Bureaucracy, Aristocracy and Autocracy* (Cambridge, Mass., 1958).

20. Hans Kohn, *The Twentieth Century* (New York, 1951), p. 5.

21. Vagt, *op. cit.,* p. 11.

22. Gerhard Ritter, *Staatskunst und Kriegshandwerk* (München, 1954), I; R. Stadelmann, *Moltke und der Staat* (Krefeld, 1950), p. 369.

23. Girardet, *op. cit., passim;* Vagt, *op. cit.,* p. 230.

24. Girardet, *op. cit.,* p. 209.

25. See the figures given by Vagt, *op. cit.,* p. 362.

26. Girardet, *op. cit.,* p. 196.

27. Vagt, *op. cit.,* p. 13

28. J. Schumpeter, *The Sociology of Imperialism* (New York, 1955), p. 92.

29. Werner Sombart, *Der Moderne Kapitalismus* (München und Leipzig, 1928), III, 1–2; F. Nussbaum, *A History of the Economic Institutions of Europe* (New York, 1933).

30. Nussbaum, *op. cit.,* p. 259.

31. Schumpeter, *op. cit.,* p. 66; W. Sombart, *Der Bourgeois* (München, 1913), pp. 194, 217, 259.

32. Schumpeter, *op. cit.,* p. 67.

33. J. Schumpeter, *Business-cycles* (New York, 1939), 2 vols.

34. Sombart, *Kapitalismus,* III, 690.

35. Nussbaum, *op. cit.,* p. 270.

36. Pierre Renouvin, *La Crise européenne et la grande guerre* (Paris, 1934), p. 41.

37. E. Kehr, *Schlachtflottenbau und Parteipolitik* (Berlin, 1930), pp. 385, 429.

38. Joachim Kühn, *Der Nationalismus im Leben der dritten Republik* (Berlin, 1920), p. 20.

39. Schumpeter, *Sociology of Imperialism,* p. 76.

40. J. A. Hobson, *Imperialism* (London, 1905).

41. Nussbaum, *op. cit.*, p. 335; H. Feis, *Europe, The World's Banker* (New Haven, 1930).

42. Th. Moon, *Imperialism and World Politics* (New York, 1926), pp. 26, 29; A. Grover Clark, *A Place in the Sun* (New York, 1936); M. Baumont, L'Essor industriel et l'impérialisme colonial (Paris, 1937); Hans Herzfeld, *Die Moderne Welt*, II (Braunschweig, 1960).

43. For the interpretation of imperialism, see the books by Hobson, Hallgarten, and Moon; also Hintze, *op. cit.*, p. 458; and more recently, John Strachey, *The End of Empire* (New York, 1960).

44. Nussbaum, *op. cit.*, p. 276.

45. Moon, *op. cit.*, p. 320.

46. Hallgarten, *op. cit.*, p. 168; Renouvin, *op. cit.*, p. 62.

47. Hobson, *op. cit.*, p. 205; F. Brie, *Imperialistische Strömungen in der englischen Literatur* (Halle, 1928); William Langer, *The Diplomacy of Imperialism* (New York, 1935), 2 vols., I, 82.

48. Moon, *op. cit.*, p. 197.

49. Langer, *op. cit.*, II, 797.

50. Hobson, *op. cit.*, p. 186.

51. Schumpeter, *Sociology of Imperialism*, p. 92.

52. L. Reiners, *The Lamps Went Out in Europe* (New York, 1955).

53. A. Camus, *The Rebel* (New York, 1954), p. 144.

54. For a good, though superficial, description of the European mood in 1914, see James Cameron, *1914* (New York, 1959).

55. Max Weber, *Gesammelte Aufsätze zur Religionsoziologie* (Tübingen, 1921), I, 252.

CHAPTER II: FOUNDING AND DESTROYING FATHERS

1. Albert Camus, *The Rebel* (New York, 1954), p. 58.

2. Quoted by Halvdan Koht, in *Goethe and the Modern Age,* The International Convocation at Aspen, Colorado (Chicago, 1949), p. 177.

3. Karl Jaspers, *Unsere Zukunft und Goethe* (Zürich, 1948), pp. 12–13.

4. Goethe, *Wilhelm Meisters Lehrjahre,* Jubiläumsausgabe (Stuttgart, 1920), p. 27.

5. *Goethes Gespräche* (Leipzig, 1909), February 26, 1824.

6. Barker Fairley, "Goethe, the Man and the Myth," in *Goethe and the Modern Age.*

7. See Gerhard Masur, *Goethe, La ley de su vida* (Bogota, 1939).

8. G. A. Borgese, "The Message of Goethe," in *Goethe and the Modern Age,* p. 12.

9. Erich Heller, *The Disinherited Mind* (Cambridge, 1952), pp. 11, 25.

10. Borgese, *op. cit.,* p. 11.

11. Goethe, *Noch ein Wort für junge Dichter,* Gesammelte Werke, XXXVIII, 325–326.

12. Arthur Schopenhauer, *Sämtliche Werke* (Leipzig, 1919), II, 3, English translation by R. H. Haldane. See also Georg Simmel, *Schopenhauer und Nietzsche* (München, 1920); Thomas Mann, *Schopenhauer* (Stockholm, 1938).

13. Schopenhauer, *op. cit.,* p. 5

14. *Ibid.,* pp. 134, 143. Simmel, *op. cit.,* p. 188.

15. Schopenhauer, *op. cit.,* pp. 195 ff.

16. *Ibid.,* p. 231.

17. *Ibid.,* p. 307.

18. *Ibid.,* p. 462. See also, E. Seillière, *Arthur Schopenhauer* (Berlin, 1912).

19. A. Baillot, *L'Influence de Schopenhauer en France* (Paris, 1927).

20. L. Lévy Bruhl, *The Philosophy of Auguste Comte* (London, 1903), p. 2. Of more recent vintage: F. S. Marvin, *Comte* (London, 1936); Jane M. Style, *Comte* (London, 1928).

21. Lévy Bruhl, *op. cit.,* p. 4

22. Auguste Comte, *Plan des travaux scientifiques nécessaires pour réorganizer la société, opuscules de philosophie sociale, 1819–1828* (Paris, 1883).

23. Charles Maurras, *L'Avenir de l'intelligence* (Paris, 1927), pp. 110–111.

24. Comte, *Cours de Philosophie Positive,* English translation by Harriet Martineau (London, 1913), 3 vols., I, 2.

25. *Ibid.*

26. André Cresson, *Comte* (Paris, 1947), p. 151.

27. J. S. Mill, *Auguste Comte and Positivism* (London, 1861), p. 8. Camus, *op. cit.,* p. 166.

28. Comte, *op. cit.,* I, 1–35.

29. *Ibid.,* p. 30

30. *Ibid.,* II, 138 ff., 182.

31. *Ibid.,* 281, 289, 300–301. See also Maurras, *op. cit.,* pp. 115–116.

32. A. L. Kroeber, *The Nature of Culture* (Chicago, 1952), pp. 4, 10.

33. Auguste Comte, *Catéchisme positiviste* (Paris, 1852); Auguste Comte, *Calendrier positiviste* (Paris, 1852). See also, E. Caird, *The Social Philosophy and Religion of Comte* (Glasgow, 1885).

34. Comte, *Cours de philosophie positive*, III, 277, 313.

35. See J. Morley's article on Comte in the *Encyclopaedia Britannica*.

36. Levy Bruhl, *op. cit.*, pp. 17–19.

37. Mill, *op. cit.*, p. 141. For Comte's influence, see D. G. Charlton, *Positivist Thought in France* (Oxford, 1959), and Lucy Prenant, "Marx et Comte" in *A la Lumière du Marxisme* (Paris, 1937), II, 26–27. James H. Billington, "The Intelligentsia and the Religion of Humanity," *Am. Hist. Review*, LXV, 807 ff.

38. G. Sabine, *History of Political Theory*, 2nd ed. (New York, 1950), p. 716; H. Marcuse, *Reason and Revolution* (New York, 1941).

39. Wilhelm Dilthey, *Jugendgeschichte Hegels*, in *Gesammelte Schriften* (Leipzig, 1914), IV.

40. Hegel, *Grundlinien der Philosophie des Rechts, 1821*, English translation by T. M. Knox (Oxford University Press, 1942). See also, T. Litt, *Hegel* (Heidelberg, 1953). Hegel, Lectures on the Philosophy of History, English translation by J. Sibree (London, 1900), p. 9.

41. B. Croce, *What Is Living and What Is Dead of the Philosophy of Hegel* (London, 1915), p. 16.

42. Hegel, *Encylopaedie der philosophischen Wissenschaften*, paragraphs 86–88, 384, English translation by Maxwell.

43. K. Löwith, *Von Hegel bis Nietzsche* (Zürich, 1941), pp. 44, 47.

44. Hegel, *Phänomenologie des Geistes*, English translation (London, 1910), II, 822–823.

45. Croce, *op. cit.*, p. 140.

46. Hegel, *Encyclopaedie*, paragraph 209, and many remarks in his *Philosophie der Geschichte*.

47. Croce, *op. cit.*, p. 61.

48. Camus, *op. cit.*, pp. 105–106.

49. Hegel, *Philosophie der Religion*, English translation by Speirs (London, 1895), I, 17; III, 29, 73.

50. Löwith, *op. cit.*, pp. 51–56, 70.

51. Hegel, *Philosophie des Rechts*, Preface; Karl Löwith, *Meaning in History* (Chicago, 1949), pp. 52–59.

52. I. Berlin, *Karl Marx* (New York, 1948); F. Mehring, *Karl Marx* (New York, 1935).

53. Löwith, *Von Hegel bis Nietzsche*, p. 132; Sidney Hook, *From Hegel to Marx* (New York, 1936), p. 18; G. D. H. Cole, *What Marx Really Meant* (London, 1934).

54. Berlin, *op. cit.*, p. 137.

55. Karl Marx, *Gesamtausgabe* (Moskau-Frankfurt, 1927), V, 533–535.

56. Karl Marx, *Das Kapital* (London, 1909); Hook, *op. cit.*, p. 15; B. Croce, *Historical Materialism and the Economics of Karl Marx* (London, 1914), p. 6.

57. Marx, *Gesamtausgabe,* V, 535; Heinrich Popitz, *Der Entfremdete Mensch* (Basel, 1953).

58. Berlin, *op. cit.*, p. 81; J. Barzun, *Darwin, Marx, Wagner* (Boston, 1941), p. 193.

59. Hook, *op. cit.*, p. 25.

60. Karl Marx, *Das Kapital,* I, 157.

61. Karl Marx, *Critique of Political Economy* (Chicago, 1911), p. 13; Croce, *op. cit.*, pp. 12, 32.

62. From Engels' oration at Marx's funeral, quoted by M. Eastman in *Marxism: Is It Science?* (New York, 1940), p. 25.

63. Marx, *Critique of Political Economy,* p. 11.

64. Karl Jaspers, "Karl Marx," in *Universitas,* VII, 226.

65. Marx, *Critique of Political Economy,* pp. 12–13.

66. *Ibid.*

67. Quoted by Sabine, *op. cit.*, p. 762.

68. Marx-Engels, *Das Kommunistische Manifest,* reprinted in *The Essentials of Karl Marx* (New York, 1946), p. 34.

69. *Ibid.,* p. 37.

70. *Ibid.,* p. 33.

71. *Ibid.,* p. 53.

72. *Ibid.*

73. Karl Marx, *Die Deutsche Ideologie,* English translation (New York, 1939), p. 22.

74. Friedrich Engels, *Herrn Eugen Dührings Umwälzung der Wissenschaft,* English translation (New York, 1935), p. 315.

75. Marx, *Das Kapital,* I, 789.

76. Eastman, *op. cit.*, p. 19.

77. Barzun, *op. cit.*, pp. 215–216.

78. Berlin, *op. cit.*, pp. 222, 265. See also, M. M. Bober, *Karl Marx's Economic Interpretation of History* (Cambridge, Mass., 1950), pp. 424–428; Edgar Salin, *Geschichte und Volkswirtschaftslehre,* 4th ed. (Bern, 1951).

79. Barzun, *op. cit.*, p. 109.

80. Charles Darwin, *Life and Letters* (Chicago, 1896), 2 vols., I, 51. See also, *Darwin, Narration of the Surveying Voyage of H. M. S. Adventure and Beagle* (London, 1839) and *Darwin's Diary of the Voyage of H. M. S. Beagle* (Cambridge, Mass., 1943).

81. Darwin, *Life and Letters*, I, 67.

82. J. A. Thomson, in *Darwin and Modern Science* (Cambridge, 1909), p. 3.

83. Darwin, *Life and Letters*, I, 85–86.

84. *Ibid.*, p. 67.

85. *Ibid.*, p. 68.

86. Darwin, *On the Origin of Species,* Modern Library edition, p. 353.

87. *Ibid.*, pp. 358, 15–50.

88. *Ibid.*, pp. 359, 51–62.

89. J. B. Haldane, *The Causes of Evolution* (London, 1932), p. 14.

90. Barzun, *op. cit.*, p. 41.

91. Darwin, *Origin,* p. 373.

92. *Ibid.*, p. 374.

93. T. H. Huxley, *Darwiniana* (London, 1907), p. 24.

94. Darwin, *Life and Letters*, I, 76.

95. Darwin, *The Descent of Man,* revised edition (New York, 1890), p. 25. See also, G. Schwalbe, in *Darwin and Modern Science,* pp. 112 ff.

96. Darwin, *The Descent of Man,* p. 56.

97. *Ibid.*, p. 93.

98. *Ibid.*, p. 619.

99. Haldane, *op. cit.*, p. 3.

100. *Ibid.*, p. 31.

101. H. Höffding, in *Darwin and Modern Science,* pp. 446, 458; R. D. E. Clark, *Darwin Before and After* (London, 1948); J. M. Baldwin, *Darwin and the Humanities* (Baltimore, 1909); W. Schmidt, *Der Kampf der Weltanschauungen* (Berlin, 1904). For the social consequences of Darwinism see: F. Brie, *Der Einfluss der Lehren Darwins auf den britischen Imperialismus* (Freiburg, 1927); R. Hofstadter, *Social Darwinism in American Thought* (Philadelphia, 1944).

102. Charles Baudelaire, *Mon coeur mis à nu* (Paris, 1943), XII.

103. *The Letters of Charles Baudelaire,* translated by Arthur Symons (New York, 1927), p. 148. I have changed Symons translation slightly.

104. Baudelaire, *Mon Coeur mis à nu,* LXXIII; see also, J. P. Sartre, *Baudelaire* (Paris, 1947), p. 87.

105. F. Porché, *Baudelaire* (Paris, 1944), p. 16. Henri Peyre, *Connaissance de Baudelaire* (Paris, 1951).

106. Porché, p. 60.

107. *Ibid.*, p. 250; Sartre, *op. cit.*, pp. 31–32.

108. Baudelaire, *Les Fleurs du mal,* ed. Y. G. LeDantec (Paris, 1918–1939), p. 136.

109. Baudelaire, *L'Art romantique* (Genève, 1945), pp. 91–92.

110. *Ibid.,* p. 94; see also, O. Mann, *Der Moderne Dandy* (Berlin, 1925).

111. Porché, *op. cit.,* pp. 171–172; Baudelaire, *L'Art romantique,* p. 326.

112. Paul Valéry, *Variety* (New York, 1938), p. 72; P. Hazard, *Quatre études* (New York, 1940), p. 17.

113. See Baudelaire's famous poem, "Correspondences," *Fleurs du mal,* p. 23; Enid Starkie, *Baudelaire* (New York, 1933), p. 186.

114. M. Raymond, *De Baudelaire au surréalisme* (Paris, 1940), pp. 17–18.

115. Valéry, *op. cit.,* p. 93.

116. E. Raynaud, *Baudelaire* (Paris, 1922), p. 289.

117. Baudelaire, *Mon Coeur mis à nu,* XIX.

118. *Ibid.,* LXXIX.

119. *Ibid.,* LXXXV.

120. Quoted by Porché, p. 304; P. Mansell Jones, *Baudelaire* (New Haven, 1952).

121. E. L. Allen, *Kierkegaard* (London, 1935), p. 1; W. Hubben, *Four Prophets of Our Destiny* (New York, 1952), p. 5; E. Hirsch, *Kierkegaard Studien* (Gütersloh, 1933), pp. 47, 78.

122. Sören Kierkegaard, *Die Tagebücher,* edited and translated by Th. Haecker (Innsbruck, 1923), 2 vols., hereafter noted as *Tagebücher.*

123. Th. Haecker, *Kierkegaard, the Cripple* (New York, 1950); R. Friedmann, *Kierkegaard* (London, 1949).

124. W. H. Auden, *The Living Thought of Kierkegaard* (New York, 1952), p. 3.

125. Th. Haecker, *Christentum und Kultur* (München, 1946), p. 109.

126. Kierkegaard, *Tagebücher,* vol. 1, p. 28.

127. *Ibid.,* p. 373.

128. *Ibid.,* II, 42.

129. S. Kierkegaard, *Concluding Unscientific Postscript* (Princeton, 1941), p. 169.

130. Haecker, *Christentum und Kultur,* p. 89.

131. Karl Löwith, *Kierkegaard und Nietzsche* (Frankfurt, 1933), p. 14.

132. Kierkegaard, *Unscientific Postscript,* p. 33.

133. Kierkegaard, *Either/Or* (Princeton, 1944); W. Lowrie, *Short Life of S. Kierkegaard* (Princeton, 1941), p. 151.

134. R. Jolivet, *Introduction to Kierkegaard* (New York, 1946), p. 124; G. Wahl, *Etudes Kierkegaardiennes* (Paris, 1949), pp. 58, 63.

135. Kierkegaard, *Either/Or*, II, 179.

136. Jolivet, *op. cit.*, p. 155.

137. Tagebücher, II, 22. See also, Martin Buber, *Die Frage an den Einzelnen* (Berlin, 1936), p. 56.

138. Allen, *op. cit.*, p. 143.

139. Jolivet, *op. cit.*, p. 225.

140. Auden, *op. cit.*, p. 21.

141. For the study of Nietzsche's life see: Charles Andler, *Nietzsche* (Paris, 1920–1931), 6 vols.; C. A. Bernoulli, *Overbeck and Nietzsche* (Jena, 1908), 2 vols.; E. F. Podach, *Nietzsches Zussammenbruch* (Heidelberg, 1930). For the meaning of his philosophy see: A. Bäumler, *Nietzsche* (Leipzig, 1931); Crane Brinton, *Nietzsche* (Cambridge, Mass., 1941); Otto Flake, *Nietzsche, Rückblick auf eine Philosophie* (Baden-Baden, 1946); Ernst Hildebrant, *Wagner und Nietzsche* (Breslau, 1924); Ernst Bertram, *Nietzsche* (Berlin, 1920); Karl Jaspers, *Nietzsche* (Berlin, 1947); W. Kaufmann, *Nietzsche* (Princeton, 1950); L. Klages, *Die psychologischen Errungenschaften Nietzsches* (Leipzig, 1926); G. Morgan, *What Nietzsche Means* (Cambridge, Mass., 1941).

142. Karl Jaspers, *Nietzsche und Das Christentum* (München, 1952), p. 70.

143. Nietzsche, *Also Sprach Zarathustra, Werke,* Karl Schlechta, ed. (München, 1956), II, 525.

144. Erich Heller, *op. cit.*, p. viii.

145. Nietzsche, *Zur Genealogie der Moral,* Vorrede, translated in *The Philosophy of Nietzsche* (The Modern Library, New York), p. 622.

146. *Ibid.*, pp. 819, 1087.

147. *Ibid.*, p. 842.

148. Thomas Mann, "Nietzsches Philosophie im Lichte unserer Erfahrungen," *Neue Deutsche Rundschau,* 1946, p. 359; Stefan Zweig, *Baumeister der Welt* (Frankfurt, 1951), p. 299.

149. Stefan George, *Der Siebente Ring* (Berlin, 1929), pp. 12–13.

150. *The Philosophy of Nietzsche,* p. 931.

151. Brinton, *op. cit.*, p. 184; Klages, *op. cit.*, p. 216.

152. *The Philosophy of Nietzsche,* p. 881.

153. Flake, *op. cit.*, p. 137.

154. Kaufmann, *op. cit.*, pp. 74 ff.; Karl Löwith, *Kierkegaard und Nietzsche, passim;* Nietzsche, *Aus dem Nachlass der Achtziger Jahre,* formerly known as *Der Wille zur Macht, Werke,* III, 557.

155. Löwith, *Von Hegel bis Nietzsche,* p. 259.

156. Nietzsche, *Aus dem Nachlass, Werke,* III.

157. Nietzsche, *Die Fröhliche Wissenschaft, Werke,* II, 202; *Also Sprach Zarathustra,* II, 466; *The Philosophy of Nietzsche,* p. 364.

158. Nietzsche, *Aus dem Nachlass, Werke,* III, 916.

159. Karl Jaspers, "Nietzsches Bedeutung in der Geschichte der Philosophie," *Neue Deutsche Rundschau,* 1950, p. 354.

160. Flake, *op. cit.,* p. 178. G. Bianquis, *Nietzsche en France* (Paris, 1929).

161. J. A. Lloyd, *F. Dostoevsky* (New York, 1948), p. 143.

162. Stefan Zweig, *Baumeister der Welt* (Frankfurt, 1951), p. 72.

163. A. Yarmolinsky, *Dostoevsky* (New York, 1934), p. 10.

164. See Freud's study in *Dostoevsky and Parricide, Stavrogin's Confession* (New York, 1947), p. 95; however, against the Freudian interpretation, see E. H. Carr, *Dostoevsky* (London, 1931), p. 37.

165. Dostoevsky, *The Insulted and the Injured,* 1, Chap. 15. All quotations are taken from Constance Garnett's translations.

166. Yarmolinsky, *op. cit.,* p. 29.

167. *Letters of Dostoevsky,* translated by E. C. Mayne (London, 1914), p. 53; see also, *Dostoevsky, Letters and Reminiscences,* translated by S. S. Koteliansky and J. Middleton Murray (London, 1923), p. 5.

168. V. Ivanov, *Freedom and the Tragic Life* (New York, 1952), p. 34.

169. *Letters of Dostoevsky,* p. 280.

170. *Ibid.,* p. 66.

171. *Ibid.,* p. 53. Dostoevsky, *The House of the Dead,* Chapter 1

172. *Ibid.,* p. 62.

173. *Ibid.,* pp. 70–71.

174. Freud, *op. cit.,* pp. 103–104.

175. Dostoevsky, *The Possessed,* last chapter.

176. Ernest Simmons, *Dostoevsky* (New York, 1940), p. 386.

177. Ivanov, *op. cit.,* pp. 9, 49.

178. *Ibid.,* p. 117.

179. Simmons, *op. cit.,* pp. 148–149.

180. *Letters of Dostoevsky,* p. 119.

181. *Ibid.,* p. 4.

182. Yarmolinsky, *op. cit.,* p. 412.

183. Simmons, *op. cit.,* p. 157.

184. Yarmolinsky, *op. cit.,* p. 168.

185. *Letters of Dostoevsky,* p. 142.

186. Carr, *op. cit.,* pp. 209 ff.

187. R. Fueloep Miller, *Fedor Dostoevsky* (New York, 1950), pp. 61, 83.

188. Carr, *op. cit.,* p. 322.

189. Quoted by Janko Lavrin, *Dostoevsky* (New York, 1947), p. 156. See also, Nicholas Berdyaev, *Dostoevsky* (New York, 1957).

Chapter III: The Self-Enchanted

1. Hugo von Hofmannsthal, *Prosa* (Frankfurt, 1950), I, p. 171.

2. E. Wechsler, *Die Generation als Jugendreihe* (Leipzig, 1930).

3. Oscar Wilde, *Intentions* (Boston, 1910), pp. 187–188.

4. André Gide, *Oeuvres complètes* (Paris, 1933), III, 473–474.

5. Oscar Wilde, *De Profundis* (London, 1949), p. 77. (This is the first complete edition of this work.)

6. The literature on Oscar Wilde is too extensive to be included here. Only the most important studies are listed: Frank Harris, *Oscar Wilde* (New York, 1918), 2 vols.; Hesketh Pearson, *Oscar Wilde* (New York, 1946); Otto Flake, *Versuch über Oscar Wilde* (München, 1946); George Woodcock, *The Paradox of Oscar Wilde* (London, 1949).

7. Woodcock, *op. cit.,* pp. 9, 12.

8. Wilde, *De Profundis,* p. 82.

9. Woodcock, *op. cit.,* p. 66.

10. F. F. Baumgarten, *Das Werk Konrad Ferdinand Meyers* (Zürich, 1948).

11. Wilde, *Intentions,* p. 125.

12. Wilde, *De Profundis,* p. 143.

13. Wilde, *Intentions,* p. 125.

14. St. John Ervine, *Oscar Wilde, A Present Time Appraisal* (London, 1951), p. 66.

15. Arthur Symons on Oscar Wilde, in *In Memoriam Oscar Wilde* (Leipzig, 1905), p. 45.

16. See the excellent book by E. Roditi, *Oscar Wilde* (Norfolk, Conn., 1946), pp. 63, 70.

17. Wilde's plays add little to our knowledge of his intellectual and emotional position. Reference to them is, therefore, omitted.

18. Wilde, *Intentions,* pp. 62–63; Woodcock, *op. cit.,* pp. 124–125.

19. Wilde, *Intentions,* p. 193.

20. Wilde, *The Soul of Man Under Socialism* (Boston, 1937), p. 6.

21. Gide, *op. cit.,* pp. 474–475.

22. Wilde, *De Profundis,* pp. 77–78.

23. *Ibid.*

24. *Ibid.,* p. 110.

25. Pearson, *op. cit.,* p. 331.

26. Hofmannsthal, *Die Prosaischen Schriften* (Berlin, 1907), II, 85–93.

27. Woodcock, *op. cit.,* pp. 238–239.

28. The literature concerning George is copious, though little of it is in English. The official biography, which received the "imprimatur" of the master, is F. Wolters, *Stefan George und die Blätter für die Kunst* (Berlin, 1930). Other sources are: F. Gundolf, *George* (Berlin, 1920); E. Morwitz, *Die Dichtung Stefan Georges* (Berlin, 1934); R. Boeringer, *Mein Bild von Stefan George* (München, 1951); Claude David, *L'Oeuvre poétique de Stefan George* (Abbéville, 1952). Also of considerable interest are those books by his friends which contain personal memories: E. Salin, *Um Stefan George* (Godesberg, 1948); C. A. Klein, *Die Sendung Stefan Georges* (Berlin, 1935); Melchior Lechter, *Zum Gedächtnis Stefan George* (Berlin, 1934); S. Lepsius, *Stefan George* (Berlin, 1935); Cyril Scott, *Die Tragödie Stefan Georges* (Eltville, 1952); B. von Heiseler, *Stefan George* (Lübeck, 1936); A. Verwey, *Mein Verhältnis zu Stefan George* (Santport, 1934); H. Steiner, *Begegnung mit Stefan George* (Aurora, New York, 1942).

29. Stefan George, *Gesammelte Werke (G.W.)* (Berlin, 1929), XVII, 52–55. There are two translations into English of George's poems: Stefan George, *Poems* (New York, 1943), Introduction by E. Morwitz, and *The Works of Stefan George,* translated by Olga Marx and E. Morwitz (Chapel Hill, 1949).

30. *Briefwechsel zwischen George und Hofmannsthal* (Berlin, 1938). See also, L. Bergel, *Voraussetzungen und Anfänge der Beziehungen zwischen Stefan George und Hugo von Hofmannsthal* (New York University, 1949); F. Hermann, *Stefan George und Hugo von Hofmannsthal* (Zürich, 1947).

31. Morwitz, Introduction to George's poems, p. 14.

32. Gide, *Oevures complètes,* V, 403. For George's evaluation of Wilde, see E. R. Curtius, *Kritische Essays zur Europäischen Literatur* (Bern, 1950), p. 156.

33. K. J. Obenauer, *Die Problematik des ästhetischen Menschen in der deutschen Literatur* (München, 1933), pp. 392–397.

34. In Boehringer's book, *op. cit.,* there are abundant examples of these masquerades in which George and his friends indulged. They were in questionable taste and rather ludicrous. See also the novel by Franzisca Reventlow, *Herr Dame* (München, 1926).

35. Scott, *op. cit.,* p. 19.

36. George, *G.W.,* VIII, 96; translation by Morwitz.

37. Scott, *op. cit.,* p. 19.

38. Illustrative in this respect are the memoirs of O. Zarek, *German Odysee* (London, 1941), p. 31.

39. George, *G.W.,* II; E. Lachmann, *Die ersten Bücher Stefan Georges* (Berlin, 1933).

40. Obenauer, *op. cit.,* pp. 397–399.

41. David, *op. cit.,* pp. 66 ff.

42. Hofmannsthal, *Prosa,* I, 283–291.

43. George, *G.W.,* IV; Boehringer, *op. cit.,* p. 62; Hofmannsthal, *Das Gespräch über Gedichte, Die prosaischen Schriften* (Berlin, 1907), I, 77.

44. George, *Poems,* Introduction, p. 21.

45. David, *op. cit.,* pp. 148–149.

46. George, *G.W.,* V. Gundolf, *op. cit.,* pp. 152 ff.; Curtius, *op. cit.,* pp. 151 ff.

47. George, *G.W.,* XVII, 74 ff.

48. Boehringer, *op. cit.,* p. 120; George, *Poems,* Introduction by Morwitz, p. 16.

49. For the Maximin chapter in George's life, see his *Gedenkbuch für Maximin,* privately printed but obtainable in a few libraries. Also, Boehringer, *op. cit.,* p. 120, and David, *op. cit.,* pp. 233–255.

50. R. Alewyn, *Hofmannsthal's Wandlung* (Frankfurt, 1948), p. 19.

51. No complete edition of Hofmannsthal's writings exists. We quote from the *Gesammelte Werke,* 6 vols. (Berlin, 1924), and the new edition, *Gesammelte Werke* (Stockholm, 1946). The literature about Hofmannsthal is almost entirely in German: R. Borchardt, *Rede über Hofmannsthal* (Berlin, 1918); W. Brecht, *Hugo von Hofmannsthal,* Deutsche Rundschau, Juni, 1930; Max Kommerell, *Hofmannsthal* (Frankfurt, 1930); Karl J. Naef, *Hugo von Hofmannsthal, Wesen und Werk* (Zürich, 1938); Grete Schaeder, *Hugo von Hofmannsthal* (Berlin, 1933); J. Wassermann, *Hofmannsthal, der Freund* (Berlin, 1930); Grete und H. H. Schaeder, *Hugo von Hofmannsthal und die geistige Welt* (Hameln, 1947); Eranos, *Festschrift für Hofmannsthal,* 1924; H. Ulrich, ed., *Hugo von Hofmannsthal* (London, 1944); Otto Henschele, *Hugo von Hofmannsthal* (Freiburg, 1949); R. Alewyn, *op. cit.,* R. Alewyn, *Hofmannsthal und diese Zeit,* Neue Deutsche Rundschau, 1949, pp. 381 ff.; E. R. Curtius, *op. cit.,* pp. 158 ff.

52. H. von Hofmannsthal, *Selected Prose,* Introduction by H. Broch (New York, 1952), p. xlii.

53. W. Brecht, "H. von Hofmannsthal sad me ipsum und seine Bedeutung," *Jahrbuch des Freien Deutschen Hochstiftes* (Frankfurt, 1930), pp. 319–331; Bergel, *op. cit.*, pp. 4–5.

54. *Das Kleine Welttheater, G. W.* (1924), I, 91.

55. See Hofmannsthal's poem, *Der Prophet, G. W.* (1946) I, 165.

56. Quoted by Broch, *op. cit.*, p. xi.

57. *The Lyrical Poems of Hugo von Hofmannsthal,* translated by Charles W. Stork (Yale University Press, 1918), p. 37. See also the translation of *Das Kleine Welttheater,* by W. Eberlein (New York, 1945).

58. Bergel, *op. cit.*, p. 5.

59. Hofmannsthal, *G. W.* (1924), I, 9 ff. (translation by Stork).

60. *Ibid.*, p. 11.

61. *Ibid.*, p. 95.

62. *Ibid.*, p. 102.

63. *Ibid.*, p. 74. See also Obenauer, *op. cit.*, p. 383.

64. Broch, *op. cit.*, p. xxv.

65. Hofmannsthal, *op. cit.*, pp. 66–67. The conflict between Life and Art in the *Death of Titian* should find a tragic climax. Hofmannsthal planned to end the play with an outbreak of the plague which would tear down the barriers between man and the artist, both of whom would go down in a frenzy of death and voluptuousness, a Venetian theme that later inspired Barrès and Thomas Mann.

66. Hofmannsthal, *op. cit.*, pp. 133 ff. The translation used in the text is, with very slight changes, by Elizabeth Walker (Boston, 1914).

67. Hofmannsthal, *op. cit.;* Walker, *op. cit.*, p. 20.

68. Walker, *op. cit.*, p. 44.

69. Quoted by Alewyn, *Hofmannsthal's Wandlung,* p. 17.

70. Hugo von Hofmannsthal, *Die Berührung der Sphären* (Berlin, 1931), p. 57.

71. Obenauer, *op. cit.*, p. 388.

72. Alewyn, *Hofmannsthal's Wandlung,* p. 22.

73. H. Steiner, "Erinnerungen an Hofmannsthal," *Deutsche Beiträge* (University of Chicago Press, 1947), p. 203.

74. See Hofmannsthal's essay on Wilde quoted above.

75. Hofmannsthal, *G. W.* (1924), II, 175 ff. The Chandos letter is translated in *Selected Prose,* p. 131.

76. Hofmannsthal, *Selected Prose,* p. 132.

77. *Ibid.*, p. 133.

78. Broch, *op. cit.,* p. xviii.

79. Grete und H. H. Schaeder, *op. cit.,* p. 34.

80. Hofmannsthal, *Selected Prose,* p. 135.

81. *Ibid.,* p. 138.

82. *Briefwechsel zwischen George und Hugo von Hofmannsthal,* p. 154.

83. Hofmannsthal, *Die Berührung der Sphären,* p. 255. See also C. J. Burckhardt, *Erinnerungen an Hofmannsthal* (Basel, 1944), p. 24.

84. Burckhardt, *op. cit.,* p. 16. For the evaluation of the later Hofmannsthal, see my essay, "Ein Fragment," *Preussische Jahrbücher,* Bd. 222, 3, 1930, which deals with Hofmannsthal's novel *Andreas,* and my essay on Hofmannsthal's *Arabella, Vossische Zeitung,* October 11, 1933.

85. H. von Hofmannsthal, *Prosa* (Frankfurt, 1950), I, p. 170.

86. T. Antongini, *D'Annunzio* (London, 1938); G. Borgese, *Gabriele d'Annunzio* (Napoli, 1909); Arthur Symons, *Studies* (London, 1904); H. D. Sedgewick, *Essays on Great Writers* (Boston, 1903).

87. Alberta von Putkammer, *D'Annunzio* (Berlin), pp. 31 ff.

88. Antongini, *op. cit., passim.*

89. Gabriele d'Annunzio, *Primo Vere* (Chieti, 1879).

90. Gonzalo Zaldumbide, *La evolución de Gabriele d'Annunzio* (Paris, 1909).

91. Zaldumbide, *op. cit., passim.*

92. D'Annunzio, *Il Piacere* (1939 edition), p. 58.

93. Lady Blennerhasset, *Gabriele d'Annunzio* (Berlin, 1901); Putkammer, *op. cit.,* pp. 31–33.

94. R. Altrocchi, *Gabriele d'Annunzio* (Chicago, 1922), pp. 7, 12; R. Altrocchi, *D'Annunzio, the Poet* (University of California *Chronicle*), vol. XXXII, No. 2.

95. D'Annunzio, *Fuoco* (Milan, 1927), *passim.*

96. Jean Dornis, *Essai sur Gabriele d'Annunzio* (Paris, 1925), p. 16.

97. Zaldumbide, *op. cit.,* p. 312.

98. Lady Blennerhasset, *op. cit.,* p. 48.

99. D'Annunzio, *Laudi del Cielo* (Milan, 1928), pp. 17 ff. F. Marinetti, *Les Dieux s'en vont; d'Annunzio reste* (Paris, 1908).

100. A. Thibaudet, *La Vie de Maurice Barrès* (Paris, 1921); E. R. Curtius, *Maurice Barrès* (Bonn, 1921); F. Duhourcau, *La Voix intérieure de Maurice Barrès d'après ses cahiers* (Paris, 1929); H. Massis, *Jugements,* vol. I (Paris, 1923).

101. Pierre-Henri Petibon, *Taine, Renan, Barrès* (Paris, 1935), pp. 139 ff.

102. Curtius, *op. cit., passim.*

103. Duhourcau, *op. cit.,* p. 77.

104. Curtius, *op. cit.,* p. 15.

105. Maurice Barrès, *Le Culte du moi; Sous l'Oeil des Barbares* (Paris, 1888); *Un Homme libre* (Paris, 1889); *Le Jardin de Bérénice* (Paris, 1891). See also, Barrès own comment in *Le Culte du moi,* "Examen des trois ideologies" (Paris, 1892).

106. Barrès, *Un Homme libre,* 1904 edition, p. 10.

107. See the preface to the 1904 edition, p. x.

108. Barrès, *L'Ennemi des lois* (Paris, 1891).

109. Barrès, *Du Sang, de la volupté et de la mort* (Paris, 1894); *Greco ou le secret de Tolède* (Paris, 1912).

110. Barrès, *Le Roman de l'énergie nationale; Les Déracinés* (Paris, 1897); *L'Appel au soldat* (Paris, 1900); *Leurs Figures* (Paris, 1901). See also, *Scènes et doctrines du nationalisme* (Paris, 1902); H. Kaeger, *Die Gesellschaftliche Entwurzelung in der Französischen Literatur* (Stuttgart, 1928).

111. *Les Déracinés,* 3rd edition, p. 248.

112. Curtius, *op. cit.,* p. 132.

113. *Ibid.,* p. 135.

114. Barrès, *La Colline inspirée* (Paris, 1913). *La grande pitié des églises de France* (Paris, 1914). The latter book was written as a protest against the neglect of the French churches which had resulted from the separation of State and Church in 1905. For Barrès' religious feelings, see the evaluation by the convert Massis, *op. cit.,* pp. 182–183.

115. Quoted by Massis, *op. cit.,* p. 184.

116. Duhourcau, *op. cit.,* pp. 230–231.

117. O. Grautoff, *Die Maske und das Gesicht Frankreichs* (Stuttgart, 1923), p. 110.

118. Duhourcau, *op. cit.,* pp. 202–203.

119. A. J. Guerard, *André Gide* (Cambridge, Mass., 1951), p. 5. Of the numerous studies dedicated to André Gide, I shall mention only those which I have found especially useful: Léon Pierre Quint, *André Gide* (New York, 1934); Paul Souday, *André Gide* (Paris, 1927); R. M. Alberès, *L'Odyssée d'André Gide* (Paris, 1952); W. Wittrock, *Der Gottesbegriff André Gides* (Marburg, 1936); Roger Martin du Gard, *Notes on André Gide* (London, 1953); Enid Starkie, *André Gide* (Cambridge, 1953); J. O'Brien, *Portrait of André Gide* (New York, 1953); Klaus Mann, *André Gide* (Zürich, 1948); E. R. Curtius, "André Gide" *Neue Deutsche Rundschau,* 1922, p. 528; "Homage à André

Gide," *Nouvelle Revue Française,* 1951; Jean Hytier, *André Gide* (Algiers, 1938).

120. Curtius, *op. cit.,* p. 530.

121. André Gide, *Si le Grain ne meurt* (Paris, 1945), p. 10.

122. Guerard, *op. cit.,* pp. 6, 12; Hytier, *op. cit.,* p. 145.

123. Hytier, *op. cit.,* p. 145.

124. Starkie, *op. cit.,* pp. 58–59.

125. Wittrock, *op. cit.,* pp. 47–49.

126. Guerard, *op. cit.,* p. 32.

127. Alberès, *op. cit.,* p. 12.

128. Starkie, *op. cit.,* p. 58; Alberès, *op. cit.,* p. 34; Gide, *Si le Grain ne meurt,* pp. 202 ff.

129. Gide, *Oeuvres complètes* (Paris, 1933), I; Quint, *op. cit.,* pp. 9 ff.; Mann, *op. cit.,* p. 67.

130. Gide, *Oeuvres complètes,* I, 73.

131. *Ibid.,* pp. 36, 42.

132. Gide, *Si le Grain ne meurt,* pp. 247 ff.

133. Marcel Raymond, *De Baudelaire au surréalisme* (Paris, 1940), pp. 30, 49–50.

134. Gide, *Oeuvres complètes,* I, 207, 215.

135. *Ibid.,* p. 365.

136. *Ibid.,* III, 479. *Si le Grain ne meurt,* pp. 342 ff.

137. Gide, *Oeuvres complètes,* I, 369 ff. Guerard, *op. cit.,* p. 69.

138. O'Brien, *op. cit.,* p. 110.

139. Gide, *Oeuvres complètes,* II, 57 ff., English translation by Dorothy Bussy (New York, 1949).

140. *Ibid.,* p. 11.

141. *Ibid.,* p. 119.

142. O'Brien, *op. cit.,* p. 129.

143. Gide, *Oeuvres complètes,* II, 57.

144. *Ibid.,* p. 227.

145. Quint, *op. cit.,* pp. 21, 49; Hytier, *op. cit.,* p. 17.

146. Guerard, *op. cit.,* p. 11.

147. Gide, *Le Retour de l'enfant prodigue* (Paris, 1932).

148. Germaine Brée, *André Gide* (Paris, 1953), p. 10. Van Meter Ames, *André Gide* (Norfolk, Conn., 1947), p. 190.

CHAPTER IV: THE DISENCHANTED

1. Wilhelm Dilthey, *Gesammelte Schriften* (Leipzig, 1914–1936), hereafter cited as *G. S.* To these must be added Dilthey's *Life of Schleiermacher,* vol. I (Berlin und Leipzig, 1922); *Das Erlebnis und die Dichtung* (Berlin, 1905); *Von deutscher Dichtung und Musik* (Leipzig, 1933). Indispensable for an understanding of Dilthey are also: *Der junge Dilthey,* Clara Misch, ed. (Leipzig, 1933); *Briefwechsel zwischen Dilthey und dem Grafen Paul York von Wartenburg* (Halle, 1923). For a bibliography of Dilthey's writings and correspondence, see H. A. Hodges, *Wilhelm Dilthey* (New York, 1944).

2. José Ortega y Gasset, *Obras* (Madrid, 1932) VI, 165–214, English translation. *Concord and Liberty* (New York, 1946); Hodges, *op. cit.,* O. F. Bollnow, *Dilthey* (Leipzig, 1936); Eduard Spranger, *Dilthey* (Berlin, 1912); Hajo Holborn, "Dilthey's Critique of Historical Reason," *Journal of the History of Ideas,* XI, 93–118; William Kluback, *Dilthey's Philosophy of History* (New York, 1956); Carlo Antoni, *From History to Sociology* (Detroit, 1959); H. S. Hughes, *Consciousness and Society* (New York, 1958).

3. *Der junge Dilthey, passim.*

4. Antoni, *op. cit.,* p. 2.

5. H. L. Friess, "Wilhelm Dilthey," *Journal of Philosophy,* XXVI, 7.

6. Hodges, *op. cit.,* p. 1.

7. *G. S.,* I, 123.

8. *Ibid.,* 15–16.

9. *Ibid.*

10. *Der junge Dilthey,* p. 81.

11. Antoni, *op. cit.,* p. 1.

12. Lecomte du Nouy, *Human Destiny* (New York, 1947), p. 89.

13. Ortega y Gasset, *op. cit.,* p. 131.

14. *Der junge Dilthey,* p. 5.

15. Antoni, *op. cit.,* 4.

16. *Der junge Dilthey,* p. 120. For the history of the term, *Geisteswissenschaften,* see Holborn, *op. cit.,* p. 98, note 25. In view of the difficulties in finding an adequate translation for the word *Geisteswissenschaften,* I have used both "human studies" (Hodges) and "cultural sciences" (Holborn).

17. Quoted by Friess, *op. cit.*, pp. 10–11.

18. Ortega y Gasset, *op. cit.*, pp. 150–164.

19. Dilthey, *Briefwechsel mit dem Grafen York von Wartenburg*, p. 247. Holborn, *op. cit.*, p. 103. See also, Max Scheler, *Vom Umsturz der Werte* (Leipzig, 1919), II, 141.

20. *G. S.*, VI, 189.

21. *G. S.*, V, pp. 402–404, 413–415. Hodges, *op. cit.*, pp. 99–101, has translated some of the most important passages from Dilthey's theory of *Weltanschauung*.

22. Hodges, *op. cit.*, p. 92.

23. *G. S.*, VIII, 232.

24. Antoni, *op. cit.*, p. 20.

25. *G. S.*, VII, 287–288.

26. *G. S.*, I, 91.

27. *Ibid.*, pp. 28–29.

28. *G. S.*, I, 37–38.

29. *G. S.*, V, 139 ff. *Ideen über eine beschreibende und zergliedernde Psychologie.* See also, *Der Aufbau der geschichtlichen Welt in den Geisteswissenschaften, G. S.*, vol. VII. Following Dilthey, a large body of theory developed around the term *Verstehen*. See: Karl Mannheim, *Essays on Sociology* (London, 1953), p. 216; J. Wach, *Das Verstehen* (Tübingen, 1926–1933).

30. *G. S.*, V, 173.

31. *G. S.*, VII, 173, 290–291.

32. *Ibid.*, 252.

33. Antoni, *op. cit.*, p. 6.

34. Holborn, *op. cit.*, p. 102.

35. *G. S.*, V, 402, ff.; VIII, vi.

36. *G. S.*, V, 402.

37. *G. S.*, VIII, 82.

38. Mannheim, *op. cit.*, pp. 15 ff.

39. *G. S.*, V, 364.

40. For an evaluation of Dilthey as a historian, see Gerhard Masur, "Dilthey and the History of Ideas," *Journal of the History of Ideas*, XIII, 94–107, and Hans Baron, "Historical Concepts of the Renaissance," *Journal of the History of Ideas*, XI, 500.

41. Antoni, *op. cit.*, p. 27.

42. Masur, *op. cit.*, 101.

43. *G. S.*, II, 90–245.

44. *G. S.*, III, 3–79; 83–200.

45. Masur, *op. cit.*, 106.

46. Antoni, *op. cit.*, p. 28.

47. *Ibid.*, p. 35.

48. Antoni, *op. cit.*, p. 22.

49. W. Windelband, "Geschichte und Naturwissenschaft," in, *Preludien* (Tübingen, 1915), II, 136 ff.

50. Heinrich Rickert, *Die Probleme der Geschichtsphilosophie,* 3rd ed. (Heidelberg, 1924), quoted as *Probleme; Kulturwissenschaft und Naturwissenschaft,* 5th ed. (Tübingen, 1921), quoted as *Kulturwissenschaft; Die Grenzen der naturwissenschaftlichen Bergriffsbildung,* 2nd ed. (Tübingen, 1913), quoted as *Grenzen.*

51. *Probleme,* p. 17.

52. *Kulturwissenschaft,* p. 6.

53. *Ibid.,* pp. 17–18.

54. *Grenzen,* p. 180.

55. *Probleme,* pp. 30–33.

56. *Kulturwissenschaft,* p. 63.

57. *Grenzen,* p. 263.

58. *Ibid.,* p. 197.

59. *Probleme,* p. 90.

60. Theodor von Laue, *Leopold Ranke* (Princeton, 1950), p. 169.

61. *Grenzen,* p. 302.

62. *Probleme,* p. 23.

63. *Ibid.,* p. 18.

64. *Kulturwissenschaft,* p. 22.

65. *Probleme,* p. 77.

66. *Ibid.,* pp. 59, 64.

67. *Kulturwissenschaft,* p. 93.

68. *Probleme,* p. 45.

69. *Ibid.,* p. 59.

70. *Ibid.,* p. 60.

71. *Ibid.*

72. *Grenzen,* p. 509.

73. *Kulturwissenschaft,* p. 157.

74. *Probleme,* p. 127.

75. See Friedrich Meinecke, "Kausalitäten und Werte," in *Schaffender Spiegel* (Stuttgart, 1948), pp. 56 ff.

76. Marianne Weber, *Max Weber, ein Lebensbild* (Heidelberg, 1950), quoted as *Lebensbild*. See also Max Weber, *Jugendbriefe* (Tübingen, n.d.).

77. *Lebensbild,* p. 558.

78. *Ibid.,* p. 564.

79. *Ibid.,* pp. 51, 62.

80. *Ibid.,* p. 562.

81. *Ibid.,* p. 64.

82. *Ibid.,* p. 68.

83. J. P. Mayer, *Max Weber and German Politics* (London, 1943), p. 18.

84. *Lebensbild,* p. 90.

85. *Ibid.,* p. 100.

86. *Ibid.,* p. 105.

87. *Ibid.,* pp. 210–211.

88. *Ibid.,* p. 112. See also H. H. Gerth and C. W. Mills, *From Max Weber, Essays in Sociology* (New York, 1946), p. 9.

89. Max Weber, *Zur Geschichte der Handelsgesellschaft in Mittelalter,* reprinted in *Gesammelte Aufsätze zur Sozial- und Wirtschaftsgeschichte* (Tübingen, 1924).

90. *Lebensbild,* p. 132.

91. Max Weber, *Die römische Agrargeschichte in ihrer Bedeutung für das Staats- und Privatrecht* (Stuttgart, 1891).

92. Antoni, *op. cit.,* p. 125.

93. Mayer, *op. cit.,* p. 16.

94. *Lebensbild,* pp. 133–142.

95. *Ibid.,* p. 150.

96. Antoni, *op. cit.,* p. 129.

97. *Lebensbild,* p. 150.

98. Antoni, *op. cit.,* p. 129.

99. *Lebensbild,* p. 189.

100. *Ibid.,* p. 190; see also, Th. Heuss, *Friedrich Naumann* (Stuttgart, 1937).

101. *Lebensbild,* pp. 190, 226.

102. *Ibid.,* p. 205.

103. Translation by Gerth and Mills, *op. cit.,* p. 35. See also, A. Bergsträsser, *Max Webers Antrittsvorlesung in zeitgeschichtlicher Perspektive, Vierteljahrshefte f. Zeitgeschichte,* V, 209.

104. *Lebensbild,* pp. 142–143.

105. *Ibid.,* p. 273.

106. Gerth and Mills, *op. cit.,* p. 29, and H. S. Hughes, *op. cit.,* p. 296.

107. See Weber's letter to his mother of April 12, 1914, *Lebensbild,* p. 561.

108. *Lebensbild,* p. 563.

109. *Ibid.,* p. 271.

110. *Ibid.,* p. 431 (Weber's italics). "Ich habe Aeusserstes an Frevel auf mir gehabt—gewiss nicht ohne tiefe und dauernde Nachwirkung."

111. *Ibid.,* p. 272.

112. *Ibid.,* p. 432 (Weber's italics).

113. *Ibid.,* p. 271.

114. *Ibid.,* p. 276.

115. *Ibid.,* p. 315.

116. *Ibid.,* p. 395.

117. P. Honigsheim, "Max Weber als Soziologe," and "Der Max Weber Kreis," in *Kölner Vierteljahrshefte für Soziologie,* I, 1; V, 3.

118. *Lebensbild,* p. 410.

119. Antoni, *op. cit.,* p. 120.

120. Max Weber, *Gesammelte Aufsätze zur Wissenschaftslehre* (Tübingen, 1922). Some of these essays have been translated by E. A. Shils and H. A. Finch, *Max Weber on the Methodology of the Social Sciences* (Glencoe, Illinois, 1949). See also, H. Grab, *Der Begriff des Rationalen in der Soziologie Max Webers* (Karlsruhe, 1927); A. von Schelting, *Max Webers Wissenschaftslehre* (Tübingen, 1934); Karl Mannheim, *op. cit.,* p. 218; Talcott Parsons, *Introduction to Max Weber's Theory of Social and Economic Organization* (New York, 1947); Dieter Henrich, *Die Einheit der Wissenschaftslehre Max Webers* (Tübingen, 1952).

121. Antoni, *op. cit.,* p. 142.

122. *Lebensbild,* p. 350.

123. Shils and Finch, *op. cit.,* p. 42.

124. *Lebensbild,* p. 356.

125. Shils and Finch, *op. cit.,* p. 113.

126. *Lebensbild,* p. 357.

127. *Ibid.,* p. 358.

128. Shils and Finch, *op. cit.,* p. 1.

129. *Ibid.,* p. 4.

130. *Ibid.,* p. 10

131. *Ibid.,* p. 52.

132. _Ibid._, p. 53.

133. Max Weber, _Wissenschaft als Beruf_ (Tübingen, 1922), translated in Gerth and Mills, _op. cit._, p. 148.

134. _Ibid._, p. 152.

135. _Ibid._, p. 128.

136. Antoni, _op. cit._, p. 137.

137. _Lebensbild_, p. 370.

138. _Ibid._, p. 366.

139. _Ibid._, p. 370.

140. Max Weber, _Gesammelte Aufsätze zur Religionssoziologie_ (Tübingen, 1922), 3 vols. See I, 18.

141. _Lebensbild_, pp. 315–345.

142. Gerth and Mills, _op. cit._, p. 62.

143. _Lebensbild_, p. 383.

144. _Aufsätze zur Religionsoziologie_, I, 14; Antoni, _op. cit._, p. 147.

145. _Aufsätze zur Religionssoziologie_, I, 17. The most outstanding critics of Weber were Rachfahl, L. Brentano, W. Sombart, and H. M. Robertson. R. H. Tawney has accepted Weber's thesis with certain reservations. About the whole controversy see: Ephraim Fishoff, "The Protestant Ethic and the Spirit of Capitalism," _Social Research_, XI, no. 1.

146. _Aufsätze zur Religionsoziologie_, I, 237.

147. _Ibid._, 1; see also Weber's _Die rationalen und soziologischen Grundlagen der Musik_ (München, 1921).

148. Antoni, _op. cit._, p. 161.

149. Gerhard Masur, "Toynbees Philosophie der Geschichte," _Hist. Zeitsch._ vol. 174, 272.

150. _Lebensbild_, p. 725.

151. _Aufsätze zur Religionsoziologie_, I, 512–536.

152. _Ibid._, 12.

153. Antoni, _op. cit._, pp. 165–168.

154. _Ibid._

155. Tübingen, 1925. English translation by A. M. Henderson and Talcott Parsons, _The Theory of Social and Economic Organization_ (New York, 1947).

156. Gerth and Mills, _op. cit._, p. 47; see also Karl Löwith, Max Weber and Karl Marx, _Archiv für Sozialwissenschaften und Sozialpolitik_, vol. 67, 53–99; 175–214. Max Weber, _Politik als Beruf, Gesammelte Politische Schriften_ (München, 1921). English translation in Gerth and Mills, _op. cit._, pp. 77–78. Wolfgang J. Mommsen, _Max Weber und die_

deutsche Politik, 1890–1920 (Tübingen, 1959); Gerhard Masur, "Max Weber und Friedrich Meinecke in ihrem Verhältnis zur politischen Macht," *Humboldt Festschrift der Freien Universität Berlin* (Berlin, 1960), pp. 702–725.

157. *Theory of Social and Economic Organization, op. cit.,* p. 328.

158. *Ibid.*

159. *Ibid.,* p. 363.

160. Gerth and Mills, *op. cit.,* p. 55.

161. *Lebensbild,* p. 703; see also Mayer, *op. cit.,* p. 62.

162. *Lebensbild,* p. 448; Mayer, *op. cit.,* p. 50.

163. *Lebensbild,* pp. 571, 572.

164. *Ibid.,* pp. 605, 631.

165. *Ibid.,* p. 652.

166. *Ibid.,* p. 686.

167. Max Petzke, *Max Weber und sein Einfluss auf die Reichsverfassung* (Leipzig, 1925); F. Meinecke, "Drei Generationen deutscher Gelehrtenpolitik," *Historische Zeitschrift,* CXXV, 248–283.

168. Gerth and Mills, *op. cit.,* pp. 77–156.

169. *Ibid.,* pp. 152, 155.

170. *Ibid.,* p. 117.

171. *Ibid.,* p. 123.

172. As does Gerth, *op. cit.,* p. 43.

173. *Lebensbild,* p. 754.

174. Karl Jaspers, *Max Weber* (Bremen, 1946), p. 42.

175. Antoni, *op. cit.,* p. 134.

176. *Lebensbild,* p. 686.

177. Gerth and Mills, *op. cit.,* p. 44; Hughes, *op. cit.,* p. 334. R. Bendix, *Max Weber* (New York, 1960), was published after the manuscript was completed.

178. A. S. Eddington, *The Nature of the Physical World* (New York, 1929), p. 4.

179. Werner Heisenberg, "From Plato to Max Planck," *Atlantic Monthly,* No. 204, p. 109.

180. John H. Randall, *The Making of the Modern Mind* (Boston, 1940), p. 467.

181. Erwin Schroedinger, *Science and Humanism* (Cambridge, 1952), p. 12. Eddington, *op. cit.,* p. 4.

182. Randall, *op. cit.,* p. 472.

183. Lincoln Barnett, *The Universe and Dr. Einstein* (New York, 1948), p. 17.

184. Schroedinger, *op. cit.,* p. 54.

185. Eddington, *op. cit.,* pp. 1–2.

186. *Ibid.*

187. Bertrand Russell, *Human Knowledge* (New York, 1948), p. 22; Eddington, *op. cit.,* p. 185.

188. Heisenberg, *op. cit.,* p. 110.

189. *Ibid.*

190. Antoni, *op. cit.,* p. 173. See also Sir James Jeans, *The New Background of Science* (Ann Harbor, 1959), pp. 232–234.

191. Barnett, *op. cit.,* p. 113.

192. Robert Oppenheimer, *Wissenschaft und Allgemeines Denken* (Hamburg, 1953), p. 9.

193. Eddington, *op. cit.,* pp. 36 ff.

194. Quoted by Barnett, *op. cit.,* p. 61.

195. *Ibid.,* p. 51; *Time* magazine, January 18, 1960, p. 44.

196. Barnett, *op. cit.,* pp. 55–59, 79.

197. Max Planck, *Scientific Autobiography and Other Papers* (New York, 1951), pp. 101–106. Heisenberg, *op. cit.,* p. 112.

198. Barnett, *op. cit.,* pp. 111 ff. Alfred N. Whitehead, *Science and the Modern World* (New York, 1956), especially Chapters IX and X.

199. Barnett, *op. cit.,* pp. 81–82.

200. Planck, *op. cit.,* pp. 117–119. Werner Heisenberg, *Das Naturbild der Heutigen Physik* (Hamburg, 1959), pp. 18–23.

Chapter V: Culture and Society

1. Raymond Cogniat, *Au Temps des impressionists* (Paris, 1954), p. 69.

2. Barzun, *Darwin, Marx, Wagner* (Boston, 1941), p. 263.

3. Richard Wagner, *Auswahl aus seinen Schriften* (Leipzig, n.d.), pp. 3 ff.

4. Thomas Mann, *Past Masters* (New York, 1933), p. 68.

5. A. Michel, *Histoire de l'art française* (Paris, 1926), VIII, 509.

6. H. Plessner, *Das Schicksal des deutschen Geistes* (Zürich, 1935), p. 81.

7. P. Francastel, *L'Impressionisme* (Paris, 1937); F. Novotny, *Die grossen franzöischen Impressionsten* (Wien, n.d.).

8. Michel, *op. cit.*, p. 577. However, the name "impressionism" may ante-date 1874; see the important work by John Rewald, *The History of Impressionism* (New York, 1946).

9. Cogniat, *op. cit.*, p. 10; Rewald, *op. cit., passim.*

10. R. Schneider, *L'Art française* (Paris, 1931), p. 3.

11. E. Waldmann, *Die Kunst des Realismus und des Impressionismus im 19. Jahrhundert* (Berlin, 1927), p. 77; A. Tabarant, *Manet et ses oeuvres* (Paris, 1947); J. Meier Graefe, *Manet* (München, 1912).

12. Th. Duret, *Histoire des peintres impressionistes* (Paris, 1939), p. 8.

13. Waldmann, *op. cit., passim.*

14. G. Bazin, *L'Epoque impressioniste* (Paris, 1954), p. 17.

15. A. Vollard, *Renoir* (Paris, 1920), p. 46.

16. Schneider, *op. cit.*, p. 97.

17. Bazin, *op. cit.*, p. 18.

18. A. Vollard, *Cézanne* (Paris, 1915), p. 76.

19. Bazin, *op. cit.*, p. 10.

20. Vollard, *Cézanne*, p. 33.

21. Schneider, *op. cit.*, p. 53.

22. Bazin, *op. cit.*, p. 12.

23. Michel, *op. cit.*, p. 578.

24. L. Venturi, *Les Archives des impressionistes* (Paris-New York, 1939), 2 vols., I, 101; T. Natanson, *Pissaro* (Paris, 1950).

25. G. Geffroy, *Claude Monet* (Paris, 1924), 2 vols., II, 95.

26. Bernheime, Jeune, ed., *Cézanne* (Paris, 1914), p. 42.

27. Schneider, *op. cit.*, p. 106.

28. *Ibid.*, p. 103.

29. H. Focillon, *La Peinture aux et XIXe et XXe siècles* (Paris, 1928), p. 202.

30. Rewald, *op. cit.*, p. 292.

31. Schneider, *op. cit.*, p. 110; Geffroy, *op. cit.*, II, 134.

32. R. Rey, *Degas* (Paris, 1954), p. 9; F. Fosca, *Degas* (Paris, 1921); G. Rivière, *Degas* (Paris, 1935); J. B. Manson, *The Life and Work of Edgar Degas* (London, 1927); J. Meier Graefe, *Degas* (München, 1920).

33. Fosca, *op. cit.*, pp. 34, 48.

34. Michel, *op. cit.*, p. 586.

35. Rey, *op. cit.*, p. 25.

36. Focillon, *op. cit., passim.*

37. *Ibid.*, p. 210.

38. F. Fosca, *Renoir* (Paris, 1923), p. 19; J. Meier Graefe, *Renoir* (Leipzig, 1929); G. Rivière, *Renoir et ses amis* (Paris, 1921); A. Vollard, *Renoir* (Paris, 1920); A. André, *Renoir* (Paris, 1923).

39. Rivière, *Renoir et ses amis,* p. 131.

40. Vollard, *Renoir*, p. 79.

41. Rewald, *op. cit.,* p. 428.

42. *Ibid.*, p. 102.

43. André, *op. cit.,* p. 21.

44. See Venturi's *Archives, op. cit.,* which contain a great number of letters by the leading artists to Durand Ruel, the dealer most interested in the new school.

45. J. Rewald, *op. cit.,* gives the details of the exhibitions and their financial success or failure. He also gives a very instructive chart of the exhibitions and the artists who participated in them.

46. J. Meier Graefe, *Impressionisten* (München und Leipzig, 1907), p. 113.

47. Ruth Moser, *L'Impressionisme français* (Genève, 1952).

48. A. Alexandre, *Paul Gauguin* (Paris, 1930), p. 32.

49. Cogniat, *op. cit.,* p. 125.

50. Moser, *op. cit.,* pp. 175, 176.

51. E. R. Curtius, *Marcel Proust* (Berlin und Frankfurt, 1952), p. 52.

52. Halvdan Koht, *Life of Henrik Ibsen* (London, 1931), 2 vols., I, 1; Bergliot Ibsen, *The Three Ibsens* (New York, 1952).

53. *Letters of Henrik Ibsen,* English translation (New York, 1908), pp. 2, 48.

54. *Ibid.*, p. 150.

55. *Ibid.*, p. 146.

56. *Ibid.*, pp. 214–215.

57. *Ibid.*, p. 233.

58. Brian W. Downs, *Ibsen, The Intellectual Background* (Cambridge, 1948), p. 143.

59. *Letters,* p. 334.

60. Miriam A. Franc, *Ibsen in England* (Boston, 1919), p. 133.

61. *Letters,* pp. 350, 353, 355.

62. *Ibid.*, p. 205.

63. *Ibid.*, pp. 208–209.

64. *Ibid.*

65. Bernard Shaw, *The Quintessence of Ibsenism* (London, 1913), p. 181.

66. *Letters,* pp. 431, 435.

67. Downs, *op. cit.,* p. 176.

68. E. Reich, *Henrik Ibsens Dramen* (Berlin, 1918), p. 250.

69. *Letters,* p. 269.

70. *Letters,* p. 367.

71. Shaw, *op. cit.,* p. 230.

72. *Ibid.,* p. 219.

73. E. von Aster, *Ibsen und Strindberg* (München, 1921), p. 25.

74. *Letters, op. cit.,* pp. 199–200.

75. M. C. Bradbrook, *Ibsen, the Norwegian* (London, 1948), p. 7. Reich, *op. cit.,* p. 553.

76. Haldane MacFall, *Ibsen* (New York, 1907), p. 246.

77. *Letters,* p. 359.

78. W. H. Eller, *Ibsen in Germany* (Boston, 1918), p. 100.

79. Ernst Robert Curtius, "Bemerkungen zum franzöischen Roman," in *Essays zur europäischen Literatur* (Bern, 1952), p. 394.

80. Emile Zola, *Le Roman expérimental* (Paris, 1918), p. 86.

81. *Ibid.,* p. 44; see also, Zola, *Les Romanciers naturalistes* (Paris, 1914).

82. Zola, *Le Roman expérimental,* p. 83; Zola, *The Masterpiece,* English translation by Thomas Walton (New York, 1959), pp. 168–169.

83. Quoted by Mathew Josephson, *Zola* (New York, 1928), p. 145.

84. *Ibid.,* p. 151.

85. Thomas Mann, *A Sketch of My Life* (Paris, 1930), p. 7; see also Victor Mann, *Wir waren Fünf* (Konstanz, 1949).

86. *Ibid.,* pp. 14–15; M. Schlappner, *Thomas Mann und die französische Literatur* (Saarlouis, 1950), p. 28; Arnold Bauer, *Thomas Mann und die Krise der bürgerlichen Kultur* (Berlin, 1946); J. M. Lindsay, *Thomas Mann* (Oxford, 1954); Henry Hatfield, *Thomas Mann* (Norfolk, Conn., 1957), p. 31.

87. T. Mann, *Grösse und Leiden der Meister* (Berlin, 1935), p. 38. See also J. G. Brennan, *Thomas Mann's World* (New York, 1942), p. 36.

88. Thomas Mann, *Meine Zeit* (Amsterdam, 1950), p. 22.

89. Thomas Mann, *Die Buddenbrooks,* English translation (New York, 1950), II, 183.

90. *Ibid.,* II, 215, 217, 219, 255, 256.

91. *Ibid.,* p. 281.

92. See the studies by Georg Lukacs, Klaus and Erika Mann in *The Stature of Thomas Mann,* Charles Neider, ed. (New York, 1951).

93. Mann, *A Sketch of My Life*, p. 36.

94. John Galsworthy, *The Forsyte Saga* (New York, 1933), Preface.

95. A. Chevrillon, *Three Studies in English Literature* (New York, 1923), p. 161.

96. *Ibid.*

97. F. Delattre, "Le Roman soçial de John Galsworthy," *Bulletin de L'Association France-Grande Bretagne* (1934), pp. 5, 18.

98. John Galsworthy, *The Forsyte Saga* (New York, 1948), p. 199. See also, E. Guyot, *John Galsworthy* (Paris, 1933), pp. 10, 51–52.

99. Galsworthy, *Foryste Saga*, Preface, p. xii.

100. *Ibid.*

101. L. Schalit, *John Galsworthy* (London, 1929), p. 50.

102. D. H. Lawrence, *Scrutinies* (London, 1928), pp. 60, 71.

103. Galsworthy, *Forsyte Saga*, Preface, p. xiii.

104. The best of these is Charlotte Rohmer, *Buddenbrooks und Forsyte Saga* (Nördlingen, 1933).

105. Josepf Schumpeter, *Social Classes* (New York, 1935), p. 118.

106. Rohmer, *op. cit.*, p. 38.

107. Chevrillon, *op. cit.*, p. 156.

CHAPTER VI: THE CONFIDENT YEARS

1. The lecture is reprinted in A. Ruhe, *Henri Bergson* (London, 1914), pp. 10 ff.

2. H. Bergson, *La Pensée et le mouvant* (Paris, 1919), English translation under the title, *The Creative Mind* (New York, 1946), p. 132. All quotations in the text are taken from the authorized translations of Bergson's writings.

3. *Ibid.*, p. 107.

4. A. Thibaudet, *Trente Ans de vie française* (Paris, 1923), vols., III, IV; *Le Bergsonisme*, III, 29.

5. Ruhe, *op. cit.*, p. 55.

6. H. Bergson, *Essai sur les données immédiates de la conscience* (Paris, 1889).

7. H. Bergson, *Introduction to Metaphysics*, in *The Creative Mind*, pp. 192, 193, 194.

8. H. Bergson, *The Creative Mind*, p. 35.

9. H. Bergson, *Matière et mémoire* (Paris, 1896); see also, his *L'Energie spirituelle* (Paris, 1919), English translation, *Mind Energy* (New York, 1920), p. 17.

10. *Mind Energy,* pp. 45, 73.

11. *The Creative Mind,* p. 42.

12. *Mind Energy,* pp. 71, 72.

13. H. Höffding, *Modern Philosophers* (London, 1920), p. 270.

14. H. Bergson, *L'Evolution creatrice,* English translation, *Creative Evolution* (New York, 1911), pp. xiii, ix.

15. *Ibid.,* p. xii.

16. *Ibid.,* pp. 7, 15.

17. *Ibid.,* p. 27.

18. *Ibid.,* p. 39.

19. *Ibid.,* pp. 87 ff.

20. *Ibid.,* p. 98.

21. *Ibid.,* p. 105.

22. *Ibid.,* p. 139.

23. See especially, *The Creative Mind,* p. 49.

24. *Creative Evolution,* pp. 153, 155, 157, 165, 176, 185.

25. *Ibid.,* pp. 264, 266.

26. *Ibid.,* pp. 270–271.

27. D. B. Kitchin, *Bergson for Beginners* (London, 1914), p. 248.

28. Quoted in Ruhe, *op. cit.,* pp. 42 ff.

29. See Erwin Schrödinger, *What Is Life?* (New York, 1947).

30. Quoted by Ruhe, *op. cit.,* p. 51.

31. See the reference to Proust in *The Creative Mind,* p. 28.

32. H. Bergson, *Les deux sources de la réligion et de la morale* (Paris, 1932); English translation (New York, 1935), p. 298. See also: Léon Husson, *L'Intellectualisme de Bergson* (Paris, 1947), and Jacques Chevalier, *Bergson* (Paris, 1948).

33. Cecil Spriggs, *Benedetto Croce* (New Haven, 1953), p. 7. Mario Corsi, *Le origini del pensiero di Benedetto Croce* (Florence, 1951); Giovanni Castellano, *Benedetto Croce* (Bari, 1936). The chapters in Hughes, "Consciousness" and "Society" (New York, 1958), are very valuable.

34. Benedetto Croce, "Soliloquy of an Old Philosopher," in *My Philosophy* (London, 1949), p. 233.

35. Benedetto Croce, *An Autobiography,* English translation (Oxford, 1927).

36. *Ibid.,* p. 32.

37. *Ibid.*, pp. 56–57.

38. Croce, *Materialismo storico ed economia marxistica,* English translation *Historical Materialism* (London, 1914).

39. Croce, "Note on the History of Communism," in *My Philosophy,* p. 68.

40. Spriggs, *op. cit.,* p. 30.

41. *My Philosophy,* p. 70.

42. *Ibid.*, p. 14.

43. *Ibid.*, p. 11; see also *Autobiography,* p. 27.

44. Croce, *What Is Living And What Is Dead in the Philosophy of Hegel* (London, 1914); Hughes, *op. cit.,* p. 207.

45. Benedetto Croce, *Storia d'Italia dal 1871 al 1915* (Bari, 1928), English translation, *A History of Italy* (Oxford, 1929); *Storia d'Europa nel secolo decimonono* (Bari, 1932), English translation, *History of Europe in the Nineteenth Century* (New York, 1933), p. 358.

46. Spriggs, *op. cit.,* p. 10.

47. *My Philosophy,* p. 228.

48. H. Wildon Carr, *The Philosophy of Benedetto Croce* (London, 1917), p. 5.

49. Croce, *Logica como scienza del concetto puro* (Bari, 1900), p. 120.

50. Carr, *op. cit.,* p. 7.

51. Benedetto Croce, *Teoria e storia del storiographia* (Bari, 1917), English translation, *History, Its Theory and Practice* (New York, 1923), p. 12.

52. *Ibid.*, p. 55.

53. *Ibid.*, p. 94.

54. Spriggs, *op. cit.,* p. 47.

55. Croce, *My Philosophy,* p. 238; Hughes, *op. cit.,* p. 227.

56. L. Kronenberger, ed., *George Bernard Shaw* (Cleveland and New York, 1953), p. ix.

57. E. Bentley, *George Bernard Shaw* (London, 1950), p. 56.

58. Shaw, *Major Barbara,* Preface (New York, 1929).

59. Richard Burton, *Bernard Shaw* (New York, 1916); Frank Harris, *Bernard Shaw* (New York, 1931); Hesketh Pearson, *George Bernard Shaw* (New York, 1942); St. John Ervine, *Bernard Shaw* (New York, 1956); A. Henderson, *Bernard Shaw* (New York, 1931); Desmond MacCarthy, *Shaw* (London, 1951); G. K. Chesteron, *George Bernard Shaw* (New York, 1909), in my opinion still one of the best books on Shaw.

60. Stephen Winsten, *Jesting Apostle, The Life of Bernard Shaw* (London, 1956), pp. 24 ff.

61. Bentley, *op. cit.,* p. 111.

62. G. B. Shaw, *Fabian Essays on Socialism* (London, 1931), p. 251.

63. G. B. Shaw, *Man and Superman* (New York, 1926), p. xxxii.

64. G. B. Shaw, *Back to Methuselah* (New York, 1921), pp. 290, 300.

65. G. B. Shaw, *Man and Superman*, p. xxxi.

66. Bentley, *op. cit.*, p. 70; Chesterton, *op. cit.*, p. 105.

67. *Atlantic Monthly*, July, 1956, p. 34.

68. G. B. Shaw, *Man and Superman, The Revolutionist's Handbook*, p. 236.

69. *Ibid.*, p. 112.

70. *Ibid.*, p. 169.

71. Chesterton, *op. cit.*, p. 160.

72. Bentley, *op. cit.*, p. 17

73. See V. S. Pritchett's Essay on Shaw, in Kronenberger, *op. cit.*, p. 242.

74. Chesterton, *op. cit.*, p. 179.

75. Winsten, *op. cit., passim.*

76. Edward Crankshaw, *Khrushchev's Russia* (Baltimore, 1960), pp. 99 ff.

77. Kenneth Tynan, "Shaw, der grimme Spielmann," *Neue Züricher Zeitung*, August 12, 1956.

78. Quoted by St. John Ervine, *op. cit.*, p. 468.

79. Georg Misch, *Geschichte der Selbstbiographie*, 2 vols. (Frankfurt, 1955). G. P. Gooch, "Political Autobiography," in *Studies in Diplomacy and Statescraft* (London, 1946), pp. 227–291.

80. L. N. Tolstoy, *Jugenderinnerungen* (Berlin, n.d.).

81. Maxim Gorki, *Meine Kindheit* (Berlin, 1917).

82. Rudyard Kipling, *Something of Myself* (New York, 1937).

83. A. Strindberg, *Lebensgeschichte*, 5 vols. (München und Leipzig, 1916).

84. H. G. Wells, *Experiment in Autobiography* (New York, 1934).

85. *Ibid.*, p. 28.

86. *Ibid.*, pp. 106–107.

87. *Ibid.*, p. 143.

88. *Ibid.*, p. 569.

89. *Ibid.*, p. 705.

90. Stefan Zweig, *Die Welt von Gestern* (Stockholm, 1944).

91. *Ibid.*, p. 16.

92. *Ibid.*, p. 17. For a very different view of prewar Vienna see W. A. Jenks, *Vienna and Young Hitler* (New York, 1960).

93. *Ibid.*, p. 43.

94. See Thomas Mann, *Stefan Zweig,* in *Altes und Neues* (Frankfurt, 1953), pp. 263–265.

95. Gustav Hillard, *Herren und Narren der Welt* (München, 1955).

96. *Ibid.,* pp. 30, 45.

97. *Ibid.,* pp. 63–64.

98. *Ibid.,* p. 149.

99. *Ibid.,* p. 136.

100. Fedor Stepun, *Vergangenes und Unvergängliches* (München, 1947), 3 vols. I owe the knowledge of Stepun's work to a suggestion from Dr. Sergius Yakobson, Library of Congress, Washington, D.C.

101. *Ibid.,* I, 25.

102. *Ibid.,* 38.

103. *Ibid.,* 184–186.

104. *Ibid.,* 208.

105. *Ibid.,* 224–225.

106. *Ibid.,* 230.

107. *Ibid.,* 240.

108. *Ibid.,* 333.

109. *Ibid.,* II, 14–15.

110. Harry Graf Kessler, *Gesichter und Zeiten* (Berlin, 1935), p. 266.

CHAPTER VII: THE SEARCH FOR THE LOST DIMENSION

1. Karl Muhs, *Geschichte des abendländischen Geistes* (Berlin, 1953), 2 vols. II. 366; Dolf Sternberger, *Panorama oder Anichten vom 19. Jahrhundert* (Hamburg, 1938).

2. For a good description of Austrian life in this period, see: H. Bahr, *Selbstbildnis* (Berlin, 1923). A more objective picture may be found in Hugo Hantsch, *Geschichte Oestreichs* (Graz and Vienna, 1947–1950).

3. M. Natenberg, *The Case History of Sigmund Freud* (Chicago, 1955).

4. Sigmund Freud, *Gesammelte Schriften* (Wien, 1925–1934), XII, 113. Of the immense literature on Freud, I shall quote only those works which I have used with benefit. S. Freud, *Aus den Anfängen der Psychoanalyse; Briefe an Wilhelm Fliess* (London, 1950); Ernest Jones, *The Life and Work of Sigmund Freud,* 3 vols. (New York, 1953–1957); F. Wittels, *Sigmund Freud* (New York, 1924); Hans Sachs, *Freud* (Cambridge, Mass., 1944); J. Jastrow, *The House That Freud Built* (New York, 1932); Stefan Zweig, *Heilung durch den Geist* (Berlin, 1932).

5. Jones, *op. cit.*, I, 5.

6. *Ibid.*, 16.

7. *Ibid.*, Preface, pp. xii–xiii.

8. *Ibid.*, 348.

9. S. Freud, *Selbstdarstellung* (Wien, 1936), English translation by James Strachey (New York, 1935), quoted henceforth as *Autobiography,* p. 13.

10. *Autobiography,* p. 14.

11. Jones, *op. cit.*, I, 41.

12. *Autobiography,* p. 16.

13. *Ibid.*, p. 23.

14. Jones, *op. cit.*, I, 8–9.

15. *Ibid.*, p. 99.

16. S. Freud, *Das Unbehagen an der Kultur, Ges. Schriften,* XII, 73.

17. See the cautious remarks by Jones, I, 139.

18. *Autobiography,* p. 29.

19. *Ibid.*, p. 34.

20. *Ibid.*

21. Jones, I, 241.

22. S. Freud, *Über Psychoanalyse, Ges. Schriften,* IV, 357.

23. *Autobiography,* p. 44.

24. *Ibid.*, p. 42.

25. Freud, *Über Psychoanalyse, op. cit.,* p. 376.

26. Freud, *Ges. Schriften,* I, 2, 4.

27. See Joachim Wach, *Das Problem der Kultur und die Aertzliche Psychologie* (Leipzig, 1931), p. 9.

28. *Autobiography,* p. 53.

29. Jones, *op. cit.*, I, 386–387. Freud attempted at some time to construct a model of the mind in the same way that Niels Bohr constructed a model of the atom. He soon discarded his essay, however, and we have to piece his ideas together from his various writings.

30. Freud, *Ges. Schriften,* I–II, 526 ff. See also Jones's comment on Freud's theory of the mind, *op. cit.*, I, 365 ff.

31. Jones, *op. cit.*, I, 401.

32. H. Marcuse, *Eros and Civilization* (Boston, 1955), p. 28.

33. *Autobiography,* pp. 58–59.

34. *Ibid.*, p. 68.

35. *Ibid.*, p. 69.

36. Freud, *Ges. Schriften,* vol. 2; Jones, *op. cit.,* I, 350.

37. Jones, *op. cit.*, I, 351.

38. *Autobiography,* pp. 74, 77.

39. Freud, *Ges. Schriften,* IV.

40. *Autobiography,* p. 85.

41. *Ibid.,* p. 86.

42. *Ibid.,* p. 38.

43. S. Freud, *Vorlesungen sur Einführung in die Psychonolyse, Ges. Schriften,* vol. 7; see also *Der Dichter und das Phantasieren, Ges. Schriften,* X, 229. Jones, *op. cit.,* p. 314.

44. Freud, *Ges. Schriften,* X.

45. *Autobiography,* pp. 122–125.

46. *Ibid.,* p. 129.

47. See Eduard Heimann, in *Das Problem der Kultur, op. cit.,* p. 81.

48. Emil Ludwig, *Der Entzauberte Freud* (Zürich, 1946), p. 97.

49. Jones, *op. cit.,* II, 422.

50. *Ibid.,* 139.

51. *Ibid.,* 134.

52. *Ibid.,* 151.

53. *Ibid.,* 152 ff.

54. Freud, *Das Unbehagen an der Kultur, Ges. Schriften,* XII, 140. I quote from the English translation, *Civilization and Its Discontent.*

55. Freud, *Das Unbehagen an der Kultur, op. cit.,* p. 42.

56. T. Reik, *From Thirty Years with Freud* (New York, 1940), p. 105.

57. Freud, *Das Unbehagen an der Kultur,* p. 47.

58. Marcuse, *op. cit.,* pp. 11, 17.

59. Freud, *Das Unbehagen an der Kultur,* p. 114. Some notable exceptions are: Marcuse, *op. cit.,* and L. Trilling, *Freud and the Crisis of Our Culture* (Boston, 1955); William Langer, "The Next Assignment," *American Historical Review,* LXIII, 283–304.

60. Even Lou Andreas Salome, in *Mein Dank an Freud* (Wien, 1931), p. 79, expresses objections to Freud's tendency to explain poetic impulse from sublimated libido. It would indeed be strange if the friend of Nietzsche and Rilke had accepted such a crude idea without reservations.

61. Freud, *Jenseits des Lustprinzips, Ges. Schriften,* VI, 232.

62. See H. Driesch, in *Das Problem der Kultur,* p. 135.

63. S. Freud, *Warum Krieg? Ges. Schriften,* XII, 360.

64. Erich Heller, "Psychoanalyse und Literatur," *Jahresringe,* 1956–1957, p. 75. F. J. Hoffmann, *Freudianism and the Literary Mind* (Baton Rouge, 1945); Jones, *op. cit.,* III, 416 ff.

65. Jones, *op. cit.,* II, 415. See also vol. 3, Appendix A, and Thomas Mann, "Freud's Position in the History of Modern Thought," *Past Masters* (New York, 1933), pp. 167 ff.

66. Charles Matton Brooks, *Vincent van Gogh, a Bibliography* (New York, 1942).

67. J. Meier Graefe, *Vincent van Gogh* (New York, 1933), p. 6. See also Th. Duret, *Vincent van Gogh* (Paris, 1919); W. Hausenstein, *Van Gogh* (Berlin, 1914); Jean Leymarie, *Van Gogh* (Paris, 1951).

68. Lawrence and Elizabeth Hanson in *Vincent* (London, 1955), p. 19, have made an attempt to find the answer to van Gogh's riddles in a childhood trauma. But there is little evidence to back up such a theory. See also: *Vincent van Gogh, Lettres à sa mère* (Paris, 1952).

69. *Lettres de Vincent van Gogh à son frère Theo* (Paris, 1937) (quoted henceforth as *Lettres*), p. 167. See also *Dear Theo, The Autobiography of Vincent van Gogh* (New York, 1946).

70. Werner Weisbach, *Vincent van Gogh,* 2 vols. (Basel 1949–1951), I, 38, 65. In my opinion this is the most scholarly work on Van Gogh.

71. *Ibid.,* p. 38.

72. *Lettres,* pp. 34–35.

73. *Ibid.*

74. *Ibid.,* p. 164.

75. Meier Graefe, *op. cit.,* p. 29.

76. *Lettres,* p. 41.

77. *Ibid.,* p. 53.

78. *Ibid.,* p. 85.

79. *Ibid.,* p. 74.

80. Weisbach, *op. cit.,* I, 110.

81. *Lettres,* p. 121.

82. Meier Graefe, *op. cit.,* p. 93.

83. Weisbach, *op. cit.,* II, 38–39; for van Gogh's encounters in Paris, see his letters: *Briefe an Emile Bernard, Paul Gauguin, John Russel* (Basel, 1941). See also, John Rewald, *The History of Impressionism* (New York, 1946), p. 402.

84. Meier Graefe, *op. cit.,* p. 105.

85. *Lettres,* p. 254.

86. *Ibid.,* p. 245.

87. *Ibid.,* p. 229.

88. Weisbach, *op. cit.,* II, 51.

89. *Lettres,* p. 199.

90. *Ibid.,* p. 187. Meyer Schapiro, *Vincent van Gogh* (New York, 1950), p. 18. See also A. Michel, *Histoire de l'art* (Paris, 1926), VIII, 990.

91. Quoted by Weisbach, *op. cit.,* II, 85.

92. Meier Graefe, *op. cit.,* p. 112.

93. Hugo von Hofmannsthal, *Selected Prose* (New York, 1952), pp. 146–148. The essay is entitled "The Colors."

94. Quoted by Weisbach, *op. cit.,* II, 207.

95. Schapiro, *op. cit.,* p. 12.

96. Meier Graefe, *op. cit.,* p. 114. See also Karl Jaspers, *Strindberg und van Gogh* (Berlin, 1926), pp. 113 ff.

97. Arsène Alexandre, *Paul Gauguin* (Paris, 1930), p. 214; see the letter by Daniel Monfreid; Charles Chasse, *Gauguin et son temps* (Paris, 1955); R. Rey, *Gauguin* (Paris, 1924); J. Rewald, *Gauguin* (London, 1938).

98. Alexandre, *op. cit.,* p. 9.

99. Paul Gauguin, *Avant et après* (Paris, 1910), English translation (New York, 1936), p. 17; Jean de Rotonchamp, *Paul Gauguin* (Weimar-Paris), 1906.

100. L. and E. Hanson, *The Noble Savage* (London, 1954), p. 31.

101. Gauguin, *Avant et après,* English translation, p. 31. See also Alexandre, *op. cit.,* p. 27.

102. Rey, *op. cit.,* p. 11.

103. Charles Morice, *Paul Gauguin* (Paris, 1918), p. 9; Pola Gauguin, *Mon Père, Paul Gauguin* (Paris, 1938), pp. 79 ff.

104. Morice, *op. cit.,* p. 8.

105. J. Maritain, *Creative Intuition in Art and Poetry* (New York, 1955), p. 25.

106. Quoted by Alexandre, *op. cit.,* p. 32; see also Gauguin's letter of January, 1885, *Lettres de Gauguin* (Paris, 1946), p. 45.

107. R. Cogniat, *The Fiery Life of Paul Gauguin* (New York, 1946), p. 29.

108. Alexandre, *op. cit.,* pp. 95 ff.

109. Gauguin, *Avant et après,* English translation, p. 154.

110. Cogniat, *op. cit.,* p. 34.

111. *Lettres de Paul Gauguin à Daniel de Monfreid* (Paris, 1919), p. 194.

112. Alexandre, *op. cit.,* p. 75.

113. See the excellent summary by Cogniat, *op. cit.,* p. 39. A very detailed analysis of the work in Brittany in Alexandre, *op. cit.,* and in Charles Chasse, *Gauguin et le groupe de Pont Aven* (Paris, 1921).

114. Quoted by Cogniat, *op. cit.,* p. 40.

115. Paul Gauguin, *Noa Noa* (Berlin), p. 54.

116. Paul Gauguin, *Lettres* (Paris, 1946), p. 221.

117. Alexandre, *op. cit.*, p. 55.

118. Gauguin, *Lettres,* p. 227.

119. Gauguin, *Noa, Noa,* p. 107.

120. Alexandre, *op. cit.*, pp. 254, 268.

121. *Ibid.,* p. 153; Jean Leymarie, *Gauguin* (Paris, 1950).

122. Cogniat, *op. cit.*, p. 51.

123. *Ibid.*

124. See Douglas Cooper, *Gauguin the Innovator* (London, 1955) (Tate Gallery), p. 11.

125. Quoted by L. and E. Hanson, *op. cit.*, p. 286.

126. Salvador de Madariaga, *Semblanzas Literarias* (Barcelona, 1924), pp. 127–161.

127. Azorín, *Classicos Modernos* (Madrid, 1919), pp. 237 ff; Hans Jeschke, *Die Generation von 1898 in Spanien* (Halle, 1934); José Ferrater Mora, *Unamuno* (Buenos Aires, 1944); Gerhard Masur, "Unamuno," *The Americas,* XXI, 2, pp. 139–156.

128. Miguel de Unamuno, *Paz en la Guerra* (Buenos Aires, 1940); Miguel de Unamuno, *Recuerdos de Niñez y de Mocedad* (Buenos Aires, 1945), pp. 75, 77.

129. Arturo Baréa, *Unamuno* (Cambridge, 1952), p. 10.

130. F. Madrid, *Genio e Ingenio de Miguel de Unamuno* (Buenos Aires, 1942), pp. 50, 61.

131. Ernst Robert Curtius, *Kritische Essays zur Europäischen Literatur* (Bern, 1952), p. 228.

132. A. del Rio, "Vida y Obra de Unamuno," in *Revista Hispanica Moderna,* October, 1934, pp. 12–19.

133. Cesar Barja, *Libros y Autores Contemporáneos* (New York, 1935), p. 39.

134. Unamuno, *Rosario de Sonetos Liricos* (Madrid, 1950), p. 44.

135. Unamuno, *Ensayos* (Madrid, 1916), vol. 1; Barea, *op. cit.*, p. 15; Marcel Bataillon's translation of Unamuno's work is entitled *L'Essence de l'Espagne.*

136. Curtius, *op. cit.*, pp. 225–226.

137. Unamuno, *Ensayos,* I, 48.

138. *Ibid.,* 43.

139. *Ibid.,* 48.

140. *Ibid.*, 211, 214.

141. *Ibid.*, 218.

142. *Ibid.*, II, 168–169.

143. *Ibid.*, 161; Barja, *op. cit.*, p. 50.

144. Unamuno, *Ensayos,* II, 201, 205.

145. *Ibid.*, 205.

146. *Ibid.*, 210.

147. Barja, *op. cit.*, p. 51.

148. Unamuno, *Ensayos,* II, 163, 172; I, 96.

149. Unamuno, *Vida de Don Quichote,* 7th ed. (Buenos Aires, 1946).

150. Curtius, *op. cit.*, p. 232; Unamuno, *Vida de Don Quichote,* p. 270.

151. Unamuno, *op. cit.;* see also *Soliloquios y Conversaciones* (Madrid, 1911), p. 111.

152. Unamuno, *Algunas Consideraciones Sobre la Literatura Hispano-Americana* (Buenos Aires, 1947), p. 106.

153. Unamuno, *Sonetos,* p. 147.

154. Unamuno, *Del Sentimiento Tragico de la Vida* (Madrid, 1912), English translation by G. E. Crawford Flitch (London, 1926), p. 1. All quotations are from Flitch's translation.

155. *Ibid.*, p. 32.

156. *Ibid.*, p. 34.

157. See the introduction by Flitch to Unamuno's *Essays and Soliloquies* (New York, 1925), pp. 23–24.

158. *Ibid.*

159. Unamuno, *Del Sentimiento Tragico de la Vida,* pp. 11, 43, 115.

160. *Ibid.*, p. 309.

161. Unamuno, *Essays,* pp. 156–157.

162. Unamuno, *Del Sentimiento Tragico de la Vida,* pp. 11, 36.

163. Julian Marias, *Miguel de Unamuno* (Madrid, 1943), pp. 21, 22, 156–157.

164. Unamuno, *Del Sentimiento Tragico de la Vida,* pp. 132, 194.

165. For the criticism of Unamuno's religious position, see Curtius, *op. cit.*, p. 239; also Mora and Marias.

166. Unamuno, *La Agonía del Cristianismo* (Madrid, 1931).

167. Barja, *op. cit.*, pp. 96–97; Flitch, *op. cit.*

168. *Cuadernos de la Catedra Miguel de Unamuno* (Salamanca, 1948), pp. 7–8, 126. Guillermo de la Torre, "The Agony of Unamuno" *New Mexico Quarterly Review,* XVIII, 150.

CHAPTER VIII: THE SOCIAL FABRIC

1. E. Wechsler, *Die Generation als Jugendreihe* (Leipzig, 1930); in Wechsler's bibliography the reader will find additional titles regarding the concept of generation.

2. Hans Kohn, "Youth Movements," *Encyclopaedia of Social Sciences,* XV, 516–520.

3. *Ibid.*

4. Howard Becker, *German Youth* (London, 1946), p. 48. Th. Herrle, *Die deutsche Jugendbewegung* (Gotha, 1921); Victor Engelhardt, *Die deutsche Jugendbewegung als kulturhistorisches Phänomen* (Berlin, 1923); W. Stählin, *Fieber und Heil in der deutschen Jugendbewegung* (Hamburg, 1923); H. Ebeling, *The German Youth Movement* (London, 1945); F. Borinski and W. Milch, *Jugendbewegung* (London, 1945); Hans Schlemmer, *Der Geist der deutschen Jugendbewegung* (München, 1922); see also "Youth Movements, Here and Abroad," *Bulletin of the Russell Sage Foundation Library* (New York, 1936), no. 135.

5. Becker, *op. cit.,* p. 47.

6. Reginald Phelps, in *American Youth,* T. Winslow, ed. (Cambridge, Mass., 1940), p. 32.

7. Charlotte Lüttke, *Die deutsche Jugendbewegung* (Frankfurt, 1925), p. 24; in my opinion, one of the best books on the subject. Th. Huber, *Die soziologische Seite der Jugendbewegung* (München, 1929).

8. Becker, *op. cit.,* p. 51.

9. Hans Blüher, *Wandervogel, Geschichte einer Jugendbewegung* (Celle, 1912), 2 vols., I, 1.

10. *Ibid.,* p. 83.

11. (Leipzig, 1908); by 1924 it had sold more than 700,000 copies.

12. Becker, *op. cit.,* p. 89; H. Höckner, *Die Musik in der deutschen Jugendbewegung* (Wolfenbüttel, 1927).

13. G. Wynneken, *Der Kampf für die Jugend* (Jena, 1920); F. W. Foerster, *Jugendseele, Jugendbewegung, Jugendziele* (München, 1923).

14. Wynneken, *op. cit.,* p. 124.

15. Elisabeth Busse-Wilson, *Stufen der Jugendbewegung* (Jena, 1925), pp. 81, 87.

16. Blüher, *op. cit.,* p. 139.

17. *Ibid.,* p. 228.

18. Else Frobenius, *Mit uns zieht die neue Zeit* (Berlin, 1929), p. 66.

19. Hans Blüher, *Die deutsche Wandervogelbewegung als erotisches Phänomen* (Berlin, 1921).

20. Johannes Schult, *Aufbruch einer Jugend* (Bonn, 1956), p. 22; Curt Bondy, *Die proletarische Jugendbewegung* (Lauenburg, 1922); Karl Korn, *Geschichte der Arbeiterbewegung* (Berlin, 1922).

21. Schult, *op. cit.*, p. 33.

22. Frobenius, *op. cit.*, p. 102.

23. O. Stählin, *Die deutsche Jugendbewegung* (Gotha, 1924), p. 25.

24. *Quickborn* was the name chosen by the Catholic youth movement. See Foerster, *op. cit.*, pp. 252–293.

25. Otto Piper, *Jugendbewegung und Protestantismus* (Rudolfstadt, 1923).

26. Herrle, *op. cit.*, p. 103.

27. *Ibid.*, p. 20.

28. W. Stählin, *op. cit.*, pp. 9–10.

29. *Ibid.*, pp. 59–60.

30. A. Messer, *Die Freideutsche Jugendbewegung* (Langensalza, 1920), p. 12; Kurt Grubbe, *Zur Charakterologie der deutschen Jugendbewegung* (Halle, 1929), p. 19; H. Buddensieg, *Vom Geist und Beruf der deutschen Jugendbewegung* (Lauenburg, 1924).

31. Messer, *op. cit.*, pp. 13, 14.

32. *Ibid.*, p. 19.

33. *Ibid.*, p. 13.

34. Klemens von Klemperer, *Germany's New Conservatism* (Princeton, 1957), p. 44.

35. *Ibid.*, p. 43.

36. *Ibid.*, p. 46.

37. Walter Flex, *Der Wanderer zwischen zwei Welten,* a book written during the First World War, has often been called the classic of the youth movement. Though it has its charm, it can hardly be ranked among great books.

38. Ebeling, *op. cit.*, p. 3; Lüttke, *op. cit.*, p. 106.

39. Lüttke, *op. cit.*, p. 109.

40. Agathon, *Les Jeuns gens d'audourdhui* (Paris, 1913) is the result of an inquiry among young French intellectuals. See also, E. R. Curtius, *Die geistigen Wegbereiter des modernen Frankreichs* (Bonn, 1919).

41. Karl Mannheim, "Youth in Modern Society," in *Diagnosis of Our Time* (London, 1943), p. 31.

42. Klaus Mehnert, *Youth in Soviet Russia* (London, 1933); Becker, *op. cit.*, p. 163; Renée Dupuis, *Jeune Europe* (Paris, 1933).

43. An example of the hostility to feminism is F. W. Eberhard, *Feminismus und Kulturuntergang* (Wien und Leipzig, 1924). For general works on the problem, see Mary R. Beard, *On Understanding Women* (New York, 1931); Winifred Holtby, *Women and a Changing Civilization* (New York, 1934).

44. Charlotte Lütkens, *Women and a New Society* (London, 1946), p. 11.

45. *Ibid.*

46. Jakob Burckhardt, *Die Kultur der Renaissance in Italien* (Leipzig, 1898), I, 237.

47. Ethel Snowden, *The Feminist Movement* (London, 1913), p. 33; Alice Clark, *The Working Life of Women in the Seventeenth Century* (New York, 1920); Georgina Hills, *Women in English Life* (London, 1896), 2 vols.

48. E. C. Stanton, *History of Woman Suffrage* (New York, 1881), I, 31; Lily Braun, *Die Frauenfrage* (Leipzig, 1901).

49. Leopold Lacour, *Trois Femmes de la révolution française* (Paris, 1900), p. 3; Braun, *op. cit.,* p. 81.

50. Braun, *op. cit.,* p. 91.

51. Th. von Hippel, *Uber die bürgerliche Verbesserung der Weiber* (Berlin, 1792).

52. Reprinted, London, 1896.

53. Braun, *op. cit.,* p. 95; Helene Richter, *Mary Wollstonecraft* (Wien, 1897).

54. Havelock Ellis, *The Task of Social Hygiene* (Boston, 1912), p. 70.

55. Léon Abensour, *Histoire général du féminisme* (Paris, 1921), p. 206.

56. André Maurois, *Lelia* (Paris, 1954).

57. Eugene A. Hecker, *A Short History of Women's Rights* (New York, 1914), p. 158.

58. *Ibid.,* p. 163.

59. J. S. Mill, *The Subjection of Women* (London, 1867); Mary R. Beard, *Women as a Force in History* (New York, 1946).

60. Hecker, *op. cit.,* p. 189; Braun, *op. cit.,* p. 124.

61. Braun, *op. cit.,* p. 209.

62. Ivy Pinchbeck, *Women Workers and the Industrial Revolution* (London, 1930).

63. Snowden, *op. cit.,* p. 36.

64. Stuttgart, 1910.

65. Bebel, *op. cit.,* p. 175.

66. *Ibid.,* p. 238.

67. *Ibid.,* p. 443.

68. *Ibid.,* p. 473.

69. *Ibid.,* p. 475.

70. *Ibid.,* p. 508.

71. Clara Zetkin, *Lenin on the Women Question* (New York, 1934).

72. Eva Curie, *Madame Curie,* English translation (New York, 1939).

73. Havelock Ellis, *op. cit.,* p. 85; E. S. Pankhurst, *The Life of Emmeline Pankhurst* (London, 1935).

74. Ellis, *op. cit.,* p. 75.

75. *Ibid.;* see also Beatrice Webb, *My Apprenticeship* (New York, 1926); Gertrud Bäumer, *Die Frau im Neuen Lebensraum* (Berlin, 1921).

76. Snowden, *op. cit.,* p. 73.

77. A. R. Wadin, *The Ethics of Feminism* (London, 1923).

78. F. Barkley Copley, *Frederick Winslow Taylor* (New York, 1923), 2 vols.; Frederick Winslow Taylor, *A Memorial Volume* (New York, 1915).

79. Copley, *op. cit.,* I, 77.

80. *Ibid.,* p. 58.

81. *Ibid.,* p. 92.

82. Frederick Winslow Taylor, *The Principles of Scientific Management* (New York, 1911).

83. Max Weber, *Ges. Aufsätze zur Religionssoziologie,* I, *passim.*

84. Copley, *op. cit.,* I, 83.

85. *Ibid.,* p. 84.

86. The House of Representatives conducted an investigation of the Taylor system and other systems of shop management in 1912. The quotation is from Copley, I, 10.

87. "Critical Essays on Scientific Management," *Bulletin of the Taylor Society* (New York, 1927), p. 67.

88. Copley, *op. cit.,* I, 99.

89. Taylor, *Principles of Scientific Management,* p. 9; Copley, *op. cit.,* I, 11, 12.

90. Copley, *op. cit.,* I, 287.

91. Stuart Chase, in *Essays on Scientific Management,* p. 67; Copley, *op. cit.,* I, 253.

92. Copley, *loc. cit.*

93. *Ibid.,* 216.

94. *Ibid.,* 223.

95. *Ibid.,* 228.

96. *Ibid.,* 326.

97. *Ibid.,* 450.

98. Chase, *op. cit.,* p. 68.

99. Copley, *op. cit.,* I, 161.

100. *Ibid.,* 2.

101. *Ibid.,* II, 403.

102. *Ibid.,* 405.

103. *Ibid.,* 414.

104. Allan Nevins, *Ford* (New York, 1954), pp. 369, 466.

105. Henry Ford, *Moving Forward* (New York, 1930), pp. 39–40.

106. *Ibid.,* p. 2.

107. *Ibid.,* p. 106.

108. *Ibid.,* p. 303. I have taken Ford's pronouncements at their face value. For a very different evaluation of Ford and his philosophy see, John Kenneth Galbraith, "The Mystery of Henry Ford," *Atlantic Monthly,* CCI, 41; F. von Gottl Ottlilienfeld, *Fordiana* (Jena, 1926).

109. Frederick W. Taylor, *Shop Management* (New York, 1911), p. 110; Copley, *op. cit.,* I, 288.

110. Copley, I, 297.

111. F. Redlich, "German Economic Planning," *Review of Politics,* vol. 6, no. 3, p. 315.

112. The article is quoted at length by Copley, I, xii.

113. Paul Olive, *Le Système Taylor* (Marseille, 1919); Henry Le Chatelier, *Le Taylorisme* (Paris, 1934).

114. Max Weber, *Wissenschaft als Beruf, op. cit.,* pp. 138–139.

115. H. S. Hughes, *Consciousness and Society* (New York, 1958), p. 41.

116. Harry W. Laidler, *A History of Socialist Thought* (New York, 1927), pp. 365–366.

117. Friedrich Engels, Introduction to Marx's *Class Struggle in France,* English translation (New York, n.d.), p. 13–14.

118. Quoted by Hughes, *op. cit.,* p. 77.

119. *Ibid.,* p. 79.

120. *Ibid.,* p. 86.

121. Max Weber, *Gesammelte Aufsätze zur Religionssoziologie* (Tübingen, 1922), I, 17.

122. *Ibid.*, note 1.

123. Hughes, *op. cit.*, p. 319.

124. E. R. Pease, *The History of the Fabian Society* (New York, 1922), p. 22. M. Beer, *A History of British Socialism* (London, 1929), I; G. M. Young, *Victorian England* (New York, 1954), pp. 254 ff.

125. Pease, *op. cit.*, p. 39, and *Fabian Essays in Socialism* by G. B. Shaw, Sidney Webb, and others (London, 1931).

126. Pease, *op. cit.*, p. 67; *Fabian Essays*, pp. 31–32.

127. Sidney Webb, *A History of Trade-Unionism* (London, 1894); *Fabian Essays*, p. xxii.

128. Pease, *op. cit.*, p. 126; D. H. Cole, *Fabian Socialism* (London, 1943), p. 171.

129. A. Millerand, *Le Socialisme réformiste français* (Paris, 1903), p. 12.

130. Peter Gay, *The Dilemma of Democratic Socialism, Eduard Bernstein* (New York, 1952), p. 26.

131. *Ibid.*, p. 61.

132. (Stuttgart, 1910); English translation, "Evolutionary Socialism" (New York, 1909); see also Eduard Bernstein, *Zur Geschichte und Theorie des Sozialismus* (Berlin, 1901); *Von der Sekte zur Partei* (Jena, 1911); and Bernstein's autobiography, *Entwicklung eines Sozialisten* (Leipzig, 1924).

133. Gay, *op. cit.*, p. 244.

134. *Ibid.*, p. 138.

135. *Ibid.*, p. 242.

136. Bernstein, *Evolutionary Socialism*, p. 147; Gay, *op. cit.*, p. 203.

137. Bernstein, *op. cit.*, p. 149.

138. Gay, *op. cit.*, p. 227.

139. Karl Schorske, *German Social Democracy* (Cambridge, Mass., 1955), pp. 24, 322; for the situation of the Austrian social democrats see Max Ermers, *Victor Adler* (Wien und Leipzig, 1932), and Julius Deutsch, *Geschichte der österreichischen Arbeiterbewegung* (Wien, 1947).

140. Thomas Hammon, *Lenin on Trade Unions and Revolution, 1893–1917* (New York, 1957), p. 9.

141. Karl Marx, *Das Kapital* (London, 1909), I, xix.

142. Gay, *op. cit.*, p. 119.

143. Hammon, *op. cit.*, p. 10.

144. *Ibid.*, p. 17.

145. V. J. Lenin, *What Is to Be Done? Collected Works,* IV, 83–258.

146. Hammon, *op. cit.,* p. 24.

147. Lenin, *op. cit.,* p. 115.

148. *Ibid.,* pp. 196, 198, 200.

149. *Ibid.,* p. 201.

150. Quoted by I. Deutscher, *Stalin* (New York, 1949), p. 278.

151. R. Humphrey, *Georges Sorel* (Cambridge, Mass., 1951), p. 1. For a more critical evaluation of Sorel see, Scott H. Lytle, *Georges Sorel, Apostle of Fanaticism,* in *Modern France,* E. M. Earle, ed. (Princeton, 1951); James Meisel, *The Genesis of Georges Sorel* (Ann Harbor, Mich., 1951); Pierre Andreu, *Notre Maître, M. Sorel* (Paris, 1953); Hughes, *op. cit.,* pp. 161 ff.

152. Humphrey, *op. cit.,* p. 9.

153. Georges Sorel, *Réflexions sur la violence* (Paris, 1908), English translation (London, 1915), p. 4.

154. *Ibid.,* p. 11.

155. *Ibid.,* p. 10.

156. *Ibid.,* p. 43.

157. *Ibid.,* p. 69.

158. *Ibid.,* p. 83.

159. *Ibid.,* p. 90.

160. *Ibid.,* p. 139.

161. *Ibid.,* p. 35.

162. Hughes, *op. cit.,* p. 176.

163. Sorel, *op. cit.,* pp. 183, 187.

164. *Ibid.,* p. 295.

165. *Ibid.,* pp. 82–83.

166. Humphrey, *op. cit.,* p. 22.

167. Hughes, *op. cit.,* p. 181. See also Michael Curtis, *Three Against the Republic* (Princeton, 1959), which deals with Barrès, Maurras, and Sorel.

INDEX

Date Due

MAR 18		
APR 21		
MAY 8		
MAY 18		

Demco 293-5